*Glo*bal Capital and National Governments

To what extent do international financial market pressures influence or constrain government policy choices? *Global Capital and National Governments* suggests that international financial integration does not mean the end of social democratic welfare policies. Capital market openness allows investors to react swiftly and severely to government policy, but in the developed world, capital market participants consider only a few government policies when making decisions. Governments that conform to capital market pressures in macroeconomic areas remain relatively unconstrained in supply-side and microeconomic policy areas. Therefore, despite financial globalization, cross-national policy divergence among advanced democracies remains likely. Still, in the developing world, the influence of financial markets on government policy autonomy is more pronounced. The risk of default renders market participants willing to consider a range of government policies. This conclusion, however, must be tempered with an awareness that governments retain choices. As evidence for its conclusions, *Global Capital and National Governments* draws on interviews with fund managers, quantitative analyses, and archival investment banking materials.

Layna Mosley is the Thomas J. and Robert T. Rolfs Assistant Professor in the Department of Political Science at the University of Notre Dame. Her research interests include the impact of global capital markets on policy choices, the governance of international financial flows, and the politics of European financial integration. Mosley received her Ph.D. in Political Science from Duke University in 1999.

Cambridge Studies in Comparative Politics

General Editor
Margaret Levi *University of Washington, Seattle*

Assistant General Editor
Stephen Hanson *University of Washington, Seattle*

Associate Editors
Robert H. Bates *Harvard University*
Peter Hall *Harvard University*
Peter Lange *Duke University*
Helen Milner *Columbia University*
Frances Rosenbluth *Yale University*
Susan Stokes *University of Chicago*
Sidney Tarrow *Cornell University*

Other Books in the Series
Stefano Bartolini, *The Political Mobilization of the European Left, 1860–1980: The Class Cleavage*
Mark Beissinger, *Nationalist Mobilization and the Collapse of the Soviet State*
Nancy Bermeo, ed., *Unemployment in the New Europe*
Carles Boix, *Political Parties, Growth and Equality: Conservative and Social Democratic Economic Strategies in the World Economy*
Catherine Boone, *Merchant Capital and the Roots of State Power in Senegal, 1930–1985*
Michael Bratton and Nicolas van de Walle, *Democratic Experiments in Africa: Regime Transitions in Comparative Perspective*
Valerie Bunce, *Leaving Socialism and Leaving the State: The End of Yugoslavia, the Soviet Union and Czechoslovakia*
Ruth Berins Collier, *Paths Toward Democracy: The Working Class and Elites in Western Europe and South America*
Donatella della Porta, *Social Movements, Political Violence, and the State*
Robert F. Franzese, *Macroeconomic Policies of Developed Democracies*
Gerald Easter, *Reconstructing the State: Personal Networks and Elite Identity*

List continues on page following the Index.

Global Capital and National Governments

LAYNA MOSLEY

University of Notre Dame

CAMBRIDGE
UNIVERSITY PRESS

PUBLISHED BY THE PRESS SYNDICATE OF THE UNIVERSITY OF CAMBRIDGE
The Pitt Building, Trumpington Street, Cambridge, United Kingdom

CAMBRIDGE UNIVERSITY PRESS
The Edinburgh Building, Cambridge CB2 2RU, UK
40 West 20th Street, New York, NY 10011-4211, USA
477 Williamstown Road, Port Melbourne, VIC 3207, Australia
Ruiz de Alarcón 13, 28014 Madrid, Spain
Dock House, The Waterfront, Cape Town 8001, South Africa

http://www.cambridge.org

First published 2003

Printed in the United States of America

Typeface Janson Text 10/13 pt.   *System* LʌTEX 2$_\varepsilon$ [TB]

A catalog record for this book is available from the British Library.

Library of Congress Cataloging in Publication Data
Mosley, Layna.
Global capital and national governments.
Layna Mosley.
    p.   cm. – (Cambridge studies in comparative politics)
Includes bibliographical references and index.
ISBN 0-521-81521-5 – ISBN 0-521-52162-9 (pb.)
1. Capital market – Government policy.   2. Finance – Government policy.
3. International finance – Government policy.   I. Title.   II. Series.
HG4523 .M67   2002
332 – dc21   2002023442

ISBN 0 521 81521 5 hardback
ISBN 0 521 52162 9 paperback

For my parents,
Janie and Steve Mosley

Contents

Figures and Tables

Figures

Tables

Acknowledgments

I first became interested in the interactions between the global economy and national governments while an undergraduate at Rollins College. Tom Lairson's general enthusiasm for international relations, and his specific encouragement of my senior research project, motivated me to pursue a career in political science. At Duke University, I encountered a variety of individuals who encouraged, mentored, and challenged me. Duke was an ideal place for graduate education – a department that was in broad agreement about its intellectual mission, filled with collegial faculty, and always prepared to engage its students. I first tackled the question of investors' preferences over government policies in Peter Lange and Beth Simmons's graduate seminar on the international economy and domestic politics. Despite the many shortcomings in my initial efforts, Peter and Beth encouraged me to pursue this issue.

In subsequent years, as cochairs of my dissertation committee, Robert Keohane and Peter Lange provided large doses of intellectual guidance, professional advice, and warm friendship. Peter's enthusiasm for questions of comparative political economy sparked my interest in the subject during my first semester of graduate school. As work on my dissertation progressed, I benefited from Peter's willingness to juggle academic and administrative burdens, as well as from his generosity with food and drink. Throughout the process, Bob offered extensive advice on research design and on the drawing of causal connections between governments and financial markets. He challenged me to consider my arguments more carefully, and my work was always better for it. Bob also joined me for runs in Berlin, Durham, South Bend, and Venice, and, when I could not be there in person, he always updated me with news of Duke's latest men's or women's basketball triumph.

Many other individuals provided insight and advice at various stages of this project. As members of my dissertation committee, Joseph Grieco, Robert Keohane, Peter Lange, and Beth Simmons offered feedback throughout the dissertation process. Bob's and Peter's interest continued long after I completed my dissertation. John Aldrich and Lori Leachman helped me to refine this project during its early stages. Michael Munger offered guidance on time series methodology, as well as on the overall project. At Duke and beyond, Sarah Brooks offered many suggestions on the domestic politics of financial market influence in developing nations and pushed me to develop further the logic of financial market–government relations. Sarah also has been the perfect roommate at academic conferences, and I am flattered to have been repeatedly mistaken for her.

While conducting the interview research for this project, I benefited from the advice and generosity of Josef Esser (who provided me with an institutional home in Frankfurt), the late Michael Hodges (who welcomed me into his research seminar at the London School of Economics), William Wallace, and Martin Wolf. I also am indebted to those institutional investors, fund managers, research directors, and credit ratings agency staff who sacrificed their time in order to advance my research agenda. Those who participated in the London and Frankfurt interview studies remain anonymous but are identified by firm in Appendix 2.1. The archival research for Chapter 7 was possible only with the assistance of archivists at the Corporation of London's Guildhall Library, ING Baring (London), the Morgan Library (New York), and N. M. Rothschild (London). For their assistance in identifying and accessing key archival materials, I am grateful particularly to Melanie Aspey, Moira Lovegrove, John Orbell, and Jane Waller. William Bernhard, Geoffrey Garrett, Mark Hallerberg, Alessandro Missale, Andy Sobel, and Duane Swank kindly provided some of the data used in Chapters 3, 4, 5, and 6.

A variety of others offered comments and suggestions on this project; in every case, these served to improve its quality dramatically. These include Suzanne Berger, William Bernhard, James Caporaso, Phil Cerny, Jonas Pontusson, Michael Wallerstein, the editors of *International Organization*, participants in the 1999 Globalization and Western Europe workshop at the Harvard Center for European Studies, participants in the UNC/NC State Historical Political Economy of Europe group, members of the "Boat Race" seminar series, and participants in the University of Chicago's PIPES Seminar. At Notre Dame, Andrew Reynolds read large portions of the manuscript, and Saika Uno offered insightful comments on the domestic

Acknowledgments

politics sections. The book also benefited from detailed responses and specific suggestions of two anonymous reviewers. The editorial staff at Cambridge University Press shepherded this book through the review and publication process, improving it along the way. None of these individuals, of course, bears any responsibility for the remaining shortcomings of this book.

Funding for the initial research contained in this book came from the Duke University Center for International Studies, the Duke University Department of Political Science, the Duke University Sawyer Seminar on Globalization and Equity, the National Science Foundation Dissertation Improvement Program, the Social Science Research Council, and the Institute for the Study of World Politics. The Institute for Scholarship in the Liberal Arts, the Kellogg Institute, and the Robert T. and Thomas J. Rolfs Professorship at the University of Notre Dame supported the archival research and the surveys of mutual fund managers. Ericka Benavides, Rosanna Castiglioni, Mark Higgins, and Michelle Petersen provided research assistance. Michelle Petersen deserves special praise; she undertook a variety of duties, including compiling databases of fund managers, surveying fund managers in the United States and United Kingdom, and editing large portions of the manuscript. Each of these things she did efficiently, accurately, and with good humor.

Friends, family, and colleagues provided a wealth of support while I worked on the dissertation and then on the book. At Duke, Sarah Brooks, Damon Coletta, Michael Ensley, Claire Kramer, Denali Mosley, and Lyle Scruggs offered advice, abundant camaraderie, and occasional distraction. At the University of Notre Dame, members of the Political Science Department and the Fellows of the Kellogg Institute facilitated the completion of my research. In particular, Frances Hagopian happily served as my official mentor; no matter how busy she was with other responsibilities, she always found time to provide professional and intellectual advice. Christina Wolbrecht helped me to understand the workings of the university as well as the profession; her continual willingness to answer the smallest – and largest – of queries eased my transition immensely. I also owe a debt of gratitude to the former members of ABBA, whose music provided me with the motivation to keep working when I wanted to give up and go home. And, as my colleague at Notre Dame and my dear friend after, Andrew Reynolds showed me the value of a friend who not only reads your work carefully and critically, but also makes you laugh hysterically.

Finally, the Mosley family was unwavering as a source of support. Although my siblings and my parents have little idea about what it is I actually *do*, they were steadfast in their love and encouragement. Since childhood, my parents placed a high priority on academic achievement; their enthusiasm was constant and their praise unlimited. In addition to instilling in me the value of learning, my parents taught me the value of money. And, perhaps without realizing it, they demonstrated to me the importance of politics. As a small display of my gratitude for these lessons, this book – about politics and money – is dedicated to them.

1

National Governments and Global Capital

A RECASTING

> More recently, however, as the downward-ratcheting logic of electoral politics has placed a death grip on their economies, they [states] have become – first and foremost – remarkably inefficient engines of wealth distribution.... Moreover, as the workings of genuinely global capital markets dwarf their ability to control exchange rates or protect their currency, nation-states have become inescapably vulnerable to the discipline imposed by economic choices made elsewhere by people and institutions over which they have no practical control.... Second, and more to the point, the nation-state is increasingly a nostalgic fiction.[1]

> For creditor states, global finance is an opportunity moderated by a measured risk. For debtor states, it can be the new tyrant.[2]

When throngs of protestors mobilized around the Free Trade Area of the Americas (FTAA) summit in Quebec, the World Bank/International Monetary Fund (IMF) meetings in Washington and Prague, and the World Trade Organization (WTO) ministerial meetings in Seattle, their target was economic globalization. Although these activists represented a variety of interests and viewpoints, they shared a refrain: a narrow set of political elites, corporations, and investors were directing globalization and global economic institutions, making them unaccountable and inherently undemocratic. In the financial realm, protestors contend that government economic policies are chosen largely by an "electronic herd."[3] This herd represents the twenty-first century analog to the British prime minister Harold Wilson's "gnomes of Zurich" (an epithet for Swiss currency traders, said to necessitate the 1967 devaluation of the pound) and to the 1980s'

---

[1] Ohmae 1995, p. 12.
[2] Pauly 1999, p. 416.
[3] Friedman 2000.

"bond market vigilantes." The electronic herd's detractors claim that it constrains all governments, but that the poorest nations experience the most severe tyranny.

For international and comparative political economy as well, the validity of the protestors' claim is a central issue. To what extent and in what ways do international financial markets influence, or even dictate, government policy choices? As antiglobalization activists have been quick to note, in an era of economic internationalization, private capital markets can appear to wield tremendous influence over national governments. For instance, dramatic capital market crises in Asia and Latin America in the 1990s prompted many governments to announce extensive pro-market reforms.

Whereas the impact of international capital markets on national governments may be most obvious in times of financial crises, many scholars maintain that financial markets also play a powerful role in routine government policymaking. For instance, a sizable body of recent scholarship argues that traditional social democracy is dying, *and* that the cause of death is the increased integration of national capital markets. This assertion is based on the assumption that global capital markets dislike – and react strongly against – key elements of redistributive, welfare-statist policies, such as high taxes and a high degree of public sector activism.

Looking at the recent growth of global capital and product markets, some observers have noted a new "impossible trinity." We can have integrated national economies, we can have sovereign and autonomous nation-states, or we can have responsive and effective domestic policymaking, but we can have no more than two of the three. The continued progression of international economic integration spells either the end of mass politics or the end of autonomous nation-states.[4] This possibility is one that may play out in coming decades, as we face choices not unlike those faced by governments and citizens at the turn of the twentieth century.[5] The more immediate question, however, is what the current implications of financial openness are for nation-states and for welfare state policies: in a period of high, albeit not complete financial openness, what can national governments achieve?

In this book, I argue that international financial integration does not necessitate the death of social democratic welfare states. Capital market openness does allow financial market participants to react swiftly and severely to changes in government policy outcomes. In the developed world,

---

[4] This revision of the "impossible trinity" is found in Rodrik 2001.
[5] E.g., Polanyi 1944.

however, capital market participants consider only a small set of government policies when making asset allocation decisions. They pay little attention to many other aspects of government policy, so that governments retain a significant degree of policy autonomy. Governments that conform to capital market pressures in select macroeconomic areas, such as overall government budget deficits and rates of inflation, are relatively unconstrained in supply side and microeconomic policy areas. As a result, international financial market forces have not rendered social democratic welfare state policies obsolete. Therefore, despite financial internationalization, we observe – and are likely to continue to observe – a significant amount of cross-national policy divergence among advanced industrial democracies. Moreover, when governments are faced with the choice between invoking the wrath of global capital markets and abandoning certain domestic policies, they do not always choose the latter. As a consequence, the diversity of national political alignments, political institutions, and economic profiles generates a multiplicity of responses to global capital market pressures.

In the developing world, however, the influence of financial markets on government policy autonomy is more pronounced. The risk of default in developing nations renders financial market participants more likely to consider a wide range of government policies when making investment decisions. Developing – or emerging market – nations are, by definition, lacking in capital endowments. They have greater needs to attract investment from abroad and, therefore, are more susceptible to capital market pressures. It is in the developing world, then, that antiglobalization activists' concerns about equity and accountability are most legitimate. Even this conclusion, however, must be tempered with awareness that governments retain some measure of choice. As in developed nations, the formulation of public policies reflects not only external financial market pressures but also domestic distributional considerations.

States and Markets: Convergence, Divergence, and the Need for Microfoundations

Structural Dependence and Interdependence

Although the contemporary era of financial internationalization is, in some aspects, historically unique, the general relationship between national states and private markets is of long-standing interest to scholars and policymakers. International economic relations, in one mode or another, always have affected the control and authority of national states.[6] In the *Wealth of Nations*, Smith points out that the imposition of taxes by national governments can provoke capital flight.[7] And in *The Great Transformation*, Polanyi argues that high levels of international economic openness are politically sustainable only when governments insulate and compensate vulnerable groups in society, by embedding market relations in a set of social institutions.[8] Without such intervention, societies choose to close their economic borders, as they did in the 1920s.

More recently, in the 1970s, comparative political economists turned their attention to the impact of domestic asset-holders on governments. The structural dependence hypothesis suggested that domestic capital holders occupied a privileged position in societies and, therefore, in policymaking. Because investment in the domestic economy is the path to economic growth, and because economic growth is the path to reelection, governments are particularly attentive to the demands of business. Different variants of structural dependence theory attributed varying degrees of influence to capital. Marxist-oriented theorists argued that capital owners possessed veto power, whereas neopluralist theorists assigned business a lesser degree of influence.[9] Later work assessed empirically the structural dependence argument by examining the responsiveness of government policy to investment patterns. For instance, Duane Swank investigates whether, when faced with low rates of domestic investment, governments respond to capitalists' activities by reducing corporate tax burdens. These studies conclude that there is some, but by no means an overwhelming, influence of business preferences on government policy outcomes.[10] Although structural dependence theorists addressed the influence of capital within polities, most[11]

---

[6] Krasner 1999.

[7] Smith 1776, book II, sections 373–379, pp. 848–849.

[8] Polanyi 1944, p. 140. More recent statements of this argument are found in Dryzek 1996 and Soros 1998, among others.

[9] Block 1977 exemplifies Marxist-oriented structural dependence theory, whereas Lindblom 1977 argues that governments need only provide a minimal level of benefits to capital owners, "without simply turning policy over to them lock, stock and barrel" (p. 183). Also see Bates and Lien 1985, Dryzek 1996.

[10] Przeworski and Wallerstein 1988, Swank 1992. More recently, Smith 1999 uses data from the United States to assess whether business exerts an overwhelming influence on public policy during economic downturns. He concludes that the structural power of business has been exaggerated.

[11] Block 1977 mentions the international dimension of capital but does not consider this dimension in his analysis. Wallerstein and Przeworski 1995 do expand their previous work to

assumed that capital owners faced a choice only between investing and not investing in their own economy, rather than between investing at home and investing abroad.

At the same time, scholars of international political economy examined the trend toward greater economic openness, labeled "interdependence," which signified changes in the capacity and roles of national states. Keohane and Nye described the "control gap" generated by transnational relations: national policymakers were less able to exercise authority over political and economic outcomes than they were in the 1950s and 1960s.[12] In such an environment, the cross-national coordination of economic policies became a functional imperative.[13] The capacity of national firms to relocate, for example, limited governments' choices over economic policies.

Contemporary Literature

The literature of the late 1960s and 1970s said little, however, about the specific causal relationships between economic interdependence and national policy outcomes; nor did it detail the interaction between international economic phenomena and domestic politics. In the mid-1980s, Peter Katzenstein's examination of small, trade-dependent European nations provided one means of integrating domestic political and international economic phenomena.[14] During the last decade, scholars devoted substantial attention to specifying the impact of economic globalization on national policy choices.[15] This theme has attracted interest not only in the academic realm, but also within media and policymaking circles. Much of the popular literature on the subject offers grim prognoses for government policymaking autonomy.

include international capital flows; they conclude that, if the cost of investment is deductible, governments retain the ability to collect taxes on uninvested profits.

[12] Keohane and Nye 1977.

[13] Morse 1969. Similarly, Richard Cooper suggested that, although international economic activity generated benefits, these benefits were derived at the expense of national policy autonomy. Cooper 1968, Cooper 1972, Dell 1987.

[14] Katzenstein 1985. In Katzenstein's account, small states are constrained substantially by the international economy, as they have little choice but to engage in trade. But at the same time, historical differences in domestic institutions generate cross-national variation in political–economic strategies.

[15] See Cohen 1996, Drezner 2001, Evans 1997, Garrett 1998c for comprehensive reviews of this literature. Sobel 1994 looks both to international and to domestic factors to explain changes in national securities market regulation. Like Cohen 1996, Garrett 2000b reviews several arguments regarding the causes of economic globalization and, specifically, the agency of national governments in the process.

The academic literature falls into two broad groups – convergence and divergence. Predictions of convergence rely on the imperatives of cross-national competition and economic efficiency; the type of convergence predicted tends to be downward, rather than a common trend toward an intermediate position.[16] Predictions of divergence, meanwhile, are based on the continued diversity of national institutions and on domestic demands for compensation. Much of this work glosses over the multifaceted nature of the globalization process, treating as similar the impacts of trade, direct investment, and portfolio capital movements.

It is important analytically, however, to distinguish among various types of economic internationalization and their effects. Trade openness and capital mobility do not necessarily covary,[17] and national resource endowments differ, so that some nations are quite open to trade but are less open to financial flows, and others are exactly the opposite. Additionally, trade flows and capital flows have different impacts on domestic economies: trade can result in increased output volatility; capital flows can induce greater volatility in investment but also can allow for consumption spending.[18] Moreover, different types of flows can generate different types of shocks. Thus, it is useful to consider the specific causal mechanisms through which capital market openness – as opposed to economic openness in general – can affect government policymaking autonomy.

Globalization, Convergence, and Efficiency

Convergence scholars argue that growing trade and financial internationalization seriously curtail government policy autonomy.[19] As governments and societies attempt to compete in an increasingly global marketplace, they reduce public involvement in the private sector. The driving force behind convergence accounts is efficiency: traditional welfare state policies are economically uncompetitive, so governments are quick to abandon them. Governments become leaner, embracing a neoliberal model of state–economy relations. They abandon the post–World War II compromise of embedded liberalism, in which governments combined increased

---

[16] On the multiple meanings of *convergence* see Kitschelt et al. 1999.

[17] Burgoon 2001, Cerny 1999, Garrett 1998c, Garrett and Mitchell 2001, Garrett and Nickerson 2001.

[18] Frankel 1986, Keohane and Milner 1996, Maxfield 1997, Maxfield and Hoffmann 1996, Sobel 1999.

[19] See Andrews 1994, Cerny 1995, Dryzek 1996, Rodrik 1997, Schwartz 1994.

openness to international trade with increased domestic protection for those dislocated by trade.[20] At the extreme, a race to the bottom ensues,[21] and global markets become masters over governments, eviscerating the authority of national states. Along these lines, Susan Strange maintains that

the impersonal forces of world markets . . . are now more powerful than the states to whom ultimate political authority over society and economy is supposed to belong. Where states were once the masters of markets, now it is the markets which, on many crucial issues, are the masters over the governments of states.[22]

Some of the convergence literature predicts not only growing cross-national similarities, but also – because financial markets have become a structural feature of the international system – a transfer of authority from national governments to private actors.[23]

In the realm of capital markets, the capacity for exit, and the political voice it confers on investors, is central to convergence-oriented accounts. While capital market openness provides governments with greater access to capital,[24] it also subjects them to external discipline. Governments must sell their policies not only to domestic voters, but also to international investors.[25] Because investors can respond swiftly and severely to actual or expected policy outcomes, governments must consider financial market participants' preferences when selecting policies.[26] Investors' credible threat of exit – assumed in the structural dependence literature but guaranteed by international capital mobility – greatly increases their voice.[27]

---

[20] Ruggie 1982, Rodrik 1997.
[21] See also Garrett 1998c and Garrett and Mitchell 2000 for a summary of the race to the bottom logic.
[22] Strange 1996, p. 4.
[23] Andrews 1994, Germain 1997. Similarly, Sassen 1996 argues that the current dynamics of the global economy threaten to undo "the particular form of sovereignty and territoriality embodied in the modern state." Also see Cerny 1999, Friedman 2000, Germain 1997, Porter 1999, Strange 1996. Sinclair 1994 suggests that a good deal of authority in international finance belongs now to credit ratings agencies rather than to national governments or to intergovernmental organizations. Ohmae 1995 labels the nation-state as "increasingly a nostalgic fiction" (p. 12). Dombrowski 1998 provides a different viewpoint, suggesting that states continue to shape outcomes in the area of international finance.
[24] See Garrett 2000b, IMF 1997b, Quinn and Inclan 1997, Quinn 1997.
[25] Burtless et al. 1998, Haggard and Maxfield 1996, Moses 1994, Pringle 1992, Simmons 1999, Strange 1996, Tanzi and Schuknecht 2000.
[26] Obstfeld 1998, Sassen 2000. Likewise, Mueller 1998 suggests that, with international factor mobility, governments' ability to impose involuntary redistribution is curtailed sharply.
[27] Hirschman 1970.

In this vein, Paulette Kurzer argues that financial markets harshly punish social democratic welfare policies and, therefore, render expansionary public programs obsolete:

In the past, governments could spend lavishly on public programs to reconcile the conflicting demands of labor and business. However, such expansionary programs produce expectations among financial asset holders that future inflation rates will drift above the rates of the country's main trading partners. This perception triggers capital outflows and foreign currency speculation.... Governments must reverse their policies to arrest future outflows.[28]

Philip Cerny offers a similar forecast: "Currency exchange rates and interest rates are increasingly set in globalizing marketplaces.... Globalization has undercut the policy capacity of the national state in all but a few areas."[29] Traditional welfare state policies are unlikely to withstand market participants' negative evaluations.[30] The prognosis is particularly dim for left-of-center governments, which receive the most unfavorable evaluations from financial asset-holders.[31]

These efficiency-based views predict a wide-ranging cross-national convergence of public policy outcomes, toward smaller governments, reduced government provision of social services, lower levels of taxation, lower levels of regulation, and lower levels of unionization. Proponents of the convergence hypothesis cite as evidence, inter alia, the rise of neoliberal policy programs and the advent of welfare state retrenchment in the 1980s in the United States, Britain, New Zealand, and Australia as evidence.[32] For at least some observers, the constraints emanating from financial openness are beneficial: they check the temptation of policymakers to "exploit a captive domestic capital market" or to pursue "unsound policies."[33] For other observers, these constraints are inherently undemocratic: national governments are accountable to a "global, cross-border economic

[28] Kurzer 1993, p. 12. Block 1996 characterizes this situation as "the dictatorship of financial markets" (cited in Evans 1997, p. 67).

[29] Cerny 1995, pp. 609, 612. Also see Grabel 1993.

[30] Germain 1997. For similar views from policymakers, see James Carville, quoted in *Economist*, October 7, 1995 survey, p. 5; Reich 1997, p. 64.

[31] Helleiner 1994, p. 296. Also see Cerny 1999, Sinclair 1994, 2000.

[32] On welfare state retrenchment and the impact of domestic political institutions on that process, see Clayton and Pontusson 1998, Dryzek 1996, Esping-Andersen 1996, Pierson 1994, 1996, Ross 1996, Tanzi and Schuknecht 2000. Germain 1997 posits that, although the constraining effect of financial market orthodoxy is most easily observed in developing nations, it is "equally at work" in industrialized countries (p. 135).

[33] Obstfeld 1998, Obstfeld and Taylor 1998.

electorate" consisting of "inflation-obsessed bondholders," rather than to citizens.[34]

Divergence, Compensation, and Domestic Institutions

The alternative perspective, which predicts continued cross-national diversity in economic policies and institutions, relies on two arguments. First, in the face of economic globalization, sustained variation in domestic institutions is not merely likely, but also possibly beneficial. The logic of comparative advantage, along with Tiebout's pure theory of local expenditure,[35] suggests that national specialization is possible within globalization. Firms and consumers have different preferences over taxation, services, and regulation; governments offer different combinations of these goods; and consumers and firms locate in the jurisdiction that best matches their preferences.[36] In the words of a former British Labour MP,

The fact is that different countries – for that matter, different regions or even different cities in the same country – can pursue competitive advantage in the global marketplace in different ways. Cost-cutting, tax-cutting, deregulation, and the rest of the Thatcherite armoury may lead to success in markets for the cheap and the shoddy.... By the same token, low real wages paid to badly trained workers are not the only attraction for inward investors. It is also possible to attract them with crime-free streets, with high quality education and training, and with a clean environment.[37]

Similarly, endogenous growth theory highlights the positive impact on economic performance of some types of government spending;[38] therefore, a large government–high-growth economy might coexist alongside a small government–high-growth economy.[39] A senior official with a major

---

[34] Sassen 1996, pp. 40, 50; also xiv, 38, 39.

[35] Tiebout 1956. Also see Hall and Soskice 2001, Mueller 1998.

[36] See Berger and Dore 1996, Garrett 1996, Kitschelt et al. 1999, Pierson 2001, Rogowski 1998. On diversity in production regimes, see Soskice 1999, Weiss 1998.

[37] Marquand in Radice 1996, p. 76.

[38] Alesina and Perotti 1996c, Barro and Sala-I-Martin 1995.

[39] In a slightly different vein, Iversen and Wren maintain that the most important change in advanced capitalist societies has not been economic internationalization, but the shift toward service sector–oriented economies. Where services, rather than manufacturing, dominate the economy, governments choose from a menu of goals, including budgetary restraint, income equality, and employment growth. Governments are able to achieve two, but not three, of these goals; divergence in government policy occurs as a result of variation in this political choice. Iversen and Wren 1998. Also see Iversen and Cusack 2000.

9

European bank summarized this viewpoint:

> It's ludicrous to suggest that all governments must have the same macroeconomic policies. All companies aren't run the same way just because they all have investors, and different companies turn in good performances.[40]

Second, economic globalization serves to heighten, rather than to reduce, pressures for government intervention. This compensation-based argument, which draws on the embedded liberalism notion, implies expanded or sustained domestic demands for government intervention. Governments have domestic political incentives to insulate individuals from externally generated insecurity and volatility; governments might pay an external economic price (in higher interest rates, for instance) for maintaining welfare state policies, but this price is offset by the internal political benefits of compensation.

The compensation view predicts a persistence of cross-national divergence in institutions and economic policy outcomes.[41] In support of this argument, for a sample of 100 nations, Rodrik finds a positive correlation between the level of a nation's exposure to international trade and the size of its government. And a nation's degree of trade openness in 1960 is a statistically significant predictor of the expansion of government size during the next three decades.[42] Rodrik's findings are rendered more convincing by his provision of several phases of evidence for the compensation mechanism.[43]

A cross-national mixture of policy outcomes also is theoretically consistent with open-economy models of aggregate fiscal and monetary policymaking. The Mundell–Fleming conditions detail the relationship between

---

[40] Interview 41. To preserve guarantees of confidentiality, I identify financial market interview subjects by interview number. A list of market participants' firms and interview dates is provided in Appendix 2.1. In a similar fashion, government officials are identified by agency and country.

[41] See Cameron 1978, Garrett 1998a, 1998c, Garrett and Mitchell 2000, Mueller 1998, Rodrik 1997. Adserà and Boix 2002 suggest that compensation is one mechanism (along with protectionism and political exclusion) through which governments can respond to increased trade openness; the compensation mechanism is more common at higher levels of democratization.

[42] Rodrik 1998. Rodrik reports that the correlation between trade and government size holds for most measures of government spending, as well as in low- and high-income samples. The result also is robust to the inclusion of a variety of control variables.

[43] For instance, Rodrik 1997 finds that external risk is positively and significantly associated with income volatility; that the effect of trade openness on government consumption is strongest in countries with more concentrated exports; and that past exposure to external risk is a statistically significant determinant of government consumption.

economic openness and the efficacy of national fiscal and monetary policies.[44] A nation may have two of the following three: open capital markets, fixed exchange rates, and an autonomously determined monetary policy. With capital market openness, a government with fixed exchange rates loses monetary policy autonomy and effectiveness. Interest rates and the money supply must be used to maintain the exchange rate peg. Fiscal policy, however, remains an effective tool for influencing domestic economic conditions, at least in the short run. On the other hand, a government with floating exchange rates retains monetary policy autonomy: interest rate policy is not subsumed to the goal of maintaining a particular exchange rate and so can be used to affect domestic demand. But, at the same time, fiscal policy loses efficacy.[45]

Open-economy models remind us that prior government decisions regarding exchange rates and capital market openness influence policy efficacy and, therefore, policy choices. If governments make similar choices regarding exchange rate regimes and capital market openness, international capital mobility reduces cross-national differences. But where governments make different choices, room for divergence remains.[46] Nations with fixed exchange rates converge in terms of monetary policy, whereas nations with flexible exchange rates should converge on fiscal policy. The loss of policy autonomy associated with capital market openness may have a greater impact on social democratic governments, as these governments traditionally employ fiscal *and* monetary policy to achieve full employment.[47] The more general point, however, is that, in a Mundell–Fleming framework, all governments face a mixture of constraint and autonomy, and this mixture varies across economic regimes.[48]

Divergence, Convergence, and the Empirical Record

Given the theoretical tension between convergence- and divergence-oriented accounts, what does the empirical record suggest about the impact

[44] Fleming 1962, Mundell 1963; also see Clark and Hallerberg 2000, Oatley 1999b. Similarly, Cohen 1996 describes an "unholy trinity," consisting of exchange rate stability, capital mobility, and national policy autonomy.

[45] See Mussa 1979, cited in Keohane and Milner 1996, p. 17, for a discussion of the standard open economy macroeconomic model. Also see Bisignano 1994.

[46] Notermans's 2000 account of the history of and prospects for social democracy is informed by such a view of externally generated constraints.

[47] Keohane and Milner 1996.

[48] Notermans 2000.

of financial openness on government policies? Recent empirical work assessing the validity of the convergence and divergence hypotheses, particularly in the advanced capitalist democracies, reveals a mixed pattern. Substantial cross-national diversity remains in areas such as government consumption spending, government transfer payments, public employment, and the public taxation,[49] but growing cross-national similarity exists in aggregate monetary and fiscal policies.[50] The latter often is associated positively with economic internationalization; the former reveals the continued influence of domestic politics and institutions.[51]

For instance, in the area of taxation, Swank finds that overall effective corporate tax burdens have not fallen in response to capital and trade internationalization. Many governments reduced marginal corporate tax rates but simultaneously broadened the tax base by closing various loopholes.[52] In fact, Swank finds a positive and statistically significant association between capital mobility and the effective tax rate.[53] Similarly, in their examination of the determinants of changes in marginal tax rates in OECD nations, Mark Hallerberg and Scott Basinger find that, although international economic openness had an indirect effect on tax changes during the 1986–1990 period – via tax competition and past economic

---

[49] Also see Boix 1997a, 1997b, 1998, Garrett and Lange 1991, Kopits 1992, Quinn 1997, Scruggs and Lange 2002, Stephens et al. 1999, Swank 1998a. On the importance of separating the effects of globalization into macropolicy and micropolicy areas, see Cohen 1996.

[50] See Frieden 1991a, Garrett and Lange 1991, Garrett 1998a, Goodman and Pauly 1993, Huber and Stephens 2001, Stephens et al. 1999. Garrett and Lange also maintain that the pursuit of different economic strategy profiles does not appear to affect economic performance.

[51] One recent example, with such mixed results, is Garrett and Mitchell's study of economic policies in 18 OECD nations during the 1961–1994 period. The reported statistical relationships between economic globalization and government spending tend to support the efficiency or convergence view, whereas the statistical relationships between economic globalization and taxation lean toward the compensation or divergence view. On the specific issue of capital mobility, Garrett and Mitchell 2001 find "scant evidence" that changes in cross-border capital flows have prompted a race to the bottom in welfare state effort. For a similar study encompassing developing as well as developed nations, see Garrett and Nickerson 2001.

[52] The net effect has been a maintenance of, or even an increase in, government revenues from corporate taxation. Kopits 1992, Swank 1998a.

[53] Swank 2001 also finds evidence of continued partisan differences in taxation: left governments rely more heavily on capital taxation; right governments tend toward higher taxes on labor.

performance – the most important influence was the structure of political institutions.[54]

Similarly, empirical studies in the Mundell–Fleming tradition reveal a mixture of convergence and divergence. In a study of 13 developed democracies for the 1968–1994 period, Oatley finds that partisan differences in economic policies do exist, but that these differences depend on the exchange rate regime and the degree of capital mobility.[55] Under fixed exchange rates, left governments run larger budget deficits than right governments, and these governments use capital controls to reduce interest rate premia. Under floating rates, monetary – rather than fiscal – policy is the preferred partisan instrument: left governments pursued looser monetary policies than right governments. In the 1990s, these partisan differences weakened; Oatley attributes this change not to a general increase in economic internationalization, but to the recession of the early 1990s and the push toward Economic and Monetary Union (EMU).[56] Recent research[57] suggests, then, that although there has been a cross-national convergence toward lower inflation rates and smaller budget deficits in the advanced capitalist democracies, divergence remains in supply-side areas. Many of these studies imply that international economic constraints are relatively small, and domestic political pressures and institutions remain central to the selection and implementation of government strategies. Nevertheless, theoretical and empirical gaps continue to characterize the field.

Far fewer empirical studies, for instance, have examined cross-national evidence from the mid- and late 1990s or focused on developing nations. Skeptics of the divergence–compensation perspective point out that although divergence persisted into the 1990s, financial globalization inevitably will produce greater cross-national policy convergence. For

---

[54] Nations with lower numbers of legislative and cabinet veto players enacted more sweeping tax changes. See Hallerberg and Basinger 1998. On the importance of separating the effects of globalization into macropolicy and micropolicy areas, see Cohen 1996.

[55] Oatley 1999b.

[56] Clark and Hallerberg also investigate the interaction between economic policymaking and Mundell–Fleming characteristics. Like Oatley, they find that government policy choices – specifically, preelectoral expansions – are constrained by exchange rate regimes and capital market openness. Unlike Oatley, however, Clark and Hallerberg 2000 do not find significant partisan influences on the use of fiscal and monetary policy.

[57] For other research that finds cross-national divergence, see Boix 1997a, 1997b, 1998 on privatization and government capital formation; Scruggs and Lange 2002 on union membership; and, more generally, the contributors to Kitschelt et al. 1999.

instance, Rodrik conjectures that, whereas high levels of international trade generate domestic demands for compensation, the ability of governments to meet these demands is constrained increasingly by international capital mobility.[58] An unraveling of empirical support for compensation-based models would be first evident empirically in changes in, rather than levels of, welfare state policies. Therefore, although economic globalization thus far has produced few reductions in national tax revenues or policies, such reductions are likely in the near future.[59]

Are developing nations more likely to experience cross-national convergence and, if so, via what mechanisms? Rodrik and Garrett assess the relationship between economic internationalization and government policies in large sets of high-, middle-, and low-income nations.[60] Garrett's analysis transcends much of the existing literature by considering trade and capital mobility as interactive, rather than independent, influences on government spending and by assessing changes in, as well as levels of, government policy outcomes. Relying on period averages for 1985–1995, Garrett finds a positive, strong, and robust relationship between the level of trade openness and the level of government spending – again, supporting the compensation view. At the same time, capital mobility appears to have no appreciable effect on the level of government spending. When Garrett considers changes over time,[61] however, different results emerge: nations in which trade grew more rapidly after 1985 also tended to experience slower growth in the public sector. This slowdown was exacerbated where capital mobility also increased quickly after 1985. Garrett's analysis reminds us that we need a better understanding not only of the cross-national trends in economic policy choices, but of the causal relationships between these trends and various facets of economic globalization.

The Need for Causal Mechanisms

Although the convergence and divergence literatures differ in terms of their outlook regarding governments' policy autonomy, they suffer from a

[58] Rodrik 1997.

[59] Tanzi 2000.

[60] Garrett 2000a, Rodrik 1998. Rudra and Haggard 2001 also consider the globalization–welfare spending relationship in developing nations; they find that domestic political institutions mediate the impact of global market forces on government expenditure. Avelino et al. 2001 conduct similar tests for Latin American nations and also find mixed empirical results.

[61] Garrett operationalizes changes as the difference between the 1970–1984 average and the 1985–1995 average.

14

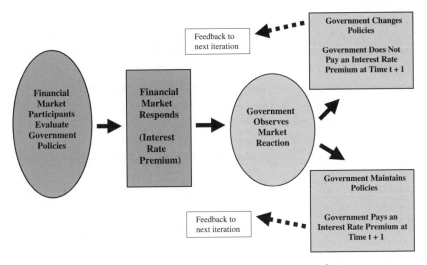

Figure 1.1 A causal model of financial market–government relations.

common shortcoming – scant exploration of the causal mechanisms under-pinning government policy selection. We need a clearer idea about what sorts of pressures are generated by financial market internationalization. For instance, how do financial market participants evaluate government policy, and how important are these evaluations for government policy choice?[62] Most research to date assumes a model of financial market operation and a pattern of government response to financial market evaluations.[63] Con-vergence arguments imply that governments elect to adopt more market-friendly policies rather than to pay the market's price for traditional social democratic policies, whereas divergence arguments suggest that – as a re-sult of the mediating effects of domestic institutions and domestic politics – governments often are willing to pay the market's price.

Figure 1.1 depicts the relationship between international financial mar-kets and national governments. On the left side, financial market par-ticipants evaluate some set of government policies and respond to these

---

[62] Cohen 1996 issues a similar challenge: "The interesting question, therefore, is not whether financial globalization imposes a constraint on sovereign states; it most clearly does. Rather, we should now be asking how the discipline works and under what conditions. What accounts for the remaining room for maneuver, and why do some countries still enjoy more policy autonomy than others?" (pp. 283–284). Also see Garrett 1998b.

[63] Recent exceptions are Leblang and Bernhard's 2000 examination of the political (and eco-nomic) determinants of speculative foreign exchange attacks in advanced industrial democ-racies and the Freeman et al. 2000 examination of foreign exchange market activity.

policies by increasing, maintaining, or decreasing the interest rate charged for government borrowing. On the right side, the government observes the financial market response. A government facing an adverse market response chooses either to alter its policies, thereby reducing its future interest rate premium, or to maintain its policies, thereby continuing to pay an interest rate premium. The interaction occurs repeatedly, as markets react to some set of government policies, and governments consider market responses when formulating subsequent policy choices. It is the right side of Figure 1.1, near the end of the causal chain, that has attracted the preponderance of attention from comparative and international political economists. This attention is neither surprising nor unwarranted: understanding the policy implications of globalization requires understanding how domestic politics and institutions refract externally generated pressures.

But, in order to comprehend correctly how government policy might change because of financial market pressures, we must know something about the financial market response function – the left side of Figure 1.1. In order to understand the conditions under which convergence or divergence occurs, we need to understand international financial market operation, which generates the external price charged to governments for their domestic policies, as well as the conditions under which governments elect to pay the market-generated price for policy autonomy. Specifying a model of financial market operation, and the sources of cross-national and over-time variation in its operation, is the central aim of this book.

The Research Project

I provide an account of how international financial market participants evaluate government policy outcomes and, therefore, of how financial market pressures affect government policy choices. In the first three chapters, I examine the means by which investors assess and respond to government policies in developed as well as in developing nations. This investigation rests on the treatment of financial market participants as rational maximizers with incentives to economize on the use of information. I assess this framework empirically by using a variety of qualitative and quantitative data. I then investigate the impact of financial market influences within domestic politics. By suggesting the conditions under which governments choose to pay the financial market price for certain policies, this section speaks directly to the government policy autonomy debate. Finally, I investigate the pre–World War I era of capital mobility, noting its similarities with the contemporary period.

My central argument is that the consideration of government policies by financial market actors varies markedly across groups of countries. In the advanced capitalist democracies, market participants consider key macroeconomic indicators, but not supply-side or microlevel policies. Market participants can charge high prices for certain government policies, but the range of policies used to set these prices is limited. In OECD nations, governments are pressured strongly to satisfy financial market preferences in terms of overall inflation and government budget deficit levels, but they retain domestic policymaking latitude in other areas. In developing nations, however, the scope of the financial market influence extends to cover both macro- and micropolicy areas. Domestic policymaking in these nations is more likely to conform to the convergence view.

The Focus: The Government Bond Market

"International financial markets" encompasses a wide range of instruments, including equities, bonds, derivatives, foreign exchange, and direct investment. Each of these categories of instrument can influence government policy through unique causal paths. For instance, as many critics of contemporary globalization argue, outsourcing or foreign direct investment abroad could generate pressures for labor market and environmental deregulation. Governments might also experience popular pressure to encourage a stable and improving stock market, particularly where national pension systems have been privatized via the local equity market, or where a majority of citizens hold some of their assets in equity markets. And, especially in trade-dependent nations, the currency's value is likely to be a central issue for national economic management.[64]

I do not deny the existence of multiple potential causal linkages between financial globalization and government policy outcomes. I elect, however, to focus on one set of financial instruments – the government bond market – and on the causal pathways associated with it. I concentrate on this segment of global finance because it provides a *most likely* location for the operation of financial market pressures. In the sovereign debt market, national governments borrow funds in order to compensate for revenue shortfalls or to fulfill other economic management objectives. Government officials

---

[64] E.g., Frieden 1991b.

announce the amount and type of financing instruments that they will issue. After this announcement, market participants submit bids: they indicate the interest rates at which they will buy government bonds. The government selects those investors offering the lowest interest rates, and those interest rates represent the government's financing costs. When market participants punish governments, they do so by increasing the interest rates at which they will purchase government securities.

Bonds are both an important source of financing for governments, as well as a central part of large institutional investors' portfolios. At the beginning of 2001, the seven major portfolio investors polled quarterly by the *Economist* magazine held an average of 42% of their assets in bonds, much of it in government debt, and approximately 80% of it denominated in euros or dollars.[65] In addition, total gross private capital flows to emerging market nations totaled $101 billion in 1999, and 29% of this amount funded sovereign borrowing. Bonds were the most common form of financing for emerging markets, representing 48.7% of total flows, compared with 13% for equities and 38.3% for loans.[66]

Moreover, there are overt linkages between types of international capital markets. For example, if a nation's exchange rate depreciates (or is expected to do so), the risk premia associated with government bonds increase. A government that experiences a declining exchange rate faces not only higher import prices, but also steeper borrowing costs.

The interest rates charged to governments for accessing the bond market also strongly influence the interest rates paid by other actors in the national economy.[67] Therefore, the impact of bond market activity on national governments is quite direct. A government that pays higher interest rates in return for a given set of policies spends a greater portion of its budget on interest payments and may have to reduce the size of other programs. And the increased financing costs experienced by private actors in the domestic economy could imply an overall economic slowdown.

Within the realm of public debt, conversations with government officials suggest that *longer-term* interest rates, such as the rates on benchmark

[65] *Economist*, April 12, 2001, p. 68. The firms surveyed include Commerz International Capital Management, Credit Suisse PB, Daiwa, Julius Baer PB, Lehman Brothers, Robeco Group, and Standard Life. During 1999 and 2000, the average holding of bonds ranged from 42% to 44% of major portfolio investors' assets.

[66] Data are taken from IMF 2000b, chapter 3.

[67] Although governments often set shorter-term rates, longer-term rates are market-determined. Gilibert 1994. See Maxfield 1997 for a similar argument.

government bonds, are particularly important to economic policymakers. Most of these officials[68] pay attention to longer-term market trends rather than to short-term (e.g., daily) market volatility. Of the 15 government officials interviewed who discussed the importance of short-term versus long-term market movements, 11 officials noted that longer-term movements were most important, 2 stated that both long-term trends and shorter-term volatility were important,[69] and 2 maintained that short-term volatility was important.

The main dependent variable with which I am concerned, then, is the interest rate on benchmark (domestic-currency denominated, 10-year maturity) government bonds – a standard instrument. Because I am more concerned with trends in the levels of rates rather than with the short-term volatility of these rates, I focus on longer-term (monthly or quarterly) interest rate movements. Although short-term volatility in government bond prices also can affect governments and private actors, this volatility often is temporary. Enduring changes in the government bond market are captured by longer-term prices. Additionally, a price measure (interest rates) is more appropriate than a flow measure (such as capital inflows/gross domestic product [GDP]), because responses to policy outcomes occur in the form of price changes, rather than quantity shifts. If governments displease financial market participants, they likely will remain able to access global capital markets, but at higher interest rate premia. Particularly in times of high market liquidity, market actors do not want governments to stop borrowing on international bond markets: government bonds are relatively safe and desirable investments, especially for risk-averse investors. Just as an individual consumer with a poor credit rating can acquire a credit card if she is willing to pay very high interest rates, so too can most governments with poor credit ratings. In the words of one market participant:

Within a wide range, governments can get away with things, provided they don't mind paying a bit more. It's like insurance: you can always find someone to insure you, as long as you are willing to pay the premium.[70]

---

[68] Interview subjects are former and current senior-level officials from the Bank of England, the British Treasury, the Bank of France, the French Finance Ministry, the Bank of Belgium, the German Bundesbank, the German Economics Ministry, and the German Chancellor's Office. Interviews were conducted from January to June 1997.

[69] Chapter 6 suggests that this view should be more prevalent among governments with higher proportions of short-term government debt. Also see Giavazzi and Pagano 1988.

[70] Interview 34.

Only when credit rationing is rife, as in the Latin American debt crisis or the August–October 1998 retreat from emerging markets,[71] is financial market influence manifested via quantity reductions rather than price increases. For instance, in April 2001, Argentina was plagued with economic problems; investors began to worry that default was inevitable. In these circumstances, the government chose to suspend an auction of government securities, hoping its credibility would improve in the following weeks. In this case, credit rationing was short-lived, and the Argentine government successfully placed bonds – albeit with a substantial risk premium – in May 2001.[72]

The Plan of the Book

Chapter 2 provides a theoretical treatment of financial market influences on government policy choice. I define financial market influence along two dimensions: strength – the capacity of financial market participants to react to policy changes – and scope – the number of policy indicators considered by financial market participants. Drawing from recent literature in finance and economics, I suggest that investors' certainty regarding governments' creditworthiness, as well as the relative costs and benefits of employing information, determine the range of government policy indicators that is salient to investors. Investors' degree of certainty varies across countries, leading investors to make different choices regarding information when dealing with different groups of nations. On this basis, I hypothesize that financial market pressures are strong *but* narrow for developed democracies. By contrast, emerging market governments face strong and broad market influence: market participants, concerned with default risk, consider many dimensions of government policy when making asset allocation decisions.

In Chapter 3, I provide two types of evidence for the "strong but narrow" proposition – data from interviews with financial market participants, conducted in London and Frankfurt in 1997 and 1998, and cross-sectional time series data for 18 OECD nations for the 1981–1995 period. The interview data strongly support the notion that financial market participants

---

[71] E.g., Cohen 1996, Edwards 1994, Epstein and Gintis 1992, Frieden 1991a, McAleese 1990. Treatments of credit rationing in economics include Bayoumi et al. 1995, Eaton and Gersovitz 1981, Jaffee and Russell 1976, and Stiglitz and Weiss 1981. For portrayals of financial market influence as credit rationing, see Helleiner 1994, Kurzer 1993, Robson 1994.

[72] *New York Times*, May 9, 2001, p. C11.

are concerned with developed country governments' "getting the big numbers right," but they are much less concerned about the partisan affiliation or the microlevel policies of these governments. As one fund manager suggests, "Governments are more constrained by their history and by their people than they are by market pressures."[73] On the quantitative side, I find that the strongest determinants of longer-term government bond rates are inflation and U.S. interest rates. Government fiscal balances, current account balances, and exchange rate levels also are significantly and somewhat strongly associated with government bond rates. I then examine the influence of microside indicators on government bond rates. I conclude that international financial markets exert relatively little influence on government policy choice in supply-side areas. Although governments may concede to financial market pressures in a few areas, they maintain autonomy in many others.

How do these results square with casual observation of the developing world, which often appears rife with financial market constraints? Building on the expectation that emerging market governments will be more broadly influenced by financial market pressures, I provide evidence that these nations, in fact, do face a strong *and* broad constraint. In emerging market economies, default risk is salient, and the quality of information is low. In addition, because of their need to attract external financing, most emerging market economies are very exposed to international capital markets. When making asset allocation decisions, market participants consider not only macrolevel policy outcomes, but also micropolicy indicators and the political landscape. The head of several emerging market investment funds makes the same point, albeit in a different fashion:

There are 108 emerging market countries, and it's like choosing among 108 pretty girls. You're going to choose the prettiest of them all and, if you're not the prettiest, you're going to have to show a lot more leg. We are international investors, attempting to get the best return possible, and deciding among competing nations.[74]

Support for my conclusions is drawn from additional interviews with financial market participants, an analysis of sovereign credit rating methodologies and outcomes, and simple cross-national statistical analyses.

---

[73] Interview 41. This fund manager went on to state, "My colleagues and I worry that governments will try to adopt a single model of economic policy – that they will go beyond tinkering – and, in doing so, that they will screw things up."

[74] Interview 28.

The next two substantive chapters take up the right side of Figure 1.1. Chapter 5 investigates how domestic economic and political institutions mediate governments' responses to a given set of financial market pressures. Figure 1.1 suggests that, when faced with financial market pressures, governments choose between changing their policies and paying the interest rate price of the policy. In the words of a senior adviser to the British government:

Markets are an important discipline, they always were an important discipline, and they always will be; it's just a question of degree.... Governments have plenty of room to do things contrary to market-friendly policies – it's crazy to think that it's not that way.... The markets will give you a price, and you only have to change your policy if the price is too high.[75]

The decision to pay the interest rate price reflects a government's assessment of the trade-offs between pursuing autonomous policies and incurring higher interest rates.[76] I posit that this assessment depends on the magnitude of the price, on the government's sensitivity to changes in economic performance caused by the price, and on the salience to governments of debt servicing costs. For instance, where voters can more easily attribute to governments responsibility for economic policy outcomes, governments are more sensitive to externally induced interest rate changes. After generating expectations regarding the relationship between various domestic factors and government responses, I consider several governments' responses to bond market disturbances of 1994. I examine the case of Sweden in detail, positing that Sweden's response – cutting the overall deficit while maintaining the broad outlines of traditional policies – reflects the impact of domestic incentives and institutions.

Chapter 6 addresses another aspect of domestic politics by exploring how governments attempt to influence the nature of their relationship with the international bond market. Particularly in the advanced capitalist democracies, governments have choices regarding the extent to and ways in which they interact with global capital markets. I evaluate three types of policies: the first category includes domestic institutions that serve to change market expectations regarding macroeconomic outcomes – politically independent central banks and fiscal-policymaking institutions. The second category of government responses covers policies that change the susceptibility of certain classes of investors to these outcomes, such as the foreign currency

[75] Interview, senior economic adviser, British government, January 1997.
[76] Also see Simmons 1994.

22

denomination of government debt or the issuance of inflation-linked debt. The final category of policies insulates national governments from financial market pressures, including lengthening the maturity structure of government debt, encouraging resident investment, and controlling capital inflows and outflows. I find, in general, that governments have choices regarding the nature of their relationship with the international financial market. The choices governments make are at least partly exogenous to economic globalization, reflecting instead domestic political contests.[77]

In Chapter 7, the final substantive chapter, I turn to an examination of historical variation in government–financial market relations. Many authors note that financial openness is not historically unprecedented; few, however, have undertaken systematic comparisons of the pre–World War I and the contemporary period. By analyzing the similarities and differences of the periods, I suggest the extent to which recent influences of financial markets on government policy have historical parallels. I compare these eras along three dimensions: the structure of the financial industry and, therefore, of sovereign borrowing practices; the governance of capital flows, both nationally and internationally; and the policy commitments and ambitions of national governments. Although there are many similarities between the periods, there also are some differences; for instance, the currency regime created greater constraints for *most* pre–World War I governments, whereas less ambitious social policies mean that pre–World War I governments were *less* affected by financial market pressures. All in all, I expect that today's governments are at least as influenced by capital markets as those in the 1880–1914 era; history may be repeating itself today, but it is doing so more loudly. To evaluate these expectations, I present primary archival evidence from lending to four nations – Argentina, Cuba, Japan, and Russia – as well as a summary of approximately 70 other sovereign lending episodes. In the pre–World War I period, the least constrained borrowers were politically important and economically hopeful, whereas the most constrained borrowers were politically marginal and economically weak.

I conclude, in Chapter 8, with a discussion of several issues raised by the book. I reflect, for example, on how the advent of a single currency in Europe might change the tenor of bond market–government relations. The elimination of cross-national currency risk may dilute the impact of resident investment, and, more importantly, heighten the salience of default risk.

[77] Oatley 1999b makes a similar argument with respect to the choice of exchange rate regimes.

The central contribution of this book is a causal model of government–financial market relations, which provides foundations for previous empirical findings of convergence and divergence. My main argument is that governments of developed democracies are not constrained broadly by financial market pressures. Financial market participants are interested principally in the aggregate economic outcomes of inflation and government budget deficits. The means by which governments achieve these outcomes, and the nature of government policies in other areas, do not concern financial market participants. Therefore, complying with financial market participants' preferences over particular aggregate outcomes leaves governments with room for maneuver. Finally, in emerging market economies, the prognosis for the autonomy of national governments is more dire. Although governments in the developing world are not fully constrained by financial market pressures, and although there is cross-national and diachronic variation in the extent to which governments are constrained, market participants do exert pressure on a wider set of policy outcomes in emerging market nations. Therefore, governments find themselves with fewer choices regarding the character of their relationship with the international financial market.

2

Financial Market Influence
on Government Policy

THEORY AND HYPOTHESES

> The Prime Minister [of Thailand] laughed, but he knew just what I meant: joining the global economy and plugging into the Electronic Herd is the equivalent of taking your country public. It is the equivalent of turning your country into a public company; only the shareholders are no longer just your own citizens. They are the members of the Electronic Herd, wherever they might be. And, as I noted earlier, they don't just vote once every four years. They vote every hour, every day through their mutual funds, their pension funds, their brokers.[1]

When a bond trader at Goldman Sachs, or a fund manager at Fidelity, sits at his desk, contemplating where to allocate investment, what information does he consider? Does he think only about inflation, the balance of payments, and the overall government budget deficit – a few figures he can gather before lunch? Does he seek more fine-grained information, considering the structure of a nation's tax system, the allocation of its budget across functional categories, and the structure of employer–union relations? Or does he keep his eyes on his Reuters screen, nervously watching for news of political developments and forecasts of government change?

This section of the book provides a theoretical framework and empirical evidence to help understand the activities of bond traders and investment managers. In this and the following two chapters, I address the financial market side of the capital market–national government nexus. Although the extant globalization literature portrays financial markets as somehow limiting governments, the precise operation of these markets and the implications of market operation for government policy choice usually are unexamined. Many political economists therefore fail to address a key piece

---

[1] Friedman 2000, p. 167.

of the globalization process: if government economic policy outcomes are due, in part, to international financial market pressures, explanations of government policy choice should include the nature of financial market operation.

In this chapter, I develop a set of expectations regarding financial market influences on government policy. These expectations are based on financial market participants' prior beliefs regarding governments' creditworthiness, on their use of information as a signal of governments' creditworthiness, and on the structure of the investment management industry. I suggest that the relative costs and benefits of employing information determine the range of government policy indicators that is salient to investors, and that this range varies across types of countries. Where investors have strong posterior beliefs regarding government creditworthiness, they are most likely to economize on the use of information. But where they are uncertain about sovereign borrowers' types, they are more likely to employ a wider range of information. I also maintain that the incentives faced by market participants – specifically, incentives to value shorter-term over longer-term performance and incentives to evaluate performance in relative terms – reinforce the impact of informational concerns on market participants' behavior.

I expect, then, that in the contemporary era, financial markets exert a "strong but narrow" influence on government policy choices in developed nations. Financial market participants are able to exact harsh punishment against governments that pursue suboptimal policies, but this punishment is meted out on the basis of a small set of indicators. By contrast, emerging market governments face a strong and broad market constraint: market participants consider many dimensions of government policy when making asset allocation decisions.

This examination focuses on professional, rather than individual, investors. Professional – or "institutional" – investors include financial institutions that "invest savings of individuals and non-financial companies in the financial markets."[2] These include pension funds, insurance companies, mutual funds, and some divisions of investment banks.[3] Institutional

---

[2] Blommestein and Funke 1998, p. 67.

[3] Hedge funds also could be categorized as institutional investors. They are, however, different from other institutional investors, in that they often are unregulated and their clients have a higher tolerance for risk. Despite the recent growth and prominence of hedge funds, however, they continue to represent a very small segment of the institutional investment market (BIS 1998).

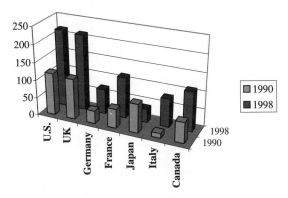

Figure 2.1 Institutional investors' assets as a percentage of GDP. *Source*: OECD 2000, p. 25.

investors are the most important actors in international capital markets, and their importance has increased dramatically during the last two decades. In OECD nations, the annual growth of institutional investors' assets averaged 12% in the 1990s.[4]

Figure 2.1 documents the growth of institutional investors' assets in the Group of 7 (G-7) nations, Canada, France, Germany, Japan, Italy, the United States, and the United Kingdom; the data indicate institutional investors' assets as a percentage of national income. Between 1990 and 1998 (the most recent year for which data are available), institutional investors' holdings increased dramatically in most nations, reaching over 200% of gross domestic product (GDP) in the United States and the United Kingdom. Total holdings of U.S. institutional investors exceeded $18 trillion in 1998; Canada, France, Italy, and Germany started at lower levels but experienced similarly dramatic increases during the decade. Only Japan, facing economic difficulties and a shaky financial system, experienced a decline in institutional investors' holdings.

Institutional investors hold a variety of assets, including bonds, equities, and loans. Although institutional investors have expanded their equity holdings in recent years, bonds remain an important component of their portfolios. As Figure 2.2 indicates, bonds constitute half or more of institutional investors' portfolios in Canada, Italy, Japan, and France, and over one-third of their portfolios in the United States and Germany. Even in

---

[4] Blommetein and Funke 1998. On the growth of institutional investors during the 1970s and 1980s, see Davis 1988 and Turner 1991.

27

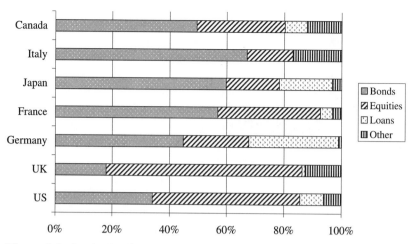

Figure 2.2 Institutional investors' assets, by instrument, 1998. *Source*: OECD 2000, pp. 32–34.

the United Kingdom, where equity holdings expanded dramatically in the 1990s, bonds remain an important investment component, particularly in periods of market volatility.

The *strength* of the financial market constraint refers to the capacity of market participants to punish governments for deviations from preferred policy outcomes. A very strong market reaction to undesirable policies involves dramatic changes in interest rates, as investors either sell their holdings or increase the risk premia charged to governments. A very weak market reaction is characterized by small or nonexistent changes in interest rates. The *scope* of the constraint refers to the number of indicators considered by financial market participants when making cross-national asset allocation decisions. When the constraint is narrow, market participants look at only a few categories of government policy. When the constraint is broad, market participants consider a wide range of government policy indicators. A more narrow constraint implies that, in many areas, government policymaking is unaffected by financial market pressures. Later, I suggest that the scope of the constraint varies across groups of countries, according to the level of concern regarding investment risks.

The strength and scope of financial market influence depend on the level of international financial openness, on investors' incentives to collect and employ information, and on the extent to which investors focus on similar types of information. The level of financial openness and the use of similar information affect the magnitude (strength) of financial market influence, measured in terms of interest rate changes; the incentives regarding the use of information establish the grounds (scope) for those changes.

Capital Mobility: A Background Condition

The extent to which investors can move their holdings from one country to another determines the capacity of investors to punish governments. With no capital mobility – and no credible threat of exit[5] – investors facing deteriorating conditions can wait and see, or convert their holdings to cash, but they cannot move their holdings to a different investment market. Cross-border investments are impossible or, at best, expensive. Under these conditions, even if capital holders are unhappy with a particular government policy choice, they can do little to express their displeasure. But, with high capital mobility and high asset liquidity, the threat of immediate exit (or increases in risk premia) becomes credible.[6] The "possibility for potential flows" changes the tenor of financial market–government relations. At higher levels of financial openness, capital market pressures should be more salient for national governments. Therefore, in the present era of relatively high capital mobility, holders of capital *can* respond sharply to particular government policy outcomes.[7]

High levels of capital mobility make such strong market reactions possible, but not inevitable. Under high capital market openness, a change in national tax policy could elicit a change in interest rate premia, or financial market participants largely could ignore it. Identifying the likelihood of such responses – that is, understanding the conditions under which strong reactions will occur – requires inquiry about the scope of the financial market constraint. Moreover, even under similar levels of capital market openness, nations are influenced differentially by international capital markets. This variation is driven by differences in types of investment risk (discussed in the following section), in national capital endowments (so

---

[5] Hirschman 1970. Similarly, Bates and Lien 1985 argue that, as the ability of capital to exit increases, the ability of governments to tax capital declines.

[6] Andrews 1994, Sinclair 2001, Thomas 2001.

[7] We can think of the impact of potential flows on governments as akin to Cooper's 1972 "sensitivity interdependence": when capital is allowed to move in and out of national borders, we should observe an increase in the cross-national sensitivities of interest rates. Also see Sinclair and Thomas 2001.

that more capital scarce nations are more susceptible to pressures),[8] and in domestic institutional structures (see Chapters 5 and 6).

Information and Investment Management

Once we allow for the *possibility* of financial market influence, we must consider the actual extent of such influence. Doing so requires a conception of how financial market participants make decisions regarding interest rate premia; these decisions rely on market participants' assumptions about governments' creditworthiness and on their resulting use of information. What are investors' prior beliefs regarding investment risks, and how do these vary across groups of countries? When deciding whether and at what level to charge risk premia to governments, at which indicators do market participants look? When making asset allocation decisions, do market participants consider a wide range of government policy indicators, or a narrow range of indicators?

I begin by assuming that professional investors have informational advantages over individual investors: that is, individuals improve the performance of their investments by delegating decision making to investment professionals.[9] Although this assumption is at odds with frameworks that assume strongly efficient markets,[10] it is consistent with a modified view of market efficiency.[11] In this view, information is costly to obtain and, as a result, provides benefits to those who collect it.[12]

---

[8] Mahon 1996, Maxfield 1997. Along similar lines, Lukauskas and Minushkin 2000 suggest that the degree and nature of financial market liberalization in developing nations vary according to their economic conditions and need for external funds.

[9] IMF 1999a. Also see Gruber 1996.

[10] The classical efficient markets view of the financial sector, based on a strong assumption of rational expectations, suggests that prices reflect all available and relevant information, so that there is no role for investment professionals. In other words, there is little reason for individuals to delegate asset management to professionals, and, if they do, there is little reason for them to expect one mutual fund to perform better than another, given appropriate diversification. For example, the Capital Asset Pricing Model (CAPM) – a relatively common model of portfolio choice – suggests that, from the point of view of uninformed individual investors, "all well-diversified investment funds will have the same expected rate of return, with actual returns distributed independently over time" (Berkowitz and Kotowitz 1993, p. 853) Also see Fama 1970, Kupiec 1993, and Malliaris and Stein 1999.

[11] Grossman and Stiglitz 1980, Ippolito 1989, Chevalier and Ellison 1999b.

[12] Chevalier and Ellison 1999a, Grossman and Stiglitz 1980, Froot et al. 1992, and Ippolito 1989 find that mutual funds are efficient in their information collecting and trading activities: funds with higher turnover, fees, and expenses earn rates of return that offset the higher expenses.

As such, delegation to fund managers reflects an optimal allocation of time by individuals: each individual could research investments on her own, but only at a cost of forgoing other, more productive activities.[13] Individuals select the investment professionals whom they expect to provide the highest risk-adjusted returns, and this selection motivates fund managers to aim for high returns. Along these lines, several studies of inflows of capital into mutual funds find strong positive correlations between past mutual fund performance and current inflows, or between poor performance and fund termination.[14] These suggest that individual investors monitor fund managers' performance, and that managers who provide superior information and performance are rewarded.[15] And because funds' incomes and managers' compensation are a function of their overall size (based usually on a percentage of assets under management, or a flat fee plus a percentage of assets), investment professionals have strong incentives to attract inflows.[16] And on the whole, fund managers appear to earn the fees they charge. For instance, Berkowitz and Kotowitz find that fund managers outperform the market by a rather significant margin, so that professional fund managers do improve the efficiency of financial markets.[17]

[13] Capon et al. 1996, Lettau 1997, Sirri and Tufano 1998.

[14] Berkowitz and Kotowitz 1993, Blommestein and Funke 1998, Ippolito 1992, Lettau 1997, Sirri and Tufano 1998. Lettau 1997 also identifies an asymmetry in the inflows/performance relationship, in that inflows are more sensitive to negative mutual fund returns than to positive ones. Sirri and Tufano 1998 find that the most recent performance information is most important to mutual fund inflows, and that this relationship is strongest among the top 20% of mutual funds. Harless and Peterson 1998 note that, despite the performance–inflow relationship identified by this literature, some consistently poorly performing mutual funds remain in existence.

[15] Chevalier and Ellison 1997, 1999a. Khorana 1996 examines managers' rewards in a slightly different way: he looks at the relationship between mutual fund performance and mutual fund manager replacement. Where mutual fund performance is poorer, the replacement of fund managers is more likely. Again, then, fund managers have clear incentives to earn relatively high returns and to attract new investment.

[16] For a brief review of the literature on compensation and performance, see Brown et al. 1996. Chevalier and Ellison 1997 explore the impact of these performance-based incentives on mutual fund investment activity. They argue that measures taken by managers to increase the fund's overall size – for instance, attempting to earn a higher return in the fourth quarter as a way of boosting year-end performance – may be at odds with maximizing risk-adjusted returns. In this way, Chevalier and Ellison demonstrate that performance incentives faced by financial agents do not necessarily fulfill the preferences of the principals. Ackermann et al. 1999 discuss the performance-based incentives faced by hedge fund managers and how these differ, in some ways, from those faced by mutual fund managers.

[17] Berkowitz and Kotowitz 1993; also see Blommestein and Funke 1998, Ippolito 1989, Otten and Bams 2000.

At the heart of my argument, then, is a conception of professional investors as rational, utility-maximizing decision makers[18] who face the challenge of distinguishing among sovereign borrowers. Their behavior takes the form of a signaling game, in which investors have incomplete information regarding governments' types.[19] In this game, governments can be of two general types – good credit risk (not prone to default) or bad credit risk (prone to default); governments know their own types, but investors do not know governments' types. Given this information asymmetry, the challenge to investors is to distinguish between types; they do so by using government policy outcomes as signals. After making inferences from these signals, investors take action by assigning an interest rate premium to government bonds.

Collecting and processing information regarding government policy outcomes – observing signals – are costly to investors. Therefore, lenders seek means of addressing informational constraints. Market participants are rational maximizers, but their maximization is subject to informational costs.[20] Market participants actively decide whether or not to collect and use particular types of information.[21] Their decisions are based on two factors – first, on their prior beliefs regarding a government's type, which are based on the nation's level of economic development, and, second, on a cost–benefit analysis of each piece of information. Where an investor has a strong prior belief that a government is of the "good credit risk" type, she will invest only a small amount in the collection of information. Identifying a government's type is a fairly simple task, one that usually can be done with a small amount of information, and at a low cost. In other words, where

---

[18] DeBondt and Thaler 1994 review literature that critiques this assumption.

[19] On signaling games, see Banks and Sobel 1987, Fearon 1994, Gibbons 1992, Morrow 1994, 1999. I thank an anonymous reviewer for suggesting the signaling framework.

[20] E.g., Coase 1937, Ferejohn 1991, Sherman and Corty 1984. My discussion of individuals' information-processing constraints is similar to that of Lupia and McCubbins 1998, who discuss informational issues with respect to individuals' political behavior. For an alternative view of human rationality, see Simon 1995. Simon maintains that, although human behavior generally is rational, there often is slippage between individuals' actions and the achievement of their goals. In Simon's view, these slippages may be due to incomplete information, to computational limits, to a multiplicity of goals, or to ignorance of potential courses of action.

[21] This concept of active acquisition of knowledge differs somewhat from a Bayesian approach, which would suggest that market participants passively receive information and then use it to update their priors. In my framework, market participants ignore useless information and employ useful information. See Lupia and McCubbins 1998, Eichengreen and Mody 1998, and Rubinstein 1998.

the marginal benefit of a piece of information is less than its marginal cost, a market participant will not collect that piece of information.[22] Where an investor does not have a strong prior belief regarding a government's type, she will invest a much larger amount in the collection of information. Here the marginal benefit of a piece of information exceeds its marginal cost, as it allows the investor to distinguish between types of borrowing governments. In these cases, market participants will devote their scarce attention and time resources to the information that provides the greatest marginal benefit. Ultimately, "information is valuable only when it improves the accuracy of predictions."[23]

The need to economize on the use of information is particularly strong when financial internationalization is high. If investment is confined to a single country or set of countries, investors are able to consider a wide range of information and to become very certain about the type of each government. But when they are able to invest in a large number of nations,[24] investors' information requirements are much greater.[25] For example, after investors diversify to 20 from 5 countries, investors who look at 5 indicators per country will have 100 rather than 25 pieces of information to consider. The constraints generated by information costs create incentives for investors to economize on the use of information;[26] collecting and

---

[22] This assertion is in line with "rational ignorance" models of political behavior, as in Downs 1957. Such models assume that the costs to individuals of acquiring information sometimes exceed the benefits of acquiring it. Also see Bianco 1994.

[23] Lupia and McCubbins 1998 refer to this model as a "calculus of attention," in which the expected return from attending to a particular stimulus is equal to the expected benefit of attention, less the opportunity costs and transaction costs associated with the stimulus. For them, the expected benefit of attention is a reduction in the likelihood of costly mistakes. For our model, attention reduces the likelihood of mispricing investment risk.

[24] On the benefits of international portfolio diversification, see Fabozzi and Modigliani 1992, French and Poterba 1991.

[25] Erb et al. 1999. Calvo and Mendoza 2000a, 2000b likewise note that international capital market openness increases the volume of available information and, therefore, the costs of information processing.

[26] Some claim that a reliance on a limited set of indicators also may lead to herd behavior, particularly when investors rely on news events or the behavior of other investors as information shortcuts. For discussions of fads and word-of-mouth communications as determinants of investment, see Shiller 1984, 1989, 2000, Shiller 1995. Calvo and Mendoza 2000a, Cole and Kehoe 1996, Frankel and Rose 1996, and Sachs et al. 1996 provide accounts of a variety of nonconventional types of behavior, including herd behavior, sun spots, and bubbles, in the 1994 Mexican peso crisis. Others claim that herd behavior – the movement of investors in a large group – is simply a rational response to market movements. I discuss herding briefly in the section on "The Similarity of Information and Relative Performance Pressures" later in this chapter.

employing information about Country A prevents a market participant from collecting and employing information about Country B.

Investment Risk and Economization

Although a wealth of information about various investment locations is available, market participants' information-processing needs – and resources – are limited. The marginal benefit of additional information varies across groups of countries, according to investors' prior beliefs regarding governments' types. Such beliefs may be more or less certain, and this certainty drives their response to risk. Investors may experience several types of investment risk: default risk, which results from a borrower's failing to repay its obligation; inflation risk, which results when an asset's purchasing power declines; and currency risk, which results from fluctuations in the value of local currency–denominated assets.[27]

When investors assign a high probability to governments' being of the "good credit risk" type, default risk is minimal; investors can focus their attention on assessing inflation risk. They need only look to broad measures of government policy outcomes as signals; provided these signals confirm their prior beliefs, they will not dig deeper. Investors will reduce or eliminate the use of information relevant to default risk; they are willing to narrow their range of indicators because additional indicators are not relevant signals of the government's type. If salient investment risks (inflation risk and currency risk) can be evaluated on the basis of a small set of indicators, and if these indicators are high in quality, the marginal benefit of employing additional information is quite small. Under these conditions, market actors will avoid the costs of additional information and will rely instead on a small set of indicators – "information shortcuts."[28] Therefore, when dealing with countries characterized by lower levels of default risk, market participants are likely to employ a narrow, less costly package of indicators.[29] It is only when a "good credit risk" government does something out of character – rapidly increasing its level of public debt to a very high level, for example – that an investor will doubt its type.

But where governments are likely to be of the "bad credit risk" type, default risk is highly salient. When investors cannot easily differentiate among

---

[27] Erb et al. 1996, Kennedy 1987, Mishkin 1992, Sobel 1999.

[28] Simon 1982.

[29] Short time horizons enhance investors' willingness to employ a narrow set of indicators. See the third section of this chapter.

types of borrowers, they must assess both inflation and default risk. They employ a wide range of information in order to infirm or confirm their prior beliefs. In such cases, investors will use a wide range of information about a government's willingness *and* ability to pay in order to gauge the government's creditworthiness. In their efforts to assess default propensity, investors will consider not only macropolicy indicators (e.g., inflation, deficits, and debt), but also supply-side policies, labor market regulation, and the composition of government spending. Small budget deficits and low inflation may indicate low future inflation risk, but they are insufficient for assessing future default risk. Considering a wide range of indicators allows for a more accurate assessment of investment risk. In addition, when uncertainty about the quality of information and the implications of information for policy outcomes is high (e.g., when it is not clear whether falling budget deficits indicate fiscal consolidation or merely "cheap talk"), market actors will gather more information. Employing a higher-cost package of indicators allows investors to reach more precise conclusions regarding governments' types.

In many cases, then, a broad range of information is not necessary to make correct assessments of investment risk. For instance, although a market participant who collects and evaluates every available piece of evidence about Sweden may generate a more accurate assessment of the future performance of Swedish government bonds, she will forgo the opportunity to make accurate assessments regarding the future of Hungarian and Czech bonds. In doing so, she sacrifices the ability to make broadly accurate assessments of many assets in return for the ability to make a very accurate assessment of a single asset – hardly rational behavior in a geographically diversified capital market, or where uncertainty regarding government type is low. In their discussion of individuals' propensity to collect political information, Lupia and McCubbins offer the extreme form of this argument: "If a person can attend to only one stimulus, then he or she will attend to the stimulus for which the expected benefits are *extremely high* relative to the expected costs."[30] Although I do not argue that financial market participants are constrained to look at only *one* piece of information, I do maintain that they often have incentives to look at a limited set of information.

The use of a limited set of information does *not* imply that market participants are unable to make correct assessments of investment risk, or that

---

[30] Lupia and McCubbins 1998, p. 29.

investors' reliance on certain heuristic principles leads to severe and systematic errors.[31] Rather, investors *could* collect and process vast amounts of information regarding each nation; I assume that they have the cognitive capacity to do so. But doing so is unnecessary in many cases, given prior beliefs regarding governments' creditworthiness.

Moreover, this description of investors' use of information does not exclude the possibility that the identity of key decision-making indicators changes over time, or that investors' categorization of particular nations into particular groups (with attendant beliefs regarding government type) changes over time. What drives changes in key decision-making indicators? Some changes are driven by events, as I discuss in Chapter 4: for instance, banking sector problems generated financial crises in Southeast Asia, leading investors to look for similar problems in other regions of the world. Other changes result from broader trends in investors' ideologies: they may revise their views regarding the sorts of government policies they deem important and appropriate. Witness, for instance, the increased prominence in the late 1990s of new growth theory in the business community. In other cases, as a result of their longer-term policy and institutional choices, nations can move across categories, from "emerging market" to "emerged" to "developed democracies" (or in the opposite direction), and these moves cause changes in financial market pressures. Investors' concerns about default risk in Portugal, for instance, likely were much more severe in the late 1970s and early 1980s than they were in the late 1990s, when Portugal had democratized and was on the verge of joining Economic and Monetary Union.

In the final category of changes are the largely unintended consequences of government actions. On occasion, governments create rules for behavior and financial market participants adopt these rules as decision-making criteria. Market participants' adoption of these rules increases their importance.[32] Although these rules are technical in nature, they have distributional consequences.[33] The most striking example of this phenomenon are the Maastricht convergence criteria for EMU. As I discuss in Chapter 3, the Maastricht criteria experience implies that, where a set of economically important nations cooperate to set rules for behavior, and where these rules

---

[31] Kahneman et al. 1982.
[32] Pauly 1999.
[33] Oatley and Nabors 1998 discuss the distributional implications of banking regulations.

appear enforceable, governments can play an active role in market participants' selection of decision-making criteria.

Changes in key indicators and in country categorizations allow for a more
dynamic portrayal of financial market influences on government policy.
They also provide for Bayesian updating among financial market participants, as these participants revise their priors regarding sovereign borrower
creditworthiness.[34] Although much of the analysis in this book is static, in
that I deal mostly with the 1990s, I do consider financial market influence
prior to the First World War in Chapter 7. I also briefly discuss emerging
changes in European bond markets in Chapter 8. Beyond this, though,
there remains fertile ground for examining how nations move between
particular groups (classified by investment risk) of nations and how market
participants' views regarding key policy indicators change over time.[35]

Developed Democracies: Narrow Influences

A central contention of this book is that investors require less information to
evaluate developed than developing nations. The propensity to economize
on information when dealing with developed nations frees wealthy nations
of many financial market influences. The signaling framework suggests
that financial market participants are most likely to rely on a narrow set
of indicators when evaluating bonds issued by governments of developed
democracies. In these nations, the potential range of policy outcomes is
quite small: although a social democratic coalition may govern in Germany,
it is very unlikely that it will increase marginal tax rates to 70% or that it will
institute capital controls. It is even less likely that the regime type will shift
from democratic to authoritarian, or that the government will declare itself
unable or unwilling to repay its obligations. As Anderson and her colleagues
point out,

an investor purchasing a bond issued by a government with a high credit
rating . . . will view both the size and the timing of the cash flows to be known with
certainty, so the primary factor influencing the investor's valuation of the instrument

---

[34] On Bayesian updating among investors, see Tomz 2001a and 2001b, who argues that,
especially when reliable cross-national data were not available, borrowers' past behavior
was a key part of investors' updating.

[35] For a model of individual investors' learning to make investment decisions on the basis of
past investment outcomes, see Lettau 1997.

will be its guaranteed rate of return. . . . Investors don't perceive default risk for developed country bonds.[36]

Investors assign a high probability to the fact that OECD nations are of the good credit risk type. The label *developed democracy* provides a degree of confidence regarding government policy, a more narrow range of possible policies, and, therefore, reduced concerns about default risk. Although investors *are* concerned about government policy outcomes in these nations and *are* aware of variance in outcomes among developed countries, they place a considerable amount of confidence in these governments. Market participants' overall confidence in government policies and in information quality leads market participants to consider only a small set of aggregate indicators. They view good performance on these aggregates – macroindicators – as indicative of low inflation and exchange rate risk. At the same time, market participants see microindicators as largely unrelated to the government's type. And, as I discuss in Chapter 3, compliance with market pressures on macroindicators does not necessitate particular changes in microindicators. Governments with small deficits and low inflation are characterized by different mixes of microside policies. The result, then, is relatively narrow financial market influence.

Emerging Market Nations: Broad Influence

On the other hand, because investors assign significant probability to the possibility that emerging market economies are bad credit risks, investors must rely on a higher-cost package of information. Given the wide possible range of investment risks that financial market participants face in emerging markets and investors' greater uncertainty regarding the salience of these risks in particular nations, investors must rely on a broad set of indicators. Almost by definition, emerging market economies lack well-developed domestic capital markets and sometimes experience difficulties repaying external loans. In emerging markets, investors often do not assume that governing parties will uphold their debt servicing obligations. It is quite possible for a government to win domestic political favor by

---

[36] Anderson et al. 1996, pp. 1–2. Similarly, Erb et al. 1998 observe that governments of developed democracies will repay their obligations, in part because they face domestic political pressures to do so from resident investors. Also see Alesina et al. 1992 and Lemmen and Goodhart 1999.

dealing harshly with foreign investors or for political instability to generate a sovereign default.[37]

Additionally, the borrowing strategies pursued by emerging market governments often serve to exacerbate investors' concerns about the ability to pay. In order to access international capital markets (or to do so more cheaply), emerging market governments often issue foreign currency–denominated, short-duration bonds. As I discuss in Chapters 4 and 6, foreign currency denomination alleviates currency risk for investors, but it also renders default risk more salient. Because default risk is highly salient in emerging markets, investors must assess the ability and willingness of governments to repay debt; these assessments require the collection of a wide range of policy indicators. Moreover, investors' incentives to consider a large number of indicators in emerging markets is strengthened by the nature and availability of information.[38] Information often is of poor quality or simply is not available. Investors often worry about the transparency, integrity, and timeliness of data released by emerging market governments. One means by which investors address informational problems is to collect a wide range of country-specific information from a variety of sources. For example, rather than relying only on statistics from the finance ministry, investors might collect fiscal policy information from several government agencies, the central bank, private industry, and intergovernmental organizations.[39]

Therefore, investors have very uncertain priors regarding the type of emerging market borrowers. Some are creditworthy, others are not, and a low-cost package of information does not allow investors to distinguish between the two. They must go beyond macroaggregates in their quest to identify the government's type. As a result, the marginal benefits of additional information are great. Market participants will worry about the ways in which emerging market governments allocate spending, the supply-side policies employed by governments, and the implications of regional and national elections. They will assess investment risks, using not only macroeconomic indicators (inflation, fiscal balances, current account deficits), but also a wide range of microside indicators (e.g., the breakdown of government spending across areas and the structure of tax systems) and the political

---

[37] Erb et al. 1996, Feldstein 1994, Sobel 1999. On the effects of regime instability on investment, see Przeworski et al. 2000.

[38] Bikhchandani and Sharma 2000.

[39] Another means by which investors can deal with informational concerns is to rely on international data standards. See Mosley 2000b and Chapter 4.

climate. Expenditures for investment, for instance, are seen to increase repayment capacity, whereas expenditures for pure consumption do not.[40] Likewise, even among emerging market economies with similar levels of public investment expenditure, we might expect investors to examine the efficiency of these investments.

These microside indicators serve as costly signals of developing nation governments' types: a good credit risk will allocate its budget in market-friendly or neoliberal ways, whereas a bad credit risk government will not. The costs of the signal are found in domestic politics: the rationalization of public pensions and health care, to take an example, often hurts governments' public approval.[41]

A broad financial market constraint does not necessarily mean that market participants make more nuanced assessments of emerging market nations, or that they consider changes in one indicator in light of changes in many other indicators. Rather, it means that, for emerging market nations, there are more policy indicators that can elicit a financial market response.[42] For example, if there is no change in market expectations regarding Belgium's government deficit/GDP ratio or rate of inflation, there probably will be no change in Belgian government bond prices. Even if, however, there is no change in Peru's government budget deficit or inflation rate, bond prices will move in response to changes in the distribution of the government budget across spending categories.

The Similarity of Information and Relative Performance Pressures

Furthermore, the degree of similarity in market participants' decision-making criteria affects the magnitude of financial market influences. If all market participants employ the same indicators – or highly intercorrelated indicators – when making asset allocation decisions, the market response to a change in one of these indicators will be relatively strong. Even in

---

[40] IMF Survey, October 20, 1997, p. 328.

[41] On costly signals and audience costs, see Fearon 1994, Morrow 1994. Also see Stokes 1999, who suggests that heterodox governments are more inclined than orthodox governments to switch to more market-friendly policies, as doing so sends a costlier – and more credible – signal to markets.

[42] Calvo and Mendoza 2000b make a similar argument: information on economic, social, and political indicators and events is more prone to large swings in emerging market nations, and this means that investors' responses to new information may well be greater than their responses to new information in OECD countries.

a thick market, where there is a great deal of trading activity, widespread reliance on similar indicators produces large market movements.[43] But if different market participants rely on different or uncorrelated indicators when assessing governments' types, market response to changes in a single indicator will be muted. Whereas some market actors will respond to a particular signal in one way, others will respond in the opposite direction, or not at all. Therefore, where there is greater consensus among market actors on the identity of decision-making criteria, financial market influences on government policy are more pronounced. Although the number of key indicators is central to determining the scope of the market constraint, the consensus among market actors on the identity of the key indicators is another important determinant of the *strength* of the financial market constraint.

I expect investment professionals to focus on similar indicators when evaluating government policies and government bonds. This behavior is driven by two factors. First, all investors have incentives to coordinate their behavior, in that doing so allows them to benefit from changes in market prices.[44] For instance, when an investor buys a stock, she hopes other investors also will buy, so that she later benefits from the accompanying rise in the stock's value. Likewise, if others are selling, an investor will be tempted to sell, so that he is not left holding a relatively worthless asset. One means by which investors coordinate their market behavior is to rely on the same type of information; if an investor uses the same indicators others are using, she can be relatively successful at anticipating the direction and magnitude of market movements.

Second, professional investors have another incentive to use similar indicators – the centrality of *relative* performance evaluation. These investors are concerned about their performance not only in absolute terms, but also relative to other, similarly situated financial market participants.[45] A poor investment decision affects absolute performance dramatically, but, if all actors take similar action, it affects relative performance negligibly. It is, then,

---

[43] For instance, Glauber (in Leland et al. 1997) points to the 1987 U.S. stock market crash as a situation in which many investors relied – implicitly or explicitly – on the same set of decision-making indicators. During the 1987 crisis, selling was very concentrated among portfolio insurers and mutual funds.

[44] I am grateful to an anonymous reviewer for highlighting this first factor.

[45] Shiller 1989, Willett 1999, Zeckhauser et al. 1991.

"better to be wrong in a group than wrong alone."[46] Friedman observes that competitive success or failure among institutional investors depends on relatives, not absolutes. Any investor who is delighted when his portfolio loses 30 percent of its value if the market is off by 32 percent and who bewails a gain of 40 percent if the market is up by 42 percent is not especially likely to be immune to socially formed opinions. Moreover, the standard that money managers seek to meet is in many cases not the performance of the market index but the index of performance of other managers.[47]

Market participants' concern with relative performance reflects the structure of the investment management industry.[48] Professional investors compete with one another to attract investment, and their clients look at performance as a means of choosing among investment professionals. Brown and his colleagues employ the metaphor of a tournament to describe this relative performance–oriented behavior. Just as winning a golf or tennis tournament depends not on obtaining an absolute score, but on outperforming other competitors, so does placing highly in the league table of investment professionals.[49] Although clients cannot observe directly the performance of fund managers – that is, they do not know what information they are collecting or how they are using this information, and they cannot distinguish between managers' abilities and managers' luck – they can use relative performance outcomes to get some sense of individual market participants' efforts and abilities.[50] In other words, evaluating performance in relative terms gives clients some sense of the extent to which a fund manager collected and acted appropriately on information. Therefore,

---

[46] Calvo and Mendoza 2000b; also see Devlin 1989, Friedman 1984, Shiller 1989, Zeckhauser et al. 1991.

[47] Friedman 1984, p. 508. Keynes identifies similar behavior in *The General Theory:* "Worldly wisdom teaches that it is better for reputation to fail conventionally than to succeed unconventionally" (1936, p. 158). For Keynes's views on market psychology, see his chapter 12.

[48] Devlin's 1989 analysis of the 1980s debt crisis treats bankers in a similar fashion: they rationally respond to incentives, but their utility functions include market share concerns as well as risk and return concerns. In my analysis, risk and return are central but are defined in relative terms.

[49] Brown et al. 1996. Also see Lunde et al. 1998.

[50] Berkowitz and Kotowitz 1993, BIS 1998, Davis 1988, Holmstrom 1982, Khorana 1996, Maug and Naik 1996, Zweibel 1995. On agency problems within the pension fund sector, see Lakonishok et al. 1992b. Eichberger et al. 1999 point out that the reliance on relative performance also could generate perverse incentives: if two managers know they are being evaluated relative to one another, one equilibrium behavior is to avoid collecting and acting on information. If both managers shirk, neither looks bad in relative terms. Of course, this result does not address the potential for competition from other fund managers.

clients not only look at mutual fund performance, but do so in relative terms.

Fund managers respond to relative performance evaluation in a variety of ways, including (for lower performers) increasing the riskiness of their portfolios at midyear,[51] focusing more on shorter-term performance outcomes,[52] and – most relevant for this study – looking at similar indicators and fundamentals. For instance, Maug and Naik maintain that where investors' performance is evaluated relative to other investors or to a market index, investors are likely to skew their investments toward the benchmark's portfolio – and, therefore, to collect and employ information similar to that collected by other investors. These actions appear to intensify over time, as the level of financial openness increases.[53] Likewise, Graham presents a reputational model of herd behavior among investment newsletters. He finds that financial market analysts, aware that they will be judged relative to the market-leading analyst, are likely to mimic the recommendation of the market leader.[54]

Market participants' concern with relative performance – and therefore with the action of other investment professionals – predicts a reliance on similar decision-making criteria. The indicators employed by one market participant will be highly correlated with those employed by other market participants.[55] And the investment strategies will be quite highly correlated among fund managers, even more so than if managers were simply spreading risk across investments in an optimal fashion.[56] For governments, this

---

[51] Chevalier and Ellison 1997. Zweibel 1995 notes that, in a relative performance evaluation situation, managers who are performing above average will become overly conservative in their investment behavior, whereas managers who are below average will become overly risk-acceptant.

[52] Brown et al. 1996, Khorana 1996.

[53] Maug and Naik 1996. Brown et al. 1996 find more pronounced effects of rankings on investment behavior in the late 1980s and early 1990s than in the late 1970s and early and mid-1980s. Chevalier and Ellison 1999a find that the incentives to pursue similar investment strategies are stronger for less experienced market participants.

[54] Graham 1999 finds that this phenomenon is most likely among analysts with high reputation or low ability – implying that analysts who stand to lose from incorrect recommendations are most likely to take into account what others in the market are doing. Also see Welch 2000.

[55] Chevalier and Ellison 1998a, however, find some evidence that younger fund managers who beat the market appear to have a better chance of promotion if their portfolio mix is more unusual. A desire for advancement, then, could offset some incentives to herd. Also see Prendergrast and Stole 1996.

[56] Eichberger et al. 1999.

implies that changes in key policy indicators can generate substantial interest rate changes. Therefore, the similarity of decision-making indicators contributes, along with international capital mobility, to stronger market reactions.

The use of similar indicators, and the underlying concern with relative performance, also could contribute to herd behavior in financial markets. Scharfstein and Stein present a model in which – as previously – professional investors worry about their reputation and career; because investors are evaluated on the basis of both the profitability of their investments and the similarity of their investments to others', market participants sometimes have labor market incentives to mimic the behavior of others. They are reluctant to act against the crowd, because doing so might damage their reputation as "sensible decision makers." And, if a manager follows the crowd into a bad investment decision, she can share the blame with others.[57]

Within the fields of international economics, microeconomics, and finance, there is much debate about the occurrence, causes, and consequences of herd behavior. Although this debate – as well as the attendant policy debate regarding how to prevent herd behavior – is not central to this book, the preceding discussion of relative performance provides an appropriate forum for a brief review of this literature. The extant literature defines *herding* quite broadly, usually as intentionally similar investment behavior by a substantial group of investors.[58] Empirically, herding occurs when there is a large imbalance in buying and selling behavior within a particular group of investors so that, for instance, on a particular day, 70% of international bond funds sell German government bonds and only 30% buy them. Recent studies of mutual fund activity suggest that some herding does occur, although the level of herding varies by country, by type of asset, and by category of mutual fund.[59] Other studies consider the prevalence of herdlike behavior in recent financial crises.[60]

---

[57] Scharfstein and Stein 1990.

[58] E.g., Bikhchandani and Sharma 2000, Kaminsky and Reinhart 2000.

[59] Chang et al. 2000, Choe et al. 1998, Grinblatt et al. 1995.

[60] For studies of foreign exchange rate crises in Europe and Latin America, suggesting that economic fundamentals in "turmoil" cases are not significantly different from fundamentals in "nonturmoil" cases, see Eichengreen et al. 1995 and Calvo and Mendoza 1996a. Similarly, Funke 1996 argues that exchange rate crises are more severe than changes in economic fundamentals would suggest, and Borio and McCauley 1996 suggest that economic fundamentals were not the proximate motivation for the 1994 turmoil in European government bond markets.

Some earlier literature treated herding as irrational; more recent work treats it as a rational strategy, driven by a desire to protect reputation, a correlation among investors' private information, the inferring of private information from earlier market activity, or an aversion to assets with particular qualities.[61] Recent studies also suggest that herding is more likely in emerging markets, where information is of relatively low quality.[62] Other recent literature points out that herding could improve, rather than detract from, the efficiency of capital markets, as large responses to changes in key fundamentals would speed market adjustment.[63]

Although our expectations regarding the impact of relative performance evaluation suggest a stronger financial market reaction to government policy outcomes, they do not allow us to resolve larger debates regarding the impact of herdlike behavior on capital market efficiency and bond price volatility. In any event, though, the rational herding literature provides further support for the reliance of market actors on similar information shortcuts. It also suggests that it would be useful empirically to identify whether there are consistent leaders in the government bond market, and, if so, who they are.

Financial Market Influences: Initial Expectations

The three determinants of financial market influence – capital mobility, incentives to collect and employ information, and similarity of decision-making indicators – suggest that financial market influence on the governments of advanced industrial democracies will be high in strength but narrow in scope. Market participants have the capacity to react sharply to changes in relevant government policies, but the set of relevant government

---

[61] See Chang et al. 2000 and Wermers 1999 for reviews of this literature. Scharfstein and Stein's 1990 treatment is based on reputational risk; Froot et al.'s 1992 is based on correlated private information; Banerjee 1992, Bikhchandani et al. 1992, and Hirshleifer et al. 1994 are based on inferring information from earlier activity. Grinblatt et al. 1985 suggest that, if investors buy assets on the basis of previous returns, it is logical that many investors buy the same, historically well-performing assets and avoid historically poorly performing assets.

[62] Bikhchandani and Sharma 2000, Chang et al. 2000. Kim and Wei 1999 investigate the occurrence of herding before and after the Korean financial crisis of 1997. They find that herdlike behavior is more likely among individuals (rather than institutions) and among nonresident investors. They suggest that this difference reflects asymmetries in information. For a similar argument, looking more generally at U.S. investors' equity holdings abroad, see Ahearne et al. 2001.

[63] Lakonishok et al. 1992b.

Table 2.1. *Possibilities for Financial Market Influences on Government Policy*

	Scope	
Strength	Broad (Salient Default Risk)	Narrow (Little Concern with Default Risk)
Strong (High Capital Mobility; Use of Similar Indicators)	I Many indicators considered Emerging markets with open capital regimes, 1990s Some nations in pre–World War I era	II Few indicators considered Developed nations with open capital markets, 1980s and 1990s Some nations in pre–World War I era
Weak (Low Capital Mobility; Less Use of Similar Indicators)	III Investors' ability to respond to changes in investment risk removed by low capital mobility; scope unimportant Developed nations, 1930s Developed nations, 1950s, 1960s, early 1970s Developing nations with closed capital accounts, 1980s and 1990s	

policies is quite small. By contrast, because of the salience of default risk and the relative value of additional information in emerging market economies, governments of developing nations will face broadly oriented *and* strong financial market influences. In Chapters 3 and 4, I assess these expectations.

The strength and scope framework also is relevant for other eras of financial market–government relations. The key determinants of financial market influence vary over time as well as across groups of countries. Therefore, financial market influences on governments also differ across time and space. Table 2.1 divides the type of influence of global capital markets on government policy into three categories: strong and broad, strong but narrow, and weak (where scope is rendered irrelevant by lack of capital mobility).[64] A refinement of these types, using continua of scope and strength, would allow for a more accurate description of market influence, but these categories are sufficient to demonstrate the possibilities for variation in market influence. The upper half of the table includes high capital

---

[64] This discussion of variance is confined to the government securities market, rather than to other types of assets.

mobility situations. In Cell I, default risk is highly salient; many indicators per country are considered, few information shortcuts are employed, and investors are able to punish bad policy quickly and cheaply. The most immediate example is the current situation of many emerging market countries. Other examples include many peripheral nations in the pre–World War I era, discussed in Chapter 7. Cell II also illustrates a situation of relatively high capital mobility, but one in which default risk is not salient. In this situation, market actors consider a small set of indicators, generating narrow market-based influences. Developed country governments in the contemporary era face this sort of environment: given the low salience of default risk and the resulting ability of market actors to employ information shortcuts, market participants consider and quickly respond to a small set of key indicators, but they are quite uninterested in many other aspects of government policy.

The lower half of Table 2.1 refers to periods of relatively low international capital mobility. With limited or no cross-border capital mobility, investors are unable to react to levels of investment risk; this renders their incentives to consider a broad or narrow range of indicators irrelevant. This irrelevance reminds us that some degree of international capital mobility is a necessary – albeit not a sufficient – condition for the influence of financial markets on government policy choices. Many situations are consistent with Cell III. One is the 1930s: after the reimposition of capital controls and the collapse of the gold standard, capital mobility was quite limited. Investors did not have a large number of potential investment locations from which to choose. Despite sometimes-high levels of partisan polarization and political instability in Europe,[65] investors' sentiments regarding government policies did not translate into strong market responses or into marked consequences for national governments. Another example is the advanced industrial democracies during the 1950s, 1960s, and early 1970s, when capital controls were widespread and largely effective.

From Table 2.1, two main hypotheses emerge:

Hypothesis 2.1: The influence of international financial markets on the governments of developed nations is strong but narrow. International capital mobility and the use of similar indicators allow for significant risk premia for "bad" policies, but financial markets consider only a small set of policies.

---

[65] Simmons 1994.

In developing nations, the influence of financial markets is more widespread:

Hypothesis 2.2: The influence of international financial markets on emerging market governments (with open capital accounts) is strong and broad: financial market participants rely on a wider set of indicators, rather than on a narrow set of policy outcomes, and are able to react sharply to undesirable values on these indicators.

In the remainder of the book, I assess these hypotheses and explore in more detail their implications for the government policymaking process. In Chapter 3, I employ interview and cross-sectional time series analyses to test the strong but narrow framework. The interview evidence supports our expectation of a strong but narrow influence of financial markets on governments of advanced industrial democracies. Financial market participants are concerned about inflation and currency risk, and not about default risk, in the developed world; therefore, they consider only a narrow set of indicators relevant to assessing inflation and currency risk.

On the quantitative side, I expect that macropolicy indicators will be associated significantly and strongly with long-term interest rates on government bonds. I also expect that more micro- or supply-side policy outcomes will not be strongly associated with interest rates. Additionally, government partisanship will not be strongly associated with long-term interest rates, as market participants make decisions on the basis of politics rather than on the basis of policy. Finally, Chapter 3 addresses the claim, implicit in the strong but narrow framework, that financial market pressure on macroindicators does not force changes in other areas of government policy. I maintain that a firewall exists between market important and market unimportant policies, so that we can expect sustained divergence in government spending by area, as well as in supply-side initiatives. Hence, a narrow market constraint does not mean that movement in the big numbers indicators captures movement in all other indicators, but simply that movement in the big numbers indicators is the only movement of central interest to market participants. In Chapter 4, I test Hypothesis 2.2 by investigating financial market influences in the developing world. Using additional interview evidence and simple statistical analyses, I consider the scope and strength of financial market influence and conjecture about the extent to which the financial market constraint changes over time.

In Chapters 5 and 6, I turn to the domestic political dimension: how do financial market influences interact with domestic interests and institutions? Government policy in developed democracies can be understood as emanating both from external and internal influences. In Chapter 5, I explore the balance between internal and external (global capital market) influences on government policy choice. I argue that, although this balance varies cross-nationally, much of what governments do remains beyond the purview of international financial markets, rooted in domestic institutional and political influences.[66] Many of the causes of national policy outcomes remain at the domestic level. Along these lines, recent quantitative work suggests that the external market constraint on government policy is weak, or perhaps is even an enabling (in terms of allowing for the pursuit of domestically determined policies) rather than a constraining force.[67]

Furthermore, market participants' use of the Maastricht convergence criteria (see Chapter 3) suggests that governments are not merely passive recipients of financial market influence. Although the convergence literature focuses on market influence on governments, we also do well to think about government influences on markets. In Chapter 6, I explore several strategies by which governments mediate the impact of international financial markets. This work suggests that, even in areas in which the market-based constraint is strong, there are several potential ways in which governments can influence – or at least develop a more refined awareness of – the nature of market constraints.

Finally, Chapter 7 considers financial market–government relations in historical perspective. I turn from an evaluation of contemporary financial market influences on government policy to an examination of financial market behavior prior to the First World War. I argue that pre–World War I merchant bankers had strong incentives to consider default risk, but that intraindustry competition and pressure from home governments sometimes mediated these concerns.

---

[66] Berger 1996, pp. 16–17; Andrews and Willett 1997.

[67] Quinn 1997 finds that international financial liberalization does not erode the corporate tax base, that capital account liberalization is positively associated with increasing corporate taxation, and that capital account liberalization and government expenditure are positively, albeit not strongly, associated. He concludes that international financial liberalization could facilitate the achievement of governments' domestically determined goals. Likewise, Sobel 1999 suggests that "the new linkages [of financial globalization] actually afford policymakers greater leeway in other domains, perhaps contributing to their autonomy" (chapter 1, p. 3; also chapter 11).

3

Financial Market Influence in Developed Nations

AN EMPIRICAL ASSESSMENT

> Ideologically, most people in the industry are against big government; they
> would rather see things provided in the private sector. But in terms of the
> way the market moves, it doesn't make any difference. . . . There really is little
> attention to micro-policies, which have a great impact on the lives of citizens
> living there, but little on the markets.[1]

What sort of influence do investors have on the policies that affect the daily
lives of citizens in advanced capitalist democracies? In this chapter, I use
qualitative and quantitative evidence to evaluate the nature of the financial market influence on government policy choice in advanced industrial
democracies. First, I analyze qualitative evidence regarding financial market influence in the contemporary era: is it, as I hypothesize in Chapter 2,
strong and narrow for developed nations? If the constraint is narrow for
developed nations, which indicators do financial market participants employ as information shortcuts? Next, I employ cross-sectional time series
data to assess this expectation further. In Chapter 4, I focus on financial
market–government relations in the developing world.

Qualitative Evidence and "Strong but Narrow" Financial Market Influence

International Capital Market Openness: A Background Condition

In Chapter 2, I propose that the strength of financial market influence
depends on two factors: a nation's level of capital market openness and
the extent to which financial market participants rely on a similar set of

---

[1] Interview 18.

decision-making indicators. In terms of cross-border capital mobility, the financial market constraint is relatively strong. Although capital is not perfectly mobile internationally, mobility currently is quite high, particularly in the advanced industrial democracies. Statutory levels of capital market openness have grown steadily in the developed world since the 1950s, reaching a point of nearly full openness in the late 1980s or early 1990s.[2] Among the advanced democracies, the few remaining national restrictions on cross-border capital mobility were removed in the late 1980s and early 1990s.

Actual levels of capital market openness, measured by covered interest rate differentials,[3] onshore–offshore interest rate differentials,[4] or savings–investment correlations,[5] also are high, albeit not perfect.[6] And the market for government bonds is quite large in developed democracies; the outstanding amount of government securities in the G-7 economies totals approximately 75% of gross domestic product. Therefore, negative changes in government policies should be met with pronounced increases in the interest rate premia on government bonds.

Information, Indicators, and Relative Performance: Interview Evidence

In order to assess the empirical veracity of the expectations developed in Chapter 2, I conducted interviews with institutional investors in two major financial centers, London and Frankfurt, from January to June 1997, as well as in October 1998.[7] The interview subjects are active in fixed income (government bond) and equity markets and make medium- to long-term (rather than short-term or daily) asset allocation decisions and recommendations. Large investment firms or institutional fund managers employ most

---

[2] IMF 1997a, Quinn 1997, Simmons 1999, Turner 1991.
[3] Bisignano 1994.
[4] IMF 1997a, pp. 60–64.
[5] Feldstein and Horioka 1980, Obstfeld 1993.
[6] E.g., Gordon and Bovenberg 1996.
[7] For discussions of the importance of London and Frankfurt as financial centers, as well as an overview of other financial centers, see *Economist*, "Survey of Financial Centers," May 9, 1998, *Financial Times*, "Survey of Pension Fund Management," May 14, 1998, Blommestein and Funke 1998, and Sassen 1999. Many of those interviewed in London and Frankfurt had worked in other markets, including New York, Paris, and Tokyo. I assume that professional investors behave similarly, regardless of the market in which they work; as a French Treasury official suggested to me in mid-1997, "traders are the same everywhere." Of course, investors in London may have better information about British politics, and those in Frankfurt may have a slightly more accurate sense of European Central Bank activities.

interview subjects,[8] and they distribute investment portfolios across a range of assets and across a range of countries, including all OECD and some emerging market nations.

The interview subjects' firms were selected from membership directories of professional organizations.[9] These firms include major institutional investors and financial institutions, such as Credit Suisse First Boston, Deutsche Bank, Goldman Sachs, HSBC, Merrill Lynch, J. P. Morgan, Prudential, Salomon Brothers, and UBS. This list was supplemented with suggestions from financial-sector journalists and, on occasion, from other market participants. I contacted potential interview subjects with a letter of introduction and project description, and I arranged interviews with those willing to participate in the study. Approximately 40% of those contacted agreed to participate. Those who did not wish to participate in the study generally cited time pressures or concerns regarding confidentiality. For those willing to participate, confidentiality was ensured via guarantees to identify only by firm (rather than by name). I conducted a total of 64 interviews, most of which lasted between 30 and 60 minutes. The interviews consisted of a set of open-ended questions regarding the identity and relative importance of indicators used by market actors, including monetary policy, fiscal policy, supply-side policies, and politics and elections.

Government economic policy – or, at least, some components of it – is of central importance to those involved in the government bond market. In contrast (and although it is artificial often to separate equity from bond market actors, as many institutional investors deal in both), many equity market participants are moving away from country-level analysis, and, therefore, away from a focus on national government policies.[10] Equity market participants do not completely ignore governments or government policy outcomes, of course: as the East Asian financial crisis suggests, equity market actors worry about government behavior when dealing with emerging market nations or when it affects economic performance in

---

[8] For an overview of the institutional fund management industry, see Blommestein and Funke 1998.

[9] In London, the Institutional Fund Managers' Association; in Frankfurt, the Bundesverband Deutscher Investment-Gesellschaften e.V.

[10] Interviews 8, 24. Indeed, most fund managers deal in both bonds and equities. Interviews with these individuals, however, focused mainly on the fixed income side of the portfolio market. Blommestein and Funke 1998 describe cross-national variation in institutional fund managers' relative involvement in equity and fixed income markets.

specific sectors.[11] Releases of monthly and quarterly economic data often do move (at least in the short term) national equity markets. Many market participants, especially in OECD nations, however, downplay the importance of government policy to equity asset allocation, suggesting "for equity investors, domestic economic policy is increasingly irrelevant."[12] Particularly in relatively internationalized sectors, equity market participants' decisions are driven by sectoral factors; many investment firms now employ sector-specific (e.g., global pharmaceutical) analysts rather than country-specific analysts. On the other hand, in part because of the nature of the assets, and in part because of relative performance concerns described later, government bond market participants continue to act as a homogeneous and country-oriented group.

The interviews provide initial confirmation of the expectations developed earlier. Professional investors note that they find ways to economize on information. As a manager who oversees $70 billion in assets points out:

A big concern for me is information overload. I can look at thousands of numbers, but they lose meaning, and it's hard to see where they all fit in. So I tend to focus on a couple of indicators, as well as on presentations by staff on key issues, such as EMU.[13]

When dealing with developed economies, government bond market participants rely on a narrow set of indicators (specifically, inflation rates and overall budget deficit levels), have short time horizons, and worry about performance relative to that of other financial market participants. Market actors forcefully demand particular values on key variables, but the number of key variables is small, so that many national economic policy choices likely reflect domestic political and institutional constraints rather than external financial market pressures.

Investment Risk: The Salience of Default The logic of signaling and information suggests that, when dealing with developed economies, government bond market participants base asset allocation decisions on a small set of indicators. Investors divide countries into groups, treating emerging market instruments as a class of assets that is fundamentally different from developed country instruments.[14] Investors assume that the governments

[11] Interviews 8, 19, 27, 33; Maxfield 1997, pp. 40–41.
[12] Interviews 5; also Interviews 15, 23, 32, 38.
[13] Interview 41.
[14] Aitken 1996.

of developed economies ultimately will repay their obligations: that is, these governments are very likely to be of the creditworthy type. Governments have both a political capacity to extract from the domestic economy and a respect for their commitments to repayment. Therefore, investors have little reason to consider microside variables. The informational framework also suggests that market participants will direct relatively great scrutiny to emerging market economies.

Interview evidence supports these expectations. In discussing asset allocation in the developed world, only 5% (2 of 38) of interview respondents mentioned default risk. On the other hand, 66% of these respondents mentioned inflation risk. This is consistent with the notion that, for developed economy market participants, "the central concern is getting their money back, which means looking at inflation. They are largely indifferent to how governments achieve these things."[15] Market participants expect stable political situations in developed economies and, therefore, pay little attention to the political process.[16] In a broader sense, the label *developed democracy* is itself a key indicator, signaling a degree of confidence regarding government policy, a more narrow range of possible policies, and, therefore, reduced concerns about default risk.

The low salience of default risk also is illustrated by differences in yield on government bonds. If we compare a nation's local currency bonds with its foreign currency bonds, and compare those in turn with relatively risk-free foreign currency bonds, we should find that investors worry about inflation or currency risk, but not about default risk. The largest differentials should be between a government's local and foreign currency bonds, reflecting the possibilities for exchange rate change, and not between a government's foreign currency bond and other foreign currency bonds, which would reflect default risk. Among developed nations, this pattern generally holds.[17] In October 2000, for instance, Italy's benchmark local currency bond, redeemable in November 2010, yielded 5.53%. Italy's Swiss franc–denominated bond, redeemable in July 2010, yielded 4.15%. A Swiss franc–denominated bond, from the European Investment Bank (EIB), with a similar maturity date and with the highest credit quality rating, yielded 4.10%. The preponderance of these differentials reflected not default risk – the

---

[15] Interview 33; also, Interviews 27, 47. Further evidence regarding the salience of default risk in emerging market economies is presented in chapter 4.

[16] Interviews 9, 30.

[17] Also see Gros and Lannoo 2000, p. 85.

Italian government was seen as only slightly more risky than the EIB – but inflation and exchange rate risk. A euro-denominated bond entailed much greater currency risk than a Swiss franc–denominated bond.

Although investors are concerned about government policy outcomes in developed nations and are aware of cross-national variance in policy outcomes, they place a considerable amount of confidence in governments. On the other hand, political risk and default risk remain salient considerations for emerging market economies. When dealing with emerging markets, investors express heightened concerns about investment risk and the "trustworthiness" of emerging market governments. Such concerns are even more severe in bear markets, during which investors rush to the safety of developed economies and avoid risk in developing nations.

Key Policy Indicators: Developed Democracies   The interviews also indicate that market participants rely on a small set of macro policy outcomes as decision-making criteria – the government deficit/GDP ratio, the rate of inflation, and (sometimes) the foreign exchange rate and government debt/GDP ratio.[18] Professional investors assume that this set of aggregate indicators captures the relevant investment risks, and they have well-defined preferences[19] regarding these indicators. Market participants want inflation rates of less than 2%, and they want relatively small budget deficit/GDP ratios. Other influences on bond market decisions include U.S. interest rate levels and (prior to 1999) judgments regarding the prospects for EMU. Market actors care about large shifts in government policy affecting performance on key indicators, but not about other policy shifts or the political debates associated with other policy choices.

Additionally, it usually is government policy outcomes, rather than policy outputs, that are important to market participants. Market actors, however, do see that a relationship exists between outputs and outcomes and sometimes react negatively to outputs that are perceived to produce suboptimal

---

[18] Also see Moses 2001, p. 83.

[19] Other empirical evidence suggests that financial market participants employ thresholds when considering levels of government debt: government debt in industrialized nations is seen as acceptable until it reaches 80%, at which point market participants strongly punish governments (Missale and Blanchard 1994). Bayoumi et al. 1995 also hint at the existence of thresholds. For a discussion of the origins of ideas regarding appropriate macroeconomic policy, see Cerny 1993, McNamara 1998, and Sinclair 2000. A recent source of these preferences, for EU and non-EU developed countries alike, are the Maastricht convergence criteria.

Table 3.1. *Indicators Employed by Financial Market Participants*

	All Respondents	Respondents Who Mention the Indicator	
	Respondents Who Mention Indicator, %	Respondents Who Cite Indicator as Important, %	Respondents Who Cite Indicator as Unimportant, %
Government Deficit	76.3	96.6	3.4
Inflation	71.1	92.6	7.4
Government Debt	50.0	42.1	57.9
How Governments Spend Money	76.3	31.0	69.0
Tax Policy	44.7	17.6	82.4
Elections	57.9	13.6	86.4
How Much Governments Spend	44.7	11.8	88.2
Labor Market and Structural Policy	55.3	9.5	90.5
Who Governs	47.4	5.6	94.4

Note: Number of interviews included: 38.

Source: Author's interviews, January–June 1997.

outcomes. For example, in December 1997, the Japanese government announced a tax cut, aimed at stimulating the sagging Japanese economy. Initially, financial markets responded positively to the announcement, with advances in the Nikkei Stock Index and the value of the yen.[20] In the next few days, however, these gains were reversed. Market actors expressed concerns that the tax cut package lacked "enough timely concrete measures to convince markets that there is no risk of a serious economic downturn in Japan," that it was a "muddle-through approach" or a "sticking-plaster solution."[21] The general sentiment – which proved correct – was that the policy output (an economic package including $6.5 billion in tax cuts) would not produce the desired policy outcome (stimulation of the Japanese economy).

Table 3.1 provides evidence regarding the indicators used by market participants. This table is based on interviews conducted during the initial (1997) study with individuals active in OECD markets. The first column indicates whether an interview subject mentioned an indicator, in terms

[20] *Financial Times*, December 16 1997, p. 2, and December 17, 1997, p. 24.
[21] *Financial Times*, December 17, p. 6, 18, p. 4, and 22, p. 22, 1997.

of either using it or not using it. The second column provides the percentage of those mentioning the indicator who cited it as important to their asset allocation decisions. The data in Table 3.1 suggest that inflation and government deficit/GDP ratios are the most important indicators for financial market actors. In open-ended interviews, 92.6% of market participants cited the inflation rate as important to their investment behavior, and 96.6% cited the government budget deficit/GDP ratio as important. Of those mentioning inflation and deficits, only 7% and 3%, respectively, of respondents stated that these indicators did not matter. This confirms our expectation that, when dealing with advanced industrial democracies, market participants' chief concern is with aggregate policy outcomes, especially on the monetary side. Additionally, because bond market actors worry about government incentives to inflate in response to debt, the total amount of government borrowing (given by the deficit for any individual year and by the debt for total accumulated borrowing) is the most important fiscal indicator.[22]

Furthermore, many aspects of fiscal policy are unimportant to market participants. Of those market participants who discussed government debt, only 42% cited it as an important indicator. Overall, only 21% of interview subjects cited debt as important; a full 50% failed to mention government debt/GDP ratios at all. Perhaps more surprisingly, of those market participants who mentioned "how governments spend their money," 69% found this to be unimportant, and a full 88% of market participants found the overall level of government spending to be inconsequential to asset allocation decisions. Similar results exist for labor market and tax policy, confirming one fund manager's claim that "there is not a feeling that a single model of economic management is superior."[23] Very dramatic policy shifts – market participants' favorite example is France under Mitterand – may generate market punishment, but such strong reactions are the exception rather than the rule.[24]

Therefore, as a result of market actors' concerns about risk and as a result of their short time horizons (discussed later), few market actors examine how governments allocate their spending across functional categories, or even look at the total size of government. To a great extent, if governments are able to finance expenditures via revenue (rather

[22] Interviews 6, 7, 16, 18, 39, 41. Also see Borio and McCauley 1996, Thorbecke 1993.
[23] Interview 46.
[24] Interview 8. Also see Chapter 5.

than via borrowing), markets are quite unconcerned about the size of government:[25]

The most important thing is how much governments borrow. The size of government only matters when government is so big as to be a burden.[26]

We don't care about where the deficit comes from; the bottom line is that the deficit has to be financed by the bond market.[27]

These things [government spending across issue areas] have implications for long-term growth, but we could sell our assets tomorrow.[28]

Ultimately, bond market participants "don't care about the micro-management of the economy."[29]

A few market participants state that they prefer cuts in government spending to increases in taxation, because spending cuts are a more certain means of reducing the deficit.[30] But, when pressed on this issue, most market actors admit that

at the end of the day, even the "very long term" people are concerned with the size of the deficit, rather than how the government finances its spending.[31]

Analysts don't care about social policy, but only about government policy as it affects interest rates and inflation.... The market controls the big picture, but the government has a lot of discretion in how it spends.[32]

The pressures of financial markets on governments are only on the macroeconomic side.... The bond market is not too interested in the supply side. They [bond market participants] may write about taxation and spending, but they never react to it.[33]

---

[25] Interviews 3, 36, 45.

[26] Interview 41; also Interviews 9, 17.

[27] Interview 11. A small minority of market actors offers a dissenting view regarding the composition of government spending. See Interviews 21, 29.

[28] Interview 12.

[29] Interview 39; also see Interviews 21, 40.

[30] Also see *IMF Survey*, January 27, 1997. "Budgetary contractions that concentrated on expenditures, especially on transfers and government wages, were more likely to succeed in reducing the public debt ratio than tax increases" (p. 24).

[31] Interview 8. A common refrain among bond market participants is "as long as the capital gains tax is low [we don't care about other tax rates, to some limit]" (Interview 28). Another market participant points out that "government spending is fine as long as it remains in proportion to what governments are able to pay. It is fine to have a bigger government sector if that can be financed with taxes" (Interview 21).

[32] Interview 19.

[33] Interview 40.

This picture is consistent with much of the divergence literature, which finds a cross-national narrowing of government policies only at the most macropolicy level. It also is consistent with those public opinion surveys in developed democracies in the 1990s that found a majority of constituents preferred higher taxes and greater provision of services to lower taxes and fewer services.[34]

The Similarity of Decision-Making Indicators: Further Evidence for Strength   The final determinant of financial market influence, the similarity of decision-making criteria across investors, also facilitates strong market influences on governments. The interviews indicate that investment professionals worry not only about the level of absolute profits or losses, but also about their performance relative to that of other fund managers. Market participants note that clients consider a particular investment fund's or fund manager's placement in a league table.[35] In a year characterized by poor market performance, a net return of 3% may place a manager in the top half of performers; in a year characterized by good market performance, the same return will doom an investor to the bottom half of the group.

In response to this incentive, fund managers often base their decisions on industry-wide benchmarks.[36] The benchmarks suggest allocations across instruments as well as among countries. Although fund managers may decide to deviate slightly from these benchmarks, they rarely stray far from them: "Fund managers are a pretty conservative crowd, and they find it best to stick with the average and to hope that they can be a little clever at the margins."[37] If the benchmark moves, individual investors move: "Managers tend to follow benchmarks, unless they are small and brave."[38] Although floor traders may make large bets in the course of daily or weekly activities, these bets are made within a longer-term, risk-averse strategy designed by managers and guided by the "prevailing wisdom."[39]

Market participants often invoke Keynes's newspaper beauty contest analogy to explain their decision-making process.

---

[34] Lipsey (in Radice 1996) reports such results for Britain, pp. 125–126.
[35] Interviews 41 and 42.
[36] Also see BIS 1998.
[37] Interview 23.
[38] Interview 34; also Interviews 5, 15, 46, 51.
[39] Interview 12.

In order to win the contest, you do not have to pick the prettiest woman. Rather, you have to pick the woman whom others believe to be the prettiest.... You could be 100 percent right [objectively], but you still may lose.[40]

We look at what others in the market are doing, and how others in the market perceive government policy. As a manager, you want to be one step ahead of the herd: there, you make money. If you are too far ahead of the herd, though, you lose money.[41]

It's not only a game between an investor and a country, where he decides whether or not to invest in that country, but also a game among many investors, where the investors want to know what others in the market are doing.[42]

One example of the focus on "what others do," or on "which indicators others use" was market participants' continued use of the Maastricht criteria (because others were using them), despite the prevailing notion that the criteria were objectively flawed (discussed later). In the mid- to late 1990s, the effect of market participants' attention to what others do was particularly salient: because almost all market participants used the Maastricht criteria in decision making, the impact on governments was strengthened. Another illustration of the impact of relative performance concerns is the propensity for discrete, pronounced (rather than continuous) reactions by market participants. A bad government policy outcome may not be met immediately with a negative market response. Rather, investors sometimes adopt a "wait and see" attitude, postponing negative reactions. From the point of view of market participants who are concerned with what others are doing, such a response is quite reasonable.[43] This pattern means that markets may not react to good *or* bad policies for some time, particularly in smaller countries. Market participants invoke a variety of metaphors to explain such behavior, including the Road Runner, who goes off the cliff but does not fall until he looks down. He is analogous to a government that pursues bad policy for some time but is not charged an interest rate premium until market participants decide to take notice.[44]

Additional Characteristics of Financial Market Behavior　　The interview evidence provides strong support for our expectations regarding the nature

[40] Keynes 1936, Interview 21.
[41] Interview 45.
[42] Interview 57.
[43] Interview 52, 53.
[44] Interview 4; also Interviews 6, 31, 35, 47.

of financial market influence on government policy outcomes. When assessing developed economies, market participants rely on a relatively small set of macropolicy indicators, and, as I demonstrate in Chapter 4, they rely on a wide set of indicators when evaluating emerging market economies.[45] Three additional aspects of financial market behavior reflect further the "strong but narrow" nature of financial market influence – professional investors' time horizons, the impact of elections on investors' activities, and the influence of governments on investors' decision-making criteria.

Market Participants' Time Horizons   In Chapter 2, I argue that fund managers' employment incentives facilitate a focus on relative performance. Another effect of these incentives is a shortening of investors' time horizons. It is not surprising that floor traders, who deal with daily and intraday market transactions, have very short time horizons. What is perhaps more surprising is that individuals involved in fund management, charged with creating the longer-term parameters that govern short-term trading activity, have time horizons averaging 1 to 3 – rather than 10 to 20 – years.[46] Of those market participants who discussed time horizons in interviews, 28% described their time horizons as "one year or less," and 61% described their time horizons as one to three years.[47] No market participant claimed to have a time horizon longer than five years. Investors' time horizons stem from competition within the investment management industry: although fund managers oversee very long-term liabilities, investment management firms compete with one another to attract new accounts, and clients focus on quarterly or annual numbers.[48]

Short time horizons reinforce the narrowness of financial market considerations; market participants pay attention only to factors that affect shorter-run asset performance.[49] Therefore, they do not consider

---

[45] See, among others, Interviews 1, 7, 29, 41.

[46] Interviews 8, 9, 12, 23, 46.

[47] Asking market participants to define their time horizons produces interesting exchanges. For example: "What is the length of your time horizon?" "Oh, it's quite long, really." "How long?" "Six months to a year." Also interesting is that market participants accuse governments of short-termism, and governments accuse market participants of the same orientation.

[48] Interview 14, 41; Cosh et al. 1992. Davis 1988 suggests that most managers operate with a one-year performance-related time horizon. Lunde et al. 1998 find that the most relevant measure of fund performance to fund survival is performance over the previous three-year period. Blommestein and Funke 1998, however, suggest that institutional investors – particularly pension funds and life insurance companies – have quite long time horizons.

[49] Froot et al. 1992 also discuss the impact of short-termism on market participants' decision-making procedures.

government policies with mostly longer-term implications: whereas market participants are very much concerned with current inflation statistics and government deficit/GDP ratios, most are unconcerned with the distribution of government spending among transfers, education, health care, and infrastructure.[50] Although market actors may agree with the propositions of new growth theory (e.g., that government spending in certain areas enhances economic growth),[51] such views do not strongly influence their allocation activities.

In the same fashion, many portfolio market participants speak strongly of the need for structural reform in continental European economies, but, when asked whether these concerns affect asset allocation, they admit that "such concerns are very long term and, as such, play little or no role."[52] Market participants are interested in the end of lower deficits, but uninterested in the means by which governments achieve this outcome.[53] Therefore, governments that can convince market actors of the shorter-run desirability of their policies (in terms of inflation performance and fiscal discipline) will find themselves relatively unconstrained in terms of longer-run or microside policies.

Elections and Government Partisanship Much of the convergence literature[54] assumes that market participants associate left-leaning governments with higher levels of inflation, government spending, and government deficits. Left governments imply lower real returns and higher default risks, so market actors charge higher risk premia to them. Therefore, elections and the partisan orientation of governments should be important to investors. Market participants suggest, however, that whereas government partisanship once was used widely as an information shortcut, it no longer receives much notice. In Table 3.1, 94% of those who mentioned "who governs" cited politics as unimportant to them; 86% of those who mentioned elections did so in the context of being unconcerned with the implications of elections for government policy outcomes and, ultimately, for investment risk. Several market actors point out that "we care about policies, but not about politics," making political risk analysis almost irrelevant.[55]

---

[50] For instance, "Investors are mainly governed by shorter-term factors, although they may pay lip service to longer-term factors, such as investment spending" (Interview 9).

[51] Barro 1997a.

[52] Interviews 4, 11, 12, 17, 22, 40.

[53] Also see Berger 1996.

[54] See Cerny 1994, Kurzer 1993, McKenzie and Lee 1991.

[55] Interview 4; also 1, 5, 15, 37, 45.

Government partisanship has ceased to be a useful shortcut with respect to developed democracies because partisan orientation often does not provide useful information about variation in macropolicy outcomes.[56] Many respondents suggest that, in past decades, left governments generally could be expected to act "left," creating variance in policy outcomes that was explained by partisan affiliation.[57] In the present period, though, left and center-left governments do not "act left" in some policy realms, and all left governments do not act alike. It is what governments achieve and credibly promise to achieve, rather than the labels attached to their parties, that is important to market participants. Market participants now tend to look at a small set of macropolicy outcomes, rather than at partisan labels, when making asset allocation decisions.

The 1997 British general election illustrates the decline of partisanship as a key decision-making indicator. Almost without exception, market participants interviewed in early 1997 were optimistic regarding the (rather certain) prospect of a Labour Party victory. They viewed the Labour Party of 1997 as quite different from Labour of the 1970s, and they found Tony Blair's pre-election policy promises (e.g., adherence to Conservative Party inflation targets) quite credible. For example, in its March 1997 investment strategy document, Deutsche Asset Management (a portfolio management arm of Deutsche Bank) noted that "with 'responsible' policies and 'responsible' policymakers in place in the Labour Party, the outcome of the election should make little difference to the economy."[58] Market participants signaled their approval of a Labour government prior to the May 1 election: preelection poll results suggesting a large Labour victory were not met with significant increases in UK risk premia.[59] As a strong but narrow framework predicts, the British election campaign was oriented toward how to allocate the government budget across and within spending categories rather than toward how much to spend overall, thereby promising not to affect the macroindicators of greatest concern to market participants.[60] Accordingly, Labour's postelection decision to grant independence to the

---

[56] Some empirical studies lead one to question whether partisanship ever was a useful proxy for government deficits. For instance, Alesina et al. 1997 find a very small and statistically insignificant impact of left governments on the size of budget deficits. Franzese 2002 presents similar evidence.

[57] See Garrett 1998a, Hibbs 1977.

[58] Deutsche Asset Management 1997, p. 4.

[59] *Financial Times*, various issues, March and April 1997.

[60] Interview, Labour Party official; interview, Labour Party MP, March 1997.

Bank of England had a more pronounced effect on market sentiment than the outcome of the general election.[61]

One might object that market participants' general views regarding government partisanship, reported in Table 3.1, strongly reflect the influence of the British election. In the first half of 1997, however, elections occurred in other developed democracies, most notably in France. And many market participants spoke with an eye toward the 1998 German election and the likelihood of a Social Democratic victory there. Despite the high potential for changes to center-left governments in France and Germany, market participants were relatively sanguine.[62] The newly elected German government confirmed the wisdom of this attitude, at least to some extent, by stressing the need for budgetary discipline.[63]

A similar attitude was seen after the September 1998 election in Sweden. Despite the loss of votes from the Social Democrats to the former communist Left Party, and the expected coalition among the Social Democrats, the Greens, and the Left Party, market participants noted that they had decided to withhold action until the implications for policy outcomes of the government change were clear. Along these lines, the credit rating agency Standard and Poor's maintained Sweden's sovereign debt rating of AA+, noting that they were not concerned about the election itself, but about its influence on policy outcomes. At the same time, Left Party officials emphasized that the party's policy platforms (such as a more egalitarian income distribution) would not increase inflation or the budget deficit.[64]

---

[61] *Financial Times*, May 2, 1997, May 7, 1997. The British Treasury estimates that the granting of operational independence to Bank of England reduced 10-year bond yields by around 50 basis points (HM Treasury 1999, p. 8).

[62] And the immediate impact of the German election on financial markets was limited. Analysts noted that the new coalition's programs would keep the overall budget deficit well within the 3% limit (e.g., Nikko Europe, Research and Strategy Division, "After Kohl," September 28, 1998, pp. 1–2). Immediately after the election, the Frankfurt stock exchange gained by 2% (*New York Times*, September 29, 1998, p. c10). Interestingly, financial market participants *did* respond markedly to the March 1999 resignation of the German finance minister, Oskar Lafontaine. Market participants stated that Lafontaine's resignation had ameliorated their concerns about inflation in Europe; prior to his resignation, Lafontaine had called on the ECB (and, before that, on the Bundesbank) to lower interest rates (*New York Times*, March 12, 1999, p. c4).

[63] *Financial Times*, October 5, 1998 p. 20. The Greens also noted that the government would have to keep a tight reign on spending, attributing the need for austerity to the "worse than expected" financial legacy of the Kohl government.

[64] Soon after the Swedish election, the deputy chair of the Left Party made a complementary point: his party wanted to maintain its policy platforms but also wanted to reassure financial

And the Social Democrats repeatedly promised continued fiscal discipline, promising "no major shift in economy policy," a continued budget surplus, and an ongoing commitment to deficit reduction.[65]

Elections are important to market participants only if they are perceived to affect key macropolicy outcomes.[66] In exceptional cases, of course, elections do affect longer-term government bond prices; these are cases in which government change is perceived to portend a significant change in government economic policy outcomes.[67] But, because the link between policy outcomes and politics, or between policy outcomes and partisanship, is now far from automatic, market participants' worries about elections and government change have become somewhat peripheral to their investment decisions. Although elections in OECD nations often produce short-term volatility in bond markets, most have few effects on longer-term interest rate levels or asset allocation decisions.

Does the lack of attention to partisanship demonstrate the limits placed on political parties by financial globalization? In one sense, the lack of concern does speak to the validity of a convergence argument: market participants dislike high inflation and high deficit/GDP ratios, and most political parties foreswear both. At the same time, however, political parties remain able to take positions – without invoking the wrath of financial markets – on a variety of other issues, such as the distribution of government spending

---

market participants. He reminded market participants that the party's policy demands would not increase inflation or harm the overall stability of the budget. Swedish Radio, *60 Degrees North*, September 23, 1998; *Economist*, September 26, 1998, p. 54.

[65] *Financial Times*, September 24, 1998, p. 9, October 6, 1998, p. 24.

[66] Likewise, Freeman 1997 provides evidence that major elections also "do not produce policy uncertainties that alter the relationship between real exchange rates and real interest rate differentials." See Leblang and Bernhard 2000 for an argument that the probability of government change, as well as the nature of that change, affect the behavior of currency market participants.

[67] An example invoked by market actors to demonstrate that "politics sometimes matters" in developed democracies is the Spanish election of 1996 (Interview 36). A few market actors made a similar argument with respect to the 1997 French parliamentary elections (Interview 12). Other aspects of electoral competition also could influence market participants' evaluations of governments, if these have implications for monetary and fiscal policy outcomes. For instance, some market participants cite New Zealand's move from a majoritarian to a proportional electoral system as troubling, given the potential implications of coalition government for fiscal and monetary policy. Interviews 8, 9, 19, 30; Alesina and Rosenthal 1995, Alesina et al. 1997, Grilli et al. 1991, Kontopoulos 1996, Roubini and Sachs 1989. Others express concerns about hung parliaments or small majorities, as these might enhance the voice of extremist elements in the governing coalition (Interviews 17, 19, 41 but also Interviews 5, 8, 29).

across issue areas and the relative importance of primary versus tertiary education. There is a good deal left – for the left, center, or right – in domestic politics.

The Role of the Maastricht Criteria   Until mid-1998, market participants used the Maastricht convergence criteria, and particularly the government deficit criterion (3% or less of GDP), as a central part of their asset allocation processes.[68] Market actors' use of these criteria represented a change, from the previous periods, in the means of evaluation of macropolicy outcomes. The criteria made financial markets' targets for government policy outcomes more explicit – violations were more obvious, and market actors responded to changes in government deficits in light of the Maastricht deficit limit. The widespread use of the criteria strengthened financial market responses to government policy outcomes.

Prior to the mid-1990s, market participants took a "less is better" view of government budget deficits. Four percent was better than 5%, and 5% was better than 6%.[69] They did not expect governments to meet a specific deficit target, or to do so by a particular date.[70] The Maastricht recommendations served as a specification and a dichotomization of an otherwise fuzzy concept: "Ten years ago, the market liked low inflation, low deficits, and good growth. Now we pay attention to specific numbers."[71] "The [deficit] constraint itself is not entirely new, but the criteria provide a common language for market actors."[72] In early 1997, then, government bond market participants watched the Italian government's actions very closely; every move was analyzed according to "Will this get them below 3% or not?"

A central reason for market participants' use of the Maastricht criteria as a decision-making instrument was that governments used the criteria. Bond market participants attempted to predict who would join the first round of EMU in 1999, so their attention to the criteria was not surprising.[73] Market actors cared not so much about the precise nature of the criteria, but about their use by governments.[74] Additionally, market actors interpreted adherence to the Maastricht criteria as a signal of governments' resolve: if a

---

[68] The criteria are found in Article 109 of the Treaty on European Union.

[69] Interview 11.

[70] Interviews 24, 25.

[71] Interview 42. Also Interview 22; interview with UK Treasury Official, Europe Division, February 1997.

[72] Interview 24.

[73] *Financial Times*, November 19, 1996, p. 18.

[74] Interview 11.

government were strongly committed to the single currency, it would find a way to meet the deficit criterion. If a government were unable to meet the 3% criterion, there was reason to doubt its future commitment to EMU.[75] The European Union (EU) politics dimension, however, was not the only facet of the Maastricht criteria's use. The criteria gained independent status: market participants routinely evaluated non-EU states according to the Maastricht criteria; for example, "Canada is in really good shape; she would qualify for EMU."[76] Others noted that "the U.S. deficit isn't really much at all, when you use the Maastricht criteria."[77]

Although market participants used the Maastricht criteria extensively, they also saw the criteria as objectively flawed. Market actors saw "no good, objective reason" to use 3% or "to make no allowance for cyclical variations in the deficit."[78] One market participant pointed out that "it is the convergence of macroeconomic factors, not the level at which they converge, that is important. If all have deficits of four percent, they should move forward."[79] Despite these objections, the widespread use of these criteria by market participants strengthened the financial market constraint: all market participants employed the deficit criterion and responded to it similarly.

At the same time, when other convergence criteria did not appear to be part of the political process surrounding EMU, market participants began to ignore them. For example, as it became evident that governments would not strictly interpret the public debt criterion,[80] market participants began to ignore it. "The sixty percent criterion has been dropped by the EU, and therefore, largely by markets."[81] As with pre-Maastricht deficits, market

---

[75] The European Commission 1995 offers a similar observation: "Compliance with the criteria is not simply a test of qualification for membership but a lasting commitment by the Member States to adhere to an economic policy conducive to sustainable growth, employment, and the maintenance of purchasing power" (p. 5).

[76] Interview 12.

[77] Interview, Monetary Affairs Division, BIS, May 1997.

[78] Interviews 6, 8, 12, 24, 41, 45; also, Interview with European Commission official, Directorate General II (DG-II), May 1997. A similar criticism has been leveled against the Stability and Growth Pact; in the summer of 2001, several EU governments suggested retooling the pact, focusing on spending targets rather than on deficit/GDP ratios.

[79] Interview 6.

[80] That is, "sufficiently diminishing and approaching the reference value at a satisfactory pace," rather than "60% of GDP" would be used.

[81] Interview 35; also Interview 16. The *Financial Times* commentator Martin Wolf explains the abandonment of the debt criterion (April 29, 1997, p. 22). "Astoundingly, Germany is one of the few members that fails on debt: its ratio has been rising and is expected to

participants preferred lower debt levels to higher debt levels, but they did not rely on the Maastricht reference value when judging levels of debt as acceptable or unacceptable. At the same time, though, market actors clung to 3% as a fiscal deficit threshold, perhaps following the German finance minister Theo Waigel's insistence that "three percent means three percent."

The impact of the Maastricht criteria on macropolicy evaluations offers two lessons regarding key indicators: first, the nature of key indicators changes over time, leading to changes in financial market influences. Second, by establishing the criteria by which they later were judged, governments are able to influence the operation of the international financial market. The development of the Maastricht convergence recommendations (as part of the treaty-crafting process) was by no means a purely technical exercise. National governments were not passive participants in these financial market–government interactions.[82] Rather, governments established criteria by which they later were evaluated. Governments that adhered to the rules quickly gained credibility with financial markets, as the case of Italy illustrates.[83] Although EU member governments do not seem to have been aware ex ante of the impact of the criteria on financial market behavior, they likely realized ex post the importance of the criteria to financial market participants. We might expect that this realization affects other EU-level decisions regarding fiscal and monetary policy, such as the existence and character of the Stability and Growth Pact.

This assertion does not go so far as to imply that governments are necessarily masters of, rather than slaves to, financial markets. Rather, along with the rest of this book, it suggests a mixed relationship between governments and capital markets; neither structural dependence of the state on capital[84] nor control of capital by the state obtains in most cases. When dealing with some types of nations, financial market participants are quite willing to evaluate governments according to a narrow set of rules. Moreover, under some conditions, governments are able to set these rules. Successful rule setting likely requires cooperation among a set of creditworthy, economically

---

reach 62 per cent at the end of this year. Arguably, other failures are Spain and Austria. Yet Belgium, with a debt ratio of 127 per cent this year, down from 137 per cent in 1993, and Italy, with a ratio of 122 per cent, down from 125 per cent in 1994, can both be judged to meet the criterion. To conclude that Germany has failed and Belgium and Italy have succeeded is palpably absurd. The solution has been simply to ignore the criterion."

[82] Mosley 1998.

[83] See Gilibert 1994, *Financial Times*, September 16, 1997, p. 9.

[84] E.g., Przeworski and Wallerstein 1988.

significant nations; it is unlikely that a group of developing nations, or a single developed nation, could set rules for financial market behavior. Successful rule setting also may require an explicit (e.g., treaty-based) statement of the rules.

Quantitative Assessments of the "Strong but Narrow" Hypothesis

The interview evidence presented previously offers two central observations regarding the behavior of international financial market participants and, therefore, the relationship between national governments and international finance. First, the nature of financial market pressures varies across groups of countries. Because investors have different beliefs regarding emerging market governments' types, these economies should experience greater external financial pressures. Second, governments of developed democracies currently experience strong but narrow financial market influences, allowing them significant opportunities for policy divergence – substantial "room to move" for government policy.

Provided developed country governments ameliorate inflation and exchange rate risks, they have considerable latitude to pursue divergent policies in other areas. This possibility is consistent with a large body of recent comparative political economy literature, which finds evidence of persistent microside divergence in the face of macroside convergence. Governments of developed democracies appear to accede to financial market preferences in a few areas, but not in others. We should continue to observe crossnational convergence across a small range of indicators, but also continued cross-national divergence in other indicators.

In this section, I employ quantitative analyses to test further the strong but narrow hypothesis: does financial market behavior, measured in terms of interest rates on long-term government bonds, comport with the macropolicy indicators story told by financial market participants? Do financial markets react strongly to movements in a narrow set of indicators but not react, or react only mildly, to changes in other indicators? When outcomes on key indicators change, market responses should be significant and sizable. When outcomes on other indicators change, market responses should be insignificant or significant but small.

In order to gauge the strength and slope of financial market influence, I estimate two sets of models, the first with macropolicy indicators and political variables, and the second with these indicators as well as a variety of more micropolicy outcomes. Cross-sectional time series analyses support the assertion that macropolicy indicators are most important to market evaluations of developed economies. Also, as market participants suggest, government partisanship exerts only a very minor influence on long-term interest rate levels. With respect to microlevel indicators, the quantitative analyses provide mixed evidence: the most aggregate of these indicators, such as the total size of government, *is* associated significantly with long-term interest rate levels. The strength of these associations, however, is rather small, so that the cost to governments for divergent policies is not great. The least aggregate of these indicators, such as the balance between workers' and employers' social security contributions, are not significantly associated with interest rate levels, as the strong but narrow framework predicts.

The Macroindicators Model

To evaluate Hypothesis 2.1 statistically, I conduct a cross-sectional time series analysis, employing data from 1981 to 1995 for a set of 19 developed democracies: Australia, Austria, Belgium, Canada, Denmark, Finland, France, Germany, Ireland, Italy, Japan, the Netherlands, New Zealand, Norway, Portugal, Spain, Sweden, Switzerland, and the UK.[85] The main dependent variable for the quantitative analyses in this section is the nominal monthly rate of interest paid on long-term, domestic currency–denominated government bonds. Long-term bond yields indicate the costs of borrowing to governments and also affect the price of borrowing for private actors in the domestic economy. Because these rates are mostly market-driven, they provide a better gauge of financial market sentiment than shorter-term rates, which are set by central banks (albeit sometimes in response to private market pressures). Additionally, I focus on longer-term (that is, monthly) interest rate movements; I am most concerned with trends in levels of rates rather than with the shorter-term volatility of these rates.[86]

Moreover, using interest rates rather than the amount of capital flows more accurately captures financial market activity. Under conditions of high international capital mobility, responses to changes in economic or policy

---

[85] Not all indicators are available for all years and countries. Where data are missing for the relevant independent variables, those indicators are not used in the analysis. Therefore, analyses using different variables have varying numbers of nations, as indicated later.

[86] See Chapter 1 for an argument that the focus on longer-term rates is consistent with the foci of most government officials. In the parlance of Orr et al. 1995, I am concerned with "low-frequency" (long-run) influences on interest rates, rather than with "high-frequency" influences.

outcomes will be interest rate changes rather than changes in capital flows. If the French budget deficit is very large, lenders may choose to remain in France but will raise the premium charged to the French government. Hence, the French government remains able to attract capital, but it must pay more to do so. As one senior French official notes:

> The external financial constraint now works through price movements. There is no problem of credit rationing. Governments can borrow any volume they want, provided they are willing to pay the price.[87]

Were we to look only at actual capital movements, we might see very small inflows or outflows from France; these likely would not capture the magnitude of actual market response. Finally, data on long-term interest rates are more reliable than those on capital flows: long-term interest rate data are transparent and straightforward. Data on capital flows often are plagued by large inaccuracies, as a look at the "errors and omissions" lines in the International Monetary Fund's (IMF's) balance of payments data quickly demonstrates.

A full description of the data used in the analysis, as well as the variable abbreviations, is found in Appendix 3.1. In order to account more completely for the time series properties of the interest rate data (and, therefore, to generate less biased and more accurate coefficients and standard errors),[88] I employ monthly – rather than annual or quarterly – data for all independent variables. When monthly data are used, the number of time periods (T) greatly exceeds the number of countries (N), increasing our confidence in the regression estimates.[89] Whereas most economic indicators (inflation, exchange rate levels) are available on a monthly basis, some government policy indicators (deficits, spending by category, debt) and institutional variables (capital controls) are available – and substantively meaningful – only in quarterly or annual series. In these cases, I interpolate the data, using cubic spline curves, to generate a set of monthly observations.[90]

---

[87] Interview, French Economics Ministry, May 1997.

[88] Stimson 1985.

[89] Beck and Katz 1995, 1996.

[90] Nonlinear interpolation was used because it prevents the existence of sharp "break points" in the data: it is reasonable to assume that government budget deficits do not sharply change from one annual data point to the next (as linear interpolation would suggest) but, rather, move smoothly from one period to another. Moreover, the estimates obtained from linear and cubic spline interpolations do not differ greatly. I used PROC EXPAND in SAS/ETS to perform the interpolations.

After examining the structure of the residuals for ordinary least squares (OLS) regressions employing these data, I conclude that OLS estimates using panel-corrected standard errors (PCSEs) are the most appropriate method for cross-sectional time series.[91] Generating estimates by using PSCEs tends to increase the standard errors of the estimates, providing more conservative assessments of the relationship between government policies and international capital markets. An examination of the autoregressive properties of the data demonstrates that it is reasonable to assume a common autoregressive (AR-1) process across the panel. I also conclude that the cross-sectional error structure is heteroscedastic, so that the variances of error processes differ across countries.[92] The models I estimate, then, employ PCSEs with heteroscedastic panels and a common AR(1) correlation.[93] Finally, in order to enhance the reliability of the coefficient estimates, as well as to gauge the impact of cross-sectional variation in independent variables on interest rates, I *do not* include a lagged dependent variable in these models.[94]

The Overall Model: Independent Variables and Expected Relationships   I first estimate a model including control variables, macropolicy outcomes, and measures of government partisanship and government change:

$$\text{Long-Term Rate} = \text{constant} + \text{USLT} + \text{INFLATE} + \text{CURRACCT}$$
$$+ \text{ERCHANGE} + \text{GOVBAL} + \text{LEFTC}$$
$$+ \text{ELECTION} + \text{CAPOPEN} + \text{error}$$

[91] Beck and Katz 1995.

[92] See Orr et al. 1995 for a discussion of cross-sectional variance in the operation of "low-frequency" fundamentals.

[93] All of the analyses presented were performed in STATA Version 5, using XTGLS and the accompanying PCSE option.

[94] See Achen 2000 for a discussion of the pros and cons of including lagged dependent variables; he maintains that a lagged dependent variable is particularly problematic when it trends and when one or more of the independent variables trend. When a lagged dependent variable is included, the model explains a higher percentage of the variation (an R^2 greater than 0.99, as expected). The results also indicate that a unit root problem does not exist: the coefficient on the lagged interest rate variable is 0.96, and a 95% confidence interval places the coefficient between 0.9486 and 0.9722. Because the coefficient is greater than 0.9 but less than 1.0, inclusion of a lagged dependent variable is unnecessary. Moreover, lagged dependent variables often cause OLS estimates to be both biased and inconsistent (Beck and Katz 1996, Maddala 1998). Therefore, I do not include lagged dependent variables in the models reported later.

Control Variables   Interviews with financial market participants, along with several econometric studies of the determinants of long-term interest rates,[95] suggest that interest rates on U.S. government long-term securities (USLT) are a key influence on other government bond rates. If we conceive of the global government bond market as one in which governments compete to attract lenders, the importance of the U.S. rate is clear. The United States has the largest and most developed government securities market, and U.S. rates are used as a benchmark with which other countries' rates are compared. When this benchmark rate increases, all other factors equal, investors will move from other countries to the United States, in order to earn higher returns. When the U.S. rate decreases, all other factors equal, other governments can reduce the rates they pay on long-term securities. Moreover, the U.S. interest rate serves as a summary of global capital market sentiment, potentially capturing a variety of factors important to long-term rates, but beyond the control of individual nations. Therefore, U.S. long-term interest rates (USLT) should be positively and strongly associated with other nations' long-term rates.

The second control variable is international capital market openness (CAPOPEN). High international capital mobility could have two opposite effects on government bond rates in the developed world. On the one hand, and as Chapter 2 suggests, increased capital mobility provides a greater capacity for exit for market participants and, therefore, an increased ability to punish governments for unsuitable policy outcomes. This effect of capital mobility should be reflected in a stronger association, as openness increases, between economic indicators and long-term interest rates, where the relationships between interest rates and key indicators are larger and/or more significant in the 1980s and 1990s (than in the 1960s and 1970s, for instance). On the other hand, increased capital mobility provides governments with a larger pool of capital from which to borrow. Rather than borrow funds only from domestic savings, governments and private individuals may borrow from any holder of capital.[96] The positive effect of capital mobility should reduce interest rates, so that higher levels of legal capital market openness are associated generally with lower interest rate levels.

In order to adjudicate between the positive and negative effects of international capital mobility, I control for capital market openness in the main

---

[95] For example, Christiansen and Pigott 1997, Orr et al. 1995.
[96] Simmons 1999. Also see Lawson 1993, pp. 70–71.

model. I also test the joint effect of capital mobility and government policy outcomes by including interaction terms (e.g., capital mobility and government budget balance) in some specifications of the statistical models. If the relationship between long-term interest rates and the government budget balance changes as capital mobility changes (so that openness is associated with greater risk premia for larger deficits), these interaction terms also should be statistically significant.

Macropolicy Indicators I include four types of aggregate economic policy outcomes in the overall model – inflation (INFLATE), government budget balances (GOVBAL), current account balances (CURRACCT), and nominal exchange rate levels (ERCHANGE). The importance of current and anticipated inflation to long-term interest rates is revealed not only via interviews and previous econometric work, but also by the relationship between nominal and real interest rates. According to the Fischer equation, nominal rates are simply the real rate plus an inflation premium. And if current inflation leads market participants to expect greater inflation in the future, they will charge an additional risk premium. Inflationary expectations can increase the cost of borrowing in both nominal *and* real terms.[97]

Indeed, trends in inflation rates in developed democracies suggest that, over time, governments have accorded greater priority to reducing inflation rates. Notermans maintains that "there is a general consensus among policy authorities in OECD nations that macroeconomic policies should have but one goal – the fight against inflation."[98] Figure 3.1 provides annual data on inflation rates for a sample of developed democracies, as well as averages for EU nations and all OECD nations (shown as a gray area in Figure 3.1).[99] The data display a cross-national, downward convergence over time. The OECD average inflation rate is 1.7% in 1998, while the EU average is 1.8%. In 1998, only Greece had an inflation rate greater than 4%, whereas, in the 1970–1977 period, all nations exceeded this rate, most did in the 1978–1985 period, and six did as late as 1993. Additionally, variance in inflation rates has decreased over time; the standard deviation of inflation rates fell from 5.1% in 1981 to 1.1% in 1998.

[97] On the inflation rate as a determinant of long-term interest rates, see Knoester and Mak 1994, Orr et al. 1995.
[98] Notermans 1993, p. 134.
[99] The inflation data are found in World Bank, *World Development Indicators 2000*. The OECD average includes only the "old OECD" nations, prior to expansion in the mid-1990s. Therefore, it excludes the "high inflation" OECD nations, such as Turkey and Mexico.

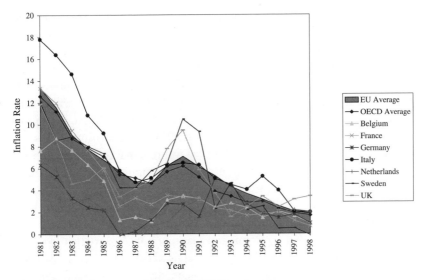

Figure 3.1 Inflation trends, select OECD nations.

The downward trend in inflation rates is likely due to a variety of factors, including changes in ideology regarding monetary policy. High inflation in the 1970s can be attributed partly to the dramatic rise in energy prices surrounding the 1973 and 1979 Organization of Petroleum Exporting Countries (OPEC) shocks. Additionally, for EU nations, lower inflation in the 1990s can be attributed partly to convergence efforts surrounding the run-up to EMU. As part of the Exchange Rate Mechanism (ERM) many EU members attempted to keep their currency's value within a narrow band; doing so meant following monetary policies similar to those of Germany, which were traditionally very inflation-averse. Moreover, the Maastricht Treaty mandated that EU members aiming to join the first round of EMU achieve an annual inflation rate only slightly greater than that of the three lowest-inflation nations. Institutionally, there has been a move toward politically independent central banks in the developed – as well as in the developing – world, and there is a fairly robust and positive association between the degree of central bank independence and the rate of inflation.[100]

---

[100] On the movement toward central bank independence, see Bernhard 1998 and Maxfield 1997, as well as Chapter 6.

Beyond these influences, however, financial market pressure likely contributed to the downward trend in inflation rates.[101] Such pressures also were one motivation for the choice of politically independent central banks in many nations. Government officials speak frequently of the importance to financial markets of "responsible" (low-inflation) monetary policy. For example, a former deputy director of the Bank of England observes, "The market constraint on the monetary side is very tough."[102] Likewise, a former president of the Bank of France warns, "If the anticipation of inflation is guided by a bad past, it will be hard to impress markets."[103] Given the existing evidence, I expect inflation rates to be significantly and strongly associated with long-term interest rates.

Financial market participants also indicate that the government budget balance is a key influence on government bond market activity. It is commonly asserted that economic internationalization, particularly on the finance side, exerts downward pressures on fiscal deficits. Along these lines, Garrett finds significant associations between increasing financial openness and smaller budget deficits.[104] Market participants dislike government budget deficits because they worry about the effect of sustained deficits on the government's ability to repay its debt (default risk) and, more importantly, because they worry that an accumulation of debt will create incentives for governments to inflate away their nominal liabilities (inflation risk).[105] Because market actors are sensitive to increases in inflation risk, I expect the government budget balance (GOVBAL) to be significantly – and somewhat strongly – associated with long-term interest rates.[106]

Again, government budgets have moved away from large deficits and toward balance during the last decade.[107] Figure 3.2 provides data on government budget balances for a sample of OECD nations for the years 1981 through 1997. Although cross-national variance in deficits persists through

[101] Kramer 1998, Kurzer 1993, Perry and Robertson 1998.
[102] Interview, former Bank of England official, March 1997.
[103] Interview, former president, Bank of France, February 1997.
[104] Garrett 1998a.
[105] IMF 1996, p. 66. Turnovsky and Miller 1984. Thomas and Abderrezak 1988 suggest that government budget deficits affect the term structure of interest rates.
[106] Giorgianni 1997 tests for the existence of fiscal-policy risk premia in Italian assets and finds that fiscal policy has a large effect on risk premia.
[107] Simmons 1999. Sinclair 2000 argues that domestic elites, wishing to contain national governments, put forward a deficit-cutting rhetoric, and that this rhetoric has gained acceptance by financial market participants and policymakers.

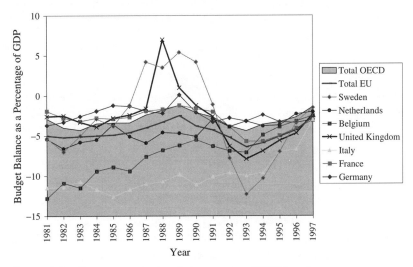

Figure 3.2   Government budget balance, select OECD nations.

the late 1990s, the size of deficits falls, quite dramatically in some cases (for example, in Greece, Ireland, Italy, and Sweden). From 1981 to 1997, 18 nations improved their budget balances; only 3 moved in the opposite direction. The average deficit for the sample of OECD nations fell from 2.9% of GDP in 1981 to 1.4% of GDP in 1997; likewise, the average deficit for EU nations fell from 5.0% of GDP in 1981 to 2.7% of GDP in 1997.[108] The deficit outcomes are consistent with the strong but narrow view.

As with inflation rates, financial market pressures are not the only influences on government budget balances. For EU members, the EMU qualification process played a central role in the mid- and late 1990s. For example, Italy's deficit ratio fell from 10.1% of GDP in 1991 to 3.0% in 1997, a fall that likely would not have been so large or quick without the incentive of EMU membership. At the same time, deficit cutting could be motivated by internal rather than external incentives.[109] Whereas many government actors publicly cite financial market pressures as the chief reason for deficit reduction, some observe privately that their underlying motivations are

---

[108] The full set of data is available in the OECD *Economic Outlook*, December 1997.
[109] Notermans 2000.

domestic – to act consistently with the government's ideology or to satisfy a particular constituency:

It is important to differentiate between the reality of market pressures and the use by governments as a cover within domestic politics.[110]

It is important not to confuse domestic with international pressures. The financial market strengthens the government's reasons for doing as it already wants to do. Political actors can use market reactions as a scapegoat for doing what is already necessary.[111]

The quantitative analyses, then, might provide insight regarding the relative importance of financial market pressures to deficit reduction. If government budget balances are significantly and strongly associated with interest rates – if the coefficients are large and the standard errors are small – we might infer that financial market pressure is an important driver of changes in budget balances. If, on the other hand, the effects of budget balances on long-term interest rates are significant but weak, or simply insignificant, we might conclude that financial market pressures are a relatively weak cause of changes in budget balances. Furthermore, if the relationship between interest rates and government balances differs between EU and non-EU nations, we can conclude that EU-based pressures exert an additional influence on government budget balances.

The final macroindicators are the current account balance and the nominal exchange rate. Both of these capture exchange rate, and possibly inflation, risk. I expect that a more negative current account balance will be associated with higher long-term interest rates. Under a flexible exchange rate regime, a current account deficit can be rectified in two ways. The first is via capital inflows. A nation may compensate for smaller current account balances (deficits) with greater capital account balances (surpluses). As the current account balance improves, the need to attract capital – by offering higher interest rates – declines, so that long-term interest rates decline. The second is via exchange rates: exchange rate depreciation should increase exports and decrease imports, thereby ameliorating the deficit. In both cases, the result of deterioration in the current account balance is upward pressure on interest rates, via increased exchange rate risk or via the need to attract inward investment. Likewise, appreciation of the nominal exchange rate should be associated with reductions in long-term interest

---

[110] Interview, senior British Treasury official, March 1997.
[111] Interview, senior Bundesbank official, May 1997.

rates.[112] Because benchmark government bonds are denominated in local currencies, investors demand higher-risk premia when local currencies are weak.[113]

Political Variables   Another implication of the interview study reported in the first section of this chapter is that, in developed democracies, the ideology – or partisanship – of governments has lost importance as an information shortcut for market participants.[114] If government policy outcomes and government partisan affiliations were highly correlated, we would expect market actors to charge increased risk premia to left governments. In this vein, Kurzer maintains that the pursuit by left-leaning governments of expansionary programs produces expectations among financial markets that "future inflation rates will drift above the rates of the country's main trading partners."[115] Expectations of expansionary government programs generate large-scale capital outflows. Similarly, in his analysis of annual government policy outcomes and long-term interest rates, spanning the period 1966 to 1990, Garrett finds that nations with left governments and strong labor movements pay higher rates than other nations. The magnitude of this effect increases as capital openness grows, from a premium of 0.3 percentage point during low capital mobility, to a premium of 0.8 percentage point under high capital mobility.[116] In a slightly different vein, Leblang and Bernhard suggest that currency market participants will employ information about government partisanship and government formation when assessing the probability of an exchange rate change; specifically, they test the expectation that market expectations of a cabinet dissolution "will more sharply increase the probability of a speculative attack if the dissolution is likely to produce a leftward shift."[117]

On the other hand, if government partisanship provides little information about macropolicy outcomes, there is little reason to expect that left governments will pay significantly higher interest rates than right governments. Perotti and Kontopolous find, for instance, that the strongest effects of ideology on fiscal policy are on the areas of transfer spending and

---

[112] IMF 1997.

[113] This exchange rate risk could be reduced via use of the forward exchange rate market, although forward contracts tend to be of short duration.

[114] On the broader impact of political regimes – authoritarian and democratic – on investment, see Przeworski et al. 2000.

[115] Kurzer 1993, p. 12.

[116] Garrett 1998a.

[117] Leblang and Bernhard 2000, p. 306.

government wages, rather than on the overall budget balance.[118] If market actors are unconcerned about more microside outcomes, they should be similarly unconcerned about ideology.

Figure 3.3 displays the bivariate correlations between government partisanship and long-term interest rates, budget balances, total government debt, and inflation.[119] Left government and the interest rates on long-term government bonds are correlated somewhat strongly during the mid- to late 1980s[120] but are only very weakly correlated in the 1990s. It is also during the mid-1980s that key macropolicy outcomes are associated with government partisanship: the correlation between left government and inflation peaks in the mid-1980s then falls considerably. The correlation between partisanship and total government debt, and between partisanship and budget balance, also peaks in the mid-1980s.[121] Given the declining association between partisanship and policy outcomes, the relationship between government partisanship and long-term interest rates should fade over time.[122] Whereas market actors once used partisanship as an information shortcut, the utility of partisanship as a decision rule has faded in recent years. Now, when making asset allocation decisions, market actors look at macroeconomic policy outcomes rather than partisan affiliations.

[118] Perotti and Kontopolous 1999.
[119] I use the LEFTC measure of partisanship. LEFTC measures left party cabinet portfolios as a percentage of all cabinet portfolios. The variable ranges from 0 (no left party cabinet ministers) to 100 (all left party cabinet ministers). The correlations between left governing legislative seats and the preceding policy indicators are very similar. LEFTC and LEFTGS rely on the left–right party scales originally developed by Castles and Mair 1984.
[120] The relationship between partisanship and macroeconomic outcomes is consistent with Franzese's 1999 study of central bank independence and inflation outcomes in the developed world. For the period 1972 to 1990, he finds that the additional impact of central bank independence on the rate of inflation is contingent on government partisanship. Where more left governments are in office, central bank independence produces a larger effect; this implies that left governments are, ceteris paribus, more inflation-prone than right governments. This conjecture, however, is not tested for the 1990s and may well disappear in that decade.
[121] Stephens et al. 1999 find strong partisan effects on government social policies in the 1960s, attenuated effects in the 1970s, and very small effects in the 1980s. Also see Kontopolous and Perotti 1999, who find that the impact of ideology on fiscal outcomes is strongest in the 1980s.
[122] On the traditional association between government ideology and economic policy outcomes, see Garrett and Lange 1991, Notermans 2000, Simmons 1994. Garrett 1998a suggests that, with respect to government spending, the combination of strong left parties and encompassing unions is associated with higher spending. The King et al. 2000 analysis of Garrett's findings confirms this finding where economic globalization is high but finds no evidence of significant partisan differences where globalization is low.

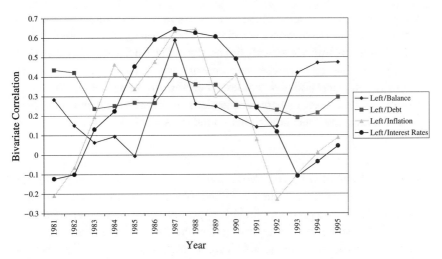

Figure 3.3 Government partisanship, interest rates and policy indicators, 1981–1995.

Therefore, although some rather strong bivariate correlations between government partisanship and long-term interest rates exist during some years of the 1981–1995 period, I expect these relationships to disappear, or to remain only weakly, in a multivariate analysis. If left governments are associated with higher long-term interest rates only because they are associated with negative macro-outcomes, once we control for these outcomes, the effects of government partisanship will disappear. To evaluate this expectation, I include the percentage of cabinet seats held by left governments (LEFTC) in the model.[123]

I also include an election dummy variable (ELECTION) in the model. This variable gauges the extent to which the occurrence of an election in a given month – or expectation regarding an election – results in an increase in long-term interest rates (during the election month or during the months preceding or following an election). The bivariate correlation between elections and long-term interest rates is very small (0.0075 for the entire sample). When the sample is divided by country, there are some negative correlations between elections and interest rates, as well as some positive correlations, but no correlations greater than 0.15. Dividing the

---

[123] Stephens et al. 1999 note that party cabinet share, rather than parliamentary seats or votes, tends to be the strongest political determinant of social policy outcomes. I also include the percentage of governing left party legislative seats (LEFTGS) in alternate specifications.

sample by year produces similar results: some negative bivariate associations, some positive bivariate associations, but no associations greater than 0.15. Similarly, interviews with financial market participants suggest that elections will matter only when a change of governments portends a change of policies in macropolicy outcomes. Therefore, in the aggregate, we might expect a weak association between elections and interest rates, in which elections occasionally affect government bond rates, but in a fairly idiosyncratic fashion.

Overall Model: Results and Discussion   The results of a macroindicators model are reported in Table 3.2. Where other assessments indicated that lagged effects were present, I include appropriate lags of independent variables in the estimation. To determine the cumulative effects of each (lagged and current) independent variable, I combine the coefficients. The total coefficients are listed in Table 3.2, where the probability that the coefficient differs from zero is given by the chi-squared estimates. The final column of Table 3.2 provides more substantive information regarding the magnitude of effects: it reports the implied effect, holding all else equal, of an increase of one standard deviation in the value of an indicator. The full results, with disaggregated coefficients for each variable, are found in Appendix 3.2.

The results reported rely on interest rate *levels* as the dependent variable (and levels of other indicators as independent variables). If interest rate *changes* are used as the dependent variable, and levels *or* changes are

Table 3.2. *Model Results*

Variable	Total Coefficient	χ^2	$P > \chi^2$	Implied Effect, One Standard Deviation Increase
USLT	0.4016***	239.02	0.0000	1.0022
INFLATE	0.2340***	113.76	0.0000	1.0746
ERCHANGE	−0.0338***	17.91	0.0000	−0.0484
CURRACCT	−0.2788***	65.11	0.0000	−0.9437
GOVBAL	−.05010**	2.08	0.0370	0.2099
ELECTION	0.1745**	6.60	0.0102	0.0270
LEFTC	0.0020**	1.961	0.0500	0.0748
CAPOPEN	0.0634	0.357	0.721	0.0415

Note: Dependent variable: long-term interest rates; number of observations: 2384; number of countries: 15; number of time periods: 169 (14 years); R^2: 0.8202.
*$p < .05$; **$p < .01$; ***$p < .001$; two-tailed test.

used as independent variables,[124] the results are broadly similar, although, in some cases, the implied relationships between independent and dependent variables (and, therefore, the degree of financial market influence) are weaker.[125] The model reported does not include country and year fixed effects (country dummies), but I do include these effects in other specifications of the models. Including these effects allows us to gauge the impact of common shocks across countries (year effects) as well as particular institutional histories of individual countries (country effects).[126] Inclusion of country and year effects does not change substantively the coefficient estimates, with two exceptions.[127] Moreover, when I exclude particular nations to assess the sensitivity of the results to their inclusion, the results remain broadly similar.[128]

The results indicate that the most pronounced and statistically significant influences on long-term government bond rates are the inflation rate, the U.S. long-term interest rate, and the current account balance. Government budget balances are significantly associated with long-term rates, but the estimated coefficient is rather small. Likewise, government partisanship is statistically significant, but its coefficient estimate and implied effects are even smaller.

Control Variables   An increase of 1 percentage point in USLT is associated with an increase of 0.40% in national long-term interest rates. At the

---

[124] See Garrett 2000a on the rationale for considering the marginal effects – captured by changes – of economic globalization on government policies. Also see Stimson 1985.

[125] The magnitude of implied effects is slightly larger for USLT and roughly equal or less for CURRACCT, ERCHANGE, INFLATE, and GOVBAL. One explanation for the difference in estimations is the nature of some of the independent variables: monthly data on fiscal policy outcomes, for instance, reflect interpolated annual values, so that the changes from month to month do not necessarily capture actual changes or changes in market expectations regarding fiscal policy. For this reason, models using changes might more appropriately employ annual observations.

[126] Garrett and Mitchell 2001 discuss in greater detail the rationale for inclusion of these effects.

[127] The coefficient estimates and significance levels are similar for USLT, INFLATE, ERCHANGE, ELECTION, and LEFTC. The estimate for CURRACCT is significant but smaller (−0.14, rather than −0.28). The estimate for GOVBAL remains quite small but is not statistically significant at conventional levels. The statistically significant (but generally substantively small) dummies are 1981, 1982, 1983, 1985, 1986, 1990, and 1994; and Belgium, Germany, Italy, the Netherlands, and Japan.

[128] The only independent variable for which results are sensitive to the exclusion of particular nations is CAPOPEN: this variable sometimes is positive and insignificant (as in original model, or with Austria or Italy excluded), sometimes is positive and significant (as with Germany excluded), and sometimes is negative and significant (Japan excluded).

same time, neither of the potential capital openness effects dominates: the coefficient for CAPOPEN is quite small and is not statistically significant. Perhaps capital market openness has two, contradictory effects on interest rates – openness provides access to greater borrowing but also facilitates greater market punishment. Alternatively, the increases in capital mobility observed in OECD nations during the 1981–1995 period may be too small to affect significantly the results. Were we to employ data for a sample with dramatic changes in capital market openness, such as a set of emerging market nations, we likely would see more pronounced coefficients on this variable.[129]

Macropolicy Indicators   The strength and significance of the coefficient on INFLATE suggest that market actors in OECD nations are most concerned with inflation risk. An increase of 1% in the annual rate of inflation (measured monthly) is associated with an increase of 0.23% in the long-term interest rate. A government presiding over an increase in inflation of one standard deviation (4.59%) might expect to pay an interest rate premium of 1.07% – a fairly significant increase. The importance of inflation rates to long-term government bond rates suggests that the most dramatic effect of international capital mobility on government economic policy is on the monetary side.[130] This finding also is consistent with trends in inflation in OECD nations, as reviewed earlier.

Additionally, as expected, as a nation's current account balance improves, long-term interest rates fall. An improvement of 1% in the current account balance/GDP is associated with a reduction in interest rates of 0.28%. A nation experiencing a deterioration of one standard deviation in its current account balance (3.38% of GDP) could expect to pay an additional annual 0.94% for government bonds. The strength and significance of the CURRACCT are consistent with the mechanism described: a current account deficit indicates the need for a capital account surplus, which requires a higher interest rate premium.

---

[129] This result increases our confidence in the assumption that the relationship between the independent variables and the dependent variables in the developed democracies is relatively constant over the 1981–1995 period. Another possibility, not yet explored in detail by political scientists, is that some sort of Markov switching process characterizes government bond interest rates. In a Markov regime-switching model, in some periods interest rates are driven by economic fundamentals; in other cases, interest rates are driven by chartist or herding behavior. For an analysis of exchange rates as the product of a Markov switching process, see Freeman et al. 2000, Hays et al. 2000.

[130] Garrett 1998a.

The other mechanism through which the current account could affect market sentiment – the potential for exchange rate depreciation – is not borne out by this analysis. Although the coefficient for ERCHANGE is statistically significant, it is quite small: a 1% depreciation in the nominal exchange rate is associated with an interest rate increase of 0.034%. Here, a change of one standard deviation (1.43) produces a smaller rise in interest rates – 0.048%. The meager size of this effect is likely due to the ability of market participants to ameliorate exchange rate risk through hedging – for example, through buying local currencies at preannounced rates on the forward market.

The final key indicator estimated earlier – and perhaps the one of most interest to comparative political economists – is the government budget balance as a percentage of GDP. GOVBAL ranges from -13.6% (a deficit) to 9.9% (a surplus), with a mean value of -3.3%. The coefficient estimate predicts that a decrease of 1% in the budget balance (toward a smaller surplus or a larger deficit) results in an increase in interest rates of 0.05%. This effect is statistically significant at the 95% confidence level, but its magnitude is perhaps surprising. If a nation were to make the substantial movement from a deficit of 10% of GDP to a balanced budget, holding all other indicators equal, the predicted improvement in the cost of government borrowing would be only 0.5%. This implied effect is noticeable, but, if we compare it to overall interest rate differentials during the period,[131] we see that it is not immense.[132] For instance, the average differential between national and German interest rates is 2.84%, substantially greater than the deficit effect.

A possible explanation for the relatively weak coefficient on the government fiscal balance variable is that the response of capital markets to budget deficits has changed over time. Perhaps capital market responses were weak in the early 1980s but strong in the mid-1990s; the result of this change, in a pooled analysis, would be a moderate coefficient estimate. To test this explanation, I added an interaction term (CAPOPEN*GOVBAL) and reestimated the model. The coefficient estimate for this term, however, was substantively small (0.0598) and not significant at the 90% confidence level. We cannot reject the assumption, then, that the relationship between

---

[131] The difference between national and German monthly long-term interest rates averages 2.84% for the entire period, with a standard deviation of 3.35%. The average difference peaks at 4.52% in 1987, then falls gradually, reaching a minimum of 1.21% in 1994, then rising slightly.

[132] See Orr et al. 1995 for a similar conclusion regarding the impact of government fiscal balances on long-term interest rates.

international financial markets and government budget positions has remained fairly constant as capital market openness has increased.

The relative magnitudes of the coefficients on inflation and deficits suggest that the influence of financial markets on government policy is much stronger on the monetary policy side than on the fiscal policy side. This is consistent with the notion that, even under flexible exchange rate regimes, financial market openness reduces monetary policy autonomy dramatically.[133] The mechanism for this reduction in autonomy is the exchange rate: if inflation leads to higher interest rates in the domestic economy, investors will enter, and the local currency will appreciate. This effect often is problematic for export-oriented sectors. The effects of fiscal policy on interest rates, however, are weaker. Contrary to some recent claims, possibilities for, and effectiveness of, fiscal policy remain.[134] Government officials may be correct to note that "markets will always constrain monetary more than fiscal policy."[135]

Moreover, the GOVBAL estimate suggests that, although we observed a reduction of government budget deficits in the OECD during the 1990s, financial market pressures are not the only drivers of these reductions. Much of the motivation for these reductions may stem from earlier political choices – particularly from EU membership – rather than from financial market pressures. In order to test for EU-driven effects, I reestimated the macroindicators model, adding a dummy variable for EU membership. The coefficient on the dummy variable is relatively large (−0.496, significant at a 92% confidence level), suggesting that EU members pay less to borrow, all else equal. Furthermore, the estimate for an interaction term on fiscal policy (EU membership∗GOVBAL) is highly significant (99% confidence): EU members with a budget deficit of 3% of GDP pay about 0.5% less than those with a deficit of 6% of GDP.[136] This result indicates that the premium paid – or the reward earned – for deficits or surpluses is higher in EU nations than in non-EU nations.

Another fiscal indicator of interest is government debt, which measures accumulated budget deficits. Some financial market participants pay

---

[133] Bisignano 1994.

[134] Clark and Hallerberg 1997, Simmons 1999.

[135] Interview, European Commission official, May 1997.

[136] In this equation, the coefficient estimates for government budget balances were similar (slightly less), but the coefficient was statistically significant at a lower level of confidence. This is likely due to collinearity between the interaction term and the budget balance measure.

attention to debt because it provides information regarding the sustainability of fiscal policy and the temptation of governments to inflate away nominal debt, or even to default.[137] If default risk were salient in OECD nations, this variable would have a strong and significant association with government bond rates. The inclusion of government debt in the regression equation (either as a substitute for GOVBAL, with which it is highly collinear, or in combination with GOVBAL to form a single fiscal indicator) does not substantially alter the results.[138] The coefficient estimates and levels of significance remain much the same, suggesting that default risk is a marginal concern for most developed democracies.[139] Again, this finding is consistent with trends over time in government debt, displayed in Figure 3.4. Downward convergence in general government financial liabilities has not occurred:[140] the gray area in Figure 3.4 indicates the average for the entire OECD over the 1981–1997 period. In the total OECD sample, all but two nations experienced a growth in debt from the 1980s to the 1990s, and the variance in debt levels remains unchanged throughout the period.

   Partisanship   Contrary to the expectations developed in the first section of this chapter, the measurement of government partisanship (LEFTC) *is* statistically significant at the 95% level. Governments with a higher percentage of left party cabinet members pay higher interest rates. The

---

[137] Alesina et al. 1992, Missale and Blanchard 1994, Orr et al. 1995.

[138] I created a fiscal policy variable (FISCAL) by standardizing the debt and government balance variables (with a mean of 0 and a standard deviation of 1), then combining the two measures. The resulting indicator ranges from -3.8 to 4.3, with negative values indicating "poor" (that is, deficit and/or debt) fiscal policies. Including FISCAL rather than government budget balance in the regression equation produces very similar results. The effects and significance of the other macroindicators and control variables remain largely the same, and the FISCAL coefficient is significant at a 94% confidence level. A negative change of one standard deviation in FISCAL is associated with a interest rate change of 0.2211% (compared with a change of 0.2054% for the same change in government balance).

[139] The specification with the strongest statistical significance (95% confidence) of debt includes a squared measure of public debt. This squared measure captures the notion that accumulated debt is most worrying to market participants at extreme values. In this model, the coefficient for "debt-squared" is 0.0003. This suggests that a government with a debt/GDP ratio of 100% will pay 3% more than a government with no debt. These findings are consistent with the Alesina et al. 1992 study of default risk in 12 OECD nations. For the 1974–1989 period, they find a significant correlation between debt and interest rate differentials, but this coefficient is quite small. The impact of accumulated debt is greatest in nations with high and quickly rising debt levels. On default risk after EMU, see Lemmen and Goodhart 1999 and Chapter 8.

[140] The full set of data is found in the OECD *Economic Outlook*, December 1997.

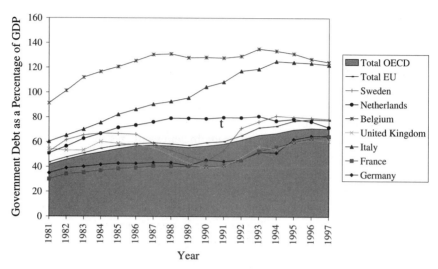

Figure 3.4   Government debt levels, select OECD nations.

coefficient on this variable, however, is very small: 0.00197. Garrett reports a similarly significant finding, although he finds a slightly larger coefficient.[141] In our model, the implied effect on government bond rates of a shift from a "fully right" government to a "fully left" government is only 0.2%.[142] Of course, most government changes, particularly in proportional representation systems, are not so extreme. In fact, many of the elections during the 1981–1995 period do not lead to a change in the partisan composition of the cabinet. When an election produces a change in the ideology of the cabinet, the average change is 37.5 (on a 0 to 100 scale), implying ceteris paribus an annual interest rate change of 0.074%. Similarly, Alesina and his colleagues find that, in the United States, a 10% change in the probability of a Democratic presidential victory is associated with an 0.05% to 0.08% change in interest rates on government bonds.[143] Whereas financial market outcomes suggest that partisanship may matter,

---

[141] Garrett 1998a. This difference may reflect the fact that I employ data for the 1981–1995 period, whereas Garrett's data end in 1990.

[142] The inclusion of a capital openness * left government interaction term does not produce a statistically significant estimate, suggesting that the effects of government partisanship on interest rates do not vary with capital market openness. Also note that the results are robust to the use of the LEFTGS variable: with LEFTGS, the coefficient is 0.0037381, the z-statistic is 2.017, and statistical significance is $p \geq 0.044$.

[143] The bonds involved are one- to four-year duration. Hays et al. 2000 confirm this effect.

in fact, to market participants, it is of only minor importance.[144] Accounting for macro-outcomes – for policies, not politics – explains much more of the variance in long-term interest rates.[145]

Elections Interviews with financial market participants suggest that elections will matter to market participants when a change of government implies a substantial change of macroeconomic policy. If market participants expect elections to create policy changes, we might find a statistically significant coefficient on the election variables. This is, in fact, the case; the total effect of elections on long-term interest rates is 0.17%, including lagged effects.[146] Again, relative to other coefficient estimates, this coefficient is quite small. It also is consistent with market participants' assertion that elections matter "occasionally."

How might we explain systematically the significance of the election variable? One potential explanation is the political business cycle: incumbent governments expand the macroeconomy (on the fiscal and monetary sides) in order to gain voters' approval.[147] If macroeconomic fluctuations coincide with the electoral calendar, market participants will demand higher risk premia in election periods. But the macroindicators model already controls for macroeconomic variables such as inflation and government budget balances.[148] And Franzese finds no increase in fiscal expenditures during the year preceding an election.[149] Furthermore, Kontopolous finds that electoral competition is not always associated with slack fiscal policies: depending on the existing level of government debt, electoral competition may lead to either fiscal tightening *or* fiscal expansion.[150]

---

[144] We might consider employing alternative measures of government partisanship. For example, the partisan affiliation of the finance minister, rather than the overall partisanship of the executive or legislative branch, could be more pertinent to financial market participants.

[145] And, as past studies have demonstrated, left-leaning governments are not necessarily associated historically with higher government budget deficits. Along these lines, Franzese 2002 finds some tendency for electorally threatened right governments to run lower budget deficits than left governments but also finds a tendency for electorally secure right governments to run higher deficits.

[146] I also tested for the significance of a lead-election term, to evaluate the effects on interest rates in the run-up to elections. The estimates for this coefficient were not statistically significant.

[147] Alesina et al. 1997, Hibbs 1977.

[148] Perry and Robertson 1998 argue that financial markets are averse not to governments of particular ideological persuasions, as a large coefficient on the partisanship variable would suggest, but to any type of major policy change.

[149] Franzese 2002.

[150] Kontopolous 1996.

Another explanation for the significance of elections is the nature of government change: if financial market participants dislike left governments (or, for that matter, if they dislike right governments), their responses to elections that produce certain kinds of governments may drive the coefficient estimates. Including a "partisanship of new government produced by an election" (ELECTION*LEFTC) measure, however, does not yield a statistically significant coefficient. Hence, we cannot reject interview subjects' assertion that elections are important occasionally – when government change implies dramatic policy change. But it is difficult to identify generalizable conditions under which elections affect long-term government bond rates.[151]

The cross-sectional time series estimates for the macroindicators model confirm the importance, revealed in the interview evidence, of certain macroindicators to financial market participants. Financial market participants do consider certain key indicators when making cross-national asset allocation decisions, but also suggest that the effects of changes in these indicators for the interest rates on government bonds may not be as extreme as a very strong financial market constraint implies. The most important of these macroeconomic outcomes is inflation performance: the constraint imposed on governments by international financial markets is strongest on the monetary side. On the fiscal side, government budget balances *are* significantly associated with long-term interest rates, but the implied effect is not nearly as large. Additionally, the results indicate that government partisanship is, in fact, significantly related to long-term interest rate levels. The magnitude of this relationship, though, is very small.

Capital Markets and National Policy Outcomes: A Microside Model

Finally, I examine the importance of more micropolicy indicators to long-term interest rates. Are micropolicy indicators significantly associated with long-term interest rates, and, if so, how strong are the effects of changes in these indicators? Interview evidence suggests that the more microside a policy indicator, the less important it is to long-term interest rate levels. Is it the case, then, that the statistical association between these indicators and long-term interest rates is either insignificant or substantively small?

---

[151] Another possibility, which might be explored in the future, is the closeness of elections: market participants could react to elections when they have high uncertainty regarding the eventual outcome. Or reactions to elections might depend on the type of electoral institutions. See Freeman et al. 2000.

Table 3.3. *Correlations between Macro- and Microindicators*

Variable	Correlation with Inflation	Correlation with Government Balance
GOVERNMENT/GDP	−0.1141	−0.3541
GTAX/GDP	−0.3948	0.0577
GCONS/GDP	−0.0990	0.0468
GCAPITAL/GDP	0.2548	−0.4602
GOODS/GDP	0.1592	−0.2265
GWAGES/GDP	0.3097	−0.4096
TRANSFERS/GDP	−0.3644	−0.3372
HEALTH/GDP	−0.1333	−0.0750
CORPTAX/PROFITS	−0.0942	0.4461
IND/CORPTAX	0.0550	−0.0189
PAYTAX/GDP	−0.0143	0.0606
WOR/EMPCON	−0.1909	0.0519

One potential objection to the strong but narrow hypothesis is that limits on macrolevel indicators necessarily imply limits on microlevel indicators. If governments are pressured to reduce inflation and government budget deficits, they also must reduce levels of government spending and alter the nature of supply-side policies. Therefore, there is no need for financial market participants to look beyond macroindicators when making asset allocation decisions. The international financial market constrains governments broadly, although its participants use only a narrow set of indicators. If this were the case – if, in fact, financial market consideration of a narrow set of indicators entails pressure on all other types of policy outcomes – we would find strong correlations between macro- and microindicators. As inflation falls, for example, so should government spending on income transfers.

This is not the case, however. Table 3.3 lists the bivariate correlations between two key macroindicators (INFLATE and GOVBAL) and a variety of microindicators. These indicators include standard measures of public intervention and welfare state effort, such as total government expenditure (GOVERNMENT/GDP), transfer payments (TRANSFERS/GDP), and tax burden (GTAX/GDP).[152] The full descriptions of these indicators

[152] Clayton and Pontusson 1998 suggest alternative measures of welfare state effort, such as social spending per poor person or social spending per unemployed person. Also see Iversen and Cusack 2000.

are listed in Appendix 3.1. None of the correlations exceeds 0.46, and several are close to 0. The strongest correlation between INFLATE and a microindicator is a negative one, between government tax revenue and inflation: lower inflation is associated with higher tax revenue. Government transfers as a percentage of GDP is similarly correlated with inflation, and government wages/GDP is the strongest positive correlation.

A similar pattern exists on the fiscal policy side. The strongest correlations are between GOVBAL and government capital spending (GCAPITAL/GDP) and between the ratio of corporate taxes to corporate profits (CORPTAX/PROFITS) and government budget balance. A more balanced budget is associated with lower capital spending and with a higher ratio of corporate taxes to profits. These results suggest that capital expenditures may be the first budget items cut during deficit reductions – as capital spending programs tend to have less well-developed domestic constituencies to support them – and that broadening the corporate tax base also might be consistent with a smaller budget deficit. Again, though, neither correlation implies a one-to-one correspondence. The bivariate relationships between GOVBAL and other micropolicy areas are even weaker – almost zero in the cases of tax revenue, government consumption, payroll taxes, and public health care spending. From the pattern of correlations presented in Table 3.3, it appears that a substantial "firewall" exists between macro- and micropolicies: financial market pressure on the macroside does not imply particular changes on the microside. This also is consistent with the notion that social democratically oriented governments have shifted their focus from macrostimulation to microlevel efforts.[153]

The existence of a firewall between macro and micro areas of government economic policy is further exemplified by the persistence of cross-national divergence in many government policy areas.[154] Figure 3.5 displays data on general government expenditures, which are the sum of current outlays and net capital outlays. Cross-national divergence in outlays persists. Although we observe a few reductions in the overall size of government within the OECD sample (Belgium, Ireland, the Netherlands, and New Zealand), on average, there is stability in the size of government, perhaps explained in part by demographic change. Figure 3.6 displays trends in the total government

[153] Boix 1997a, 1997b, Hall 1999.
[154] Also see the literature reviewed in Chapter 1.

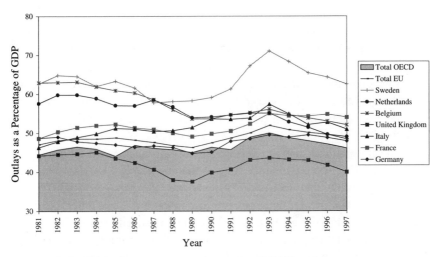

Figure 3.5 General government outlays, select OECD nations.

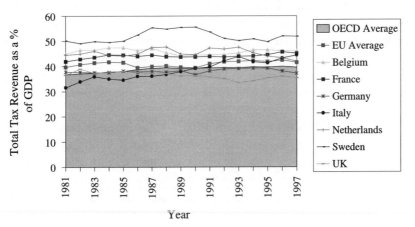

Figure 3.6 Government tax revenue, select OECD nations.

tax take.[155] This indicator, essentially the flip side of government outlays, also suggests a continued pattern of cross-national diversity. On average, tax revenue increases over time, from 36.7% of GDP in 1981 to 39.5% in 1997. In a longer-term perspective, from the 1974–1989 to the 1990–1995 period,

[155] The government outlays data are from OECD *Economic Outlook*, various years. Data on tax revenues are from OECD, *Revenue Statistics of Member Countries*, various years.

19 governments increased their tax revenues, while only 2 nations' tax revenues declined. Variance in tax revenues persists over time, decreasing only from 7.4 in 1981 to 6.8 in 1997, with some volatility in the intervening years.[156] Similarly, government consumption spending – a component of total expenditure, shown in Figure 3.7 – and public health care spending (in Figure 3.8) are characterized by stability over the 1980s and 1990s.[157] Average consumption levels remain relatively constant in the OECD, ranging from 17.7% of GDP (1989 and 1997) to 18.9% of GDP (1993). Public health care spending also remains quite constant through the 1990s.

These patterns of divergence suggest that micropolicy indicators might be unimportant to financial market participants; alternatively, some of these indicators *could* affect long-term interest rates, but governments might judge the effects to be an acceptable cost of domestically determined policies. In order to test the importance of a variety of micropolicy indicators to financial market outcomes, I estimate a series of models, including the independent variables from the macroindicators model (U.S. interest rates, current account balance, inflation rates, government fiscal balance, exchange rate levels, capital market openness, elections, and government partisanship) and various "microindicators," as listed in Table 3.3. Because many of these microindicators are somewhat collinear (e.g., government consumption, total government outlays, and total government revenues), I include one microside variable in each equation and estimate a series of cross-sectional time series equations.

In Table 3.4, I report the results of these estimations, in terms of total coefficients (including lagged effects, where present), the direction of the effect predicted by a strong and broad financial market constraint, the probability that the total coefficient estimate differs from zero (the chi-squared test), and the effect of a one-standard-deviation change in the microindicator, as suggested by the coefficient estimates. The shaded rows indicate a confidence level of 90% or more. The estimates for most other independent variables remain very similar, in terms of significance and coefficients, to those reported in the macroindicators model. In some cases, however, the government fiscal balance coefficient decreases in significance and/or

---

[156] For a recent analysis of OECD tax policy, see Steinmo and Swank 1999, who argue that tax systems *have* changed over the last two decades, but that these changes are not explained satisfactorily by changes in economic globalization.

[157] The data contained in Figures 3.7 and 3.8 are from World Bank, *World Development Indicators 2000*.

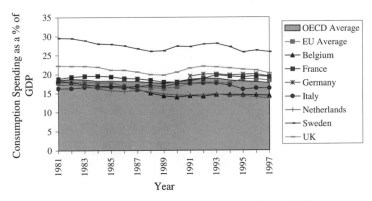

Figure 3.7   General government consumption, select OECD nations.

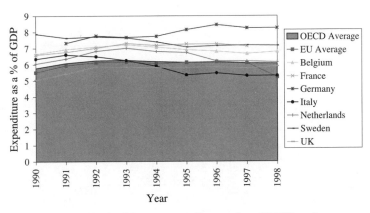

Figure 3.8   Public health care expenditure, select OECD nations.

size. This is likely due to the moderate collinearity between this and some of the microside variables.

These indicators are listed in terms of their "microness," with the most aggregate first. The first variable is measure of the overall size of government (GOVERNMENT/GDP). This is a relatively macrolevel indicator, as it expresses the presence of the government sector in the economy. Even if we accept the idea that the financial market constraint facing developed democracies is somewhat narrow, we might not be surprised to find an association between the size of government and long-term interest rates. Indeed, the results suggest that larger governments pay higher interest rates, and the coefficient estimate is statistically significant at the 98% level.

95

Table 3.4. *Estimated Effects of Microindicators*

Variable	Number of Countries	"Strong Influence" Effect on Interest Rates	Total Coefficient	$P > \chi^2$	Confidence Level, %	Effect, Standard Deviation Change
GOVERNMENT/GDP	15	Positive	0.024742	0.018	98	0.2253
GTAX/GDP	15	Positive	0.043314	0.012	98	0.3215
GCONS/GDP	15	Positive	0.108238	0.0003	99	0.4542
GCAPITAL/GDP	14	Negative	−0.439259	0.000	99	−0.4955
GOODS/GDP	15	Positive	−0.005749	0.875	12	0.01185
GWAGES/GDP	13	Positive	0.09075	0.210	79	0.2670
TRANSFERS/GDP	14	Positive	−0.011409	0.659	34	−0.054
HEALTH/GDP	14	Positive	22.37452	0.131	87	0.1882
CORPTAX/PROFITS	15	Positive; Ambiguous	0.001803	0.925	7	0.0097
IND/CORP TAX	15	Negative	−0.026933	0.410	59	−0.1019
WOR/EMP CONTRIB	13	Negative	−.0689923	0.535	46	0.0429
PAYTAX/GDP	15	Positive	−0.12684	0.280	72	−0.1034

The coefficient on this variable is, however, rather small: a change in the size of government of one standard deviation (9.1% of GDP) leads to a corresponding change in interest rates of 0.23% – a penalty, but a modest one. Likewise, the government tax revenue variable (GTAX/GDP), another relatively "macro" measure of the degree of government involvement in the private economy, is statistically significant at the 98% level. The implied effect of a one standard deviation change in the tax revenue variable is 0.32 percentage point.

The next two variables are relatively comprehensive measures of how governments allocate spending across functional categories. Government capital/GDP (GCAPITAL/GDP) includes all government expenditures for capital investment – for example, projects relating to national infrastructure. Government consumption/GDP (GCONS/GDP) includes government expenditures for consumption purposes – including, but not limited to, social security transfers and subsidies to industries. If financial market participants care about how governments allocate their budgets in advanced democracies, as they appear to do with respect to emerging market economies, the coefficients on these indicators will be large and statistically significant. In fact, in both cases, the coefficients *are* statistically significant: higher rates of capital spending are associated with lower interest rates, and higher levels of government consumption are associated with higher interest rates.[158]

This suggests that, despite some interview evidence to the contrary, financial market participants do have some concerns about the division of government spending between consumption and investment. Such a result is consistent with the idea that certain types of government spending promote economic growth or with the argument that the most effective fiscal consolidations rely mostly on expenditure cuts rather than tax increases.[159] Again, however, we must also consider the size of these effects: a government that increases its consumption/GDP ratio by one standard deviation (4.19% of GDP) can expect to pay an additional 0.45% in interest rates, whereas a government that increases its capital spending by one standard deviation (1.13% of GDP) can anticipate a drop in interest rates of almost half a percentage point. Under some domestic political conditions, we could

---

[158] When I estimate this regression by using changes, rather than levels, for the dependent and independent variables, the overall size of government variable is not significantly associated with interest rates.
[159] Alesina and Perotti 1995, Barro 1997a, IMF 1996, pp. 59–61, Tanzi and Schuknecht 1996.

imagine governments paying these prices and maintaining high levels of consumption and/or low levels of investment. I identify these conditions in Chapter 5.

Moreover, there likely is a trade-off between changing the size of the deficit and changing the size of government capital spending. A government that cuts capital expenditures in order to balance its budget may well pay lower interest rates overall. For instance, in 1997, Italy reduced its overall budget deficit to less than 3% of GDP. It did so via a combination of tax increases and cuts in capital expenditure.[160] Although the cut in capital expenditure could have longer-term economic effects, financial markets rewarded the overall budget outcome. This response is consistent with investors' emphasis on macroindicators, as well as their focus on shorter-term outcomes.

Interestingly, the consumption/GDP variable is the only one of the microside variables for which an interaction term including capital market openness is significant (at the 99% level). The negative coefficient implies that, as openness increases, government bond rates are less sensitive to levels of government consumption. This may reflect the fact that, as financial markets have opened, investors' confidence in developed nations has improved (and perceived default risk has fallen). Alternatively, it could reflect the fact that governments can more easily finance consumption when capital markets are more open, as they have access to a wider range of financing sources.

The next group of variables measures other, more microlevel aspects of the distribution of government spending – spending on goods and services (GOODS/GDP), on the wages of government employees (GWAGES/GDP), on social security transfers (TRANSFERS/GDP), and on health care (HEALTH/GDP). It is these types of variables, that, according to the divergence literature, should be driven by domestic politics and institutions rather than by international capital market pressures. On the other hand, according to a strong globalization view of financial market–government relations, these indicators should be significantly, and somewhat strongly, associated with interest rate levels. In fact, the results in Table 3.4 reinforce the conclusion that financial market consideration does not extend to these more microlevel policy outcomes. None of the coefficient estimates for these indicators is significant at a confidence level

---

[160] Government of Italy, Treasury Department, *Economic Bulletin* no. 26, February 1998, pp. 1–8.

of 90%. Moreover, the coefficient estimates are not of the expected sign for GOODS/GDP and TRANSFERS/GDP, and the implied effects of a one standard deviation increase in these indicators are quite minor.

The final group of indicators measures different aspects of the structure of tax systems: the ratio of corporate income taxes to corporate profits (CORPTAX/PROFITS), the balance between individual and corporate taxes (IND/CORP TAX), the balance of workers' to employers' social security contributions (WOR/EMPCON), and the ratio of payroll taxes to GDP (PAYTAX/GDP). Again, a strong globalization explanation of financial market–government relations predicts that these variables will be significantly and strongly associated with government bond rates. For instance, private capital markets, averse to "big government," would object to an increase in the corporate tax burden.[161] Three of the four coefficient estimates are in the direction predicted by such a hypothesis, but the coefficient estimates for all four indicators are somewhat small, and none is statistically significant. The largest predicted effect of a one-standard-deviation change is −0.10% (for payroll tax as a percentage of GDP), but this effect is in the opposite direction and not statistically significant.

The analysis of microindicators' relationship to long-term government bond rates reveals several interesting conclusions regarding financial market–government relations in an era of open capital markets. First, as the evidence in Figures 3.4 through 3.8 and Table 3.3 suggests, convergence in aggregate fiscal and monetary policies does not necessitate convergence in more micropolicy areas. Macroeconomic and microlevel indicators do not necessarily move in tandem; for example, a government that undertakes deficit reduction may or may not reduce its expenditures on social security transfers and health care. Second, despite this conclusion, the quantitative analysis suggests that financial market pressures *do* extend to the most aggregate of microindicators, although the effects of the consideration of these indicators are somewhat moderate. For instance, whereas an increase of one standard deviation in government consumption might cost an OECD government 0.5% in interest rates, an increase of one standard deviation

---

[161] The predicted relationship between corporate tax burdens and government bond rates is somewhat ambiguous. If market participants are averse to all business-unfriendly policies, including higher tax rates, the relationship will be positive. If, however, government bond market participants are concerned only about the overall government budget deficit – rather than about conditions for firms in the private sector – they might welcome higher corporate tax rates. In any case, the actual coefficient and its level of significance are quite small. I thank an anonymous reviewer for pointing out the ambiguity of this relationship.

in the inflation rate will cost the government 1.34% in long-term interest rates. Third, financial market influences do not extend to more microindicators. Of the eight indicators tested, only one estimate is significant at a level greater than 90%, and the coefficient estimate for that variable is very small. In these cases, government policy is of little interest to financial market participants, and scholars would do well to look at domestic sources when explaining these types of government policy outcomes.

Again, these findings have implications for the nature of policymaking in advanced capitalist societies. As with inflation and government budget deficits, government officials often are quite aware of this evidence regarding financial market activity. Many of the senior policymakers interviewed note that, provided they pursue appropriate macropolicies, governments have autonomy in micropolicy areas.

The market does not like huge mistakes, especially in monetary policy ... but there is still a lot of room for governments to move. In many areas, these [policy] questions are open – governments have some choice. You can give a variety of answers, as long as you are consistent.[162]

The government does have more room on the fiscal side. It is generally O.K. vis-à-vis the markets, provided its aggregates are doing well. There is room to move at the margins, as long as the numbers are right.[163]

Markets often only look at the large numbers.[164]

Findings of interviews with several other policymaking officials in Belgium, Britain, France, and Germany are consistent with the views quoted: in more micropolicy areas, governments are relatively unconstrained by financial market pressures.

The analysis in this section, then, suggests a modification of our hypotheses regarding financial market influences on government policy. For the most macro of microindicators, government policy outcomes do seem to affect market participants' assessment of investment risk. Perhaps they worry about potential linkages between government size and inflation, or between government size and the sustainability of government finances. Long-term interest rates are affected by more than the narrowest set of key indicators (implying a slightly broader set of criteria), but the effects are quite moderate (implying a weaker influence). "Strong but narrow" might be labeled more aptly "not quite so narrow, and not quite so strong."

---

[162] Interview, former senior French Treasury official, May 1997.
[163] Interview, former British Labour MP and current cabinet minister, March 1997.
[164] Interview, director, Bank of Belgium, May 1997.

Conclusion: Government Policymaking and Strong but Narrow Influences

The evidence in this chapter provides qualified support for the hypotheses developed in Chapter 2: developed economies face fairly narrow financial market pressures. Whereas interview evidence suggests that the financial market constraint is both very narrow and very strong, the quantitative evidence suggests that the constraint is not quite so narrow, nor quite so strong. In the aggregate, financial market participants do respond to broad characteristics of government spending, such as the overall size of government, but they do not respond to a broad range of more micropolicy indicators, such as government outlays for social security transfers or health care, or the balance between individual and corporate taxation. At the same time, the strength of the financial market response often is not tremendous. Although the effects of changes in inflation rates on government bond rates are relatively great, the effects of changes in the government fiscal balance are quite mild. Even at the aggregate fiscal level, the international financial market may be relatively mild in its treatment of developed economies; these nations may be able to compete in the global economy while retaining many of the hallmarks of post–World War II social democracy.[165]

Therefore, we can conclude that the evidence provided by interview research is fairly robust: it does not correspond perfectly with aggregate financial market outcomes, particularly at the micromacro margins (e.g., total size of government), but it corresponds quite well with aggregate outcomes in terms of the consideration of microindicators, the importance of aggregate monetary policy outcomes, and the relative unimportance of government partisanship. This evidence gives further weight to the expectation that what markets ultimately care about "is overall performance, and governments could put together several different combinations of macro- and microeconomic policies leading to such performance."[166]

In the next chapter, I investigate the financial market constraint faced by developing nations. Is it, as Chapter 2 suggests, stronger and broader than the constraint facing developed economies? Does the salience of different types of investment risk lead to a greater financial market constraint?

---

[165] Also see Marquand, in Radice 1996, p. 75.
[166] Interview, former senior British government official, January 1997.

4

Financial Market–Government Relations in Emerging Markets

> Politics are much more important [in developing countries] than in developed markets. Every aspect of policy/performance generates politically-related concerns. Who governs matters in these markets.... It's hard to know what a government will do.... There are not necessarily clear priorities for these governments; there are so many issues, it's hard to know how they will prioritize.... The problems experienced in the developing world are totally non-existent in the developed world.[1]

I now turn to the question of financial market influence on government policy choices in the developing world. How does the influence of financial markets in developing nations differ from that in developed nations, and what explains the difference? In the preceding chapters, I have demonstrated that financial market influence on advanced industrial democracies is strong, but nevertheless narrow. As long as governments perform to financial market participants' satisfaction on a set of key indicators, they are relatively unconstrained in other policy areas. In general, differences in microlevel policy outputs or outcomes are not associated with the rate of interest charged on government bonds, and the implied effects of government partisanship on bond rates are small.

In Chapter 2, I hypothesized that financial market influence on developing world governments with open capital accounts would be strong *and* broad. Investors are uncertain regarding these governments' types, and there is a significant probability that these governments are potential defaulters. Therefore, market participants rely on a wide set of economic policy indicators and political variables when making investment decisions. Their capacity to respond sharply to poor performance on these indicators

[1] Interview 60.

allows for greater market influence. This "strong and broad" pattern stems from financial openness, from the types of investment risk present in developing nations, from the quality of available information, and from uncertainty regarding the relationship between policy outcomes and financial market activity in emerging markets. Although emerging market governments are not always constrained to follow the dictates of global capital markets, the cost of defying global capital markets is often high.

I begin the first section of this chapter with an empirical overview of investment in emerging markets in the 1990s. The second section discusses the rationale for why we should expect strong and broad market influence in emerging nations. In order to assess these expectations, in the third section, I present empirical evidence from a variety of sources – basic quantitative analyses, interviews with, and surveys of, financial market participants – and describe the methodology and outcomes of sovereign credit rating agencies. The last section addresses the seeds of variation in financial market influence *among* emerging market nations. The primary purpose of this chapter, however, is to contrast the treatment of emerging market economies with that of advanced industrial democracies. Even in periods of relative optimism regarding emerging market nations, financial market pressures remain broader than in developed democracies.

Emerging Markets Overview

Financial market participants label a nation an *emerging market* if it is characterized by a recently instituted, or recently revitalized, set of domestic financial markets. In many ways the term *emerging markets* has replaced "LDCs" or "the Third World" or "developing nations" in the parlance of market participants.[2] In fact, in the mid-1980s, the International Finance Corporation (IFC), the arm of the World Bank charged with promoting investment in developing nations, coined the phrase *emerging markets* as a more appealing alternative. The first emerging markets fund was launched shortly afterward, in 1986.[3]

The IFC defines an *emerging market* as a country that meets one of two criteria: (1) it is located in a low- or middle-income economy[4] and

---

[2] E.g., George 1994, Posner 1998.

[3] *New York Times*, February 15, 1999, p. A10.

[4] This classification is found in many World Bank publications, including the 1998 *Global Economic Prospects* report. Until 1995, the IFC's categorization was based solely on criterion (1), but, with fluctuations in dollar-based GDP figures, this definition became insufficient.

Table 4.1. *IFC Country Classifications*

Developed	Emerging		Frontier
Australia	Argentina	Nigeria	Bangladesh
Austria	Brazil	Pakistan	Botswana
Belgium	Chile	Peru	Bulgaria
Canada	China	Philippines	Cote d'Ivoire
Denmark	Colombia	Poland	Croatia
Finland	Czech Republic	Portugal (through 98)	Ecuador
France	Egypt	Russia	Estonia
Germany	Greece	Saudi Arabia	Ghana
Ireland	Hungary	Slovakia	Jamaica
Italy	India	South Africa	Kenya
Japan	Indonesia	Sri Lanka	Latvia
Netherlands	Israel	Taiwan	Lithuania
New Zealand	Jordan	Thailand	Mauritius
Norway	Korea	Turkey	Romania
Spain	Malaysia	Venezuela	Slovenia
Sweden	Mexico	Zimbabwe	Trinidad and Tobago
Switzerland	Morocco		Tunisia
United Kingdom			Ukraine

(2) its investable market capitalization is low relative to its most recent GDP figures. Nations graduate from emerging markets status once their income per capita exceeds the upper-income threshold for three consecutive years, and once their investable market capitalization/GDP ratio is near the average ratio for "developed markets" for three consecutive years. Nations that retain or introduce investment restrictions (capital controls) remain categorized as emerging, reflecting the IFC's opinion that "pervasive investment restrictions on portfolio investment should not exist in developed stock markets."[5] In 1996, the IFC introduced a new category, frontier markets. This grouping includes nations that have equity exchanges, but on which trading activity is very thin. When liquidity in these portfolio markets increases, frontier nations graduate to the IFC's set of emerging market nations.

Throughout this chapter, I rely on the IFC's classifications of developed, emerging market, and frontier market nations. These nations are listed in Table 4.1. As I suggest in Chapter 2, the classification of nations into distinct groups can have implications for the extent of financial market pressures in

[5] IFC 1999, p. 3.

these nations. If a nation moves from the emerging to the developed group, it likely will face a more narrow set of capital market pressures. In future research, political economists may assess how investors place nations into these broad groups and, perhaps more importantly, the conditions under which they move nations from one group to another.[6]

Capital market openness in emerging states has expanded over the last two decades, suggesting a strong financial market constraint. The capacity of international participants to enter and exit national capital markets has grown, and the reliance of emerging markets on foreign portfolio financing has increased.[7] Although international capital long has flowed to the developing world, these flows have varied over time in terms of both amount and type. High levels of flows, mostly in the form of bank loans, characterized the 1970s.[8] After the resolution of the 1980s debt crisis, portfolio and foreign direct investment flows to developing nations expanded dramatically, reflecting both the trend toward disintermediated finance in global markets and shifts in national policies toward greater capital market openness.[9] The Brady Plan, aimed at resolving the 1980s debt crisis, spurred the creation of a new financial asset, the Brady Bond. These bonds represent U.S. government–guaranteed and IMF-supported commercial bank loans, usually denominated in dollars, to Latin American governments. In exchange for loan guarantees, debtor governments promised to undertake economic policy reforms. Rather than keeping these loans on their books, banks sold them to portfolio investors, further spurring a shift toward disintermediated finance. Many governments – eighteen at last count – continue to issue Brady Bonds.[10]

Rather than borrowing directly from large international banks, then, emerging market borrowers now turn to international portfolio markets,

---

[6] Along these lines, Devlin 1989 notes that banks in the 1970s placed nations into broad categories as well.

[7] Also see Mahon 1996.

[8] On capital flows to the developing world prior to the First World War, see Chapter 7. On debt flows during the 1970s and early 1980s, see Devlin 1989, Edwards 1994.

[9] E.g., Bisignano 1994, Friedman 2000, Manzocchi 1999, Maxfield 1997, Posner 1998, Sobel 1999, Turner 1995. For a discussion of the benefits of disintermediated finance, see World Bank 1998b, p. 26.

[10] Friedman 2000. As emerging market nations have reestablished their position in the international financial system, however, the use of Brady Bonds has declined. Brady Bond trading accounted for 61% of total trading in emerging markets debt in 1994, but for only 35% of total trading in 1999 (Emerging Markets Traders Association, www.emta.org).

issuing either bonds or equities.[11] Disintermediation has gone hand-in-hand with an expanded role for institutional investors: as much as 90% of the portfolio assets invested in developing nations involve institutional investors.[12] The large quantity of assets managed by institutional investors (estimated at $20 trillion by the IMF in 1998) implies that even an incremental movement into emerging markets can have profound consequences. Furthermore, whereas sovereign borrowers can negotiate lending terms with banks, as Latin American governments did in the early 1980s, it is nearly impossible for them to negotiate lending terms with disintermediated financial markets. Witness, for example, the Russian government's attempts to reach agreements with its creditors after the August 1998 quasi default.[13]

These investment flows are concentrated in middle-income nations – those with a per capita income between $786 and $9,655. In 1997, these countries received 89% of resource flows to developing nations. Table 4.2 presents data for 1997, the latest year for which complete data are available, on net resource flows to select developing nations. Included are the largest 20 destinations for these flows, measured in terms of percentage of aggregate net flows. The table also provides information regarding two specific categories of portfolio capital – debt and equity.

The data highlight several key facts. First, although many developing nations attract investment from abroad, this investment is quite concentrated; the top 20 nations account for nearly 83% of net resource flows. Second, although the percentage of total world investment directed to emerging market economies remains small in relative terms, the importance of foreign investment to individual emerging market economies is great.[14] This is true not only for large importers of capital, such as Brazil and Argentina, but also for smaller importers, such as Pakistan and Peru. Moreover, outside the largest 20 capital importers, the ratio of investment

---

[11] For an overview of sovereign debt markets in a select set of developing nations, see Del Valle Borraez et al. 1998.

[12] Haley 1999. Haley argues, furthermore, that a few large institutional investors dominate the developing nation asset market, and that these investors coordinate their behavior. As evidence for this claim, Haley notes that there are differences in the asset allocation behavior of United States–based, Europe-based, and Japan-based mutual funds. It is not clear, though, whether deliberate coordination or differences in clients' preferences and managers' expertise drive these differences.

[13] Also see Eichengreen 1999, Maxfield 1997. On cooperation among bondholders before the First World War and after the Second World War, see Suter and Stamm 1992.

[14] BIS 1998, pp. 89–90; Grabel 1996a.

Table 4.2. *Distribution of Capital Flows among Developing Nations, 1997*

Country	Aggregate Flows, % of GNP	Net Aggregate Flows, % of Developing Nation Total	Net Debt Flows, % of Developing Nation Total	Net Equity Flows, % of Developing Nation Total
China	7.38	19.74	11.98	29.23
Brazil	5.08	12.30	11.35	13.25
Argentina	6.10	5.87	10.74	7.73
S. Korea	3.71	4.89	8.26	N/A
Mexico	3.98	4.69	2.3	7.1
Russia	3.16	4.57	4.89	4.17
Turkey	6.3	3.69	8.31	2.00
Indonesia	5.54	3.50	8.56	10.29
Chile	12.54	2.81	4.07	1.68
Colombia	10.01	2.76	2.25	0.40
Thailand	5.85	2.64	3.65	1.06
India	2.32	2.49	0.15	9.31
Malaysia	8.71	2.46	5.44	1.69
Poland	4.93	2.01	1.26	3.26
Venezuela	6.84	1.76	1.03	1.48
Philippines	5.24	1.36	4.72	0.25
Peru	7.03	1.29	1.23	2.39
South Africa	3.03	1.15	0.11	4.82
Egypt	4.55	2.05	0.30	6.27
Pakistan	4.95	0.95	1.08	0.87
TOP 20 TOTAL		82.98	87.01	90.48
All middle-income developing nations	5.08	89.24	94.14	91.80
All low-income developing nations	4.38	10.75	5.86	8.20

flows to income is even larger – 11% for Vietnam, 13% for Croatia, 17% for Azerbaijan, 18% for Panama, and 44% for Guyana. Even when flows are not large relative to the global pool of capital, they can be a very significant part of domestic economies, helping to fund current account and government budget deficits.[15] Finally, the data in Table 4.2 suggest that different nations rely on different types of capital inflows – FDI, equity, and debt. Chile, for instance, accounts for 4.07% of net debt flows, but

---

[15] BIS 1998, Mahon 1996.

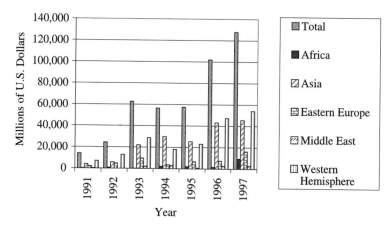

Figure 4.1 Emerging market bond issues. *Source*: International Monetary Fund, World Economic Outlook, 1998.

for only 1.68% of net equity flows; South Africa displays the opposite pattern.[16]

Turning to bonds, the specific focus of this chapter, Figure 4.1 displays the total amount, by year, of bonds issued by emerging market governments and corporate entities. Total bond issues in emerging markets increased from $13.9 billion in 1991 (0.3% of developing country GNP) to $127.9 billion (2% of developing country GNP) in 1997.[17] Likewise, the governments of Latin America and Eastern Europe issued only $2.3 billion of international bonds in 1991, but $34 billion of international bonds in 1997.[18] Although issuance of bonds by emerging market countries fell substantially in 1998, issues recovered again in 1999.[19] Figure 4.1 also reveals that these debt issues are concentrated in Latin America, Asia, and Eastern and Central Europe. Bond issues from the economies of Africa and the Middle East have increased over time but remain a small proportion of total issues. Similarly, Figure 4.2 provides data on secondary market transactions – that is, the buying and selling of previously issued assets – in emerging market debt. Again, market activity in these instruments increased

---

[16] Brooks and Mosley 2000 discuss the implications of this variation for domestic policy-making.

[17] Also see Eichengreen and Mody 1998, Summers 2000.

[18] Aronovich 1999, p. 464.

[19] Also see the data presented in World Bank 2000, p. 36.

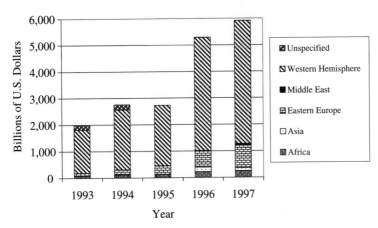

Figure 4.2 Secondary market transactions in emerging market debt instruments. *Source*: International Monetary Fund, World Economic Outlook, 1998.

dramatically during the 1990s, nearly trebling from 1993 to 1997. Similarly, from a survey of market participants, the Emerging Markets Traders Association reports that total emerging markets debt instrument trading grew from $734 million in 1992 to $5.9 billion in 1997, before falling in 1998 and 1999.[20]

Financial Market Influence in Emerging Markets: Theory and Expectations

Because developing nations long have relied on capital from abroad, the existence of external economic influences in emerging markets is not unique to the contemporary era. In the 1950s and 1960s, for instance, developing nations often were subject to overt political demands from foreign aid donors.[21] What are more unique to the contemporary era are the nature and degree of external capital market influences. Governments are less subject to overt demands from bilateral aid providers, but more subject to the demands and policy preferences of portfolio (and direct investment) market participants.[22] As in developed nations, the central question regards the mechanisms by and extent to

[20] Emerging Markets Traders Association, *Bulletin*, second quarter 2000, p. 1.

[21] Armijo 1999, Wood 1986.

[22] And we can expect that different types of capital inflows create different pressures on government policy. Armijo 1999, Table 2 and p. 23; Maxfield 1997, chapter 3.

which financial market influence operates. For instance, to what extent do portfolio capital flows create pressures for a variety of neoliberal policy reforms?[23]

Expectations Regarding Financial Market Influence

The two dimensions of financial market influence are strength and scope. Openness to and reliance on international capital determine strength. The scope of financial market influence, meanwhile, reflects concerns about investment risks and the quality of available information. In emerging markets, investors face both greater risk and greater uncertainty.[24] For this reason, I hypothesize that financial market influence in developing nations will be "strong and broad."

The Strength of Financial Market Influences   Capital market openness is a background condition for the operation of financial market influence. When a nation's capital markets are very open, the capacity of market participants to punish or reward governments is high. With closed economies, developing nations are capital-poor.[25] Capital is necessary to finance consumption and investment, but much of this capital is unavailable domestically. Capital flows from abroad increase the efficiency of the allocation of resources, benefiting individuals, firms, and governments in both sending and receiving economies.[26] Notwithstanding the benefits of capital inflows, capital market openness is accompanied by risks, as financial crises in Latin America and Southeast Asia demonstrate. Inflows sometimes are associated with overborrowing, with financial sector difficulties,[27] with greater constraints on national macroeconomic policies, and with exchange rate volatility. At the extreme, inflows can contribute to the destabilization of

---

[23] For an argument that emerging market governments are very constrained, see Grabel 1996b.

[24] Risk implies that an investor has firm knowledge about possible outcomes and the approximate likelihood of these outcomes; uncertainty is defined by the absence of knowledge about probabilities associated with outcomes. Here, a lack of high-quality information generates uncertainty. Friedman 1983. Also see Sobel 1999.

[25] Maxfield 1997.

[26] Summers 2000. Of course, inefficient firms will be harmed by greater capital market openness, assuming capital markets discipline poorly behaving equity and bond issuers.

[27] For a concise summary of the causes and consequences of the Asian financial crisis, see Goldstein 1998. Also see Kahler 1999, Devlin 1989.

political regimes and social order.[28] Moreover, removing restrictions on capital outflows deprives governments of a captive market for their bonds. Finally, certain domestic groups – such as local capital owners – have reasons to favor the retention of capital market controls.[29]

Despite these potential disincentives to capital account liberalization, the average level of restriction on the capital account has fallen since the late 1980s.[30] This trend likely reflects a variety of factors – the desire to access a wider pool of capital and to compensate for low domestic savings rates,[31] political pressures from domestic financial intermediaries and capital owners, the technical difficulty of maintaining capital controls, and the hope of signaling to foreign investors a commitment to fiscal and monetary discipline.[32]

Relatively open capital markets in middle-income developing nations allow for strong market responses to government policy changes.[33] Other factors can render these pressures even stronger: first, emerging market nations' reliance on foreign capital is greater than that in developed democracies; governments have fewer choices regarding how to access international capital markets. Second, emerging markets face the problem of capital flow volatility. Investment in emerging market economies often is driven by efforts at portfolio diversification and at high risk-adjusted returns.[34] Investment flows to emerging markets are more volatile than flows to developed nations. For instance, in the 1990s, the volatility of returns on emerging

---

[28] Armijo 1999, Grabel 1996b, Haggard 1985, Haggard et al. 1993, Kaufman 1985, Rodrik 1999, Starr 1999. For a contrasting view, see Maxfield 1998.

[29] See Chapter 6 for a more detailed discussion of capital controls.

[30] Eichengreen and Sussman 2000, IMF 1998b, IMF 1997a, Kastner and Rector 2001, Maxfield 1997.

[31] Kingstone 1999 examines this motivation in Brazil in the 1990s.

[32] Eichengreen and Sussman 2000. On the determinants of financial openness in the developing world, see Haggard and Maxfield 1996, who look at trends in financial openness in Indonesia, Chile, Korea, and Mexico, and Quinn and Inclan 1997.

[33] Armijo 1999 argues that nations with a high reliance on portfolio inflows are under "high implicit pressure to adopt neoliberal economic policies" (p. 34). Along these lines, Garrett 1998b estimates the impact on interest rates of a 1% increase in government consumption spending in a sample of developed and emerging market economies. He finds that, for countries with capital controls for all of the 1985–1995 period, an increase over the period in consumption spending of 5% of GDP would have been associated with a real interest rate increase of 1.3%. In a nation without capital controls, the same increase in consumption would have been associated with a real interest rate increase of 3.9%. This finding demonstrates the potential impact on the strength of the financial market constraint that is generated by capital market openness.

[34] Barth and Zhang 1999, Cavaglia et al. 1997, George 1994, Posner 1998.

market debt consistently and substantially exceeded that of returns in developed nation markets.[35] The occurrence of high levels of volatility implies that financial market pressures can be very strong at some points in time, but rather weak at others. I return to this issue in the last section.

The Scope of Financial Market Influences   The signaling and informational framework developed in Chapter 2 suggests that the expansion of global capital markets creates informational challenges for financial market participants. Market participants require information about a large range of investment locations, and they make rational calculations about how to expend their information-gathering resources. When faced with a diverse range of investment locations, market participants collect a narrow amount of information for nations with low default risk and a broad range of information for nations with high default risk. In emerging market economies, inflation and exchange rate risk remain important, but market participants also consider the risk of default.

Almost by definition, emerging market economies lack well-developed domestic capital markets and sometimes experience difficulties in repaying external loans.[36] Default risk is "for all intents and purposes, absent" in developed nations but is a salient factor in developing nations.[37] Scholars of developing country borrowing generally treat default as the result of a series of events, reflecting both a government's willingness and its ability to repay debt.[38] Simplified treatments of default assume that governments compare the costs of default (market access and reputation, for instance) to the benefits of default. Where benefits exceed costs, governments default.[39] This treatment of default implies large information asymmetries: governments know more than lenders about their utility functions and cost–benefit analyses, and perhaps even about their levels of indebtedness. In order to address the asymmetric information problem,

---

[35] IMF 1998b, p. 23. On differences between emerging and developed markets in equity market volatility, see Richards 1996. Patel and Satar 1998 find that stock market crises in emerging market economies differ systematically from those in developed economies. Precrisis price increases are larger in emerging markets, and crises in emerging equity markets tend to be quicker and steeper, with longer recovery periods.

[36] Bisignano 1994, p. 29.

[37] Dym 1994, p. 61.

[38] Eaton et al. 1986. Also see Balkan 1992, Larrain et al. 1997. See Eaton and Fernandez 1995 for a review of literature on sovereign default and debt.

[39] See, for instance, Cohen and Sachs 1986, Eaton and Gersovitz 1981, Jaffe and Russell 1976, Nunnenkamp and Picht 1989.

investors look at indicators that will give them insight regarding governments' utility functions, cost–benefit analyses, and current economic and political constraints. Therefore, investors should collect a broader set of information.

Previous research on the relationship between default risk and interest rate premia in developing nations suggests that default risk *is* a central consideration in developing nations.[40] In the 1980s, economists tested a variety of hypotheses regarding which indicators were associated with higher default risk and, therefore, with either credit rationing or higher risk premia.[41] From an analysis of both bank loans and sovereign bond issues from 1976 to 1980, Edwards concludes that the default risk premium is related positively and significantly to the level of debt and debt service, and related negatively and significantly to the level of investment in the domestic economy.[42] The latter result suggests that, where capital market expectations of future growth are higher, default risk is less salient.[43] Other work suggests that, at least for some sets of observations, the current account balance, the ratio of reserves to GNP, and the ratio of debt to GNP are associated with default risk premia.[44]

More recent studies echo these conclusions. A 2001 IMF review[45] cites solvency considerations as key in emerging markets lending. The IMF points out that assessing the willingness to pay is the most difficult aspect of risk analysis.[46] This study also notes a relatively robust association between interest rate spreads on government bonds and the ratio of government debt to exports. Likewise, in an analysis of bond spreads in emerging markets during 1990–1995, Min finds significant positive associations between the interest rate spreads and debt/GDP, the debt service ratio, the inflation rate, and the real exchange rate, as well as significant negative associations between the interest rate spread and the terms of trade and the level of international reserves/GDP.[47]

---

[40] Devlin 1989 argues, however, that banks did not price this risk adequately prior to the Third World debt crisis.

[41] For example, see Edwards 1984, 1986, Eaton et al. 1986, and Nunnenkamp and Picht 1989.

[42] Edwards 1986.

[43] Edwards 1986 also suggests that the effect of the level of investment is more pronounced in the bank loan than in the bond market (p. 581). Also see Maxfield 1997 for a theoretical discussion of the differences in behavior between bank and bond lenders.

[44] See Balkan 1992, among others.

[45] IMF 2001.

[46] IMF 2001, p. 8, paragraph 25.

[47] Min 1998.

Furthermore, default risk is exacerbated by the strategies emerging market governments sometimes employ. In order to access international capital markets, or to do so more cheaply, governments (and private firms) sometimes assume the risks typically borne by investors. For this reason, their debt is more likely to be short-duration and denominated in foreign currency, whereas developed economies have longer-term debt denominated in domestic currencies.[48] Foreign currency denomination is appealing to investors because it allows them to avoid currency risk:[49] an investor purchasing Thai dollar–denominated bonds does not have to worry about the value of the Thai baht or about inflation in the Thai economy. Because dollar denomination transfers these risks to governments, interest rates on dollar-denominated securities generally are lower. In some cases, investors purchase only dollar-denominated government debt. In 1999, approximately 65% of international bond issues in emerging markets were denominated in dollars.[50] By contrast, the issuance of dollar-denominated bonds is rare in developed nations, even among higher-debt countries.

Foreign currency denomination transfers currency risk to governments, thereby sharpening the risk of default.[51] It is easier for governments to repay home currency–denominated debt than foreign currency–denominated debt; at the limit, the monetary authority can print the necessary currency.[52] But governments must generate foreign exchange to repay dollar-denominated debt. If currencies depreciate or are devalued, or if a country has difficulty generating foreign exchange, the government will have difficulty repaying its obligations, as Mexico did in December 1994.

Similarly, the issuance of shorter-term securities renders governments more susceptible to changes in market sentiment.[53] Many emerging market countries issue securities with maturities of one year or less, rather than longer-term securities. Under most circumstances, shorter-term

---

[48] See Chapter 6.

[49] Gavin et al. 1996.

[50] Institute for International Finance, "Capital Flows to Emerging Market Economies," April 13, 2000, p. 6.

[51] Cline 1996, Conti and Hamaui 1994, Devlin 1989, Maxfield 1997, Missale et al. 1997.

[52] For this reason, ratings agencies tend to assign higher ratings to domestic currency than to foreign currency sovereign debt.

[53] Krueger 2000, Liederman and Thorne 1996, p. 12; Summers 2000, World Bank 2000, chapter 4.

114

borrowing rates are lower than longer-term rates. This is particularly true when market expectations of future inflation are high.[54] For most emerging market governments, short-term debt is the less expensive choice; for some governments, short-term debt is the only option.[55] For instance, in the mid-1990s, Russian debt issues were very short-term, as only 5% of loans had a duration longer than three months.[56] Frequent refinancing of outstanding obligations, however, forces governments to "face the markets" more often. A brief but sharp change in financial market sentiment can render governments unable to refinance outstanding debt and, therefore, push them toward default.[57] For instance, in its September 1998 downgrading of Brazil's sovereign credit rating, Duff and Phelps (DCR) cited the increasingly short duration of government debt and the associated growth in "monthly rollover needs." As these needs increased, so did the likelihood of default.[58] More generally, several studies suggest that financial crises are more likely, all else equal, with shorter debt maturities or unevenly distributed stocks of debt.[59]

Given these characteristics of emerging markets, I expect that investors will continue to have concerns about governments' willingness and ability to repay debt. Investors assume that, no matter which political parties are in office in developed economies, governments will uphold their debt servicing obligations. But in emerging market economies, market participants often *do not* make this assumption. It is not unthinkable for a government to win domestic political favor by dealing harshly with foreign investors, or for political instability to generate a sovereign default.[60] Therefore,

---

[54] Aronovich 1999, Missale and Blanchard 1994, Federal Reserve Bank 1997, p. xxi; World Bank 2000, p. 82. Along these lines, Eichengreen and Mody 1998 find a positive association between interest rate spreads on emerging market bond issues and the maturity of debt.

[55] Debt maturity structures also are discussed at greater length in Chapter 6.

[56] Genesis Investment Management 1997, p. 28.

[57] Detragiache 1996 suggests that some such crises are the result of self-fulfilling prophecies: "creditors do not lend because they think that the debtor will not repay. Without the option of rolling over some of his debt, the debtor ends up defaulting, thus validating the pessimistic expectations" (p. 546).

[58] "DCR Downgrades Brazil's Local Currency Rating to 'BB–'," Press Release, September 28, 1998. Consistently with the "broad financial market pressure" argument, the following year, DCR described its outlook on Brazil as contingent on tax and social security reform. "Stable Brazil Outlook Explained in New DCR Report," press release, November 2, 1999.

[59] Canzonero 1995, p. 6; Frankel and Rose 1996, pp. 355, 359; Milesi-Ferritti and Razin 1996, p. 12.

[60] Erb et al. 1998.

market participants consider a wide range of indicators, including not only macroindicators (inflation, fiscal balances, current account deficits), but also microindicators (e.g., the breakdown of government spending across areas and the structure of tax systems). They also analyze the political climate, for example, the type of the governmental coalition expected after a general election, and the capacity of new democracies to implement tax and spending changes.[61] Recent financial crises in emerging markets strengthen investors' incentives to collect a wide range of information: particularly in Asia, the crises were due in part to structural problems – weak domestic financial systems and corporate governance.[62]

Finally, investors in emerging markets worry about the quality of information available.[63] Because of their role in recent financial crises, information problems have become a central concern of policymakers and investors alike.[64] Although policymakers debate about the importance of information to the prevention of financial crises, almost all agree that high-quality public and private sector information plays some role in crisis prevention. For investors in emerging markets, information problems require more effort, relative to the effort expended for developed nations, to collect the same amount of information – or to gather information characterized by the same confidence intervals. The information provided by governments in emerging markets often is of poor quality; it may not reflect standardized accounting procedures, it may be inaccurate, or it may be published with long lags or at sporadic intervals. Some kinds of information simply are not available.[65]

Investors may respond to informational problems in three ways. First, they will look to other investors and external agents (the IMF, credit ratings agencies) for insight regarding appropriate risk premia. Second, market participants will attempt to collect information from a wide range of sources. Third, investors will advocate better data standards; they, for instance, may exert pressures on national governments and on private industries to adhere to internationally determined accounting

---

[61] On extraction and regime type, see Cheibub 1998.

[62] IMF, *World Economic Outlook*, May 2000, p. 40.

[63] Aronovich 1999, p. 468; Friedman 1983.

[64] See IMF 1998b, pp. 55, 61; Trichet, Mishkin, Greenspan, Litan, and Fischer et al. in Federal Reserve Bank 1997.

[65] Kim and Wei 1999 argue that information problems are more severe for foreign than for resident investors, particularly in emerging markets. See Chapter 6.

standards.[66] These responses contribute, again, to broad financial market influence.

The existence of a broad financial market constraint does not imply high levels of financial market sophistication. Investors may consider a wide range of indicators, but a change in any one or two of these indicators can generate a significant market reaction. As I suggested earlier, international diversification allows investors to change asset allocation decisions on the basis of relatively thin information; relative performance concerns also can contribute to superficial assessments. And when these concerns are combined with informational concerns, we can expect investors to respond quickly and sharply to changes in single indicators. They may conclude, for instance, that a change in short-term debt figures portends changes in other indicators, which simply have not been captured because of poor data quality.

For this reason, different types of indicators can be associated with different crises, and the indicators viewed as important may change somewhat rapidly. In the recent crises in Mexico and Thailand, very different key indicators were important. In Mexico, market participants became concerned – at least ex post – about the consumption/investment balance of government spending,[67] whereas in Thailand, investors examined the activities of the central bank in the forward exchange rate market.[68] In each case, these indicators had received little attention prior to the crisis. As the crises unfolded, investors began to pay attention to these indicators in other markets – to assess the prospects of "similarly situated" economies.[69] Market participants behaved in the same way as the general who likens the current war to the last war and bases his strategy on past experience. They focus on the indicators that were associated with the most recent crisis. For example, after the depreciation of the Thai baht in July 1997, some nations with relatively strong fundamentals, but with a few similarities to Thailand, were hit by negative market sentiment.[70]

---

[66] Mosley 2000b.

[67] Liederman and Thorne 1996.

[68] Grabel 1999.

[69] IMF 1998b, p. 62

[70] Along these lines, Willett provides a "too little, too late" model of financial market behavior: there are zones of vulnerability inside which a country is not certain to face a crisis, but in which the economic fundamentals are not strong enough to guarantee against a crisis. Willett 1999. Also see Interview 57.

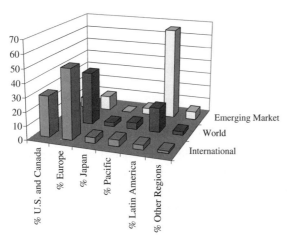

Figure 4.3 Regional asset allocation, bond funds.

The Range of Investment Locations and the Variance of Government Policy Outcomes

Expectations of strong and broad financial market influences are based on two assumptions. First, investors allocate assets across a range of developing nations. This diversification provides benefits but also poses informational challenges. Second, the range of policy outcomes in emerging markets is wider, rendering investors less able to assume that all governments pursue a fairly similar set of policies, or that every government is of the creditworthy type. Therefore, they must look closely at each nation and its propensity for default.

The Diversity of Investment Locations and Assets   A survey of asset allocation by several categories of mutual funds provides evidence regarding the diversity of investment locations. Figure 4.3 offers information on the regional distribution of three categories of mutual funds – world bond, international bond, and emerging market bond. The percentages reported are averages calculated from all funds listed in Morningstar's Principia Pro mutual fund database and reflect allocations in April 2000.[71] Of these three types of funds, international bond funds are least diversified geographically, holding 53% of assets in Europe and 32% in the United States and

[71] Also see Knight 1998.

Canada. World bond funds are slightly more diversified. Emerging market bond funds, not surprisingly, are weighted heavily toward Latin America; these funds also hold some assets in the "emerging" nations of Europe – Poland and Hungary, for instance – as well as in Asia.

Figure 4.4 provides country-specific information on the allocation of the 25 largest emerging-market debt mutual funds. These data reflect asset allocations in September 1999 and indicate a substantial level of geographic diversification. As does Table 4.2, Figure 4.3 reveals the allocation of these funds across a group of approximately 20 middle-income developing nations. A few nations, such as Brazil, Mexico, and Argentina, account for large amounts of these mutual funds' holdings, but many other nations – in a variety of geographic areas and with a variety of political institutions – also are represented.

Last, Figure 4.5 provides information regarding the quality of debt held by internationally oriented bond mutual funds (as in Figure 4.4). International bond funds hold nearly 60% of their assets in U.S. government or other AAA (highest)–rated securities. A very small portion of assets are rated BBB or below. World bond funds hold approximately 50% of assets in AAA securities, including U.S. government bonds; just over 20% of their assets are rated BB or below. More importantly, assets held by emerging market bond funds are lower-quality, higher-risk instruments. Only 4% of holdings are in top-rated assets, and 82% of assets are in the BBB to B credit rating range. Given that emerging market funds deal with higher-risk instruments, attention to a variety of investment risks – inflation, exchange rate, and default – is rational.

The Diversity of Government Policies   The diversity of government policies also contributes to investors' information needs. If all developing nation governments were characterized by similar economic policies and policymaking processes, financial market participants could look less carefully at country-specific information. They could assume that default risk was relatively constant across nations and price default risk accordingly. If, on the other hand, some nations were characterized by high debt and others were characterized by low debt, market participants would have incentives to look more carefully at country-specific information.

A comparison of developed and developing nations suggests that the latter is true. There is greater economic policy variation among developing nations. Table 4.3 provides the standard deviations for a variety of aggregate

120

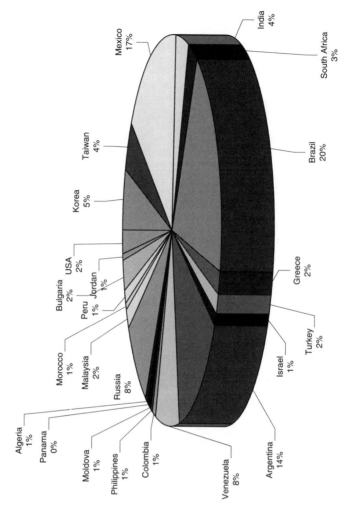

Figure 4.4 Asset allocation for 25 largest emerging market debt funds, September 1999.

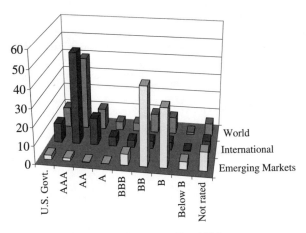

Figure 4.5 Bond fund asset quality, 1999.

Table 4.3. *Variance in Policy Outcomes, 1990–1998*

Indicator	Developed Nations	Emerging Market Nations	Frontier Market Nations
Government budget balance/GDP	3.74 ($n = 131$)	3.96 ($n = 207$)	4.25 ($n = 87$)
Annual rate of inflation	1.85 ($n = 153$)	18.20 ($n = 253$)	15.44 ($n = 105$)
Current account balance/GDP	3.55 ($n = 152$)	4.63 ($n = 263$)	4.86 ($n = 142$)
Government debt/GDP	29.55 ($n = 93$)	39.37 ($n = 140$)	52.50 ($n = 41$)
Government expenditure/GDP	8.70 ($n = 131$)	11.3 ($n = 207$)	8.48 ($n = 87$)
Annual change in real effective exchange rate	0.06 ($n = 153$)	0.11 ($n = 163$)	0.15 ($n = 61$)

Note: Numbers are standard deviations. *N* refers to the number of country-years.

Source: Calculations are based on data from World Bank 2000, World Development Indicators database.

economic policy indicators for groups of developed, emerging market, and frontier market economies, as listed in Table 4.1 These standard deviations are calculated by using data available for the 1990–1998 period.[72]

---

[72] I exclude the 16 country-years (contained in the emerging and frontier nations) in which inflation was greater than 100% annually. Excluding these nations serves to reduce

Table 4.4. *Annual Comparisons of Economic Policy Variance*

Indicator	Emerging Market Variation Greater than Developed Nation Variation, Number of Years	Frontier Market Variation Greater than Developed Nation Variation, Number of Years
Government budget balance/GDP	7 (except 1993, 1995)	6 (except 1993, 1995, 1998)
Annual rate of inflation	9	9
Current account balance/GDP	7 (except 1995, 1997)	9
Government debt/GDP	9	8 (except 1990)
Government expenditure/GDP	9	7 (except 1995, 1997)
Annual change in real effective exchange rate	8 (except 1993)	8 (except 1993)
TOTAL	49 (of possible 54)	47 (of possible 54)

These data demonstrate that economic policy outcomes display more cross-national variation in emerging and frontier market nations than in developed nations. Only in one case – inflation – is frontier market variation less than emerging market variation, and only for government expenditure/GDP is frontier market variation less than developed market variation. In all other cases, cross-national variation is smallest in developed nations. The table also suggests that the availability of comparable indicators cross-nationally is poorest in frontier market economies.

The data in Table 4.3 might mask changes during the 1990s. It is possible that cross-national variation in emerging markets narrowed substantially over time, so that, by 1997 or 1998, policies were much less variable. In order to check this possibility, I also calculate standard deviations for each year during the period. Table 4.4 indicates the total number of years (ranging from zero to nine) in which emerging and frontier market policy variation (again measured by the standard deviation) is greater than developed nation policy variation. Again, in all but 12 of 108 cases, policy variability is greater in less-developed economies.

crossnational variance in inflation but changes the standard deviations of other variables only marginally.

Financial Market Influences: Empirical Evidence

In this section, I employ a variety of empirical evidence to assess the strong and broad hypothesis. A cross-sectional time series analysis could assess the extent to which changes in macro- *and* microindicators are associated with interest rate premia on government bonds. Unfortunately, the lack of reliable, comparable cross-national time series data for emerging market nations makes this sort of analysis difficult, if not impossible, to perform. Although there exist data on macroindicators for a relatively wide set of indicators for the late 1990s, data for earlier periods are less comprehensive.[73] Moreover, although all OECD nations issue comparable government securities, the pattern of issue (in terms of maturity and currency denomination) varies widely across emerging market nations. Further, data on micropolicy indicators – for instance, on the division of government spending among education, transfer payments, and infrastructure – are available only for a very limited set of nations. Because of these limitations, cross-sectional time analysis would suffer from serious estimation problems. Our conclusions, based on the small set of countries (fewer than 10) and short period for which a sufficient set of data is available, would lack external validity.

I address these data limitations by employing a variety of other types of evidence. Although each type, in isolation, makes only a partial case, the total evidence makes a compelling case regarding the strong and broad hypothesis. I draw first on qualitative accounts of financial market behavior, taken from secondary studies as well as from interviews with financial market participants. I also present information from mutual fund manager surveys, credit rating agencies, and simple quantitative tests.

Qualitative Evidence

Extant qualitative discussions of emerging market investment highlight the salience of default risk, the role of informational concerns, and investors' preferences for neoliberal economic policies. According to these discussions, investors prefer a stable fiscal and monetary policymaking environment; as a result, nations with politically independent

---

[73] *IMF Survey*, February 23, 1998, p. 52.

central banks and fiscal authorities often pay lower interest rate premia.[74] Market participants also prefer stable (and, where fixed, credible) exchange rates.[75]

This literature also emphasizes the differences between investing in developed and investing in emerging markets. For instance, in a handbook intended for investors in emerging markets, Posner notes that emerging markets "carry greater country risk than do developed markets. Risk of political turmoil, hyperinflation, and social unrest, while not unknown in developed markets, are much higher in emerging markets."[76] He also points out that, despite their problems, developed countries do not have "hyperinflation, 'ethnic cleansing,' general strikes that paralyze the nation, and national leaders looting billions from the Treasury."[77] Similarly, Papaioannou and Tsetsekos underline the salience of political risk in emerging market economies, noting that "the consequences of adverse policies are often more dramatic in emerging markets."[78]

In terms of specific policies, investors are said to prefer neoliberal policy mixes. Posner describes "good" emerging markets as those that have a government budget moving toward balance or surplus; a free and open market; a privatization program under way or in the planning stages; a falling debt burden (and debt much lower than the OECD norm of 60% of GDP); relatively low inflation; and a high degree of economic freedom.[79] Likewise, Grabel notes that a viable investment climate is characterized by falling government budget deficits, restrained inflationary pressures, and privatization programs.[80] In a more pessimistic but similar account, Armijo maintains that investors' preferences for neoliberal policies tie the hands of governments, "forcing them into politically (and sometimes economically) risky behavior such as 30 to 50 percent slashes in already low levels of social

---

[74] Armijo 1999, Maxfield 1997, 1998, Milesi-Ferretti and Razin 1996, Summers 2000.

[75] Dym 1991, Frankel and Okongwu 1995.

[76] Posner 1998, pp. 5–6. Balkan 1992 analyzes the relationship between political structures and the probability of debt rescheduling, using data from 33 nations during the 1971–1984 period. He finds that, as the level of political instability increases, so does the likelihood of rescheduling. And, as the level of democracy increases, the probability of rescheduling falls.

[77] Posner 1998, p. 227.

[78] Papaioannou and Tsetsekos 1997, p. 41. Also see Aizenman et al. 1996, Bekaert et al. 1996, Haley 1999, Milesi-Feretti and Razin 1996.

[79] Posner 1998, pp. 193–194. Also see Haley 1999.

[80] Grabel 1996a, p. 6.

spending, often just as democratization finally is giving the poor a voice in politics."[81]

Interviews with financial market participants offer a similar, albeit more nuanced, picture. The main interview study for this book, described in Chapter 3, focuses on the differences between emerging market and developed nation assessments and, specifically, on financial market–government relations in advanced capitalist democracies. In order to assess the constraints facing emerging market economies, I conducted a second, smaller series of interviews during the fall of 1998; interview subjects were London-based participants in emerging markets fixed income markets. As do the market participants interviewed in 1997, these individuals make longer-term recommendations regarding asset allocation, and most deal with nations in a variety of geographic regions. Interviewees answered a set of open-ended questions regarding asset allocation in emerging market economies. If the strong but narrow model of financial market influence is accurate, respondents should demonstrate a concern with default risk, with a broad set of government policies, and with information quality.

Default Risk and the Scope of the Constraint   Again, market participants view the investment risks in emerging markets as relatively great.[82] They point out that, in addition to inflation risk and currency risk, they consider default risk. Although defaults or near-defaults in Russia and Ukraine – and more recently in Ecuador – have raised the salience of default risks for market participants, default risk has long been a factor in emerging market asset allocation.[83] Therefore, market participants are very concerned about governments' ability and willingness to pay.[84] They consider a wide variety of indicators.

Macropolicy Indicators   As in developed nations, market participants consider macro-outcomes, including the inflation rate and the deficit/GDP ratio.[85] Additionally, because a government's ability to repay depends on its capacity to generate revenues, market participants also consider the

---

[81] Armijo 1999.
[82] Interviews 52, 60. Interviews 51 through 64 refer to interviews conducted during October 1998.
[83] Interviews 52, 56, 61. Also see *New York Times*, September 29, 1999, p. C2.
[84] Interview 53.
[85] Interviews 52, 53, 57, 59, 60, 62, 63.

sources of government revenue, the balance of payments position, access to further funds (from private or official lenders), existing government debt, and the structure of government borrowing. Furthermore, because of the prevalence of foreign currency denomination, exchange rate considerations also are very important.[86] These concerns are magnified in countries with fixed exchange rates, where exchange rate adjustments can be sharp and sudden.[87]

Market participants' examination of the government's fiscal position also entails an examination of the character of government debt; knowledge of the overall level of outstanding debt is not sufficient. Rather, market participants seek information about how government borrowing is financed, in terms of the maturity structure and currency composition of debt.[88] More generally, market participants are concerned about the nature of the capital account: does the nation depend principally on short-term portfolio capital or on longer-term direct investment?[89]

Micropolicy Indicators   Market participants also look at micropolicy indicators. For instance, they consider not only a government's aggregate fiscal stance but also the components of its fiscal policy. One market participant points out,

In emerging markets, I require a greater appreciation of how governments spend their money, of how wealth is generated, of what the assets and liabilities of government and the private sector are.[90]

Along these lines, market participants consider the sources of tax revenue and the government's capacity to collect taxes.[91] On the expenditure side, market participants consider how resources are allocated across spending categories.[92] Are public funds used for consumption or for (growth-enhancing) improvements in infrastructure?[93] How is the pension system structured? What is the role of government subsidies in the economy?[94] Furthermore, market participants consider a government's level of fiscal

---

[86] Interviews 57, 60.
[87] Interview 56.
[88] Interviews 56, 57, 60, 63.
[89] Interviews 52, 62.
[90] Interview 54.
[91] Interviews 60, 63; also BIS 1998.
[92] Interview 59.
[93] Erb et al. 1998, Liederman and Thorne 1996.
[94] Interview 60.

126

flexibility: in a crisis, is the government able to change or reallocate spending?[95]

As in developed nations, market participants have well-defined preferences regarding appropriate micropolicy outcomes. If we look at the conditions contained in recent IMF standby agreements, which market participants often use as a seal of approval for emerging markets, we see a precise specification of policy targets. This specification has intensified over time, as private capital flows to emerging markets have grown in importance.[96] In the 1980s, the conditions attached to IMF loans expanded from macro-outcomes to supply-side policies and structural adjustment.[97] Using IMF archives, Gould generates a data set of 249 IMF conditionality arrangements, involving 20 borrowers during the 1952–1995 period. She identifies several trends, including a lengthening of IMF agreements and an increase in the total number of binding conditions. In addition, Gould demonstrates an increase over time in the use of procedures – which dictate not only the ends needed but also the means to achieve them – rather than targets – which indicate only an end.[98] The increased use of procedures evidences a broadening of concerns in emerging market economies. It is not only that the IMF – and, by extension, private investors – wants countries to do well in macroterms, but also that they want a certain set of microside policies and procedures to result.

The IMF's fall 1998 agreement with Brazil exemplifies the breadth of IMF agreements. Market participants were particularly concerned about Brazil's fiscal and current account deficits. They suggested specific policy changes – social security reform, modifications to state–federal fiscal relations, changes in labor law, and bureaucratic reform.[99] In keeping with these concerns, the IMF agreement outlines four broad goals: major fiscal

---

[95] Interviews 62, 63.

[96] Gould 2001 argues that changes in IMF conditionality are caused not by changes in state (U.S.) preferences, but by changes in the importance of and demands by private investors. She finds a relatively robust correlation, for emerging market nations, between private capital inflows and the number of binding conditions in IMF agreements. Kapur 2000 maintains that changes in conditions are, at least in part, an effort to address the functional problem of incomplete contracting. Also see Krasner 1999, Pauly 1999, and the contributors to Williamson 1983.

[97] Dale 1983, Polak 1991, Williamson 1983.

[98] Gould 2001. Also see Dale 1983, Kapur 2000.

[99] E.g., Interview 58; Genesis Investment Management Strategy Document (October 1998, confidential). *Financial Times*, October 20, 1998, p. 6, November 20, 1998, p. 9; *Economist*, March 28, 1998, p. 68; *Economist*, October 31, 1998, p. 73.

tightening, the maintenance of the exchange rate regime (a failure), a firm monetary policy stance, and wide-ranging structural reforms.[100] The agreement also specifies the precise procedures by which the Brazilian government is to meet these targets – increases in the financial transactions tax, increases in social security contributions by public employees, cuts in discretionary and capital spending, constitutional reforms of the civil service and social security, and (institutionally) the passing of new budgeting laws.

A similar pattern characterized the fund's 1997 negotiations with Argentina. For the first time, the agreement (concluded in February 1998) extended IMF conditionality beyond macroindicators to include elements of "good governance," such as spending on health care and education, tax reform, social security reform, labor market reform, and transparency in government bookkeeping.[101] More generally, the IMF repeatedly has noted the "importance of reducing unproductive public spending."[102] It warns, "Capital flows into the region [Eastern and Central Europe] have increasingly been used to finance widening current account deficits that mainly mirror increases in consumption . . . rather than investment."[103] A more recent IMF study argues that "economists should be more restrained in their praise of high public sector investment spending, especially in countries where high-level corruption is a problem."[104] In the aftermath of the Asian financial crisis, in which investment/consumption ratios were high but investments were unproductive, we can expect an even more finely tuned focus on how government spending is allocated across functional categories.

Domestic Political Coalitions and Platforms The second component of default risk, willingness to pay, reflects political decisions. The political climates in emerging markets are much less predictable than those in developed democracies, making country risk analysis an essential part of the asset allocation process.[105] As market participants point out:

It's a far more dynamic environment than in developed democracies. It is always true that politics are more important in emerging markets than in developed economies.[106]

---

[100] IMF 1998d.
[101] *New York Times*, July 15, 1997, p. C1; BIS 1998, p. 50; Camdessus 1997.
[102] E.g., IMF 1995.
[103] IMF Survey, December 11, 1995, p. 383; also Sobol 1996.
[104] Tanzi and Davoodi 1998, p.10.
[105] Interview 60; also Interviews 7, 15, 29.
[106] Interview 52.

Government policy matters most for emerging markets asset allocation...the shifts in policy are so much greater, as is the uncertainty.[107]

Politics is huge for emerging markets. It's a far more dynamic environment than in developed democracies.... There is much less certainty and homogeneity in emerging markets. Anything can happen, and big policy shifts are always possible.... The game is to get in the head of the finance minister. The technocratic element is small, so you have to figure out the political.[108]

In emerging markets, "who governs" does matter for market participants, and political shocks can contribute to market reactions, as they did in Mexico in 1994.[109] Furthermore, political party labels may provide little evidence regarding policy platforms or eventual policy outcomes, and policy outcomes may be the result of individual personalities and conflicts rather than of an institutionalized policymaking process.[110]

Market participants point out that they are most concerned with the predictability and stability of government policy.[111] In emerging market economies, market participants view the range of possible policy outcomes as relatively wide: some governments pursue capital-friendly policies, but others may advocate policies hostile to international investors.[112] A change in government can have large implications for policy outcomes.[113] For instance, immediately after a strong electoral showing in Venezuela by the former coup leader Hugo Chavez, the local equity market index fell 8%. Market participants cited fears about Chavez's promises of radical political reform and his rejection of the "savage neo-liberal economic model."[114] In other cases, however, where government change does not seem to portend economic policy change – as in Chile in

---

[107] Interview 41.

[108] Interview 53. As an example of "getting in the head of the finance minister," this investor offered Argentina in 1995 and 1996. "A political consultant in Argentina found 91 fallings-out between Cavallo and Menem. Each time it happened, the market fell. And after they reconciled, a few days or weeks later, the market recovered. So it had nothing to do with economic variables, but was all about the political game."

[109] Interview 53, Mishkin in Federal Reserve Bank 1997, p. 76.

[110] Interviews 53 and 60.

[111] Interviews 56, 60, 61, 62, 63. Predictability is often more important than the form of government to market participants. Several point out that stability of policy is more important than the degree of democracy. See Armijo 1999, Mahon 1996.

[112] Interviews 52, 53, 56, 57.

[113] Interview 59.

[114] *Financial Times*, November 24, 1998, p. 20; November 16, 1998, p. 21; November 10, 1998, p. 9.

January–March 2000[115] – investors are more sanguine about political risks. Nevertheless, because of the importance and variability of political variables to investment risk in emerging markets, market participants include elections and the political orientation of governments in their set of key indicators as a rule.

Concerns about Information The interviews also suggest that the quality and availability of information are, in fact, important considerations. Of those participants interviewed in October 1998, 11 of 13 cited informational concerns as a factor in their emerging market asset allocation behavior, and 8 of these 11 described information as a *very central* concern.[116] In the words of one professional investor:

> On information, first of all, there's none. It's not available. There is no culture of information and transparency [in emerging markets], and governments don't want to tell you anything. The information that is there is often late in coming, irregular, and not comparable even over time.

The preface to a recent report on Russia from a large fund-management agency reflects similar concerns:

> Caution should be exercised regarding the quality of the publicly available financial statistics.... Even when derived from official sources the data should always be considered critically. The absence of uniform methodologies and the inconsistency of data compilation by the official agencies often result in a situation where a single source produces ambiguous and even contradictory statistics. Frequent revisions of previously published data are also usual.[117]

Information problems have a variety of causes, including national statistical offices' lack of resources, failure to adhere to internationally accepted data standards, and difficulties associated with measuring nonofficial economic activities.[118] The timing of data releases also creates challenges: data may

---

[115] *Financial Times,* January 19, 2000, p. 22. Richard Lagos, the Socialist victor in the Chilean presidential election, offered the muted market response to the election as proof that he "is no Salvador Allende" and that his economic policies differed little from those of his center-right opponent.

[116] Also see Summers 2000, Walter 1996.

[117] Genesis 1997, p. I.

[118] Interviews 59, 63.

be released with a long lag or may be substantially revised several years later.[119]

In response to information problems, some market participants simply use the publicly available information but take it with a grain of salt. Others attempt to gather a wide assortment of information from a variety of sources, such as monetary authorities, fiscal authorities, multinational firms, local research centers, and international institutions. Market participants may make research visits to emerging market nations in order to assess the situation in qualitative terms. One notes, "If the statistics say that there is a lot of spending on infrastructure, but you visit the country and don't see any cranes, you begin to worry."[120] In many cases, low information quality leads to an increase in the country risk premium.[121] A final response of market participants to problems of information entails support for an international statistical standard, both for government statistics and for private sector accounting.

Market participants' and policymakers' concerns about the quality of information also are reflected by the recent attention given to the IMF's Special Data Dissemination Standard (SDDS). This standard was created in 1996 in order to "enhance the availability of timely and comprehensive statistics" and to "contribute to the improved functioning of financial markets."[122] Subscription to the SDDS is voluntary, and subscribing governments commit themselves to providing data in 17 categories, in monthly or quarterly form, as well as information regarding the statistical techniques used to generate the data. The SDDS became fully operational in 1998. A government's participation in the SDDS is intended to send a signal to investors regarding the availability and quality of information.[123] As of May 2002, 50 nations, including 19 developed and 31 emerging market economies, had subscribed to the standard. Appendix 4.1 lists the indicators required by the SDDS, the indicators encouraged by the SDDS, and the periodicity of the data required. The number and range of indicators included demonstrate that investors in emerging market economies prefer high-quality, frequent data in a variety

---

[119] Interviews 59, 62, 63.

[120] Interview 59.

[121] Interviews 52, 56, 62, 63.

[122] IMF 1998c.

[123] *Financial Times*, October 19, 1998, p. 4. On the extent to which the SDDS has accomplished this goal, see Mosley 2000b.

of policy areas – again, giving rise to a broad pattern of financial market influence.

Survey Evidence

Another means of gauging financial market participants' behavior is via survey research. Surveys of mutual fund managers allow us to inquire, in a more standardized fashion, about the importance of various criteria to asset allocation decisions. In this section, I report results from a survey of mutual fund managers, conducted in two rounds, during May and July 2000. The survey subjects for the first round were managers of the largest internationally oriented U.S. mutual funds, ranked according to assets under management.[124] After elimination of duplicated managers, the sample consisted of 178 individuals. The subjects for the second round of surveys were drawn from a database including mutual funds of all sizes, Morningstar's Principia database; I selected those funds with substantial activity outside the United States.[125] This database generated a pool of 486 potential subjects.

Each subject received a four-page questionnaire, along with a brief description of the purposes for which the data would be used. Part I of the survey requested basic descriptive information, such as the number of and size of funds managed, the type of assets held, and the geographic allocation of capital. Part II asked respondents to rate the importance, on a scale of 1 to 10, of 13 policies or political factors. The final part of the questionnaire inquired about fund managers' views on information and their awareness and use of the IMF's Special Data Dissemination Standard.[126] A follow-up reminder regarding the survey was sent two weeks later.

A total of 47 surveys were returned, 15 in May and 32 in July. After elimination of those surveys that did not reach the intended recipients, the resulting rate of response was approximately 8%.[127] The very low response rate is not surprising, given the time demands faced by fund managers.[128] By comparing the characteristics of the respondents to those of the entire

---

[124] Ratings are based on data from CBS MarketWatch; several categories of mutual funds – including International, Global, and Emerging Market – were used to compile the survey pool.

[125] Data are from the April 2000 release of the Principia CD-ROM. The fund categories of International Hybrid, Diversified Emerging Markets, Asia/Pacific Stock, Foreign Stock, World Stock, Latin America Stock, and Europe Stock were used.

[126] Results of this part of the survey are reported in Mosley 2000b.

[127] This reduced the May sample size to 161 and the July sample size to 432.

[128] On the general problem of survey nonresponse in political science, see Brehm 1993.

Table 4.5. *Fund Manager Allocation, by Asset Type*

	May Respondents	July Respondents	Total Respondents
Equities	59.0% of assets	91.9	81.5
Government Bonds	18.5	2.0	7.2
Corporate Bonds	18.1	0.9	6.4
Cash and Other	4.4	5.2	4.9

sample, however, we can increase our confidence that the bias generated by survey nonresponse is acceptable. Among respondents, the number of funds managed by respondents ranged from 1 to 86, with the median number managed as 4. Average fund assets under management were $17.5 billion in the May survey (reflecting the selection of participants, which was based on fund size), $4.7 billion for the July respondents, and overall $8.9 billion. The median fund size was considerably smaller, at $1.5 billion.

To compare the respondents with the total potential pool of managers, the average fund size in the Principia database was $332 million. The average fund size for respondents – calculated by dividing total assets under management by the number of funds managed – was $1.1 billion.[129] Similarly, the median fund size is $34 million in the Principia database and $318 million in the May and July responses. The responses reported later, then, are biased toward larger mutual funds. This may reflect the fact that the managers of smaller funds are more concerned with improving their reputation and therefore are less likely to devote time to responding to surveys. In any case, larger mutual funds are more able to impact the fortunes of emerging market nations, so a bias toward these funds is acceptable.

Table 4.5 details the allocation of fund managers' assets by asset category. The data suggest, not surprisingly, that equities constitute the majority of assets. Government bonds were more important among the May survey sample and, on average, constituted 7.4% of assets in the total sample. The geographic distribution of assets is very similar in the May and July survey samples; data for the entire sample, therefore, are presented in Figure 4.6. The overall asset allocation results from the survey indicate that, on average, 86.9% of fund managers' assets are invested in OECD, or advanced capitalist, nations, and the remaining 13.1% are invested in emerging

---

[129] There is very little difference in fund size between the May and July survey groups; the average size for May respondents is $1.09 billion and the average for July respondents is $1.05 billion.

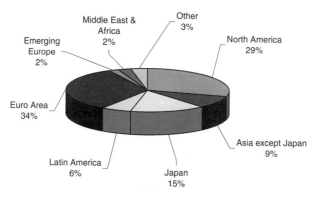

Figure 4.6 Geographic allocation of respondents' mutual funds.

market economies. On average, 34% of investment is in the euro-area, 29% in North America, and 15% in Japan. Other investment locations include Latin America (6%), emerging Europe (2%), and the Middle East and Africa (2%). Again comparing this allocation with that of the wider Principia database, the allocations generally are similar.[130]

Part II of the survey asked fund managers to rate the importance of a series of policies and political factors to their asset allocation decisions. The scale ranged from 1 to 10; lower values denoted "not at all important" and higher values denoted "very important." This evidence allows us to compare fund managers' treatment of emerging market and developed nations; if the strong and broad pattern holds in developing nations, we should observe marked differences in the importance of these factors, as well as a pronounced attention to default risk in emerging markets.

Table 4.6 reports these results. The first column lists the indicator, using the wording from the survey. The second column lists the overall average score. This column indicates that the most important indicators are the expected rate of inflation and the ability and willingness of governments to repay debt. When we divide the sample on the basis of geographic allocation, however, important differences appear. The third column reports the average for those fund managers with more than 25% of assets invested in

---

[130] The categories used by Principia are slightly different from those used in the survey. The geographic breakdown is United States and Canada (10%), Europe (40%), Japan (15%), Asia-Pacific (16%), Latin America (6%), and others (3%). The breakdown between developed and emerging in Principia is 73% and 25%, with 2% of assets coded as not available, "N/A."

Table 4.6. *The Importance of Policies and Political Factors to Asset Allocation*

Factor	All Respondents	Emerging Markets (>25% Assets)	All Other Respondents
Expected rate of inflation	6.93	8.5[a]	6.84
Political independence of national central bank	6.15	7.8[a]	6.03
Expected government budget deficit	5.73	7[a]	5.59
Political independence/ insulation of fiscal policymaking authorities	5.95	7.3[a]	5.89
Overall level of government debt (e.g., debt/GDP ratio)	6.27	6.5	6.24
Total size of government sector (e.g., government spending/GDP)	5.73	6	5.7
How governments allocate spending across functional categories (e.g., public investment spending vs. transfer payments)	4.88	5.8	4.84
Tax policy (e.g., marginal rates of taxation)	6.39	5.8	6.59
Degree of government intervention in labor markets	6.07	7.0	6.08
Ability of government to repay sovereign debt	7.27	8.7[a]	7.14
Willingness of government to repay sovereign debt	7.46	8.3[a]	7.41
Partisan orientation of government (e.g., Social Democrats, Liberals, Christian Democrats)	4.98	5.33	4.97
Expected changes in government (e.g., upcoming elections)	6.29	7.67[a]	6.08

[a] Indicates a difference from "All others" that is significant at a 90% or greater level of confidence.

emerging markets ($n = 7$); the fourth column reports averages for all others in the sample ($n = 40$). For all but one factor (tax policy), the importance of these factors is greater in emerging markets. In 7 of 13 cases, the difference between groups of respondents is statistically significant. Particularly large differences exist for the ability of governments to repay debt, monetary policy, fiscal policy, and expected changes in government. If we define emerging markets more loosely – as more than 10% of assets in emerging markets – the results are similar, albeit with less statistical significance.[131] The survey results, then, provide additional confirmation for our expectation that investors treat developed and emerging markets differently and that default risk is more salient for emerging market investors.

Credit Ratings: Outcomes and Methodologies

Another means of gauging financial market concerns in emerging market economies – and of comparing these with concerns in developed economies – is to investigate the methodology employed by sovereign credit ratings agencies. This investigation reveals two facts implied by Hypotheses 2.1 and 2.2: first, default risk is salient in emerging market economies, but assumed to be nonexistent in developed economies. Second, greater uncertainty surrounds ratings in emerging market economies. Assessing default risk by rating sovereign borrowers has been common practice for several decades. In the 1970s, when international bank lending expanded to developing nations, banks began to generate standardized measures of country risk. These measures relied on a combination of expert opinion, quantitative analysis, and qualitative assessments.[132] In the contemporary period, banks continue to generate in-house country risk assessments.

At the same time, several independent agencies provide investors with quantitative and qualitative risk assessments; these ratings are used by a variety of market participants.[133] These services, which include the Economist Intelligence Unit (EIU), Business Environment Risk Information (BERI), Euromoney, Institutional Investor (II), International Country Risk Guide (ICRG), and Political Risk Services (PRS), target different types of audiences. Some, including BERI, ICRG, and PRS, provide information for firms that seek to make direct investments in foreign locations. Others, such as Standard and Poor's, Moody's, Duff and Phelps (DCR), and Fitch-IBCA, rate sovereign and corporate debt instruments.

---

[131] There are 20 respondents with more than 10% of assets invested in emerging markets. For 10 of 13 factors, the average is greater among this sample than among the "all others" group ($n = 27$).

[132] Devlin 1989, Erb et al. 1998. Friedman 1983 and Group of Thirty 1982 provide summaries of the country risk assessment procedures of several international banks.

[133] IMF 1999a, p. 185.

These agencies sell their ratings to institutional investors and other portfolio market investors. Still other agencies, including Euromoney and II, target individual participants in the financial services industry. The various ratings agencies also differ somewhat in their methodologies; most, however, employ a combination of qualitative and quantitative indicators. Investors tend to consider several agencies' sovereign ratings: they believe not that one agency has a superior methodology, but that an evaluation of many agencies' ratings will allow them to make better decisions. This is exactly the sort of behavior that can be expected in an environment characterized by poor information, uncertainty, and high levels of investment risk.[134]

The Role of Ratings   The use of sovereign credit ratings can reduce investors' information costs, thereby playing a key role in the pricing of a sovereign debt.[135] Credit ratings agencies point out, however, that sovereign ratings are not designed to guide shorter-term asset allocation.[136] Ratings sometimes fail to anticipate major events, downgrading sovereign borrowers *after* political and economic crises occur, as in Mexico in 1994– 1995.[137] Moreover, many financial firms also evaluate sovereign borrowers in-house, and these evaluations are not always consistent with ratings agencies' judgments. For instance, in early 1999, Malaysian government debt was assigned junk-bond status by ratings agencies. At the same time, though, many major fund managers ranked Malaysia's sovereign bonds as among the most attractive in Asia.[138]

In many instances, though, ratings *do* affect financial market behavior. For example, on December 24, 1997, Moody's Investor Service announced a downgrading of Korean, Indonesian, and Thai sovereign bonds to noninvestment grade. The next trading day, the Korean won fell by 9%,

---

[134] Sobel 1999.

[135] IMF 1998b, p. 52.

[136] "The ratings agencies view their ratings as providing a forward-looking indication of the relative risk that a debt issuer will have the ability – and willingness – to make full and timely payments of principal and interest over the life of a particular rated instrument. The agencies do not regard their ratings as providing either a prediction of the timing of a default or an indication of the absolute level of risk associated with a particular financial obligation" (IMF 1999a, p. 192).

[137] E.g., Aronovich 1999, World Bank 2000, pp. 36, 48–52. Another potential problem is that ratings agencies avoid downgrades because they do not want to set off self-fulfilling financial market panics.

[138] *Singapore Business Times*, February 27, 1999, p. 4.

the Indonesian rupiah by 3%, and the Thai baht by 2%. The following day, Standard and Poor's downgraded Korea even further, and the won fell an additional 15%.[139] Conversely, after Korea's February 1998 ratings upgrade by Standard and Poor's (from B+ to BB+, still below its 1997 rating of AA), investors happily returned to Korean government bonds.[140] These correlations, of course, should be interpreted cautiously.[141] It is quite likely that a third factor – changes in policy outcomes or in publicly available information – often drives both market responses and ratings changes.[142] Changes in ratings often occur at the same time as other events, such as concern about debt rollover, so that financial market behavior likely is not driven entirely by ratings changes. In a study of investment risk and country credit ratings during the 1987 to 1996 period, Larrain and colleagues provide evidence to support this conjecture: statistical tests demonstrate a reciprocal causality between yield spreads on government bonds and credit ratings, suggesting that each influences the other.[143]

Moreover, firms in the sovereign credit rating business earn a large part of their income from governments that request ratings.[144] Ratings agencies might therefore be reticent to provide a negative assessment, for fear that competing agencies will provide a better ranking and, therefore, access to future ratings business. Along these lines, smaller credit ratings agencies appear to rate sovereign debt higher than the two main agencies, Moody's and Standard and Poor's (S&P's).[145] Ratings agencies respond to this criticism by pointing out that they have reputational incentives to provide accurate ratings.[146]

Despite these criticisms, there exist other reasons to expect that sovereign ratings are important to market participants. First, many institutional

---

[139] BIS 1998, p. 110.

[140] *New York Times*, April 9, 1998.

[141] The IMF 1998b discusses the timing of rating agency actions in Asia and the extent to which these actions influenced financial market activity. Also see *Economist*, May 15, 1999, p. 82; *Financial Times*, May 8, 1998, p. 21.

[142] BIS 1998, p. 110; World Bank 2000, p. 49.

[143] Larrain et al. 1997.

[144] The IMF 1999a reports that the major ratings agencies acknowledge that 90% or more of their total revenues are from the fees they charge for granting ratings. Also see World Bank 2000, p. 51.

[145] Larrain et al. 1997, p. 9.

[146] Cantor and Packer's 1997 study of U.S. corporate debt ratings supports this claim. They find no specific evidence that firms seek ratings from smaller ratings agencies as a means of achieving higher ratings levels.

investors are required to hold assets of some minimal credit rating.[147] Because of these restrictions, ratings changes can generate substantial re-allocations.[148] Second, Cantor and Packer find that rating announcements have immediate and independent effects on interest rate spreads, particularly for higher-risk debt issues. Interestingly, these effects were significant when ratings were upgraded, but not when ratings were downgraded.[149] Third, Keefer and Knack[150] find a significant and positive association between components of country credit ratings and the level of private investment.

Ratings Methodologies   The ratings methodologies employed by three firms – Euromoney, II, and Standard and Poor's[151] – imply narrow considerations of developed economies, but broad considerations of emerging market nations. These agencies take for granted that default risk is very low in advanced industrial democracies, even when outstanding debt is high. Ratings agencies devote the preponderance of their attention to emerging market economies and, in doing so, consider a wide range of government policy indicators.

Appendix 4.2 details the methodologies employed by each firm.[152] The services vary in the weights they assign to quantitative versus qualitative factors and in the relative importance of economic and political risk. All, however, focus on components of the willingness and ability to pay. Euromoney relies on quantitative assessments; it includes measures of overall debt and of access to international financing, as well as assessments of political risk. S&P's relies on both publicly available data and annual country visits.[153] These ratings include balance of payments flexibility, the external financial position, and fiscal policy and public debt, as well as political risk.

---

[147] BIS 1998, IMF 1998b.

[148] On the impact of ratings agencies, also see Sassen 1996 and Sinclair 1994.

[149] Cantor and Packer 1996. In a follow-up study, however, Reisen and von Maltzan 1999 find significant effects on risk premia *only* for downgrades – just the opposite of Cantor and Packer.

[150] Knack and Keefer 1995, 1997.

[151] Also see IMF 1999a, chapter 5 and appendix 5; Sobel 1999. PRS's and ICRG's methodologies are similar to those employed by Euromoney and II, whereas DCR's and Fitch-IBCA's are similar to Moody's and S&P's.

[152] The IMF provides brief results of a survey of four agencies – S&Ps, Moody's, Fitch IBCA, and DCR – in its 1999 report (IMF 1999a).

[153] The World Bank 2000 argues that sovereign ratings are based primarily on publicly available information, rather than on private information (p. 49).

Political risk is a broadly defined concept, including the form of government, the degree of consensus on economic policy objectives, and income distribution.[154] Although II's ratings rely explicitly on subjective expert judgments, these judgments appear to include assessments of similar criteria (see Table 4.7).

Given that developed nations vary on many of the dimensions listed in Appendix 4.2, we might expect different developed democracies to be rated differently. This is not the case: because default risk is central to credit ratings, and because default risk is viewed as minute in developed nations, variance among developed nation ratings is very small.[155] In developed nations, credit ratings experts assume the willingness and ability to repay debt. This assumption goes hand in hand with the notion that governments of developed countries have a well-developed respect for the rule of law, including a commitment to honor outstanding fiscal obligations.[156]

It is not surprising, then, that per capita income is associated positively and strongly with sovereign ratings.[157] For example, in 1997, Standard and Poor's rated all developed nations, with the exception of Greece and Iceland, as AAA.[158] This happened despite the fact that some of these nations had large debt GDP ratios. After the advent of EMU (and the associated increase in default risk), however, EU member ratings displayed slightly more dispersion.[159] Moreover, the ratings of high-credit sovereign borrowers are very stable: in general, sovereigns tend to remain in the same ratings category over time, but this effect is strongest at the top end of the scale. The IMF reports that over 97% of nations rated AAA by S&P's in one year will be rated AAA in the following year; of nations rated A, 92.3% will be rated

---

[154] Moody's and DCR employ similar measures.

[155] Interview, director of sovereign risk, Standard and Poor's, March 1997; Interview, director, Political Risk Services, February 1997.

[156] Standard and Poor's, March 27, 1995. Likewise, Sobel 1999 argues that "governments in developed nations are all 'above threshold' in their relations to private investment activity."

[157] Cantor and Packer 1996, Reisen and von Maltzan 1999. Garrett 1998b finds, however, that nations with higher GDPs per capita tend to have higher real interest rates, "going against suppositions that wealth, ceteris paribus, increases market confidence among lenders" (p. 34).

[158] Until the late 1990s, many fund managers and institutional investors categorized Greece as "emerging European," rather than as developed. In late 1998, however, the *Economist* removed Greece from its list of emerging market economies for which it reports weekly data.

[159] Standard and Poor's Creditweek, January 5, 2000, pp. 231–232.

A the following year. And of nations rated B, 75% will receive the same rating in the following year.[160]

Along similar lines, Ul Haque and colleagues'[161] study of rating methodologies and outcomes finds that different groups of countries are treated differently by ratings agencies, above and beyond their objective economic characteristics. Euromoney assigns ratings to Europe and Asia that are 10 to 20 points higher, after controlling for economic fundamentals, than those given to Latin American and African nations. Similarly, the EIU's ratings tend to be highest for European nations. When assigning scores to OECD nations, Euromoney errs on the side of "no default risk": where data on certain debt indicators are absent, all OECD countries receive the maximal score.

In emerging markets, however, ratings agencies assume neither willingness nor ability to repay.[162] As Moody's Investor Service points out:

Countries as diverse as Poland, Argentina, South Africa and the Philippines have defaulted on or have rescheduled their foreign debts to commercial banks for other than strictly economic or financial reasons. Very often, a mixture of political, social and cultural considerations – such as the inability to impose austerity, radical or political uprisings, or lack of public confidence in the central authorities – were at the root of a country's liquidity crisis.[163]

Ratings services examine emerging market nations with a fine-toothed comb. They consider not only aggregate fiscal outcomes in these economies but also the breakdown of government spending, the structure of the tax system, and the nature of government regulation. For instance, S&P's considers not only trends in inflation and public debt, but also the purposes of public sector borrowing.[164] It also evaluates supply-side policies, including the tax code, domestic regulation, and national investment policies.[165] In light of recent financial crises, ratings agencies also have begun to place stronger emphases on the strength of domestic banking systems and the degree of reliance on foreign capital inflows.[166]

Table 4.7 provides further evidence regarding the types of investment risk considered by ratings agencies. The table displays the relative

---

[160] IMF 1999a, p. 204.
[161] Ul Haque et al. 1997.
[162] Interview, director, IBCA, January 1997.
[163] Quoted in Sinclair 1994, p. 457.
[164] Standard and Poor's, March 27, 1995.
[165] Standard and Poor's, August 1992.
[166] IMF 1999a; *IMF Survey*, August 17, 1998, pp. 259–260.

Table 4.7. *Factors in Institutional Investor Country Risk Ratings*

Factor	OECD 1979	OECD 1994	Emerging 1979	Emerging 1994	Rest of World 1979	Rest of World 1994
Economic Outlook	1	1	2	3	3	4
Debt Service	5	2	1	1	1	1
Financial Reserves/Current Account	2	3	4	4	4	3
Fiscal Policy	9	4	9	7	6	6
Political Outlook	3	5	3	2	2	2
Access to Capital Markets	6	6	7	9	8	9
Trade Balance	4	7	5	5	5	5
Inflow of Portfolio Investment	7	8	8	8	7	8
Foreign Direct Investment	8	9	6	9	9	7

Source: Erb et al. 1996, Table 1.

importance of various factors to II's ratings. In 1979 and 1994, II's ratings experts were asked to rank the importance of several factors. Their responses demonstrate the differences between developing ("rest of the world" and emerging) countries and developed nations, as well as the changes over time in investors' decision-making criteria. The Pearson correlation between developed nations and emerging market scores is 0.74 in 1994, suggesting some similarity in indicators used to assess each type of country. The difference between developed nations and "rest of the world" (lower-income developing nations) is greater, with a correlation of 0.67 in 1994. Although Table 4.7 indicates some similarities in assessments of developed and emerging market nations (for instance, the importance of current account balances), it also reveals several differences.

Political outlook has declined in importance in OECD nations, as is consistent with the argument that government partisanship is not a key indicator for market participants. At the same time, fiscal policy and debt service have become more important indicators for OECD nations; perhaps the Maastricht guidelines focused market participants' attention on fiscal outcomes. In general, if we look at the correlations between the rankings of these factors, we find some change over time – a correlation of 0.58 between OECD rankings those in 1979 and those in 1994.

The ratings criteria for emerging market economies exhibit less change over time, with a correlation of 0.87 between 1979 and 1994.[167] The most important indicator in both periods is debt service; this is followed, in 1994, by political outlook, economic outlook, and debt service. The importance of these four factors suggests that the ability to pay remains a very salient part of the evaluation of developing countries. Finally, the switch in the relative positions of economic outlook and political outlook between 1979 and 1994 might hint at the increasing importance of willingness to pay considerations.[168]

Ratings Outcomes I conclude this examination by considering some of the outcomes of ratings agencies. If default risk is salient in emerging market economies, but not in advanced industrial democracies, ratings for developed democracies will, on average, be higher. Additionally, the greater uncertainty regarding information and political outcomes in emerging market economies should generate more variance in the ratings of emerging market economies, both across a sample of emerging markets rated by a single agency and between different agencies' ratings of a single country. Along these lines, in a study of ratings from 1981 to 1992, Sobel finds that the standard deviation for Euromoney ratings for developed nations is 11.58, whereas it is 19.99 for developing nations.[169] Calvo and Mendoza observe that, for the 1979 to 1996 period, "the variability of credit ratings is very low both in countries that represent 'good risks' [OECD nations] and in countries that are 'bad risks'."[170] Credit ratings are most variable among the intermediate group of countries – emerging market nations.

Appendix 4.3 lists ratings scores, as well as ordinal rankings, from Euromoney, II, and Standard and Poor's, released during March 1997. This table includes the 134 nations rated by II.[171] As expected, the ratings are

---

[167] The correlation for "rest of the world" in 1979 and 1994 is even higher, 0.93.

[168] The contributors to Armijo, ed. 1999 also note the importance of political considerations to market participants. They argue that institutional investors' concerns about political risk and desire for government stability often run counter to democracy.

[169] Sobel 1999.

[170] Calvo and Mendoza 2000b, p. 19.

[171] Euromoney ranks a total of 179 nations, whereas Standard and Poor's ranks only 69 nations. Standard and Poor's rankings are, for this reason, somewhat self-selecting. Standard and Poor's assigns a rating only at the request of a sovereign borrower and "only

Table 4.8. *Standard Deviations of 1997 Ratings*

Sample Set	Institutional Investor	Euromoney
Entire Sample ($n = 135$)	24.37	25.19
Developed Nations ($n = 21$)	8.64	3.58
Emerging Markets ($n = 37$)	15.67	15.40
Frontier Markets ($n = 18$)	10.63	11.68
Other Developing Nations ($n = 59$)	13.63	18.87

generally higher for developed nations. The average II rating for developed nations is 79.6 (82.5 when Greece, Portugal, and Iceland are excluded) and is 32.3 for developing nations. The average Euromoney rating is 91.6 for developed economies (93.1 excluding Greece, Portugal, and Iceland), but 47.9 for emerging market economies.[172]

Moreover, there is considerable dispersion within ratings, particularly for some categories of countries. Table 4.8 provides information regarding the variance of Euromoney and II ratings, with nations grouped according to IFC classifications. The standard deviation for developed nation ratings is 8.64 for II and 3.58 for Euromoney. When Greece and Iceland, the two lowest-rated developed nations, are excluded, the standard deviation drops further. The low standard deviations for developed nation ratings compare with standard deviations of 15.67 (II) and 15.40 (Euromoney) for emerging market nations. For frontier market and other developing nations, standard deviations are higher than for developed nations, but lower than for emerging market nations, suggesting again that uncertainty regarding appropriate ratings is greatest for emerging markets.

We also can look at the correlations between rating agency outcomes as a means of assessing uncertainty. Were there no uncertainty regarding the formulation of sovereign credit ratings, all agencies would produce very similar scores. The overall correlations between sets of 1997 ratings are, in fact, relatively high – 0.96 for II and Euromoney, 0.87 for Euromoney and

when adequate information is available." We might expect, then, that poorly performing nations would not request an assessment; that would explain why there is no rank lower than B in Appendix 4.3.

[172] Two Euromoney rankings are displayed in Appendix 4.3: the ordinal ranking within the entire Euromoney sample and the ordinal ranking within the smaller II sample. For the calculations later, I employ the ratings, rather than the rankings, as these more accurately reflect ratings assessments.

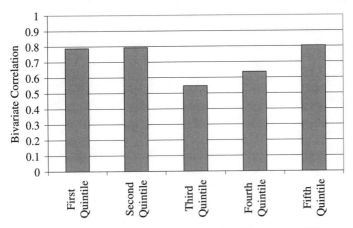

Figure 4.7 Correlations between Institutional Investor and Euromoney ratings.

S&P's, and 0.89 for S&P's and Euromoney.[173] When these correlations are calculated for different groups of countries, the degree of agreement varies. Figure 4.7 graphs the bivariate correlations within each quintile of the Euromoney and II ratings. These correlations are highest at the extremes: the correlations in the first, second, and fifth quintiles approach 0.8. In the second and third quintiles, however, the correlations are lower, 0.55 and 0.64, indicating less agreement.[174] These results suggest that, when dealing with intermediate groups of countries, uncertainty about investment risk and the quality of information is greater.[175]

Quantitative Evidence

I now turn to simple quantitative analyses regarding financial market treatment of emerging market versus developed nations. One means of dealing with quantitative data limitations for emerging markets is to pool developed and developing nations into a single sample and/or to use period averages or

---

[173] To calculate correlations, S&P ratings were assigned a number on an incremental 0 to 100 scale, with AAA receiving 100 and B* (a B rating for foreign currency issues, with no local currency issue rating) receiving 0. Ratings for foreign currency issues were placed 5 points lower than the equivalent ranking for local currency issues.

[174] One could argue that the greater variance across agencies in emerging market economies also is due to the difficulty of judging intermediate cases. An analogy might be the difficulty of placing intermediate nations on a polychotomous democracy–authoritarian scale (Przeworski et al. 2000).

[175] Also see Interview 62.

changes between periods as dependent and independent variables.[176] Such an analysis, however, assumes that the same causal mechanisms underlie the relationship between interest rates and policy outcomes in both the developing and the developed world. As a result, regional dummy variables tend to be highly significant. Additionally, average levels of indicators over a 5- or 10-year period are unlikely to provide accurate insight regarding financial market–government relations. Period averages obscure much of the shorter-term variation that drives market movements.

I elect to employ cross-sectional analyses, undertaken for individual years during the mid-1990s. Using the year as the unit of aggregation also allows us to take note of variability over time in the nature of financial market–government relations. The strong and broad model of financial market influence on governments implies that, because of the salience of default risk, emerging market nations and developed nations are treated differently. That is, the constraint is broader, and perhaps stronger, not merely because governments of emerging market economies pursue a different set of macropolicies than governments of developed economies, but also because emerging market governments are characterized by greater policy uncertainty, by less accurate information, and by higher levels of default risk. *Even when* emerging market economies have outcomes on macropolicy indicators that are similar to developed nations' outcomes, they should pay higher interest rate premia.

The dependent variable in these analyses is the interest rate spread – the difference between the interest rate charged by banks on loans to prime customers (LIBOR, the London Interbank Offer Rate)[177] and the interest rate paid by banks for demand, time, or savings deposits. Unlike data on government bond prices and rates, this measure is cross-nationally comparable and widely available. Where national data on treasury bill rates exist, they are closely correlated (greater than 0.9) with the interest rate spread variable. Additionally, using an interest rate spread measure controls for changes over time in global credit conditions.

I begin by estimating annual OLS regression models, using the combined set of developed, emerging, and frontier market nations, as listed in Table 4.1. The independent variables include several macropolicy indicators – the rate of inflation, the current account/GDP ratio, and the

---

[176] E.g., Garrett 2000a.

[177] The LIBOR spread reflects the differences in risk between loans in national markets and low-risk interbank, dollar-denominated loans.

Table 4.9. *Interest Rate Spread and Macroeconomic Indicators, All Countries*

Year	N	R^2	Inflation	CurrAcct	GovtBal	Constant
1994	44	0.36	0.41***	−0.83**	−0.14	5.86**
1995	42	0.54	0.68***	−0.59**	0.04	4.11**
1996	38	0.47	0.40***	−0.79***	0.04	5.96***
1997	30	0.65	0.46***	−0.94***	−0.68**	2.99**

Note: ***99%, **95%, *90% level of confidence.

Source: All data are from the World Bank 2000, World Development Indicators database.

government budget balance/GDP. I report models for 1994 through 1997; these years are characterized by both relatively high levels of capital mobility in emerging market economies and wide data availability.

Table 4.9 suggests that, although the relationship between interest rate premia and government policy indicators varies from year to year, some regularities exist. Higher rates of inflation are associated significantly, at a 99% confidence level, with higher interest rate spreads, and the substantive impact of inflation is quite large. A nation with a 10% inflation rate is predicted to pay between 2% and 3% more in interest than a nation with 5% inflation. This result is similar to that reported in Chapter 3 and is consistent with Maxfield's finding of a positive association between the level of central bank independence and the level of private investment in developing nations.[178]

Current account balances[179] also are significantly associated with interest rate spreads – larger deficits imply higher spreads. Again, these effects are fairly substantial, ranging from 0.6% to 0.9% for a 1-point shift in the current account balance/GDP ratio. This again is consistent with the results in Chapter 3. The results for the government budget balance are less consistent: in 1994, the effect is negative, so that larger deficits are associated with higher interest rates, as Chapter 3 suggests. This association, however, is not statistically significant. In the next two years, the coefficients are neither statistically significant nor in the expected direction. The final year of the sample is the only one in which the government budget balance estimate is both statistically significant and substantively meaningful: here, a nation with a 5% deficit/GDP ratio would pay approximately 2% more in interest than a nation with a 2% deficit/GDP ratio.

[178] Maxfield 1997. Axilrod 1996 discusses the importance of anti-inflationary monetary policies to investors.
[179] Negative numbers indicate a deficit, and positive values indicate a surplus.

Table 4.10. *Macroeconomic Indicators and Country Dummy Variables*

Year	N	R^2	Inflation	Current Account	Govt Balance	Country Category	Constant
1994	44	0.40	0.31***	−0.66*	−0.38	5.01*	2.55
1995	42	0.59	0.62***	−0.46*	−0.24	4.43**	0.73
1996	38	0.61	0.33***	−0.54**	−0.25	6.20***	1.60
1997	30	0.64	0.42***	−0.84***	−0.61	1.24	2.59*

Note: ***99%, **95%, *90% level of confidence.

Source: All data are from the World Bank 2000, World Development Indicators database.

These basic models do not include an exchange rate variable because that measure is highly correlated with the rate of inflation. Unfortunately, similar information for other, more micropolicy indicators, such as the distribution of government spending across functional categories, is available only for a subset of these nations. The resulting bivariate correlations between interest rates and micropolicy indicators are sometimes quite weak,[180] a result that likely stems both the small number of cases and the need to control for other factors in order to isolate the relationship between these indicators and interest rates.

Next, I estimate models that include a "country category" variable. This variable is coded as 0 for developed nations, 1 for emerging market economies, and 2 for frontier markets. This variable gauges the extent to which, once macroeconomic outcomes are accounted for, emerging market and frontier market nations *still* pay higher interest rates than developed nations. A positive and significant coefficient on this variable indicates that two nations, one developed and one emerging or frontier, with similar macroeconomic fundamentals are treated differently by financial market participants.

The results in Table 4.10 generally confirm this expectation. In three of four years reported, the country category variable is positive, statistically significant, and substantively large. The significance, substantive and statistical, of the other independent variables remains similar.[181] If we compare

---

[180] In some pooled cross-sectional models, however, there is a positive and statistically significant association between government consumption and the interest rate spread, suggesting that nations with higher levels of government consumption pay higher interest rate premia.

[181] I also estimated a set of models including government expenditure/GDP (an overall measure of the government sector). Including this variable did not change the preceding results in any meaningful fashion but served to reduce the sample size. In some years, the

these results with those in Table 4.9, we see that the constants in the latter models are smaller, suggesting that part of the unexplained variation in the constants is due to country category. The "category" variable likely serves as a proxy for financial market participants' concerns about the attributes of emerging and frontier markets – high default risk, political uncertainty, and poor information quality, for instance. This result provides evidence for the expectation that market participants do differentiate between developed and emerging market and frontier nations.

There are other potential means for confirming the differences in treatment of developed and emerging market economies. For instance, in-depth case studies of nations with similar economic fundamentals but different categorizations should reveal similar differences in financial market–government relations. In the mid- to late 1990s, possible pairs – based on similarity of macrofundamentals, but different categorizations – are Italy and South Africa, Sweden and Argentina, and Chile and New Zealand. Another piece of evidence comes from rates on local and foreign currency–denominated bonds. In developed nations, the spread between U.S. benchmark bonds and other nations' dollar-denominated bonds should be quite small, reflecting the fact that currency and inflation risk, rather than default risk, is the main determinant of interest rate premia. In developing nations, the spread between U.S. and other dollar-denominated instruments is greater, reflecting an enduring concern with default risk.[182]

Emerging Markets and Government Policy: Push vs. Pull Factors

The implications of strong and broad financial market influence for government policy autonomy are rather severe. Because the interest rates charged to governments are related directly to a wide range of economic policies, social policies, and institutional features, governments that want to please international market participants are highly constrained.[183] We are likely to observe many instances of emerging markets governments' attempting to

---

coefficients on the expenditure variable were positive; in other years, they were negative. In none of the four years was the expenditure coefficient statistically significant at a level exceeding 90%.

[182] Frankel and Okongwu 1995.
[183] Grabel 1996a.

please promarket constituents and international lenders rather than other domestic interest groups.[184]

This picture, which describes much of the reality for emerging and frontier market nations, assumes that country-specific, or "pull," factors dominate investors' assessments. Investors consider a set of policy indicators and base risk premia on the levels of these indicators and the potential for change in these indicators.[185] It does not consider the influence of global factors on capital flows to emerging market economies. Under some circumstances, though, exogenous ("push") factors, rather than country-specific evaluations, drive activity in global capital markets.[186] These exogenous factors include investors' attitudes regarding risk, changes in U.S. interest rates, and savings/investment rates in wealthy nations.[187] Eichengreen and Mody, for instance, find that changes over time in emerging market bond spreads are explained "mainly by shifts in market sentiment rather than by shifts in fundamentals."[188] Moreover, Gavin and associates note that, in Latin America, "the flow of capital . . . is very largely determined by developments in the world economy which are essentially exogenous."[189] If these push factors dominate, the link between capital flows and government policy outcomes is more tenuous.[190] In such periods, market participants might seek the high returns available in emerging markets and be willing to charge risk premia that are lower than economic fundamentals imply. Governments will be less constrained.[191] And in periods of flight from emerging markets the risk premia charged to governments far exceed those implied by economic fundamentals.[192] In these situations, governments can do little to attract foreign capital.

---

[184] See Calvo et al. 1996, Garrett 1998b, Haley 1999, and Manzocchi 1999 for preliminary evidence on this point.

[185] E.g., see Min 1998.

[186] Aronovich 1999, Doukas 1989, Eichengreen and Mody 1998, p. 38; Papaioannou and Tsetsekos 1997, p. 148. Goldstein and Turner 1996 note that movements in world interest rates could explain between one-half and two-thirds of the surge in private capital flows to developing nations in the 1990s.

[187] Germain 1997, Haley 1999, Maxfield 1997, Pou in Federal Reserve Bank 1997.

[188] Eichengreen and Mody 1998, p. 4.

[189] Gavin et al. 1996.

[190] Mahon 1996, Manzocchi 1999.

[191] Haley 1999, Maxfield 1997, 1998.

[192] This is not to deny that such periods of market sentiment do not occur in OECD nations – the ERM crisis may be one example. But I do assert that these events are more common in emerging markets.

Table 4.11. *Global Market Environments and the Nature of Financial Market Influence*

Global Market Environment	Normal Market Conditions	Mania	Panic
What Drives Investment Behavior?	National economic and political fundamentals	Global sentiment: desire for high returns; fundamentals but less important	Global sentiment: desire for low risk; contagion, very low levels of information
Who Borrows?	Some emerging markets, with appropriate risk premia	Most emerging market economies, with lower risk premia	Very few, if any, emerging markets; credit rationing common
Nature of Financial Market Influence	Strong and broad	Not as strong, not as broad	Very strong

Thus we are left with a second type of variation in financial market influence – over time, rather than across groups of countries – to explain. Table 4.11 offers three general possibilities for the global financial market environment: a normal market environment (the focus of this chapter), a mania, and a panic. In a normal market environment, market participants demand some amount of low-risk, low-return securities, and these are provided by developed nations. Market participants balance these securities with higher-risk, higher-return assets, provided by emerging market economies. Investors differentiate among various emerging market economies, charging higher premia where economic fundamentals are weaker and political risk is higher. Financial market influence in developing nations is strong and broad.

For example, in mid-1999 to early 2000, financial market treatment of emerging market economies approximated a normal market environment. Private capital flows to emerging markets recovered from the 1997–1998 crises but did not reach the extreme levels seen in 1996 and early 1997.[193] Investors offered credit to developing nations but differentiated among emerging market countries on the basis of credit risk.[194] Where economic fundamentals were stronger, as in East Asia, governments were able to

[193] World Bank 2000, p. 22.
[194] IMF 2000a, World Bank 2000, *Economist*, April 24, 1999, pp. 21–23; *New York Times*, November 28, 1999, p. C1.

access international markets at relatively low interest rate spreads. Where economic fundamentals remained weaker, as in most of Latin America, market access entailed higher interest rate premia.[195] Moreover, although there were some difficulties with debt service during this period – Ecuador defaulted on its Brady Bonds in October 1999[196] – these difficulties did not spill over to other emerging markets. Investors were careful to distinguish among emerging market nations.

In a mania environment, market participants are highly risk-acceptant. Driven by their preferences for high returns and/or the maintenance of market share, they are willing to lend to many borrowers. Emerging market governments can borrow at rates that are low relative to their economic fundamentals. During such periods, the "marginal moron, the person who would never get funded in a more cautious or recessionary period," is able to attract capital, and investors' rush into emerging markets can be described as rational herd behavior.[197] Nations with better fundamentals should be able to attract investment more easily, but, in general, governments are able to borrow on international capital markets as long as they pay a relatively small premium. Market participants also are likely to overlook microside problems, such as banking sector weaknesses. The early to mid-1990s period exemplifies a mania environment.[198] Declines in asset yields in the advanced economies made emerging markets increasingly attractive, and risk premia declined across emerging market nations.[199] Most nations paid interest rates that were lower than economic fundamentals implied.[200] Such situations embody one fund manager's description – offered in early 1997 – of the situation facing emerging markets:

There's a boundary [of acceptable policies] and governments that cross this will pay higher rates, or even have trouble getting access to credit... [but] a country can step a fair way out of line before being slapped on the knuckles by the market.[201]

Finally, in panic situations, risk-averse investors, seeking safety rather than high returns, dramatically increase the risk premia charged to, or fully

---

[195] IMF 1999a, p. 64. Also *Economist*, April 3, 1999, pp. 61–62.
[196] *New York Times*, September 2, 1999, p. C2.
[197] Friedman 2000, p. 124. Also see Chapter 2.
[198] Eichengreen and Mody 1998.
[199] Calvo et al. 1996, IMF 1998a, p. 340; World Bank 1998b, p. 13; *Economist*, March 21,1998, p. 87; *Financial Times*, March 21 1998, p. 22.
[200] Cline and Barnes 1997, IMF 1999a.
[201] Interview 8.

avoid, emerging markets. They reallocate their holdings to safe invest-ments, such as U.S. Treasury Bills.[202] Solid economic fundamentals pro-vide no guarantee of capital market access; all emerging market economies tend to be treated similarly.[203] They may face credit rationing.[204] In panic phases, investors also are more likely to use small amounts of informa-tion for decision making. For example, in mid-1997, market participants noted that, like Thailand, the Czech Republic had a large current account deficit. They discovered that, from 1994, there was a noticeable correla-tion between the returns on koruna-denominated and baht-denominated instruments. On the basis of this information, market participants pres-sured the koruna at the same time as they pressured the baht, resulting in the spread of the financial crisis to the Czech economy. In the end, the correlation between baht and koruna returns was an artifact of the way in which the two currencies were managed,[205] but in a panic en-vironment, this piece of information was sufficient to provoke a market response.

The market situation of August–October 1998 illustrates a panic, or a "negative herding," environment. Gross capital flows to emerging markets fell from $400 billion in 1997 to nearly 0 by August 1998.[206] After expe-riencing losses from the Russian default, investors sought safe investment locations.[207] Heavily leveraged investment funds worried that shareholders would redeem their shares. In their rush to transfer assets from emerging to mature markets, many investors sold their most liquid assets; investors sold "what they could" rather than "what they wanted to."[208] Hungary, which earlier had impressed investors with its good economic fundamentals and its relatively liquid capital markets, was among the first to be hit by the financial downturn.[209] Rather than collect country-specific knowledge that might differentiate between Argentina and Mexico, or between Hungary

[202] Sobel 1999.
[203] IMF 1998b, p. 72.
[204] Eichengreen and Portes in Federal Reserve Bank 1997; also Detragiache 1996.
[205] BIS 1998, p. 52, 108–109. The correlation was a result of the fact that the baht and the koruna both were managed tightly against baskets containing the dollar and the German mark.
[206] *IMF Survey*, November 2, 1998, p. 340
[207] BIS 1998, p. 90; Interviews 52, 53, 57, 58 61, 62, 64.
[208] BIS 1998, p. 109; Detragaiche 1996, IMF 1998b. Glauber (in Leland et al. 1997) describes the 1987 U.S. stock market crash in similar terms (p. 1186).
[209] Interviews 60, 61, 62. Also see *Economist*, February 13, 1999, p. 74; *Financial Times*, September 14, 1998, p. 7. Szapary (Federal Reserve Bank 1997) anticipates this (p. 119).

and Russia, investors simply avoided all emerging market economies, or all Asian economies.[210]

The result of this flight to safety was a crisis global in scope.[211] With the exception of an issue by the Lebanese government, which was purchased mostly by residents, no emerging market debt was issued between mid-August and mid-October 1998. Total bond issuance by emerging market issuers fell from $108 billion in 1997 to $74 billion in 1998.[212] On the other hand, in developed nations, the situation was just the opposite. Investors' search for safety drove interest rates in developed democracies, especially the United States, to historic lows, almost independently of their economic fundamentals. The demand for developed nation government bonds increased, while the supply remained constant or declined.[213] This again highlights the asymmetry between developed and emerging market nations.

Figure 4.8 illustrates the variation over time in overall sentiment regarding emerging market government debt. The graph tracks the progress of four of the government bond indexes calculated by J. P. Morgan – the Emerging Markets Bond Index Plus (EMBI Plus),[214] Argentina, Mexico, and Russia – from January 1994 to June 2001. The index shows periods of flight from emerging markets, such as late 1994 and early 1995, periods of market recovery; and periods of strong enthusiasm for emerging market assets. The close comovement of country indexes hints at the importance of broad market trends for individual country performance, as well as the variability over time of financial market pressures.

The variability over time in the constraint facing emerging market economies, as well as the relative importance of national versus global factors, has implications for the degree of government policy autonomy and

---

[210] During this period, the *Economist* referred to these nations as "submerging," rather than emerging, markets. *Economist*, December 19, 1998, p. 101.

[211] Greenspan, quoted in *Financial Times*, October 8, 1998, p. 1; *Economist*, September 26, 1998, p. 71; Interview 58; *Financial Times*, September 30, 1998 p. 2; Merrill Lynch *Currency and Bond Market Trends*, September 3, 1998, p. 2.

[212] Institute of International Finance 1999.

[213] BIS 1998, pp. 82–83; IMF 1998a, p. 8.

[214] The EMBI Plus indicates overall returns for external debt securities with secondary markets and at least $500 million outstanding. These securities include foreign currency–denominated Brady Bonds, loans, and Eurobonds, as well as U.S. dollar local markets instruments. Countries included are Argentina, Brazil, Bulgaria, Mexico, Morocco, Nigeria, the Philippines, Poland, Russia, and South Africa. Market participants use the EMBI Plus as a benchmark for emerging market debt performance.

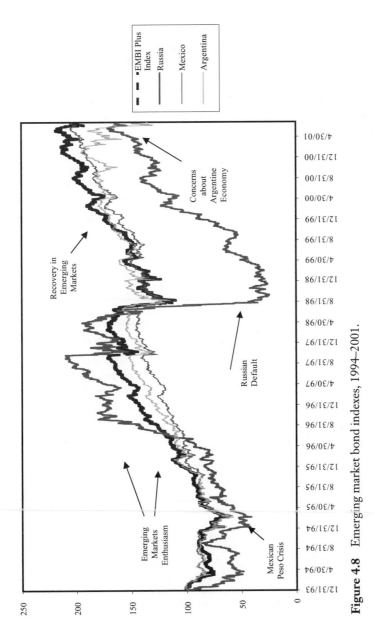

Figure 4.8 Emerging market bond indexes, 1994–2001.

for the ability of governments to attract foreign portfolio flows. In a normal market environment, emerging market governments are constrained in a broad range of policy areas.[215] In a mania situation, however, emerging market governments are less constrained. They are able to access international capital markets and to do so relatively cheaply, despite shortcomings in their economic and political fundamentals. Conversely, in a panic situation, governments of emerging market economies can do nothing right: even if they pursue appropriate macro- and micropolicies, they may not be able to access capital markets. If these expectations are correct, we should observe variance in policy that is correlated with variance in global market sentiment. For instance, when global liquidity is high, we should observe more cross-national diversity among developing nation policies. Alternatively, governments' desire to access markets in the future – after global sentiment changes – could prevent policymakers from abandoning market-friendly policies; rather, governments might retain them. Such a decision will depend, in large part, on domestic political alignments and institutions, which are the subject of Chapter 5.

Ultimately, if we want to understand the means by which emerging market economies might ameliorate the influence of global capital markets, we should seek out causal explanations for changes in global attitudes regarding emerging markets. It also is useful to realize that, under most conditions, a combination of push and pull factors drives capital flows. Whereas the overall amount of flows depends on push factors, the division of flows among nations likely is due to pull factors.[216] In conclusion, the evidence shows that regardless of external conditions, emerging market economies are treated differently than developed economies. This finding provides confirmation for Hypothesis 2.2: the financial market influence experienced by emerging market economies is quite broad and quite strong, especially in comparison to that faced by advanced capitalist democracies.

---

[215] Grabel 1996a, p. 6.

[216] Haley 1999, p. 77. See Manzocchi 1999 for a similar point (p. 62). Manzocchi notes that, when pooled together in a regression, external factors can explain between 30% and 50% of the time series variation in capital flows during the early 1990s. He also suggests that external factors appear more relevant in Latin America than in Asia (p. 62).

5

Politics Meets Markets

DOMESTIC RESPONSES TO
FINANCIAL MARKET PRESSURES

Governments can tax wealth in an open capital regime. . . . The reason they don't do this is because of domestic political concerns. . . . And governments need to realize that, by signing onto an open capital regime, they are signing on to certain constraints on their policy: they are making a deliberate choice, with foreseeable effects, so they should not complain about these effects in the future.[1]

The presence of all these [international] constraints means it is not parliament or public opinion that constitutes the most important sounding board for government policy but, rather, markets, and especially financial ones. Astute government officials will therefore anticipate and attend to the reactions of markets, and not to those of legislators, interest groups, or the public.[2]

How do domestic political factors interact with global economic forces, and with past choices regarding economic policy? The majority of this book is concerned with specifying the nature of financial market pressures on government policymaking. By providing a causal mechanism linking financial globalization with government policy outcomes, this endeavor greatly enhances our understanding of government policymaking in an era of financial globalization. In order to understand fully this linkage, and the process by which cross-national policy divergence occurs, however, a second causal mechanism – the effect of financial market pressures within domestic politics – is necessary. We need to connect events in global capital markets with changes in government policy, and we must consider how various domestic institutions and ideologies mediate these changes. In other words, under what conditions do governments accede to financial market influence,

[1] Interview 40.
[2] Dryzek 1996, p. 26.

resist financial market influence, or attempt to insulate themselves from financial market influence?

This chapter and the next offer preliminary evidence regarding this subject. Although a full examination of the role of external financial pressures in domestic politics is beyond the scope of this book, we formulate expectations regarding the ways in which financial market pressures play a role domestically. In this chapter, I consider three determinants of democratic governments' responses to financial market influence – the magnitude of financial market influence, the vulnerability of governments to financial market influence, and the ability of governments to avoid blame for the results of financial market penalties.[3] In Chapter 6, I consider the various policies that governments sometimes employ to alter the nature of financial market–government relations.

Financial Market Influence in Democratic Societies

Chapters 2, 3, and 4 paint a picture of financial market influence that varies over time, with both the level of capital market openness and the salience of default risk. In the contemporary era, financial market influence in advanced capitalist democracies is fairly strong but also fairly narrow, suggesting that market influence should play an important role in the development of aggregate fiscal and monetary policies, but a much smaller role in the formulation of supply-side policies or in the allocation of public spending across functional categories.

This finding comports with many other studies, in which domestic political affiliations and institutions remain key determinants of government policy outcomes. External pressures are refracted by a variety of internal conditions, including the extent of democratic governance, the relative strength of interest groups, electoral systems, and political party dynamics.[4] In addition, financial market pressures allow for multiple models of economic management, provided that each achieves key macroeconomic outcomes. Recent research suggests, for example, that the managed path to monetary

---

[3] My examination focuses on democratic nations. For a discussion of the interaction between democratization and economic policy, see Haggard and Kaufman 1995, Przeworski et al. 2000.

[4] See, for example, Andrews and Willett 1997, Adserà and Boix 2001, Berger and Dore 1996, Garrett 1998a, Garrett and Lange 1996, Kitschelt et al. 1999, Leblang 1999, Notermans 1993, Rudra and Haggard 2001, Simmons 1999, Swank 2002.

discipline, based on coordinated wage bargaining, can improve the efficacy of central banks, thereby helping to ameliorate investment risk.[5] Similarly, there are different means by which governments can achieve lower deficits, choosing between spending cuts and tax increases, as well as among different types of cuts and increases.[6]

Financial market influence in developing nations, however, is fairly broad, so that capital markets can significantly affect the development of microside, as well as macroside, public policies. Again, this conclusion provides insight regarding the *possibilities* for financial market influence on government policymaking, and a causal framework, which supports contemporary patterns of cross-national divergence and convergence. What they do not do, however, is explain *how* external market pressures filter through domestic politics – the right side of Figure 1.1.

And, as Chapter 7 points out, the ultimate impact of capital markets on government policy depends not only on the demands made by these markets, but also on the impact of these demands on the policymaking process. Where, as in many pre–World War I cases, market participants prefer smaller public sectors *and* national governments have few domestic incentives to provide for generous welfare benefits, the preferences of investors are consistent with the preferences of governments. There is little independent impact of financial market pressures. Likewise, in some contemporary cases, governing parties have long-standing ideological predispositions toward neoliberal policies. Where national governments prefer, for ideological or domestic political reasons, to reduce budget deficits, rather than to maintain or increase them, financial market pressures serve to reinforce fiscal rectitude. But they do not cause governments to change their overall course of action.[7]

In other cases, however, the preferences of global capital markets are clearly at odds with the preferences of policymakers. Sometimes policymakers accede to financial market pressures; other times, they resist, paying the price for autonomously determined policies. The experience of the French Socialist government under Mitterand is, perhaps, the modern archetype of accession, taking the form of a postelection change in the government's

[5] Iversen 1999, Hall and Franzese 1998. More generally, see Soskice 1999, Weiss 1998.

[6] Iversen and Wren 1998.

[7] Mahon 1996 makes this point about Mexican economic policy in the late 1980s and early 1990s; Maxfield 1997 presents similar logic regarding the reelection of Carlos Menem in 1995: voters believed that he would sustain a credible commitment to monetary stability, to central bank independence, and, therefore, to international investors (p. 47).

platform.[8] In May 1981, the Socialists won control of both the presidency and the National Assembly; the governing coalition, which comprised Socialists and Communists, embarked on a dramatic program of redistribution, entailing a significant revision of government–market relations.

In an effort to stimulate demand and reduce unemployment, the government increased spending in health care, housing, pensions, and salaries and encouraged reductions in workweeks as well as early retirements. Although these programs did help to reduce unemployment and to improve the overall economic standing of the poorest individuals, they also were associated with economic difficulties. The French budget deficit grew from 0.4% of GDP in 1981 to 3.4% of GDP in 1982, and inflation remained high (above 10%) in 1981 and 1982. The annual yield on benchmark government bonds grew from 13.79% in January 1981 to 17.4% in September 1981; in Germany, the equivalent September rate was 11.1%. France also experienced a tremendous balance of payments crisis: investors responded to France's reflation strategy by battering the franc, and this left France in a particularly precarious position, given its reliance on oil and other imported goods.

The French government ultimately concluded that pursuing an expansionary strategy, especially while other European nations were not doing so, was far too costly. Global capital markets rendered the French program rather intractable, spurring the government to change its course.[9] In order to rectify its currency and balance of payments problems, the French government reversed its policies, imposing an austerity program in June 1982. When this austerity program failed to stem the franc's decline, the government imposed an additional program of tightening. The March 1983 program included new taxes on the middle class and drastically cut government spending. The French government also negotiated

[8] This account draws from Hall 1986, Keeler 1993, Ross 1996. Also see Andrews 2001. On the unresponsiveness of governments to their preelection mandates, see Stokes 1997, who finds that, in 30% of competitive presidential elections in Latin America between 1982 and 1995, governments switched policies after taking office. Dryzek (1996, p. 49) notes a similar phenomenon in New Zealand during the 1980s.

[9] The prevailing view of the French U-turn is that global market pressures drove it. Cameron 1996, however, argues that, even in the face of market pressures, the French government had choices, and that the ultimate policy choices reflected struggles within the Mitterand government: "It [the government] did so not because it was *forced* to shift by external constraints, but, rather, because it *chose* to do so. And it made that choice not because of unavoidable external constraints but, rather, because the supporters of a contractionary policy triumphed over the adherents of an alternative policy in a protracted, *political* struggle that preoccupied the government during its first two years" (p. 58).

Table 5.1. *A Schematic of Financial Market–Government Preferences Regarding the Size of the Public Sector*

Domestic Political Pressures	Financial Market Pressures	
	Expand/Hold Constant/Indifferent	Contract
	I	II
Expand/Hold Constant (Traditional Social Democratic)	Consistent pressures; public sector expansion Example: Japan, late 1990s	Conflict: government adjudication among inconsistent pressures Example: France 1981–1983; some states in Latin America, 1980s
	III	IV
Contract (Neoliberal Reform)	Conflict: government adjudication among inconsistent pressures	Consistent pressures; contraction Example: Britain, 1980s; some states in Latin America, 1980s

a series of franc devaluations, in October 1981, June 1982, and March 1983.[10]

It is this sort of case, in which, absent international market pressures, governments would act differently, that is of central theoretical interest. Table 5.1 displays four possibilities for the preferences of financial market actors and national governments; government policy is divided, crudely, into "expand" or "contract/maintain." Although financial markets rarely prefer expansionary government policy, they may be indifferent to expansion if it has few consequences for overall deficit and inflation levels, or they may prefer expansion where growth is severely depressed, as in Japan in the late 1990s. More common, however, are market preferences for contraction. In Quadrants I and IV, the preferences of external market actors and national governments are consistent: both prefer either expansion or maintenance (Quadrant I) or both prefer contraction (Quadrant IV).

Arguably, the policies of Britain under Thatcher fit Quadrant IV, in that they ultimately were motivated as much by party ideology as by capital

---

[10] Stokes 1997 suggests that the German government's actions in 1976 also fit this model: immediately after winning the election and forming a new government, the SPD reneged on a campaign promise to raise old age pensions by 10%.

market incentives.[11] According to many observers and policymakers, the British Conservatives undertook cuts for ideological reasons but often attributed their behavior to financial market pressures. For instance, Nigel Lawson, chancellor of the Exchequer under Thatcher, suggests that external constraints are desirable, in that they minimize political intervention into economic policy. In his view, whereas the ERM definitely constrained the British government, "a constraint of this kind is highly desirable, and should be welcomed by all true 'Thatcherites.'"[12] More recently, a senior British Treasury official, as well as a senior adviser at the German Bundesbank, made similar arguments:

International openness is wholly a good thing, as a way to ensure the application of sensible policies. Yes, portfolio investors place pressure on government policy, but their views are consistent with the views of the government.... So I don't see much at all of an opposition between what the government wants and what the markets want.... When the government wants to do something that's a bit unsavory, they sometimes do use the justification that, if they don't do it, the exchange rate will collapse, or foreign investment will go elsewhere.[13]

It is important to separate out domestic from international market pressures. For example, the Clinton administration's concern about the performance of financial markets.... has a lot to do with public opinion and domestic markets.... The market strengthens the government's reasons for doing as it wants to do anyway. Political actors can use market reactions as a scapegoat for doing what is already necessary.... But I see no direct market influence on the behavior of politicians.[14]

At the same time, domestic demands and international pressures are not necessarily independent of one another: where international conditions contribute to a severe economic crisis, domestic constituents could come to demand a resolution to the crisis. In such cases, the government is empowered to take dramatic actions, and these actions are supported both domestically and internationally.[15]

---

[11] Hall 1986, Simmons 1999. On the same phenomena in developing nations, see Eichengreen and Sussman 2000, Weyland 1996.

[12] Lawson 1993, p. 504. Lawson goes on to note that, despite the appeal of ERM on these grounds, in mid-1985, Margaret Thatcher remained opposed to it.

[13] Interview, January 1997. Along these lines, one investment bank research director observed that "seventy-five percent of the change in the Labour Party platform is internally driven: they weren't looking at international influences, but just trying to win elections" (Interview 10).

[14] Interview, Bundesbank adviser, April 1997.

[15] See Keeler 1993 for an argument that extraordinary policymaking is possible only where the government achieves an impressive mandate or when a severe socioeconomic crisis hits.

Alternatively, Notermans maintains that, in the 1970s and 1980s, social democratic governments used international markets to justify their shift toward neoliberal policies, even where market pressures did not necessitate such policies.[16] Even when the preferences of markets and governments are consistent, then, we might imagine governments' invoking financial market pressures as a scapegoating device.[17] Pursuing such a course of action could allow governments to make cuts while avoiding all blame, but scapegoating also could be risky, as it might give rise to antiglobalization backlash.[18]

Quadrants II and III, on the other hand, contain cases in which governments must choose between pleasing markets and pleasing domestic constituents:[19] in Quadrant II, which is much more common than Quadrant III, the government has some domestic political incentives to expand – or to sustain current policy – but faces financial market pressures to keep monetary and fiscal policy in check.[20] An extreme example of this situation would be Latin America in the mid-1980s. Governments faced capital flight and intense needs for capital inflows, as well as pressure from the IMF, but they also had domestic incentives not to impose austerity.[21] In response, many Latin American governments embarked on programs of liberal economic policy reform. The most decisive reformers of the late 1980s and early

---

In his view, Thatcher's initial successes stem from the British sterling crisis in 1976, and from the 1978–1979 Winter of Discontent.

[16] Notermans 2000, pp. 172–173, 232–235.

[17] See Lichtensztejn 1983 for a similar claim with respect to IMF agreements with developing country governments: "There are cases in which economic policies are modified in the direction of the IMF's conditionality for basically domestic reasons.... In these circumstances, conditionality may at most precipitate a decision process that was already underway" (p. 210). Likewise, in mid-1998, the Polish finance minister pointed to crises in Asia and Russia as evidence used against domestic groups who opposed fiscal expansion that financial discipline was necessary (*Financial Times*, June 3, 1998, p. 7).

[18] Buiter et al. 1993, Pierson 1996, Rodrik 1997.

[19] Tanzi and Schuknecht 2000. Likewise, Simmons 1994 views a government's decision to adjust domestically – and to maintain its commitment to the interwar gold standard – as a choice between maintaining international obligations and servicing domestic constituencies. Eccleston 1998 characterizes Australian fiscal policy during the last two decades in this fashion.

[20] Pierson 1996, Turner 1995.

[21] Haggard 1985, Kaufman 1985, Stokes 1997. Stokes suggests that the most pronounced demands for domestic security–oriented policies occurred when output and employment were declining and when inflation was relatively low. This view contrasts with that of Armijo 1996, who suggests that it was the working classes who lost most from the hyperinflations of the 1980s. In Brazil, for instance, financial institutions reaped substantial benefits from inflation, while the poor suffered.

1990s were those facing the most severe financial situation – Argentina, Mexico, and Venezuela.[22]

Quadrants II and III present choices for governments; both choices have costs. Although government officials generally acknowledge *some* awareness of financial market pressures, particularly on aggregate monetary policies, and to a less extent on overall fiscal policies,[23] different governments resolve these trade-offs in different ways. Even in Latin America in the 1980s, the degree of neoliberal policy reform varied cross-nationally,[24] reflecting a diversity of national responses to similar external pressures.[25] Under what conditions, then, do governments accede to financial market pressures or, alternatively, defy financial markets and "pay the market price" for their policies?

Determinants of Government Response

Recent empirical work on OECD nations suggests that the impact of international capital market pressures on government policy outcomes is highly dependent on the type of collective interest representation, the centralization of policymaking authority, and the degree of universalism inherent in welfare state policies.[26] Likewise, I maintain that, in democratic societies,[27] a government's resolution of the trade-off between financial market penalties and domestic political concerns depends on three factors: (1) the magnitude of the financial market price, (2) the government's sensitivity to changes in economic performance induced by financial market reactions, and (3) the nation's external financial vulnerability. Each of these factors, in turn, is mediated by domestic institutional structures, particularly in advanced democracies.[28]

---

[22] Mahon 1996. Stokes 1997 suggests that, in some cases, voters did not recognize ex ante the merits of contractionary policies but saw their value ex post.

[23] See Chapter 3.

[24] Mahon 1996.

[25] E.g., Katzenstein 1985. For an analysis of another sort of domestic political trade-off, among fiscal restraint, employment, and wage equality, see Iversen and Wren 1998.

[26] Swank 2002.

[27] Dryzek 1996, citing Bowles and Gintis 1992, suggests that governments of more democratic nations are more likely to be punished electorally for acceding to financial market pressures. Therefore, it may be that "life in the international political economy is easier for more authoritarian states" (pp. 80–81).

[28] Cohen 1996.

The Magnitude of the Financial Market Price

First, all other factors equal, governments will be less willing to pursue policies that are more costly. Increases in government bond rates produce increases in domestic interest rates. Higher interest rates can lead to higher unemployment, lower investment, poorer equity market performance, and lower economic growth. Higher interest rates also can contribute to exchange rate appreciation, which damages export-oriented industries; particularly where the competitiveness of national industries is at stake, governments have clear incentives to keep a careful eye on externally induced interest rate changes.[29] These effects will be most pronounced in small, open economies, which are price-takers on world capital markets.[30]

If we assume that democratically elected governments are motivated by a desire to remain in office (that is, they are office- and/or vote-seeking),[31] and that voters respond to economic conditions,[32] we can expect all governments to be sensitive to the impact of interest rate changes. Even when a governing coalition has a strong policy commitment to public sector expansion, its desire to maintain office and to maximize votes may override this commitment.[33] In addition, in emerging markets, the interest rate price of expansionary policies is lower when global markets are risk-acceptant; in such periods, governments are more likely to choose domestic goals over international market preferences. And, for EU members, an increase in the magnitude of punishments and rewards likely occurred in the mid-1990s, when financial market participants focused on the propensity to qualify for EMU.

Sensitivity to Changes in Economic Performance

Notwithstanding the general salience of interest rates, governments' sensitivities to interest rate changes vary cross-nationally.[34] An increase in

---

[29] Cerny 1999, Tanzi and Schuknecht 2000. Put differently, governments are more likely to retrench in cases of severe economic downturns.

[30] Simmons 1999. In his examination of British public opinion during the 1970s, Hibbs 1982 finds that manual workers' opinions of the government are particularly sensitive to changes in the exchange rate. This may well be the result of their exposure to international trade.

[31] Downs 1957, Mayhew 1974, Mueller and Strom 1999.

[32] Lewis-Beck 1988.

[33] Mueller and Strom 1999, p. 281.

[34] These sensitivities also may vary over time, as voters become more sophisticated in their knowledge of economic relationships.

interest rates of 0.5% is more salient in a nation with a poor economic outlook than in a nation with a robust economy. Likewise, exchange rate appreciation is more worrisome for governments when the export sector is large. More importantly, the impact of economic conditions on voting behavior – and, therefore, on electoral costs and on government policy choices – depends on political institutions.[35]

The Clarity of Responsibility and Blame Attribution   Recent extensions to the general economic voting argument – that voters consider either prospective or retrospective economic performance, in terms of either personal or sociotropic outcomes[36] – suggest that voters behave differently, depending on the institutional context. Voters appear to recognize that, as a result of institutional structures, some governments have more control than others over economic performance. For instance, Powell and Whitten report that the strength of economic voting is affected by the "clarity of political responsibility." Voters can assign blame more easily to single-party governments with high political party cohesion. In coalition governments, or where party cohesion is low, the responsibility for economic policymaking is diffuse, and voters are less able to blame or reward the incumbent government for economic performance.[37] Therefore, where responsibility is clear – in nations with single-party governments, cohesive political parties, and few veto points – economic voting is more prevalent.

The implication of this finding is that, where voters are more able to blame specific parties for economic outcomes, governments will be more sensitive to interest rate changes. Where attributing blame is more difficult – where there are multiple veto points, or coalition governments, or low party cohesion – voters are less able to blame or reward the incumbent government for economic performance. Members of coalition governments likely are aware of voters' difficulties in blame assessment and are more likely to accept interest rate penalties. Therefore, governments of nations with majoritarian electoral systems and well-disciplined parties will

---

[35] Also see Haggard and Kaufman 1995, Keohane and Milner 1996.

[36] Kitschelt 1999 notes that the magnitude and nature of economic voting effects remain unknown. Pacek and Radcliff 1996 suggest that, in the developing world, the impact of economic conditions on electoral fortunes is asymmetric, so that governments are punished for downturns but not rewarded for upturns. Duch et al. 2000 suggest that individuals' evaluations of the economy vary according to information, political attitudes, and demographic characteristics, among other factors. Also see Hibbs 1982, Lewis-Beck and Paldam 2000.

[37] Powell and Whitten 1993. For different approaches to assessing the impact of political institutions on economic voting, see Anderson 2000, Royed et al. 2000.

be more sensitive to changes in interest rates, as they expect to receive most of the public's blame for economic downturns. Quinn and Inclan make a similar argument about political responsibility and capital controls: capital controls will be more attractive where political responsibility is clearer, as governments with heavy responsibility could be unwilling to give up some of their economic policy tools. In support of this conjecture, they find a significant statistical relationship between capital controls and majoritarian political institutions.[38] Similarly, Bernhard and Leblang find that, in developed democracies, politicians in proportional representation systems are more likely to peg their exchange rates than their counterparts in majoritarian systems. Where single political parties can more easily be held responsible for economic outcomes, politicians seek to retain control over domestic monetary policy.[39]

The clarity of political responsibility is driven by a variety of domestic institutional factors.[40] The size of governing coalitions – operationalized by the average number of political parties in the cabinet, or by an index of cabinet fractionalization – is one measure of clarity. Coalition size, of course, is related to the electoral rules in place, so that inclusion of a large number of governing parties is more likely under more proportional electoral systems.[41] Therefore, where nations change their electoral systems (as in Italy, Japan, and New Zealand in the mid-1990s), their responsiveness to external market pressures also should change, all other factors equal.

Another aspect of the clarity of responsibility is political party cohesion; where political parties are cohesive – or, more exactly, where voters view political parties as cohesive and disciplined – blame is more easily attributed.[42] More cohesive political parties should be more sensitive to interest rate changes. Yet another determinant of clarity is the extent of centralization or federalism; where a large degree of economic policy responsibility belongs to subnational entities, national governments will bear less of the

---

[38] Quinn and Inclan 1997.

[39] Bernhard and Leblang 1999; their argument rests on the fact that in majoritarian systems, the costs of electoral defeat are higher, so politicians strive to retain control over domestic monetary policy levers. Leblang 1999, however, reaches the opposite conclusions for a sample of 76 developing nations. Among developing nations, democratic regimes are more likely to float their exchange rates; among democratic regimes, politicians in proportional representation systems are more likely to choose floating rates.

[40] Also see Anderson 2000, Royed et al. 2000.

[41] Lijphart 1984.

[42] On the effect of political system fragmentation on the prospects for economic reform, see Haggard and Kaufman 1995.

blame for economic outcomes.[43] Therefore, unitary states will be more sensitive than federal ones to interest rate changes. Each of these variables could be understood as an aspect of economic policy veto players: where the number of veto players[44] is high, voters are less able to blame governments, and governments are more able to tolerate financial market penalties. This expectation parallels Swank's findings, which suggest that welfare state retrenchment is less likely in multiparty or consensus democracies.[45]

Security of Tenure in Office   Another determinant of governments' sensitivity to changes in interest rates is the security of their tenure in office. Politicians' attempts to influence shorter-term interest rates underlie a good deal of the political business cycle literature.[46] This literature is based on the assumption that, as elections approach, political actors become more attentive to economic performance. A government facing a closely contested election in the near future will be much more sensitive to the effects of international financial markets than one facing a relatively noncompetitive election in the more distant future.[47] Of course, where election timing is endogenous, governments are more able to time elections to coincide with positive economic performance. But even where timing is endogenous, deadlines exist for elections, and a government approaching the deadline is more likely to worry about the impact of interest rate penalties. Therefore,

---

[43] In his study of 46 developing nations, Wibbels 2000 finds that federalism has a negative impact on macroeconomic prospects and reform. In federal systems, the argument goes, subnational governments have few incentives to bear the burden of national economic adjustment measures, as they are not held accountable for the overall state of the national economy. Wibbels suggests, however, that federalism has a lesser impact in developed democracies, where federal systems have largely succeeded in overcoming collective action problems.

[44] Tsebelis defines a veto player as "an individual or collective actor whose agreement is necessary for a change of the status quo" (1999, p. 593). See Kastner and Rector 2001, Tsebelis 1995, Tsebelis 1999.

[45] Swank 2001. Huber and Stephens 2001 also consider the impact of domestic institutions on the process and degree of welfare state retrenchment.

[46] Alesina et al. 1997, Clark and Hallerberg 2000, Hibbs 1977.

[47] Also see Keeler 1993, Mueller and Strom 1999, Schultz 1995, Schwartz 1994. Keeler finds that the most ambitious governments, in terms of policy change, are those with large mandates and many years until an election. The security of tenure in office also may interact with ideology. For instance, where a large proportion of a government's supporters prefer a generous welfare state, a government approaching reelection may maintain – or even increase – social spending, even in the face of financial market pressures. Alternatively, such governments may attempt consolidation near the beginning of their terms and increased expenditures near the end of their terms. On the interaction between ideology and the political business cycle, see Alesina et al. 1997, Clark and Hallerberg 2000.

governments with long terms remaining and with good reelection prospects will be least responsive to the changes induced by international financial markets.

The security of governments' tenure in office also mediates the role of public opinion and partisan ideology in national responses to market pressures.[48] In parliamentary systems, an aspect of security is the size of the governing party or coalition's majority. Where the governing party has a significant majority, and where it does not rely on the support of other parties, it is most able to pursue its own policy preferences. But in cases of minority government or multiparty coalitions, governments will be more sensitive to the policy preferences of other parties. For instance, if a Social Democratic party relies on a far-left party for support, it will be less likely to accede to financial market pressures. And if a Christian Democratic party relies on an economically liberal party for support, it will be more likely to accede to financial market pressures. The impact of a government's security in office, therefore, depends both on the time remaining and on the type of government – single-party majority, majority coalition, or minority coalition.

Insulation from Conditions in the Private Economy   The third influence on governments' sensitivity to interest rate changes is the extent to which constituents are exposed to or shielded from market determined economic conditions. How quickly and to what extent do individual voters experience the results of an increase in longer-term interest rates? Many factors feed into voters' insulation or exposure, including trade openness, the importance of personal equity investment (as with privatized pension systems),[49] and the use of fixed versus variable home mortgage rates. The most important insulating factor is the size and nature (e.g., residualist vs. social citizenship model) of the public welfare system.

---

[48] For general discussions of ideology and international economic policy, see Garrett 1998a, 1998c, and Simmons 1999.

[49] Where individual share ownership is greater, we should expect equity market performance to be more salient in domestic politics. This suggests a difference between the United States and continental Europe, but also a change over time. In continental Europe, equity ownership is small, but on the rise (*Economist*, March 10, 2001, pp. 73–74; *Economist*, May 5, 2001, pp. 7, 20–21). In the United States, 10% of households owned mutual funds in 1984; by 1998, this number had grown to 44% (Investment Company Institute 1999). On the relationship between stock market performance and presidential approval in the United States, see Alter and Goodhart 2001.

In some nations, large welfare states insulate individuals from market determined economic conditions. By doing so, such programs can help to sustain public support for international economic openness, particularly where welfare state policies are universalistic.[50] They also often help to achieve ideological goals of income redistribution and social protection. If a substantial portion of voters' material needs is provided by the public sector, rather than in a market setting, voters are less affected by changes in economic conditions.[51] As such, they are less likely to punish governments for increases in interest rates.[52] Moreover, citizens in these states are more likely to resist cuts in social spending, as entrenched constituencies support such spending.[53] Therefore, governments with large public sectors, such as Sweden, should be more willing to pay interest rate premia than governments with smaller public sectors, such as Britain.

This expectation does not, however, address the longer-run sustainability of generous welfare states. Although voters receive benefits from generous welfare state policies, they may be averse to bearing the costs of these policies. As international financial integration increases, though, voters may be asked to do just this. Mueller posits that, in a world of mobile factors, governments will supply redistributive policies only when voters are willing to fund such policies via taxes.[54] Therefore, welfare state insulation may be less common in the future.[55] Alternatively, voters will continue to demand and support welfare state policies as a means of insulation from globalization,[56] and governments will be enabled, rather than constrained, by access to international capital markets.[57] At present, a substantial degree of variation

[50] Katzenstein 1985, Kramer et al. 2000, Rodrik 1997, Scheve and Slaughter 2001, Summers 2000, Swank 2002.

[51] Along these lines, Radcliff 1992 suggests that voters' responses to economic adversity (in terms of the decision whether to vote) depend on the size of the welfare state. His data analysis reveals that individuals' responses to economic conditions are related, in a nonlinear fashion, to the extensiveness of social security provisions. Also see Leblang 1999, who argues that the absence of generous welfare states in developing nations creates incentives for politicians to attempt to retain monetary policymaking autonomy.

[52] Pacek and Radcliff 1995.

[53] Moses 2001, Tanzi and Schuknecht 2000.

[54] Mueller 1998. Mueller's model assumes, however, that all factors are equally mobile, so that labor is as able as capital to threaten exit.

[55] Burtless et al. 1998.

[56] Friedman 2000, Notermans 2000, Pierson 1996, Rodrik 1997, Swank 2002, *Economist*, January 23, 1999, p. 19.

[57] Quinn 1997 makes such an argument: he finds a positive association between capital mobility and corporate tax burdens, which does not support a "race to the bottom" argument.

in welfare state policies persists, so we can expect that voters living in more social-democratically oriented welfare states will be less sensitive to interest rate changes.

Trade Openness   A final influence on government sensitivity is the importance of the internationally oriented sector of the economy. As Frieden suggests, firms and individuals involved in the international economy will have preferences different from those of firms and individuals not involved in the international economy.[58] At the cross-national level, polities with more exposure to trade will, all else equal, be more sensitive to the effects of interest rate changes, via two mechanisms. First, interest rate increases can dampen the competitiveness of local goods in international markets. Along similar lines, several scholars argue that firms and workers in the trade-exposed sectors of the economy will be concerned about maintaining competitiveness and, therefore, might pressure governments for public sector reform,[59] just as financial markets would pressure governments. Second, interest rate changes often are associated with exchange rate changes. Exchange rate changes – either general volatility, or appreciation and depreciation – will be more politically salient where trade openness is greater. Therefore, we can use trade as a percentage of national income as a rough indicator of this dimension of government sensitivity.

The impact of trade openness on government responses also provides for an interesting combination of influences: high trade openness and large welfare states often go hand-in-hand, reflecting an earlier compromise of embedded liberalism. But, where large welfare states can mediate against the impact of international financial market pressures, high trade openness can make the same pressures more salient. So, the combined effect of *both*

One potential explanation is that voters desire economic openness, as it is associated with higher growth, but they also want insulation from external market forces, and they prefer to have these paid for via corporate, rather than individual, taxation. In Quinn's view, financial internationalization might serve to allow governments to achieve the goals demanded by voters.

[58] Frieden 1991b.

[59] Clayton and Pontusson 1998, Iversen 1999, Schwartz 1994. Huber and Stephens 1998, as well as Weiss 1998, however, argue that social democracies such as Sweden have always been rather open to trade, so trade-related pressures on welfare state policies should not change over the course of the 1980s and 1990s. Soskice 1999 maintains that, depending on their type and competitive advantages, different firms prefer different national systems of regulation.

high trade openness and a large welfare state might be negligible. In some cases, the determinants of sensitivity are likely to push in opposite directions; for instance, a government with a large welfare state, a high degree of trade openness, an upcoming election, and a coalition government has some incentives to ignore increases in government bond rates and other incentives to respond to these increases.

Vulnerability to Changes in Financial Market Conditions

Finally, we can expect governments to consider the impact of changes in interest rates on debt financing costs and, more generally, on capital flows from abroad. The propensity of governments to accept an increase in financing costs depends on the existing level of debt, on the current debt structure, and on the willingness to make trade-offs across other budget categories. Increases in government bond rates raise future government financing costs. When faced with increases in debt servicing, a government can allow its expenditure to grow; or it can make cuts in other budget areas and maintain the same overall balance; or it can attempt to achieve cost savings via changes in debt management, such as shorter-term or foreign currency–denominated debt. If a government chooses to run a larger deficit, it may well face another round of interest rate increases, making this choice relatively unattractive.

Where government debt – and financing costs – already is high, as in Italy during the mid-1990s, governments are more reluctant to pay an interest rate premium. Furthermore, if existing debt is of relatively long maturities, or denominated mostly in local currency, governments have the option of restructuring debt. By issuing debt that is shorter-term and/or foreign currency–denominated, a government lowers its interest rate. There are limits to this strategy, however: governments are averse to very short maturities or to complete foreign currency denomination. Therefore, nations with already short debt maturities and high levels of foreign currency denomination – again, Italy in the mid-1990s fits this mold – will be more sensitive to interest rate increases.

These expectations reflect that governments are influenced not only by current domestic and international conditions but also by their own past behavior. Belgium's borrowing in the late 1980s, for instance, affected its responses to financial market developments in the mid- and late 1990s. Belgium's central government expended nearly 10% of GDP on interest payments in 1995, whereas most OECD nations spent less than 5%

of GDP.[60] Moreover, when governments rely extensively on international capital markets for funding – rather than on borrowing from captive domestic capital markets – financial market pressures are exacerbated.[61] At the same time, where governments perceive other items in the budget as necessary – where they see little fat to trim from the budget – they also will be less willing to pay the interest rate premium. This situation might characterize EU members at present; paying higher financing costs would entail either reducing other areas of spending or violating the EU's Stability and Growth Pact. Therefore, I expect Belgium – an EU member with high debt servicing costs – to be much less willing to pay an interest rate price than Australia or Canada. And more externally vulnerable emerging market economies are more likely to accede to financial market pressures. In emerging markets, international capital market pressures are more likely to override the effects of domestic institutions and ideology.

Summing Up: Expectations about Government Choices

Table 5.2 summarizes the expectations developed, again dividing the influences on government response into three categories. The key domestic factors may push governments in opposite directions, and they may vary in magnitude. Assessing the relative weight of each factor and the interactions among factors is a complex process. Using the expectations developed previously and summarized in Table 5.2, however, we can array governments according to the extent to which they should respond to changes in international financial market conditions. In nations characterized by high political sensitivity to changes in economic performance and high vulnerability to changes in debt servicing costs, governments should respond markedly and swiftly to increases in government bond prices. On the other hand, where sensitivity and vulnerability are low, governments are less likely to respond to an increase in bond prices.

If we consider the factors listed in Table 5.2, we find that few governments face pressures that push exclusively in the direction of resisting or acceding to financial market pressures. It is difficult to find cases – particularly among advanced capitalist democracies – of nations with single-party

---

[60] Tanzi and Schuknecht 2000.
[61] Maxfield 1997, Simmons 1999. Similarly, Leblang and Bernhard 2000 suggest that nations with current account deficits and high levels of economic openness are vulnerable to speculative currency attacks.

Table 5.2. *Expectations Regarding Determinants of Government Response*

Category of Influence	Influence	Potential Operationalization/ Measurement	Increase in Variable Should Be Associated with
Magnitude of Price	Benchmark interest rate on government bonds	Interest rate, premium over U.S. or Germany	More accession to financial market pressures
Sensitivity to Changes in Economic Performance	Clarity of government responsibility/blame attribution	Coalition size Party cohesion Federalism Veto points	More accession as clarity increases
	Security of government's tenure in office	Proximity of election Length of term in office	More accession when election nears or term is short
		Importance of coalition partners or other parties	More attention to other parties' policy preferences in coalition or minority government
	Insulation of individuals by public sector	Size of welfare state	Less accession
	Trade openness	Imports and exports/GDP	More accession
Vulnerability to a Change in Debt Servicing Costs	Accumulated debt	Debt/GDP level Interest payments/ GDP	More accession
	Debt maturity structure	Average time to maturity of public debt	Less accession

government, a highly centralized political system, high trade exposure, a widening current account deficit, high outstanding debt, and an approaching election. Brazil in the late 1990s, an open economy with fiscal problems and an election due in 1998, might be closest to fitting this picture. But Brazil's political system was both fragmented and decentralized, reducing political responsibility for economic outcomes. Nor are cases characterized by a high degree of federalism, a large number of coalition partners, a distant election, low trade exposure, a current account surplus, and a low level of outstanding debt easy to identify. Rather, most cases fall somewhere in the middle, albeit closer to one extreme or the other.

One means of assessing the expectations developed in Table 5.2 is a cross-sectional time series analysis. Table 5.2 predicts that government policy outcomes at time $t + 1$ will reflect, to some extent, the interaction between financial market pressures and various domestic institutional and economic conditions at time t. Once other determinants of monetary and fiscal policy are accounted for, the annual change in inflation or the government budget balance should reflect government bond rates, as well as the interaction between these rates and "sensitivity factors," and the interaction between these rates and "vulnerability" factors. For instance, an interaction term between the financial market penalty and trade openness should be associated with fiscal and monetary tightening, as this combination of factors renders governments more sensitive to market movements. Likewise, interest rate penalties should interact with the clarity of political responsibility, producing the strongest effects in single-party, federal governments.

In order to ensure methodological integrity, such statistical analyses require a long series of data (preferably monthly or quarterly, rather than annual) and require sophisticated measures of a variety of complex political factors. Additionally, given the degrees of freedom required by a model with many independent and interactive variables, the sample should comprise a relatively large number of nations. Assessing the domestic politics–global capital markets nexus in this fashion, and at this level of detail, is an important task, but one that I leave for another major research project. I elect, instead, to present in the following a set of cases that illustrate the utility for understanding national policy choices of the expectations developed.

Initial quantitative analyses, however, including data only for a set of 14 developed nations, spanning the early 1980s to mid-1990s, suggest that many of the preceding expectations are accurate. Inflation at time $t + 1$ is associated negatively with the interest rate spread at time t, positively with endogenous election timing and with the number of years until an election is necessary, and negatively with an interactive partisanship–interest rate spread interaction term (so that right-leaning governments are more responsive to financial market penalties).[62] Assessing the complete set of

---

[62] All reported relationships are significant at a 90% level of confidence or higher, using a cross-sectional time series model. The χ^2 statistic for this model is 152.35, and the model R^2 is 0.61. The total number of observations is 107. The model also includes inflation at time t as an independent variable, and this variable is associated positively and significantly with inflation at time $t + 1$.

independent and interactive variables found in Table 5.2, and doing so for a wide set of nations, for the entire 1990s decade, is a worthwhile future project.

Government Responses: Initial Evidence

The year 1994 was marked by volatility in the bond markets of many developed nations; this volatility was due to both push and pull factors and, in many cases, generated marked increases in government bond rates. National experiences in 1994 offer an opportunity for a first-cut analysis of the factors presented in Table 5.2; developed nations faced similar global market conditions yet were characterized by different domestic political institutions and pressures, as well as by different degrees of dependence on global markets. Moreover, the 1994 time period is fairly recent and, therefore, a time of extensive capital market openness; at the same time, however, it largely precedes EU members' efforts to qualify for the single currency, allowing us to compare among future EMU members, future EMU opt-outs, and non-EU nations.

In Table 5.3, I summarize the characteristics of five nations that experienced bond market volatility – and, particularly, increases in government bond rates – during 1994. Sweden faced large penalties in government bond markets, high vulnerability in the forms of rising and short-dated government debt, and a high clarity of political responsibility. Other factors served to mediate this susceptibility, including a recent election, insulation of individuals by welfare state policies, and only a moderate degree of trade openness. In the same year, we would expect Britain's high clarity of political responsibility to provide incentives for a rapid response to financial market pressures, but its low debt levels, small current account deficit, long maturity of existing government debt, and relatively low level of trade openness mediate against such a response. As a first cut, then, we can expect Britain to respond less dramatically than Sweden to similar turmoil in government bond markets in 1994.

Sweden: An Illustration

In order to illustrate the influence on government responses to market pressures of both internal and external pressures, I examine one of these cases, that of Sweden, in more detail. Among the cases listed in Table 5.3,

Sweden is the most likely case for financial market influence. In 1994, many other nations experienced bond market volatility, but market pressures on Sweden appear to have been tightly tied to economic policy concerns (pull factors). In other nations, the market pressures often were instead the result of global market conditions (push factors).[63] In Sweden, the clarity of political responsibility was high, and Sweden relied on its export sector to carry its economic recovery. At the same time, the minority Social Democratic government faced domestic pressures – in terms of public opinion and party competition – to retain many of its traditional policies. Therefore, Sweden should respond to external pressures with consolidation but do so in a way that is sensitive to traditional welfare state aims.

Background As a social democratic welfare state, Sweden traditionally had a high level of taxation, a high level of public goods provision, a high degree of labor union density, and an egalitarian income distribution. Central public policies included "full employment, a generous welfare state, and a tax regime supportive of production and redistribution."[64] The Social Democrats (SAP) dominated Swedish politics from 1932 to 1976, governing alone or in coalition throughout that period. Labor unions held a prominent position within the political system, and centralized collective bargaining was the rule. In 1976, the SAP's modern governing monopoly ended; from 1976 to 1982, several nonsocialist governments were in place.

In 1982, the Social Democrats returned to power, holding office until 1991. During this time, the party began to pursue a "third way," undertaking some market liberalization, devaluing the kroner by 16%, seeking EU membership, and concentrating on growth via the external sector.[65] This strategy served to improve economic performance in the early 1980s, but, by the late 1980s, Sweden again faced difficult economic conditions. The removal, in the early 1990s, of the remaining barriers to capital flows both freed and constrained the Swedish government, allowing it easier access to capital, but also subjecting it to externally determined interest rate and currency swings.[66]

---

[63] Borio and McCauley 1996.
[64] Huber and Stephens 1998, p. 356.
[65] Kitschelt 1999, Martin 2000.
[66] E.g., Huber and Stephens 1998.

Table 5.3. *Domestic Politics, Vulnerability, and Predicted Responses in 1994*

	Sweden	UK	Denmark	Australia	Ireland
Clarity of Political Responsibility	From Sept 1991: center-right coalition From Sept 1994: Social Democratic government; system fairly centralized at national level	From April 1992: Conservative government, with 60% of legislative seats; system strongly centralized	From Jan 1993: 4-party coalition led by Social Democrats From Sept 1994: 3-party coalition led by Soc Dems; system quasi-federal	From March 1993: single-party Labour government, 54% of lower house legislative seats; system decentralized, federal	From November 1992: coalition between Labour and Fianna Fail; system is strongly centralized
Security of Government's Tenure in Office	Proportional electoral system Next election in September 1998, but Social Democratic government a minority (46% of seats)	Majoritarian electoral system Next election due by May 1997; Conservative Party in beginning decline, Labour strengthening, but election distant	Proportional electoral system New government in minority (42% of seats), relying on two small left parties Government reshuffle in Dec. 1996; next election due by 1998	Majoritarian electoral system Next election due in 1996	Proportional electoral system Next election due in 1997; governing coalition: 60% of parliamentary seats
Insulation or Exposure: Trade Openness, Welfare State	Govt/GDP = 49% Trade/GDP = 69%	Govt/GDP = 42% Trade/GDP = 54%	Govt/GDP = 44% Trade/GDP = 66%	Govt/GDP = 27% Trade/GDP = 38%	Govt/GDP = 33% Trade/GDP = 126%
External Vulnerability	Debt = 81% GDP and rising Maturity = 2.9 years Current Account = 1.5% GDP	Debt = 54% GDP and falling Maturity = 6.8 years CA = −0.4% GDP	Debt = 77.5% GDP and falling Maturity = 3.6 years CA = 2.1% GDP	Debt = 43% GDP and stable Maturity = 4.8 years CA = −4.7% GDP	Debt = 92% GDP and falling; Maturity = 3.7 years CA = 2.9% GDP

Magnitude and Nature of Interest Rate Changes	Several monthly increases, including 71 BP in March, 109 BP in June, 101 BP in September Net calendar year increase of 87 basis points	Several monthly increases, including 42 BP in February, 64 BP in March, 40 BP in May; net calendar year increase of 18 basis points	Pronounced monthly increases in April (60 BP), June (93 BP), August (51 BP), and September (51 BP); net calendar year increase of 34 basis points	Pronounced monthly increases in February (69 BP), March (90 BP), June (84 BP), September (97 BP); net calendar year increase of 176 basis points	Monthly increases in February (60 BP), March (61BP), and May (82 BP); net calendar year increase of 47 basis points
Predicted Response to Market Pressures	High: most factors suggestive of market pressure salience	Moderate: high clarity of political responsibility, but some government security and low vulnerability	Moderate to high: relatively high clarity of responsibility, high exposure, but government security and history of reform	Moderate: high clarity of political responsibility; low to moderate vulnerability; moderate interest rate increase	Moderate to low: past history of reform, relatively secure government, but high clarity of responsibility; no strong left-wing alternative
Annual Changes in Macropolicy, 1994–1995	Attention to market pressures, including decline in fiscal deficit; but consolidation via expenditure cuts and tax increases	Worsening budget deficit (1.3% increase), rising debt and inflation	Slight fall in government share of economy (0.7%), debt (3.9%), budget deficit (0.2%), increase in tax revenue (1.1%); economic growth slowing	Slight increase in government share of economy (0.4%), as well as tax revenue (1.1%); modest debt increase (0.7%), but deficit fall (by 2.1%)	Decline in government share of economy and taxation (both 2%); significant drop in debt (6.6%), slight increase in deficit (0.3%); economic growth improved

In 1991, the SAP's electoral strength reached its nadir; as the governing party in a time of rising unemployment and falling output, the SAP received only 38% of the vote share. That year, a four-party coalition among the Moderates, the Christian Democrats, the Center Party, and the Liberals came into power. The coalition, a minority government holding 170 of 349 parliamentary seats and led by Prime Minister Carl Bildt, pursued a policy platform that stood in marked contrast to traditional social democratic programs. The government – largely with the cooperation of the opposition SAP – attempted to communicate to international markets its commitment to fiscal discipline and the credibility of the kroner's peg to the ECU.[67] The coalition called for the reduction of public expenditures, economic deregulation, tax reforms, and the partial privatization of social services and education. In pursuit of these goals, the government enacted a series of tax and expenditure cuts, particularly in established welfare entitlements. From 1980 to 1994, the size of the public sector labor force declined by 12%, and the funding of public health care was shifted partly to employee-paid payroll taxes.[68]

Various economic pressures, the most important of which were inflation[69] (which exceeded 10% in 1990) and a pronounced economic recession, appeared to necessitate some of the Bildt reforms. As falling growth and rising unemployment cut revenues and increased expenditures, the Swedish government had gone, in a matter of four years, from having the largest government budget surplus among OECD nations to having the largest deficit. Despite the apparent economic need for policy change, the governing coalition's popularity suffered as its term progressed. Many Swedish voters, who had favored *some* trimming of welfare state provisions, appeared to believe that the coalition had gone too far in its market reforms. Public opinion polls in 1992 indicated "overwhelming support" for social spending.[70] Stagnating economic growth (per capita GNP growth contractions of more than 2% in 1992 and 1993) as well as continued high unemployment further served to reduce the government's popularity. Moreover, the Swedish kroner fell victim to the September 1992 ERM crisis, and domestic banking crises emerged, further damaging the Bildt government's standing.

---

[67] Iversen 2000.
[68] Clayton and Pontusson 1998, Kurzer 1993.
[69] Iversen 2000.
[70] Pierson 1996, p. 172.

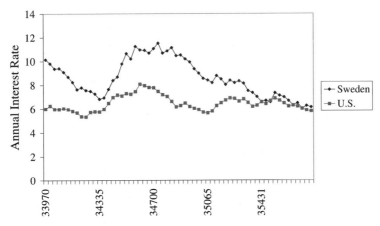

Figure 5.1 Swedish government bond rates, 1994–1997.

Further, as the recession of the early 1990s progressed, Sweden's fiscal position deteriorated: even without the expansion of entitlements, expenditures rose. Many traditional job training and creation programs became too expensive, prompting the government to attempt to narrow their scope.[71] Deficit financing became the norm, as the government budget deficit/GDP ratio climbed to 16% in 1993 and 13.1% in 1994.[72] As the deficit climbed, so did Sweden's level of outstanding public debt. In July 1994 Prime Minister Bildt warned that, if the government was to stabilize its debt/GDP ratio by 1998, as planned, it would have to intensify its efforts at fiscal consolidation.

Financial Market Pressures and External Vulnerability   Sweden's deteriorating fiscal position, as well as the approaching election in September 1994, led to rising government bond rates throughout the year. Government bond markets throughout the developed world were characterized by large swings in 1994, but the movements in Sweden were among the largest and most negative. Figure 5.1 displays the monthly interest rate on Swedish benchmark government bonds, as well as the comparable rate for the United States. The Swedish rate began to increase sharply in 1994, remaining several points above the U.S. rate until mid-1996. In several months during 1994, Swedish bonds experienced relatively dramatic changes in interest rates, including increases of 71 basis points (0.71%) in March, 109 basis

[71] Olsen 1999.
[72] World Bank, World Development Indicators, 2000.

points in June, and 101 basis points in September. For the 1994 calendar year, the net increase in interest rates was 87 basis points; for a government with a large and growing level of public debt, such an increase put additional pressure on fiscal policy.

Market participants tended to cite concerns about Sweden's fiscal position during this period, making clear that the path to lower interest rates was via fiscal tightening. In late June, Skandia Group Insurance AB, a major resident bondholder, announced that it had sold its portfolio of Swedish debt, "pending government proof that it is able and willing to reduce the budget deficit."[73] The Social Democrats, as members of the official opposition, responded by demanding that the ruling coalition convene its financial committee during the government recess. Days later, however, an auction of Swedish government bonds was oversubscribed, suggesting to some that financial markets *had* recognized the Bildt government's efforts at fiscal reform. Other observers, particularly on the left, argued that the successful auction was due to the high interest rates available rather than to market confidence.

Although such financial market pressures could influence a wide range of governments, these pressures were more salient in Sweden because of the country's reliance on exports and its high and rising debt level. The average effective maturity of Sweden's government debt stood at 2.9 years in 1994 (compared with 6.8 years in the United Kingdom), creating a need to refinance debt with some regularity.[74] The welfare state that, in the past, had served to insulate Swedish citizens from the volatility of international markets,[75] had grown to rely on these markets for its existence, particularly when public revenues declined. Moreover, Sweden's openness to trade stood at 69% of GDP in 1994. Although this level of imports and exports is considerably less than that of many European nations (for instance, Ireland), it may have been quite salient for the Swedish government, as the export sector was the main engine of economic recovery.[76] Finally, the impact of high interest rates on economic growth was already evident in 1994: the forecast for growth for 1995 was cut in half because of the impact of high interest rates on new spending and investment.

---

[73] AFP-Extel News, July 1, 1994.

[74] Debt figures are from Missale 1999. Also see the discussion in Chapter 6.

[75] E.g., Rodrik 1997.

[76] Pierson 1996 notes, however, that Sweden has not been characterized by clashes between internationally oriented private sector workers and domestically oriented public sector workers.

In this context of financial market unease and external vulnerability, elections were held in September 1994. In the run-up to the election, financial markets were again unsettled, possibly because they worried that a Social Democratic government would lack the wherewithal to implement fiscal rectitude and stabilize public debt.[77] Financial markets also were upset, in the days immediately preceding the election, by opinion polls suggesting that support for the Left and Green Parties had increased. This raised the specter of a minority government and sent yields on five-year government bonds to just over 11%.

At least in part to counter these market fears, the Social Democrats announced in late August that, if elected, they would retain the budgetary cutbacks introduced by the Bildt government. According to their public statements, rising public debt left them little choice but to accept large parts of the government's economic policy; as the election approached, stabilization of the public debt by 1998 was something on which all major political parties agreed.[78] The domestic political issue, then, became the means to achieve fiscal consolidation and debt stabilization – via spending cuts, revenue increases, or some combination of the two. At a more microlevel, spending cuts themselves were an issue for domestic politics and institutions, as different parties favored cuts in varying areas and programs.

Domestic Political Factors   On September 18, the SAP won 45% of the vote, with an additional 6% going to the Left and 5% going to the Greens. Rather than form an official coalition with any one or two parties, the SAP decided to form a minority government, stating that it preferred to rely on various parties for support of different parts of its program. As a single-party government, holding 46% of parliamentary seats in a unicameral legislature and centralized system,[79] the SAP government had clear political responsibility. At the same time, however, it had to rely on other parties for legislative support, and the existence of parties to its left likely served to prevent it from moving too far to the right, even when it desired fiscal consolidation.

The election outcome – not only the swing back toward the Social Democrats but also the increase in vote shares to other left parties – evidenced the extent to which the government was constrained by domestic

---

[77] *Financial Times*, September 14, 1994, p. 8.

[78] *Financial Times*, August 20, 1994, p. 12.

[79] Although the Swedish system is unitary rather than federal, the provision of many welfare services is made at the local level.

public opinion. One observer concluded that the election demonstrated that Swedish voters "are simply prepared to pay higher taxes for better services."[80] Similarly, the ratings agency IBCA (now Fitch-IBCA) wryly noted that, on the basis of a campaign platform that featured tax increases, the Social Democratic victory was "one of the very rare instances of a political party gaining popularity on the basis of promises to [raise] state revenues."[81]

Indeed, in its presentation of fiscal plans before and after the election, the Social Democrats, led by Prime Minister Ingvar Carlsson, offered a combination of tax increases and spending cuts. Although the government was determined to cut the overall budget deficit, thereby getting right an important macroindicator, it also was sensitive to a large domestic constituency that opposed radical reform. In their August proposed budget plan, for instance, the SAP vowed to cut expenditure by SKr33.6 billion and to increase revenues by SKr27.4 billion, via an increase in the marginal income tax from 50% to 55%, a restoration of taxes on dividends, and higher capital and wealth taxes. (Interestingly, marginal rates of corporate taxation were and remained low, at 28%.) The Bildt government's proposed program, on the other hand, included only SKr15 billion in new tax revenues, relying mostly on cuts in transfer payments and other forms of public consumption.

The Outcome After its election victory, the SAP announced an "austerity budget" calling not only for further reductions in several types of public expenditures, but also for an increase in taxes as well as a restoration of the previous government's cuts to unemployment and sickness benefits. As part of its longer-term plan, covering the new government's four-year term, Carlsson asked every government department and state authority to cut spending by 20%. The longer-term plan, however, also contained a major role for tax increases. The business and financial communities, both inside and outside Sweden, did not view this route to deficit reduction in the most favorable light. Industry and business leaders were quick to criticize the new government for not focusing more on expenditure cuts; immediately after the election, yields on 10-year government bonds rose by a quarter of a percentage point. Moreover, at the end of October, Moody's Investor Service placed Sweden's foreign currency–denominated sovereign debt rating on

---

[80] Agence France Press, September 19, 1994. Also see Swank 2001, 2002.
[81] IBCA, Sweden: Country Report, March 1996, p. 9.

review, indicating that it might downgrade Sweden. (In the same month, however, Standard and Poor's affirmed its AA rating of Sweden.)[82]

During its first months in office, the new Social Democratic government maintained its pledge to achieve fiscal consolidation, but – if at all possible – to do so in a way that used spending cuts *and* revenue increases. In January 1995, the official budget for the 18 months ending in December 1996 included an additional SKr21.7 billion in spending cuts, as well as an SKr42 billion package aimed at reducing unemployment. The government predicted that the budget deficit would fall below 7% of GDP in 1996 and that debt would be stabilized by 1997. In addition to announcing such plans, the Social Democrats also led a campaign for EU membership, urging voters to choose accession in the November 1994 referendum.

International capital markets remained skeptical of the government's plans, occasionally sending government bond rates higher. The markets welcomed Sweden's positive vote on EU accession. The January 1995 budget statement, however, was received coolly in financial markets.[83] In the same month, Moody's followed through on its rating review, downgrading Swedish foreign currency debt from Aa2 to Aa3. Interest rates on Swedish government bonds spiked upward again in March 1995; Figure 5.1 shows that rates remained high until late 1995.

In the later months of 1995, however, it became evident that the Social Democratic plans, as well as the nascent economic recovery, were allowing for fiscal consolidation. The government budget deficit fell to 7.3% of GDP in 1995, and growth improved to 3.6%. General government debt, as measured by the IMF, fell from 79% of GNP in 1994 to 78.2% of GNP in 1995 and, eventually, to 75.1% of GNP in 1997. There was a virtuous circle quality to this outcome: as fiscal consolidation continued, interest rates fell, and, as interest rates fell, fiscal consolidation became easier to achieve. The export sector continued to do well, helping to account for a current account surplus of 4.5% of GDP in 1995. Inflation also fell in the mid-1990s, reaching 2.5% in 1995 and less than 1% in 1996.

At the same time, the overall share of government in the economy fell from a high of 71% in 1993 to 65.4% in 1995 and 64.3% in 1996. This fall is attributable, at least in part, to improving economic conditions: as unemployment fell, fewer individuals turned to automatic stabilizer programs. The reduction also represents some changes in spending policy, including

[82] *Financial Times*, October 3, 1994, p. 10.
[83] *Financial Times*, December 19, 1994, p. 9; January 11, 1995.

that of the Ministry of Health and Social Affairs. Similarly, government revenue, which had fallen from 52.8% of GDP in 1991 to 49.8% of GDP in 1994, grew steadily to 54.2% in 1996. Again, this reflects not only the government's focus on revenue-side fiscal measures, but also an improving economy. In 1995, Swedish government expenditure on subsidies and transfers was 35.7% of GDP, compared with 30.4% of GDP in 1980, and with a small-country OECD average of 25.3%.[84] In many areas, government intervention was trimmed, but modestly; for instance, public health care spending was 7.9% of GDP in 1990, 7.4% in 1994, and 7.2% in 1996 and 1997.[85]

Later in its term, the Social Democratic government began to suggest that some of the earlier cuts might be reversed to some degree. Indeed, as fiscal deficits declined, the government gained more room to fund new spending programs, seeking to reduce unemployment and to maintain welfare state provisions. For instance, prior to 1993, the rate of replacement of income under UI (the income-related unemployment insurance program) was 90% of daily income. The Bildt government cut this rate to 80% in July 1993, and the Carlsson government cut it to 75% in January 1996. Later that year, however, Göran Persson, who assumed the office of prime minister in March, suggested that he wanted to return the replacement rate to 80%. Predictably, financial markets reacted negatively the next day, but the government maintained the promise regarding UI, including it in the April 1997 budget.

By the end of 1995, financial markets appeared to have taken note of aggregate fiscal changes in Sweden. Although some observers, such as the IMF, expressed a continued preference for spending cuts over revenue increases, market reaction was generally favorable. Interest rates on benchmark government bonds stood at 8.6%, similar to the level seen in early 1994, and with a smaller spread over U.S. interest rates. In the following years, government bond rates continued their downward trend.

Causes of the Outcome What does the Swedish case demonstrate about the interplay between external financial market pressures and domestic political pressures? Of the cases described in Table 5.3, Sweden is the country that we might expect to react most strongly to financial market pressures. With single-party, minority government (albeit a recently elected one),

---

[84] Tanzi and Schuknecht 2000.
[85] World Bank, World Development Indicators 2000.

high and growing debt, a fragile economy, and large interest rate risk premia, Sweden appears a prime candidate for accession to financial market pressures. And, to some extent, this accession occurred under the Social Democrats. Fiscal deficits fell dramatically, and public debt was stabilized. In some areas, such as pensions and sickness benefits, welfare state policies were trimmed, albeit not eliminated,[86] and, when making these cuts in the early 1990s, the government simultaneously increased outlays for active labor market policies.[87] In sum, Sweden's economic policy in the mid-1990s focused more on cutting the costs of programs and expanding state revenue than on eliminating entire programs or reorienting the general degree of welfare statism.[88]

This pattern is consistent not only with a strong but narrow view of financial market influences, but also with a view that emphasizes the interaction of domestic politics with international market pressures. In Sweden, domestic ideology and public opinion, as well as electoral competition, were particularly salient; they impacted strongly the nature of fiscal consolidation. Specifically, the presence of left-leaning alternatives to the Social Democrats created incentives for the ruling party to moderate its response to financial market pressures. In the 1994 (and 1998) election, voters expressed their dissatisfaction with the degree of fiscal consolidation and the level of unemployment, defecting from the Social Democratic to the Left Party. This exemplifies a dilemma faced by many contemporary social democratic parties – although they may get pushed into the opposition because of their aversion to neoliberal economic policies (in Sweden, from 1991 to 1994), they also may be punished by their traditional constituents for embracing such policies while in power.[89] Even in an age of global capital markets, ideology can be an important determinant of government policies,[90] particularly when electoral competition is high.

In fact, although Persson expressed the desire to build a self-financing welfare state, so that "no Swedish finance minister will ever again have

---

[86] Also see Iversen 2000.

[87] Huber and Stephens 1998, Swank 2002.

[88] For a debate regarding the extent to which welfare state reform in Sweden involves "programmatic" versus "systemic" retrenchment, see Clayton and Pontusson 1998, Moses 2001, Pierson 1994, 1996, Stephens et al. 1999.

[89] Iversen 2000, Kitschelt 1999. On the electoral punishment of reformist governments in developing nations, see Friedman 2000.

[90] Perotti and Kontopolous 1998.

to travel to New York and London to explain himself to leering twenty-five year old market brokers,"[91] the Social Democrats' strategy was one aimed at balancing global market and domestic pressures. In the run-up to the 1998 election, and facing its lowest level of approval for decades, the government focused on the domestic side of the equation. It presented a 1998 budget that included increased financing for a variety of social services and educational programs.[92] Ultimately, this proposal was not enough to prevent continued voter defections to other left parties, but it serves to demonstrate the importance of domestic politics to the impact of financial market pressures.

The examination of the Swedish case also resonates with a larger debate regarding the importance of external and internal factors to changes in social democracies. Some posit that changes in Swedish policies are due in large part to economic globalization, on either the trade or the financial side.[93] Others locate the problem in domestic economic and political conditions,[94] including economic policymaking mistakes,[95] while acknowledging the tendency of political leaders to invoke global market forces as a justification. Notermans, for instance, maintains that many of the changes in Sweden resulted from the domestic imperative to contain inflationary pressures. In his account, the abandonment in Europe in the late 1980s and early 1990s of some traditional social democratic policies is correlated with, but not caused by, financial internationalization.[96]

We also could point to the role of the EU and the Maastricht convergence criteria (a more distant influence for Sweden)[97] or to demographic pressures on welfare state policies. The number of people in Sweden aged 65 and older more than doubled between 1950 and 1999, and Sweden has the largest proportion of over-65 individuals in the world.[98] As in many advanced industrial democracies, this creates pressures for pension system

---

[91] Cited in Thompson 1997, p. 107.

[92] Olsen 1999.

[93] E.g., Olsen 1999, Moses 1994.

[94] Esping-Andersen 1996, Swank 2002, Weiss 1998.

[95] Huber and Stephens 1998.

[96] Notermans 2000.

[97] For instance, Gilibert 1994 argues that variation in national responses to the ERM crisis was driven by variation in the degree of political commitment to EMU. France and Italy were highly committed, whereas the United Kingdom was not. As a result, Italy maintained fiscal restraint after the crisis, while Britain embarked on a more expansive macroeconomic program.

[98] Olsen 1999.

reform and, more broadly, for fiscal consolidation. Moreover, one also could argue that the Swedish welfare state – and many other European welfare states – had reached its natural limits: by the late 1980s, further growth was impossible, and some retrenchment likely was unavoidable. The political choice in Sweden was between a defense and a rollback of welfare state policies, and this was to be expected.[99] In the end, Swedish policy decisions likely result from a combination of these factors; to forget the role of domestic institutions, interests, and ideologies in mediating the response to financial market pressures would be to omit one side of the coin.

At present, Sweden appears to have transformed itself into a strong economy, with higher growth than most euro-currency area nations and relatively low unemployment. Although the government recently has embraced entrepreneurship and some deregulation, it continues to finance health care, education, and many social services. Sweden has addressed pressures on the welfare state by trimming and modifying existing programs, rather than by making fundamental changes to its universalistic welfare state principles.[100] Sweden also has consolidated its fiscal position, eliminating the large budget deficits of the early 1990s. In 2001, Sweden succeeded in keeping central government expenditure below the ceiling set by the Riksdag (parliament); the government ended the year with a surplus equivalent to 4.8% of GDP. This surplus was cosiderably larger than the Riksdag target of 2.5% of GDP. For 2002, the Swedish government anticipated another budget surplus but also planned to increase expenditures for education, job creation, health care, and the elderly.[101] To some observers, then, Sweden is evidence that multiple models of capitalism can flourish[102] – or that governments have room for policy maneuver (and for attention to domestic politics and institutions) once their aggregate fiscal and monetary houses are in order.[103]

Other Cases

In the other nations that experienced significant bouts of bond market volatility in 1994, the link among financial market pressures, domestic politics and institutions, and macroeconomic outcomes is less evident. In none of the other four countries was the decline in the budget deficit, nor the

---

[99] Stephens et al. 1999.
[100] Pierson 1996.
[101] Government of Sweden 2001.
[102] *New York Times*, October 8, 1999, p. A4.
[103] Kitschelt et al. 1999.

overall degree of fiscal consolidation, as pronounced as it was in Sweden. Of course, the highest of these countries' deficits in 1994 was 6.9%, in Britain, so there was less need for consolidation. In all but Ireland, deficits fell modestly the following year; in Ireland, the deficit increased incrementally.

United Kingdom   For internal as well as external reasons, the British government did not respond markedly, if at all, to bond market activity in 1994. Despite monthly increases in government bond rates in February, March, and May, the United Kingdom experienced a relatively small net increase in rates in 1994, amounting to 18 basis points. And because of the United Kingdom's relatively long debt maturity and relatively low level of public debt, the government found itself more insulated from shorter-term changes in bond market volatility. With few refundings to finance,[104] it was better able to avoid placing bonds on the market when market conditions were negative. Domestically, the Conservative government was clearly responsible for economic outcomes, given centralization and single-party governance. At the same time, the Conservatives were – despite an election three years away – facing a loss of support to the Labour Party.

Most analysts at the time attributed bond market volatility to overall market conditions rather than to poor British policies.[105] Accordingly, there was little economic policy change in response to increases in interest rates. As economic growth slowed and automatic stabilizers began to operate, both the debt and the government budget deficit rose – the opposite pattern we might expect from a government that was highly sensitive to financial market pressures. More generally, despite the image of welfare state cutbacks that persisted while the British Conservatives were in office, and despite earlier financial market pressures, Pierson makes a solid case that, in the mid-1990s, the British welfare state, "if battered, remains intact."[106] Although public expenditure fell for much of the 1980s, by 1996 total public spending was just 2% of GDP below its peak (in 1983).[107]

Denmark   The annual increase in government bond rates in Denmark in 1994 was approximately twice that of the increase in the United Kingdom. In several months, particularly in the run-up to the September election,

[104] *Financial Times*, July 21, 1994, p. 22.

[105] *Times of London*, March 3, 1994, p. 12.

[106] Pierson 1994, 1996, points out that overall social expenditure remains about the same, despite cuts in public housing and pension programs.

[107] Tanzi and Schuknecht 2000.

Danish bond rates increased by substantial amounts. At the same time, the clarity of political responsibility was lower in Denmark, which – as a result of its proportional electoral system and low threshold for parliamentary representation – was governed by either a three- or a four-party coalition during 1994. Moreover, the Danish system is quasi-federal, so that governments at several levels are responsible for economic outcomes. With such low clarity, we might expect the Danish government to resist financial market pressures. On the other hand, individuals in Denmark were less insulated (compared to those in Sweden) from international pressures, as the welfare system lacked an active labor market policy.

In the first nine months of 1994, the government faced an upcoming election, with attendant pressures to ensure good economic performance. As the election approached, the Socialist People's Party, a left-wing member of the coalition, pressured the other governing parties to slow the pace of neoliberal economic consolidation. The Social Democratic finance minister, however, vowed to resist these pressures.[108] As in Ireland, Denmark had pursued fiscal consolidation since the 1980s; this consolidation aimed at moving toward budget balance and at signaling a commitment to monetary policy discipline.[109] As a further means of reassuring financial markets in light of the September election, the government moved forward the publication of its 1995 draft budget, which included reduced expenditure and increased revenue.

Denmark's public debt continued to decline in 1994, reaching 77.5% of GDP; whereas the effective time to maturity of its government debt was low, at 3.2 years, the maturity had begun to rise, climbing to 3.6 years in 1995. Denmark also had a current account surplus. Overall, then, we would expect outcomes in Denmark to reflect an attention to market pressures, albeit in a less pronounced fashion than in Sweden. And in fact, from 1994 to 1995, the Danish budget deficit and the total size of the public sector fell slightly and tax revenue increased. The Danish Social Democrats, however, bore electoral costs for their public sector tightening, losing votes in the 1994 election despite favorable economic performance.[110] Moreover, in 1995 and beyond, we would expect greater responsiveness to domestic demands for a slowdown in reform, as the minority government – a less secure government, albeit the norm in Denmark – attempted to retain control.

---

[108] *Financial Times*, August 27, 1994, p. 4.
[109] Iversen 1999, 2000.
[110] Kitschelt 1999. Here, retrospective economic voting appears to have been outweighed by concerns with public sector policies.

Ireland The increase in Ireland's government budget deficit from 1994 to 1995 did not obscure Ireland's continued progress in fiscal consolidation – progress stemming not from the market pressures of 1994, but from the government's decision in 1987 to undertake a dramatic program of fiscal consolidation.[111] After several years of large fiscal deficits, Ireland's public debt peaked at 120% in 1987. In order to reduce the debt and address its sources, the fiscal consolidation program included various reductions in government expenditure and a base broadening in the taxation system. These efforts successfully lowered fiscal deficits and public debt and contributed to the economic boom in Ireland in the 1990s.

As it faced increases in government financing costs in 1994, the Irish government did so from a relatively strong domestic position, holding 60% of parliamentary seats, with an election due in three years. In addition, there was no substantial challenge to its economic policies from left-of-center parties. Ireland's level of trade openness was among the highest in Europe, and its public sector was relatively small, suggesting high exposure to international economic pressures. At the same time, however, it had already made progress in its macrofundamentals, with falling debt, a current account surplus, and a lengthening (albeit still relatively low) time to maturity of government debt. In the wake of bond market volatility in Ireland in early 1994, there were declines in the overall share of government in the economy, as well as in taxation, and another significant decline in debt. These actions were consistent with fiscal consolidation, but they were part of a long-running consolidation effort, rather than a reaction to the particular pressures of 1994. In the months that followed the bond market volatility of 1994, Moody's upgrading of Ireland's foreign debt rating (Aa2) reflected financial markets' further recognition of Ireland's continued consolidation.[112]

Australia The 1994 bond market volatility also impacted Australia, with a substantial increase in government bond rates over the course of the year. After the yield on the benchmark 10-year government bond reached a 20-year low in late January, increases in bond rates were most pronounced in February, March, June, and September. The government that faced these increases was a single-party Labour government, elected in March 1993 with 54% of lower house legislative seats. The government, however,

[111] Tanzi and Schuknecht 2000.
[112] *Financial Times*, September 12, 1994, p. 13.

lacked an outright majority in the Senate, leaving it dependent on the Green Party and the Australia Democrats to pass legislation in the upper house. In 1993, these smaller left-leaning parties had expressed opposition to the tax proposals contained in that year's budget, calling for more progressive taxation. The clarity of political responsibility was diminished as well by Australia's federal political system. And, although the Labour Party's popularity dipped in mid-1994 (the party ultimately would suffer a crushing defeat in the 1996 election), its standing in public opinion polls was again high by September 1994. Given the clarity of political responsibility and the security in office of the Australian government, as well as its traditional orientation toward liberal or means-tested welfare policies, we can expect an intermediate response to financial market pressures.

In the area of vulnerability to external capital market pressures, Australian governments had pursued a moderate program of fiscal consolidation since the early 1990s,[113] eventually achieving a budget surplus in 1998. Inflation averaged 8% per annum during the 1980s but had fallen to less than 2% in 1994. Public debt was relatively low, at 43% of GDP, and stable. The average effective maturity of this debt was 4.8 years, less than that of the United Kingdom but more than that of other nations in Table 5.3. Additionally, the Australian economy was somewhat insulated from international developments, with a low openness to trade. Moreover, as a nonmember of the EU, Australia did not experience nascent Maastricht Treaty–based pressures. On the other hand, the country had a relatively large current account deficit (4.7% of GDP), increasing its reliance on attracting capital from abroad. Again, these factors suggest a moderate responsiveness to financial market pressures.

In terms of policy outcomes, the 1994–1995 budget, unveiled in May 1994, did not contain particularly expansionary measures, but it also did not include a dramatic reduction in the deficit. Rather, it contained a higher-than-expected budget deficit, driven in part by the creation of a new jobs program aimed at cutting double-digit unemployment. The government claimed that this program would be paid for mostly via accelerating growth, so that the overall macrolevel fiscal outcome would remain unaffected. In October 1994, the Reserve Bank of Australia raised interest rates to counter inflationary pressures stemming from the economic recovery; this move, the second increase in two months, was met with a decline in government bond rates. At the same time, however, financial market participants continued

---

[113] Tanzi and Schuknecht 2000.

to press the Australian government for further deficit reduction.[114] In fact, from 1994 to 1995, the government budget/GDP ratio fell, suggesting continued consolidation and attention – at least at the most macrolevel – to financial market pressures. The Australian outcome, then, appears to reflect some attention to financial market pressures, albeit within the constraints of domestic ideology and accountability.

Responses to Financial Market Pressures

The preceding episodes, particularly the case of Sweden, suggest that government responses to financial market pressures in advanced industrial democracies are driven by both internal and external factors. Where electoral competition renders governments susceptible to criticism in terms of cutting traditional welfare state policies, and where individuals are insulated from global capital market effects, financial market pressures will influence policy choices less strongly. On the other hand, where governments are economically vulnerable and clearly responsible for economic performance, financial markets will exert stronger influence. And despite the constraints on overall fiscal and monetary policy stemming from financial internationalization, the fact remains that "societies still have political choices regarding the types of welfare states they want to maintain."[115] This conclusion is not necessarily limited to developed democracies. For instance, in an examination of social security reform in a broad array of developing nations, Brooks finds cross-national divergence in outcomes (in the extent to which pension systems are more market- or collectively oriented) that is due not only to variance in external constraints, but also to variance in domestic political factors.[116]

While illustrating the role of domestic factors in response to external pressure, the cases of 1994 bond market volatility also demonstrate the methodological difficulties associated with tracing the impact of financial market pressures on national governments. As Table 5.1 exemplifies, in many cases, governments have independent reasons – their own ideology or domestic economic difficulties – for pursuing fiscal and monetary consolidation. It is not always clear whether a government should be placed in Quadrant II or in Quadrant IV of Table 5.1. When governments, as

[114] *Financial Times*, October 25, 1994, p. 23.
[115] Stephens et al. 1999, p. 193.
[116] Brooks 2002.

in Ireland, embark on programs of fiscal consolidation, we assume that financial market pressures influence these choices, but it is difficult to weigh the impact of these pressures versus that of other types of influences. Additionally, Weyland notes that, in the late 1980s and early 1990s, several Latin American governments implemented economic reform programs in part for domestic reasons, using "foreign pressures as an excuse to advance market-oriented ideas they had long espoused." In Latin America, the programs implemented sometimes were tougher and more wide-ranging than those demanded by international financial institutions; where citizens faced dire economic prospects, they were willing to support drastic adjustment measures.[117] Fiscal and monetary policy outcomes are driven by a variety of domestic and international causes, and disentangling these causes is an empirical challenge.

Moreover, it may be analytically inaccurate to treat ideology and external market forces as two independently operating influences. Rather, external market forces may influence ideology (as well as the electoral fortunes of certain parties) at time t, which in turn would influence the nature of policy responses at time t + 1. Here, ideological and institutional factors are the proximate determinants of government behavior, but market forces also indirectly influence behavior. Economic internationalization in the 1980s and early 1990s may prompt the domestic spread of neoliberal ideology,[118] at both the individual and political party levels, and ideology may then affect government policy choices.

Where a government that was elected on a left-of-center platform proposes or implements neoliberal economic policies, a stronger case for the role of external pressures can be made. On the other hand, where a government is in a strong position vis-à-vis financial markets (with low debt, a current account surplus, and good rates of growth), the adoption of neoliberal policies is more likely to signal the independent impact of ideology.[119] Therefore, to the extent that Swedish Social Democrats undertook market reforms of traditional welfare state policies, or to the extent that Hungary's socialist-dominated coalition implemented an austerity program in the mid-1990s, we can conclude that external pressures were highly salient. More generally, we face the challenge of identifying the motives behind

---

[117] Weyland 1996, pp. 186–190. This contrasts with Stokes, who portrays international financial actors and domestic groups as at odds with one another.

[118] Stephens et al. 1999.

[119] Mahon 1996. As noted, Britain in the 1980s and early 1990s demonstrates the role of domestic ideology.

government policy choices – a task that is difficult to complete even via interviews of policymakers.

Furthermore, responses to interest rate changes probably are not the only cases of "government response to market pressures." When market pressures occur in the form of interest rate changes, it is possible to gauge the effects of market pressures. On the other hand, when market pressures occur in the form of threats of interest rate changes, their impact is much more difficult to gauge. The case of France in 1981 clearly is one of "market punishment then policy change," but if other governments learn from these changes, and therefore either avoid certain policies or change certain policies, we will not observe the pattern of "market reaction then government response." Rather, as governments preemptively change either their preferences over strategies or their utility functions, they will avoid certain types of behavior.

Government Policy Choices beyond the Overall Trade-offs: Accession and Compensation

This chapter reinforces an argument made in Chapters 2 and 3: even where governments make the political decision to accede to financial market pressures, they have secondary choices regarding how to achieve monetary and fiscal discipline. Financial market participants desire low inflation and low deficits, but there are many ways of achieving lower deficits. Likewise, there is more than one means of attaining low inflation – governments might employ the free market path (with no minimum wages and no wage bargaining) or the managed path. Provided governments achieve the desired outcomes, in OECD nations, market actors often do not worry about which means is employed.

For instance, the case of Sweden reminds us that a government that wants to reduce its budget deficit, thereby pleasing financial markets, can pursue one of several paths. It can reorient the welfare state entirely, moving from universalistic to residualist policies. Instead, it can retain an array of welfare state policies but place stricter limits on these policies. And once a government elects to cut spending, it must decide what to cut – a classic comparative politics question of "who wins, who loses, and who gets compensated?" Alternatively, rather than cutting spending, governments can maintain a given level of expenditure but increase revenue via tax base broadening or tax rate increases, as several OECD governments did during the 1990s.[120] Even if a government decides to increase tax revenue, there is some latitude regarding what sorts of taxes to employ – corporate versus individual or direct versus indirect. The domestic dimension of this process was illustrated graphically in the run-up to EMU. Although all EU governments were attempting to meet the same deficit criterion, they employed different measures. In 1997, France, which wanted both to qualify for EMU and to ameliorate high unemployment, imposed some increases in corporate taxation.[121] These increases were used to fund job creation programs. Because France's growth improved later that year, the new taxes were sufficient to fund these programs and to allow France to meet the Maastricht deficit goal. Italy also used taxation as one part of its plan to qualify for EMU, imposing a one-time "Euro tax" on its citizens.

Capital market openness, therefore, in no way eliminates domestic distributive politics or the potential for distributive conflict. And, in emerging market nations, capital market openness can exacerbate distributional pressures. Kingstone notes that when foreign capital entered Brazil in the early and mid-1990s, it allowed for renewed growth and larger public sector deficits. Governments used many of the proceeds from foreign inflows to purchase support from key domestic groups via social policies.[122] Later in the decade, when international financial markets became anxious regarding Brazil's fiscal position, the Brazilian government had to decide which domestic groups should bear the costs of adjustment. In general, these costs fell to the least advantaged members of society,[123] creating the potential for a backlash against austerity and financial openness. In a nation with a different welfare state tradition or different political institutions, these costs may well have been parsed out in a different fashion.

Finally, when we consider the impact of domestic politics on national responses to external pressures, we are reminded that the constraints faced by government at time t reflect the government's policy choices at time t − 1. This applies not just to existing levels of debt or debt maturity, but also to the degree of capital market openness and to the exchange rate regime. As I discuss in Chapters 1 and 8, the exchange rate regime – fixed, flexible, or some intermediate arrangement – influences the capacity

[120] Swank 2001.
[121] *New York Times*, July 22, 1997, p. A5; *Financial Times*, August 18, 1997 p. 1.
[122] Kingstone 1999.
[123] *New York Times*, February 5, 1998, p. A1.

for monetary and fiscal expansion.[124] A government that finds itself subjected to capital or exchange market pressures may accede to the pressures, resist the pressures, or redefine the nature of its relationship with international markets. In this chapter, I focus on the two former choices, taking the latter as given. In the longer term, however, governments also have choices regarding how to structure their relationships with international capital markets. These choices reflect not only technological influences but also earlier domestic political decisions.[125] For this reason, there remain significant cross-national differences in the degree and form of integration into the global economy.[126] It is to the range of such differences, and their impact on financial market–government relations, that I turn in the next chapter.

[124] Also see Notermans 2000.
[125] Friedman 2000, Kitschelt et al. 1999, Sinclair and Thomas 2001.
[126] Garrett 2000b.

6

Alternative Domestic Responses

CHANGES TO FINANCIAL
MARKET–GOVERNMENT
RELATIONS

Soros and those like him have opportunities because the government allows
them those opportunities.[1]

How do governments' institutional choices affect the operation of financial
market pressures? In the previous chapter, I consider some of the means by
which domestic political institutions affect government responses to financial market pressures. In this chapter, I consider another facet of the impact of national institutions on financial market–government interactions.
I evaluate various institutional means by which governments can alter their
relationship with global capital markets. Particularly in the advanced capitalist democracies, governments have choices regarding the extent to and
ways in which they interact with global capital markets. Nations are differently integrated into the global capital market;[2] the choices governments
make regarding integration are at least partly exogenous to economic globalization, as well as to purely economic considerations. They reflect instead domestic political contests.[3] In other words, I suggest that, in many
cases, governments can and do respond to international market pressures
by changing some institutions, rather than by changing economic policies.

I evaluate three types of policies: policies that alter market participants'
expectations regarding macroeconomic outcomes, policies that insulate

---

[1] Interview, European Monetary Institute (now ECB) official, April 1997.
[2] E.g., Garrett 1998c, Porter 2001.
[3] Oatley 1999b makes a similar argument with respect to the choice of exchange rate regimes;
Lukauskas and Minuskin 2000 examine the domestic influences on the style of financial
liberalization in developing nations. Missale 1999 estimates the economically optimal shares
of various types of debt for OECD nations; the estimates often differ sharply from the actual
shares.

particular groups of investors from certain kinds of investment risks, and policies that insulate governments from activity in international financial markets. In general, I argue that, particularly in advanced capitalist democracies, governments have *some significant degree* of choice regarding these policies: they are not forced by financial market pressures to make particular institutional changes. The policies pursued reflect governments' considerations of their costs and benefits, depend on domestic distributional concerns as well as external economic pressures, and, therefore, vary cross-nationally.

Government Interactions with Financial Markets: An Overview of Strategies

Table 6.1 provides summarizes the policies – or "strategies" – I examine and their implications for national governments. The first group of policies change market participants' expectations regarding key macroeconomic outcomes; these include politically independent central banks and fiscal policymaking institutions. In both cases, more politically independent institutions should reduce government borrowing costs, as lenders' perceptions of investment risk decline. At the same time, however, these institutions reduce government policymaking autonomy, often in pronounced ways.[4] Many governments have selected independent central banks and fiscal policymaking institutions in recent years. Especially in developed economies, the nature and timing of these choices reflect not only financial market pressures, but also domestic political motivations and supranational (e.g., EU-wide) motivations.

The second set of policies change the susceptibility of certain classes of investors to investment risks. These policies allow governments to borrow from a group of market participants that, under normal circumstances, would not purchase sovereign debt or would demand greater interest rate premia. The issuance of foreign currency–denominated debt and the issuance of inflation-linked bonds can facilitate reductions in sovereign interest rates. They also require, however, that the government assume inflation or currency risk. Empirical evidence suggests that not all governments with high debt and high inflation find it necessary to issue indexed or foreign currency-denominated securities, and not all governments that issue such securities have macroeconomic problems. Particularly in advanced

---

[4] Grabel 1996a, Starr 1999.

Alternative Domestic Responses

Table 6.1. *Government Policies and International Financial Markets*

Effect of Policy	Examples	Implications for Government Policy
Alters Market Participants Expectations Regarding Macroeconomic Outcomes	Independent Central Banks Independent Fiscal Policymaking Institutions	Lower interest rates, but government cedes policymaking autonomy in the fiscal or monetary area
Insulates Particular Groups of Investors	Indexed Government Debt Foreign Currency Denomination	Lower interest rates, but government bears costs of inflation or depreciation
Insulate Government from Market Activity	Capital Account Restrictions Maturity of Public Debt Resident Investment	Governments may pay higher borrowing costs, but less susceptible to international market developments

capitalist democracies, debt management policies are driven by factors other than economic necessity.

The final row of Table 6.1 contains policies that insulate governments from financial market pressures. These include (at the extreme) instituting controls on capital flows, as well as altering the maturity structure of government debt and encouraging resident investment. The pursuit of an insulating strategy often entails higher borrowing costs for governments, but, in exchange for these higher rates, governments are less susceptible to international capital market developments. Our empirical evidence suggests that controls on capital flows tend to increase the nominal interest rates paid by governments and that there is a moderate association between macroeconomic fundamentals and levels of resident investment. We also find some, albeit not a perfect, correspondence between macroeconomic fundamentals and the extent to which governments are able to issue longer-term bonds.

Figures 6.1 and 6.2 represent these strategies in the context of financial market–government relations. The first model recalls that presented in Chapter 1: financial market participants evaluate some set of government policies and respond to these policies by increasing, maintaining, or decreasing the interest rate charged for government borrowing. A government facing an adverse market response chooses between altering and

201

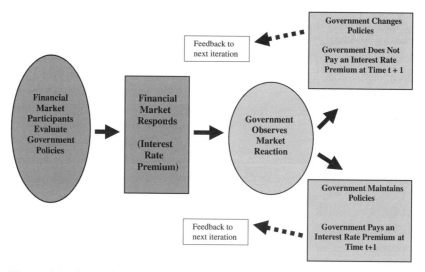

Figure 6.1   A causal model of financial market–government relations.

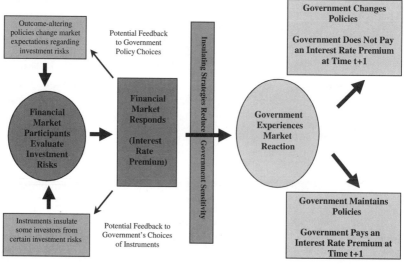

Figure 6.2   A causal model with government strategies.

maintaining its policies. Figure 6.2 includes the impact of different types of government strategies. In the upper left corner, outcome-altering strategies, such as establishment of independent central banks, change market partic-ipants' overall assessments of investment risks. Changes in these overall assessments lead to changes in interest rates. In the lower left corner of Figure 6.2, investor-insulating strategies alter investment risks for some classes of market participants. In both cases, the responses of financial market participants may have feedback effects for government policy: if a policy is successful at lowering interest rates, governments may be encouraged to maintain or enhance the policy. At the next stage, after financial market decisions regarding interest rates, insulating strategies take effect. A government that is more insulated from international capital markets experiences market activity in a more limited sense. For example, a government that rolls over its international debt infrequently may be able to defer its borrowing until market conditions are very favorable. Therefore, the same market response, in terms of interest rate changes, can have different effects cross-nationally.

The objective of this chapter is to assess the various choices governments make regarding the ways in which they interact with international financial markets. I also consider the extent to which the policies that governments pursue are strategic choices, made independently of international financial markets. I describe each category of government policy and its use; I then explore the incentives – economic and political – to adopt the policy. And, where appropriate data are available (mostly for developed democracies), I use quantitative analyses to determine the extent to which the use of a particular policy is associated with macroeconomic conditions. For example, do governments with high inflation and high debt levels issue foreign currency debt more extensively? I assume that, if a particular policy at time t is *not* associated significantly with various macroeconomic conditions at time t − 1, the policy likely is not an effect of those conditions. If a government policy is associated significantly with (lagged) macroeconomic conditions, I conclude that it may be an effect of macroeconomic conditions. At the same time, if the policy in past periods is associated with current macroeconomic outcomes, that policy may be a cause of those outcomes. In some cases – for instance, inflation and central bank independence – a policy may be both a cause and an effect of macroeconomic outcomes. I conclude the analysis of each policy with a discussion of its costs and benefits.

Strategies to Alter Market Expectations: Monetary and Fiscal Institutions

Governments of democratic societies often have difficulty making credible commitments to monetary and fiscal discipline. They face a time inconsistency problem:[5] although it is rational to commit to restraint at time t, it also is rational to renege at time t + 1, engineering a positive inflation surprise. This surprise serves to produce an output gain, benefiting both the local economy and the policymaker. Rational economic agents, however, anticipate such surprises and the inflation they produce; therefore, they bid up wages and prices preemptively. And in financial markets, lenders demand higher risk premia. Similarly, on the fiscal side, governments have domestic political incentives to increase budget outlays.[6] Various other institutional configurations, such as coalition governments or short-duration governments, may exacerbate issues of fiscal control.[7]

One solution to this credibility problem – and to the associated interest rate premia – is a commitment to a fiscal or monetary policy rule. This rule cannot be subject to easy modification; otherwise, policymakers would simply abandon the rule when it became inconvenient.[8] Rather, the policymaking body, in order to be perceived as credible by market participants, must be politically independent. According to the wide literature on central bank independence, only an entity that is legally prohibited from deviating from its rules can succeed in altering private agents' expectations and assessments of investment risk. Politically independent policymaking institutions reduce governments' interest rate costs but also require them to surrender policymaking capacity.[9]

Monetary Institutions

Many studies of the impact of central bank independence (CBI), focusing mostly on the advanced democracies, reveal strong and positive correlations

---

[5] Alesina and Tabellini 1988, Forder 1998a, Iversen 1999, Kydland and Prescott 1977, Persson and Tabellini 1994, Rogoff 1985.

[6] See Alesina and Tabellini 1988, Alesina et al. 1997, Franzese 1999, von Hagen and Harden 1994, 1995.

[7] On coalition governments, see Alesina and Perotti 1995, Alesina et al. 1997, Roubini and Sachs 1989. On short-duration governments, see Alesina and Perotti 1995, Grilli and Milesi-Ferretti 1995, Olzer and Tabellini 1991. In a contending view, Hallerberg and von Hagen 1999 argue that electoral systems influence the choice of fiscal institutions but do not directly influence fiscal outcomes. In proportional electoral systems, coalition members are not willing to delegate fiscal authority to a single actor. They argue that the resulting differences in fiscal institutions – strong in majoritarian systems but weak in proportional systems – drive budget deficits.

[8] Barro and Gordon 1983.

[9] Cohen 1996.

between CBI and inflation rates.[10] This correlation suggests that CBI serves to alter economic actors' perceptions and governments' reputations. In this vein, Freeman and associates argue that independent central banks mitigate currency market participants' fears regarding inflation and government change.[11] And by refusing to provide unlimited financing to the public sector, independent central banks also can pressure governments to reduce debt and deficits.[12] Moreover, as an instrument to effect anti-inflation credibility, independent central banks can be a substitute for a fixed exchange rate arrangement.[13] As a result, independent central banks have been hailed widely by international financial institutions and neoliberal policymakers especially as an instrument for developing countries. Between 1990 and 1995, at least 30 governments legislated increased independence for their central banks.[14] In Europe as well, CBI was a key feature of the move toward a single currency; the European Central Bank's charter makes the restraint of inflation the bank's central policy goal.[15]

More recently, the robustness of the CBI–inflation relationship has been called into question. Some critics point to the problems associated with measuring independence, where legal indexes can overstate operational autonomy. This problem is most severe in developing nations.[16] Others note that the relationship between CBI and inflation could be spurious, reflecting the impact of an underlying, common causal factor, such as domestic preferences for low inflation. Central bank independence simply could be endogenous.[17] Moreover, the impact of CBI on monetary policy outcomes could be contingent on other domestic factors, such as the structure of labor market institutions.[18] Still others challenge the notion that a monetary policymaking institution can have full operational independence: independent central banks are aware that governments can

---

[10] Alesina and Summers 1993, Alesina and Perotti 1996b, Cukierman 1992, Grilli et al. 1991.

[11] Freeman et al. 2000.

[12] Franzese 2002, Grilli et al. 1991. Additionally, Alesina and Summers 1993 find no measurable impact of central bank independence on real economic performance – it neither detracts from nor contributes to growth.

[13] Clark and Hallerberg 2000, Frieden and Martin 2001.

[14] Maxfield 1997.

[15] Berman and McNamara 1999.

[16] Berman and McNamara 1999, Cukierman 1992, Forder 1998a, 1998b, Mangano 1998, Oatley 1999a.

[17] Alesina and Grilli 1992, Forder 1998a, Posen 1998.

[18] Hall and Franzese 1998, Iversen 1999.

Table 6.2. *Increases in Central Bank Independence, Developed Democracies*

Country	Year of Change	Average Inflation before Change (from 1974)	Average Inflation after Change (to 1997)	Average Long-Term Interest Rate Level before Change	Average Long-Term Interest Rate Level after Change
Belgium	1993	5.72	1.89	9.84	6.73
France	1993	7.75	1.66	10.65	6.74
Italy	1992	12.32	3.95	13.68	10.07
New Zealand	1989	13.04	2.50	11.99	8.46
Portugal	1992	18.96	4.22	16.37	9.27
Spain	1994	11.79	3.40	13.79	8.35

Sources: Maxfield 1997a, for dates of change; Chapter 3 data for inflation and long-term interest rates. For Portugal, data begin in 1985.

revoke their mandates, so they give some consideration to government preferences.[19]

Despite these critiques, and given market participants' tendency to accept the conventional central bank–inflation wisdom,[20] I expect that governments with more independent central banks will pay lower government bond rates, as they will have some success in changing market participants' expectations regarding inflation. Simple bivariate relationships confirm this expectation: for the late 1980s and early 1990s – the most recent period for which accurate measures of CBI are available – there are moderate negative correlations between independence and inflation and between independence and government bond rates.[21] Higher levels of CBI also are associated with lower levels of volatility of long-term interest rates.[22]

Likewise, if we compare levels of inflation and interest rates before and after increases in CBI, we see a decline over time in inflation and long-term interest rates. Table 6.2 reports recent changes in CBI in the advanced democracies. After increases in CBI, rates of inflation and long-term interest rates decline. Although the table does not control for other influences on interest rates or inflation, it offers preliminary evidence that the adoption of

[19] Lohmann 1992, Simmons 1996, Keefer and Stasavage 1998, Drazen and Masson 1994.
[20] Interviews 3, 6, 8, 10, 21, 30, 33, 37, 40, 45, 46.
[21] Annual correlations range from −0.43 to −0.57. Central bank measures rely on Cukierman 1992 and Maxfield 1997.
[22] Interest rate volatility is measured as the annual variance of monthly interest rates on benchmark government bonds. Again, annual correlations are approximately −0.5.

Table 6.3. *Increases in Central Bank Independence, Emerging Market Economies*

Country	Year of Change	Average Inflation before Change (from 1981)	Average Inflation after Change (until 1996)
Chile	1989	20.19	14.72
Ecuador	1992	38.54	29.93
Egypt	1992	17.21	10.79
Mexico	1993	64.86 *	25.45
Pakistan	1993	7.59	11.70
Poland	1991–1992	107.67	32.48

Sources: Inflation data are from World Bank 1998. Data are from 1981 to the year before the change, and from the year after the change through 1996.

more independent monetary institutions aids in the reduction of inflation rates and, therefore, of government borrowing costs.

Table 6.3 provides similar evidence for a set of emerging market economies;[23] only inflation data are used, as reliable interest rate data prior to 1990 are difficult to obtain. Inflation fell dramatically in Mexico and Poland and also fell in Chile, Ecuador, and Egypt. Only in Pakistan did the average annual rate of inflation increase. Because CBI appears to be a route to lower government bond rates, we might hypothesize that nations with a history of inflation and high interest rates are motivated to free their central banks. Recent literature provides mixed evidence regarding the impact of past economic performance, capital market pressures, and domestic politics on national choices of monetary institutions. International pressures are most pronounced in the developing world, as we might expect from the discussion in Chapter 4. For instance, Maxfield maintains that improving the government's standing vis-à-vis international financial markets is an important motivation for CBI in the developing world.[24] The founding and freeing of central banks are more common during periods of high financial market openness, as governments compete to attract foreign investment.[25] Additionally, in developing nations, the creation of an independent central bank often is an element of IMF conditionality. At the same time, however, another explanation may be that voters in emerging markets demand antiinflationary policies because they worry about the purchasing power

[23] These are the economies for which there was a substantive change in central bank independence, as reported in Maxfield 1997, and for which an appropriate time series of inflation data is available.

[24] Maxfield 1997.

[25] Haggard et al. 1993, Keefer and Stasavage 1998.

207

of their own currencies, or that governments in the midst of a democratic transition delegate monetary authority in order to restrain the powers of future governments.[26]

The case for external financial market influences on CBI is weaker in developed nations. Although CBI has become the norm, central banks were granted independence at different times, and this timing likely reflected domestic political dynamics. For example, Bernhard argues that a government frees its central bank when it does not trust its new coalition partners to fulfill its policy preferences.[27] Additionally, the movement to CBI in Europe also reflects the *political* choices embodied in the Maastricht Treaty. When required to increase the operational independence of their national central banks, national governments did so in diverse ways. Some central banks' mandates mention only the control of inflation; others call for a joint consideration of inflation and employment.

In the end, we can imagine governments' weighing the costs and benefits of CBI, just as they weigh the costs and benefits of acceding to financial market influences. As in Chapter 5, different governments weigh costs and benefits in diverse ways. CBI can provide lower inflation and lower interest rates, which will please both financial markets and some domestic constituents. But CBI also reduces government officials' ability to influence the macroeconomy.[28] As recent calls for a central bank focus on employment rather than on inflation demonstrate, CBI not only constrains opportunistic politicians but also gives rise to issues of democratic accountability.[29] Therefore, to understand the determinants of CBI, political economists should look not only at financial market or international institutional pressures, but also at domestic politics and distributional considerations.

Independent Fiscal Institutions

On the fiscal side, politically independent institutions also can enhance government credibility, affect market participants' concerns about default and inflation risk, and lower government bond rates. Fiscal policymaking institutions fall into three broad categories: numerical targets, procedural

---

[26] Also see Forder 1998a, who argues that, to reassure financial markets, governments need only use foreign currency denomination and indexed debt. His suggestion, then, is that other factors drive the choice of central bank independence.

[27] Bernhard 1998.

[28] Clark 1998, Rodrik 2001.

[29] Pauly 1996.

rules that govern the formulation of the budget, and rules that affect the transparency of the budget.[30]

Numerical targets establish limits for budget outlays, deficits, or debt; these are found in many U.S. states,[31] as well as in the EU's Maastricht Treaty and Stability and Growth Pact. Similarly, the British and German governments have "golden rules," which suggest public borrowing only to fund public investment (rather than consumption).[32] Procedural rules govern various phases of the budgeting process – the formulation of the budget within the executive branch, the approval of the budget in the legislature, and the implementation of the budget by the bureaucracy. These rule systems can be classified as "collegial" or "hierarchical." Hierarchical systems are characterized by a top-down approach, in which the finance minister has a dominant position vis-à-vis spending ministers. Unlike spending ministers, the finance minister has incentives to consider the total size of the budget and its impact on the median taxpayer; this results in greater fiscal stringency.[33] As a former British Treasury secretary suggests, budget targets not only discipline the finance minister, but "discipline the Cabinet in its capacity as a bevy of spending Ministers."[34]

In the legislature, hierarchy means that few or no amendments to the budget are allowed. Collegial systems, on the other hand, allow for increased consultation with and input from cabinet ministers and legislators. For example, in Ireland, Italy, Belgium, Greece, and Portugal, the finance minister has no special status, and many amendments to the budget – rather than only a vote up or down – are permitted in the legislature. Collegial procedures are likely to lead to looser fiscal policies, as there are more opportunities for political influence on the final budget. Empirically, hierarchical procedures are associated with greater fiscal discipline – which market participants likely prefer – whereas collegial procedures are associated with more moderation and compromise.[35] Finally, transparent fiscal institutions are rules that allow the general public, opposition political parties, and international financial market participants to assess more easily

---

[30] Branson et al. 1998. I employ the typology of fiscal institutions offered by Alesina and Perotti 1996a, 1996b, and von Hagen and Harden 1994. For another classification, see Hahm et al. 1996.

[31] Alt and Lowry 1994, Poterba 1996a.

[32] Allsopp and Vines 1998, Tanzi and Schuknecht 2000.

[33] Alesina and Perotti 1996a, Hallerberg and von Hagen 1999, von Hagen and Harden 1994.

[34] Lawson 1993, pp. 70–71.

[35] Alesina et al. 1997, chapter 9.

the nature and implications of the budget.[36] More transparent rules should result in more accurate expectations regarding the budget deficit and tax burdens, thereby increasing market participants' confidence in current and future fiscal policy outcomes.

Fiscal institutions often combine elements of targeting, transparency, and procedural rules; the character of budget institutions varies widely across countries. In Germany, for example, the finance minister has veto power in the cabinet and can change the budget bids of individual spending ministers after consultation with them. Likewise, the French prime minister and finance minister unilaterally decide the overall budget targets. In Italy and Portugal, however, the finance minister has no formal special authority in the cabinet-level budget process. On the legislative side, there are no limitations to parliamentary amendments to budgets in Belgium, Greece, the Netherlands, and Portugal. In Italy, amendments are permitted, but they cannot change the overall budget balance. Finally, amendments to British government budgets can neither increase existing taxes nor create new taxes, and parliamentary legislation involving new expenditures requires the consent of the government.[37] More generally, budget institutions range from quite hierarchical, in France, Britain, and Germany, to quite collegial, in Italy, Sweden, Ireland, and Belgium. In Latin America, Colombia, Jamaica, and Chile are characterized by very hierarchical institutions, the Dominican Republic, Bolivia, and Brazil by very collegial institutions.[38]

Recent empirical work suggests that politically independent fiscal institutions are associated with lower government debt and deficits. In the 1980s and early 1990s, European governments with more hierarchical budget procedures also had tighter fiscal policies.[39] In Latin America during the 1980–1993 period, governments with more hierarchical and transparent budget procedures displayed greater fiscal discipline.[40] In the American context, state-level fiscal institutions are, under some conditions, significantly associated with fiscal outcomes.[41] As a result, U.S. states with the

---

[36] Liebfritz et al. 1994.

[37] Von Hagen and Harden 1994, appendix A.

[38] OECD information is based on scores for the early 1990s from von Hagen and Harden 1994, 1995. Latin American information, for the mid-1990s, is drawn from Grisanti et al. 1998.

[39] Von Hagen and Harden 1994, Hallerberg and von Hagen 1999. Also see Hahm et al. 1996.

[40] Alesina et al. 1996, Grisanti et al. 1998.

[41] Alt and Lowry 1994, Poterba 1996b.

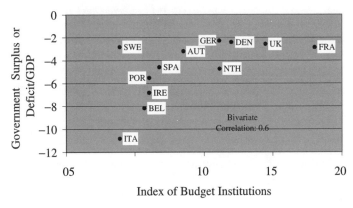

Figure 6.3   Budget institutions and fiscal performance in Europe.

most restrictive fiscal limits pay slightly lower public bond rates than states with average fiscal limits.[42]

As in the case of central banks, some have questioned the veracity of the causal link between fiscal institutions and fiscal outcomes.[43] Financial market participants, however, *do* appear to assign more credibility and less investment risk to nations with such institutions. Independent fiscal institutions seem to play a role in convincing market participants that governments will honor their fiscal commitments. Therefore, I expect to observe a positive relationship between the independence of fiscal policymaking institutions and government fiscal outcomes as well as between fiscal institutions and government bond rates.

For data from advanced industrial democracies, I employ the cumulative indexes created by von Hagen and his colleagues,[44] which measure hierarchy, numerical targets, and procedural rules annually for the 1981–1994 period. Von Hagen and Hallerberg also provide dichotomous data on the presence of a strong finance minister and the presence of negotiated budget targets at the cabinet level. Whereas the indexes remain constant for the period of data coverage, the latter two variables do change (albeit in only a few instances) during this period. Figure 6.3 displays the relationship between budget institutions, where higher values represent greater political independence, and the average deficit levels in 12 European nations for

---

[42] Goldstein and Woglom 1992, Poterba and Rueben 1997.
[43] Alesina and Perotti 1996b, Alesina et al. 1997, Corsetti and Roubini 1996, Poterba 1996b.
[44] E.g., Hallerberg and von Hagen 1999.

Table 6.4. *Strong Finance Ministers, Fiscal Targets, and Economic Outcomes*

Finance Minister	N	Mean Balance/ GDP Ratio	Mean Interest Rate Level	Fiscal Target	N	Mean Balance/ GDP Ratio	Mean Interest Rate Level
Strong	42	−2.56	9.42	Target	57	−2.32	9.11
Weak	140	−4.82	11.48	No Target	125	−5.20	11.64

the 1981–1994 period. The chart reveals a positive, and relatively strong, bivariate relationship between budget institutions and government budget balance outcome, with a correlation of 0.62. The bivariate correlation between interest rates and fiscal institutions is more moderate (−0.41) but still suggests some relationship between more independent fiscal institutions and lower interest rates on government bonds.[45]

Similarly, Table 6.4 displays the relationships among three sets of variables: fiscal institutions (either a strong finance minister or the existence of fiscal targets); the government budget balance; and long-term interest rates. As previously, governments characterized by a strong finance minister or by the existence of a fixed fiscal target have, on average, lower budget balances and pay lower rates of interest on government bonds. In Latin America, the other region for which fiscal institutions have been analyzed comparatively, a similar relationship exists. For the 1990–1995 period, the bivariate correlation between budget institutions and the average government budget balance is 0.53.[46] This again suggests smaller interest rate premia where fiscal institutions are relatively independent.

Given this benefit, what explains diversity in national fiscal institutions? Little empirical work thus far has addressed the selection of fiscal institutions.[47] Changes in national fiscal institutions are somewhat rare, but they provide some clues to motivations of governments, particularly if they come on the heels of poor economic performance or severe financial market punishment. A recent case of change is the adoption in New Zealand of the

[45] These relationships also exist when the Hahm et al. 1996 "strength of fiscal bureaucracy" measure is used.

[46] I use the Stein et al. 1998 composite index, which includes constitutional constraints on the budget deficit, borrowing constraints on the government, the authority of the finance minister, rules regarding the presentation and modification of the budget, and the fiscal relationship between national and subnational governments.

[47] Hallerberg and von Hagen 1999 are one exception. Also see Mosley 1999.

1994 Fiscal Responsibility Act. The act provides a set of fiscal policymaking procedures, aimed at increased budget transparency and responsible fiscal management. The act requires that technocrats, rather than political officials, make budget forecasts and that policymakers disclose the impact over a three-year period of all budget measures. Although the act does not set specific budget rules for a given year, it does encourage "balanced budgets on average over reasonable periods of time."[48] In passing the act, the New Zealand government aimed "to address New Zealand's history of poor fiscal performance, reduce public debt, and improve fiscal management."[49] These motivations suggest that past economic fundamentals were an important determinant of institutional choice. At the same time, discussions of the motivations for the Fiscal Responsibility Act highlighted the interaction between fiscal and electoral institutions; as New Zealand moved from a majoritarian to a multimember plurality electoral system (in 1996), it wanted to provide reassurances about fiscal management under future coalition governments.[50] The New Zealand case, then, offers an example of the potential interactions between domestic political and international financial incentives that seem to characterize choices regarding economic policymaking institutions.

As in the case of monetary institutions, fiscal institutions likely reflect a variety of motivations: although these institutions serve to change investors' expectations, they are not driven entirely by investors' demands. The New Zealand case suggests that more independent fiscal institutions are useful to tie the hands of future governments or future coalition partners. This pattern is consistent with recent work on the determinants of CBI.[51] In addition, some fiscal institutions represent functional responses to past problems, such as the German economic crisis of the mid- to late 1960s and the Italian fiscal difficulties of the mid-1970s.[52]

In political terms, there exists a trade-off between the costs and benefits of politically independent fiscal institutions. A government that elects to institute a numerical target is able to commit itself more credibly to fiscal rectitude, thereby pleasing market participants and perhaps some domestic groups, but this government also cedes flexibility.[53] The lack of

[48] IMF 1996, p. 48.
[49] Grisanti et al. 1998, p. 146.
[50] Tanzi and Schuknecht 2000.
[51] Bernhard 1998. Also see Alesina and Rosenthal 1995.
[52] Allen 1989, Della Sala 1988, Friauf 1975.
[53] Bayoumi and Eichengreen 1995.

flexibility may be particularly problematic in periods of economic downturn or in periods of fierce electoral competition. Under such circumstances, the government can ignore or revoke the target, but this behavior would have reputational – and perhaps financial – costs. Likewise, a legislature that approves changes in amendment procedures, so that the government's budget proposals occupy a privileged position in the fiscal policymaking process, may expect greater fiscal stringency, but loses the ability to amend the budget when it disagrees with the executive branch's spending priorities.

In emerging market economies, external influences on institutional choice are likely to be more pronounced. Cross-national variation in fiscal institutions is smaller in Latin America and Central Europe than in Western Europe.[54] For instance, the reforms of fiscal institutions in Central Europe in the mid-1990s, carried out under IMF supervision, produced broadly similar (albeit not identical) institutions in several nations. In Latin America, Colombia has a long history, dating to at least the 1920s, of altering its budgetary institutions in order to attract foreign investment.[55] On the other hand, some cross-national differences in institutions remain: the fiscal institutions of Colombia and Chile are significantly different from those of Bolivia and Brazil. If the debt crises of the 1980s did not prompt a revision of fiscal institutions in Bolivia and Brazil, it is difficult to imagine that the need for external finance is a sufficient explanation for institutional choices. And Chile's stringent fiscal limits, contained in Article 64 of the 1980 Constitution, appear to reflect Pinochet's distrust of bargaining among elected officials rather than an outward-oriented reform.[56] At present, we can conclude that fiscal institutions affect and are affected by financial markets, but that neither of these relationships is fully isomorphic.

Assuming Investment Risks

Policies in the second category render particular investors less susceptible to certain types of investment risk. I investigate two such policies – the indexation (or linking to inflation) and foreign currency denomination of government debt – with a focus on their use in developed democracies.

[54] Branson et al. 1998.
[55] Drake 1989, Hommes 1996.
[56] Baldez and Carey 2001.

Inflation-Linked Government Debt

Inflation-linked, or indexed, bonds are instruments for which the principal and interest payments are tied to the rate of inflation. The nominal return on indexed securities increases with inflation, thereby holding the real return constant.[57] Therefore, index-linked bonds transfer inflation risk from the investor to the government. The government's assumption of inflation risk can lower borrowing costs, particularly where market expectations of inflation are overstated. Indexation also provides governments with an incentive to restrain inflation: when the government must pay inflation premia, reducing nonindexed debt via high inflation is less attractive, and reducing indexed debt via inflation is impossible.[58] Indexing debt can allow governments to insure investors against inflation risk without necessarily bearing the additional costs associated with central bank independence.

Although several developed nations have issued indexed debt in recent years, its use in developed nations remains quite limited.[59] Britain issues the largest volume of indexed securities, approximately 15% of total debt. The British government began issues of indexed debt in 1981, as a means of improving its antiinflation credibility and of reducing the costs of government borrowing.[60] This strategy has succeeded in lowering the British government's overall borrowing costs. Australia, Canada, Greece, Iceland, Israel, Italy, Sweden, New Zealand, and the United States also issue inflation-linked debt. In Canada, New Zealand, and Sweden, indexed debt was introduced when governments thought that rates on nonindexed debt overestimated future inflation.[61] Israel, on the other hand, has long relied on index-linked debt, first issuing such securities in 1955.[62] The United States

---

[57] Tobin 1963, p. 449. Anderson et al. 1996 provide a technical discussion of the details of indexation – for example, the choice of an inflation index to be used in calculating inflation premia (pp. 137–140).

[58] Giovannini 1997, Missale and Blanchard 1994. In his memoir, Nigel Lawson, former British chancellor of the Exchequer, points out: "The indexation of longer-term Government debt was an even stronger deterrent [to inflation]. For, if both the principal and the interest are indexed, the cost of servicing the debt increases as inflation rises. This is a stark contrast to conventional gilts, where the servicing burden declines when inflation accelerates" (Lawson 1993, p. 114)

[59] Foresi et al. 1996, Missale 1999.

[60] Anderson et al. 1996, Campbell and Shiller 1996, Evans 1998, Hale 1996, Missale 1999.

[61] Anderson et al. 1996, Hale 1996.

[62] Campbell and Shiller 1996.

launched index-linked bonds in January 1997, hoping that this new instrument might appeal to institutional investors and mutual fund managers.[63] Portugal, Greece, Austria, Italy, and Denmark employ an alternate form of indexation, tying the returns on some of their long-term government bonds to a short-term market-determined interest rate.[64] Emerging market nations – particularly when facing periods of high inflation and difficulty in obtaining credit – also issue index-linked securities. In recent years, Argentina, Brazil, Chile, Colombia, and Mexico have used indexation as part of their debt management policies.[65]

To what extent is the issuance of index-linked debt determined by macroeconomic conditions? That is, are nations with high levels of inflation or government debt required to use index-linked debt in order to access international financial markets? Some of the main issuers of index-linked debt *have* experienced high rates of inflation (Italy) or fiscal problems (Canada and Ireland), particularly in the 1980s. Other issuers, such as the United Kingdom, however, have not. And some nations with high debt and inflation, such as Spain and Portugal, have not turned to indexation. I expect that, in advanced democracies, there exists a weak relationship between economic fundamentals and the use of indexation. Additionally, I expect that the issuance of indexed debt exerts only mild pressures on future inflation; other influences on inflation rates, including the nature of monetary policy institutions, affect inflation more strongly. In investigating these questions, I rely exclusively on data for the advanced industrial democracies. Unfortunately, systematic data regarding the use of indexation in the developing world do not exist, making it impossible to compare the two groups of countries. On the basis of the evidence provided in Chapter 4, as well as anecdotal evidence regarding indexation, I assume that if indexation is rendered necessary by economic fundamentals in developed nations, it also will be necessary in emerging markets.

I begin by examining the potential determinants of indexation. Table 6.5 reports the results of a Cochrane–Orcutt regression with the percentage of debt that is index-linked as the dependent variable.[66] The independent variables are the current account balance/GDP, government debt/GDP, and inflation rate, all lagged by one year. Each observation represents a

---

[63] *Financial Times*, January 29, 1997, p. 21.
[64] Alesina et al. 1990, Missale 1999.
[65] Missale and Blanchard 1994, Goldfajn 1998.
[66] This variable ranges from 0 to 12, with a standard deviation of 1.857.

Alternative Domestic Responses

Table 6.5. *Indexation as a Dependent Variable, 1981–1996*

	Coefficient Estimate	Standard Error	$P > t$
Inflation	−0.59*	0.03	0.076
Debt	−0.006	0.005	0.216
Current Account	−0.083*	0.048	0.083
Constant	1.332***	0.405	0.441

Note: $N = 259$; $p > F = 0.02$; transformed Durbin–Watson = 2.00.

country-year, and data are for advanced industrial democracies during the 1981–1996 period. There are statistically significant associations, at a 90% confidence level, between indexation and inflation, and between indexation and the current account balance. The inflation coefficient is negative, suggesting – oddly – that higher inflation in the past period is associated with lower indexation in the current period. At the same time, the negative sign on the current account variable implies that a deteriorating current account is associated with higher indexation. As economic agents worry that current account deficits will lead to currency depreciation, and perhaps then to inflation (as imported products increase in price), they may demand more indexed securities. Again, however, the magnitude of this coefficient is quite small, suggesting that a 1% decline in the current account balance is associated with less than a 0.1% increase in the level of indexed debt. The coefficient on the debt indicator is not statistically significant, and the sign on the coefficient is negative. More generally, these variables explain very little of the variance in levels of indexation. Cross-national variation in the use of indexation, then, appears largely not an effect of earlier levels of debt or inflation.

I then consider, in Table 6.6, whether indexation leads to lower inflation in developed democracies. The lagged independent variables include indexation, debt, the current account balance, the exchange rate, and the degree of central bank independence.[67] The results indicate that although indexation does affect inflation performance, its effects are much smaller than those of other variables. The strongest coefficients are those on the level of central bank independence, the current account balance (a deteriorating balance is associated with higher inflation), and change in the nominal exchange rate (negative changes are associated with higher inflation). The

---

[67] An analysis that uses observations from the current year, rather than from a previous year, as independent variables produces similar results.

Table 6.6. *Indexation and Inflation*

	Coefficient Estimate	Standard Error	$P > t$
Indexed Debt	−0.161*	0.089	0.074
Debt	−0.024***	0.008	0.003
Current Account	−0.590***	0.068	0.000
Central Bank Independence	−1.069***	0.119	0.000
Exchange Rate	−0.146***	0.034	0.000
Constant	11.16***	0.876	0.000

Note: $N = 212$; $R^2 = 0.53$; $p > F = 0.00$; transformed Durbin–Watson = 2.00.

coefficient on the government debt variable, although significant, implies – paradoxically – that higher debt in the previous year is associated with lower inflation. Finally, the coefficient on indexation is negative and significant at the 90% confidence level. A higher level of indexation is associated with a lower level of inflation. This is consistent with the notion that when governments index a larger percentage of their debt, they have greater incentives to control inflation. A one standard deviation increase in indexation implies a 0.297% decrease in the rate of inflation. By comparison, an improvement of one standard deviation in the current account balance implies a 2.06% decrease in the rate of inflation. Therefore, indexation creates an additional pressure, but a relatively small one, on monetary policy.

The results reported in Table 6.5 suggest that in developed nations indexation is more a matter of domestic debt management choices and domestic politics than of economic necessity. One cost of indexation is the assumption of inflation risk: if a nation experiences high levels of inflation, the government's cost of repayment increases, at least in nominal terms. Additionally, indexation reduces the government's ability to inflate away conventional debt. Another potential pitfall is liquidity risk: if a government issues only a few index-linked securities, market actors will demand additional interest rate compensation, and this may offset the interest rate savings associated with indexation.[68] At the same time, if market expectations regarding inflation exceed actual inflation, indexation allows for cheaper government borrowing. Another benefit of indexation is that, by comparing the interest

---

[68] The Swedish government experienced this problem in the mid-1990s. It responded by increasing the volume of index-linked debt from 0.5% of total debt in 1994 to 7.6% of total debt in 1996. Even the British government, the leader in indexed debt, has reported problems with liquidity. See Anderson et al. 1996, Bekaert et al. 1998, Missale 1999, Mylonas et al. 2000.

rates on indexed bonds with those on nonindexed bonds, policymakers can estimate more accurately inflationary expectations.[69] In some cases, such as the United Kingdom and Australia, indexation has produced cost savings. In other cases, for instance, Canada and New Zealand, indexation has proved more expensive for governments than issuing of nonindexed securities at the prevailing market rate. In those cases, investors have reaped the benefits of indexation.

Foreign Currency Denomination

Foreign currency denomination, the issuance of government bonds denominated in a major international currency, is a more comprehensive insulating strategy. Foreign currency denomination insulates investors from both inflation *and* exchange rate risk. An investor purchasing dollar-denominated Mexican bonds does not have to worry about the value of the Mexican peso or about inflation in the Mexican economy. She must worry only about the value of the U.S. dollar and the risk that the government will fail to repay its debt. Therefore, borrowing in foreign currencies generally is cheaper than borrowing in home currencies.[70]

Foreign currency denomination is employed by both developed and emerging market nations but again is more prevalent in emerging markets. Even "higher-risk" developed nations issue relatively small amounts of their debt in foreign currencies; in OECD nations, there has been a general trend away from the use of foreign currency denomination since the 1980s.[71] Figure 6.4 summarizes the use of foreign currency issues (as a percentage of total debt) in European nations.[72] The EU-wide average, indicated by the shaded area, ranges from 12% to 18% of total debt. Whereas Ireland, Finland, and Sweden issue relatively substantial quantities of foreign currency debt,[73] Germany and the Netherlands issued no foreign currency denominated debt in the 1990–1997 period. Less than 10% of debt issued in France, Spain, Italy, and the United Kingdom during the 1990s

[69] Campbell and Shiller 1996.
[70] Alternatively, foreign currency debt may have similar interest rates, but a longer maturity.
[71] Missale 1999.
[72] Data are taken from European Monetary Institute, *1998 Convergence Report*. Similar data are found in the data appendix of Missale 1999. These series of data have a correlation of 0.97.
[73] For a discussion of Sweden's turn toward foreign currency denomination, and its potential domestic political consequences, see Moses 2001.

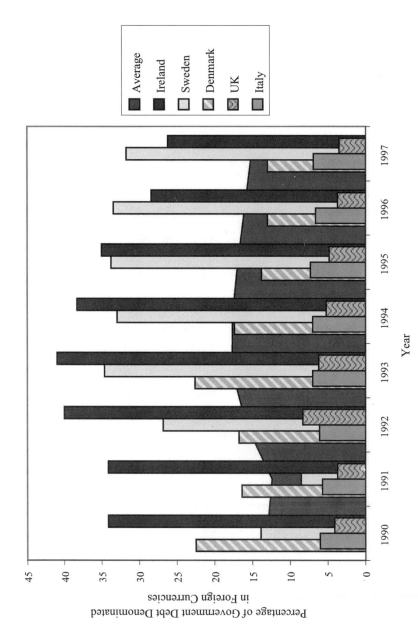

Figure 6.4 Foreign currency denomination in Europe.

was denominated in foreign currencies. Similarly, the Canadian government borrows in foreign currencies *only* to purchase foreign exchange reserves – about 5% of outstanding market debt in 1997.[74]

At the same time, because the largest component of interest rate differentials between developed and developing nations is expectation of local currency depreciation,[75] borrowing in foreign currencies can provide substantial cost savings for developing nations. Brady Bonds, created in the wake of the Latin American debt crisis, are now a widely traded class of dollar-denominated government securities. In 1999, 52% of all long-term debt issued by developing countries was denominated in U.S. dollars, 11% in Japanese yen, and 8% in German marks.[76] During the 1990–1997 period, an average of 57% of long-term government debt in Latin America was denominated in U.S. dollars; the average rate of dollar denomination was 49% in the Czech Republic, 56% in India, 58% in Bulgaria, and a whopping 92% in South Africa.[77]

In emerging market economies, foreign currency denomination is a necessity, rather than a choice: governments that cannot attract investment in domestic currencies must issue debt in foreign currencies.[78] In the advanced industrial democracies, foreign currency denomination likely is associated with exchange rate risk: as a nation's exchange rate deteriorates, investors are less willing to buy local-currency debt, and the percentage of foreign currency debt increases. Additionally, anecdotal evidence – for instance, the increase in foreign currency denomination in Ireland during the 1970s and early 1980s, as budget deficits accumulated[79] – suggests an association between fiscal performance and the issuance of foreign currency debt.

Using a measure of the percentage of government debt denominated in a foreign currency, I assess the association between economic fundamentals and foreign currency denomination in EU nations during the 1990–1996 period. Table 6.7 reports the results of a Cochrane-Orchutt regression, using an iterative estimation process to account for autocorrelation in the

---

[74] Canadian Treasury 1997, pp. 11–12; Missale 1999.
[75] Frankel and Okongwu 1995.
[76] World Bank 2000.
[77] Data are from World Bank 1999.
[78] An alternative to foreign currency denomination, with greater implications for government policy autonomy, is a currency board exchange rate system, as is used in Hong Kong and Argentina. See Williamson 1995. On dollarization, another alternative, see Alesina and Barro 2001.
[79] Missale 1999, p. 99.

Table 6.7. *Regression Results for Foreign Currency Denomination*

	Coefficient Estimate	Standard Error	$P > t$
Exchange Rate	−0.17**	0.08	0.048
Government Budget Balance	−0.35	0.22	0.115
Inflation Rate	−1.33***	0.38	0.518
Domestic Savings	0.19	0.30	0.001
Constant	4.16	51.6	0.936

Note: $N = 53$; $R^2 = 0.25$; $p > F = 0.0011$; transformed Durbin–Watson = 1.85.

data.[80] The independent variables in this model are the annual change in the nominal exchange rate, the government deficit/GDP ratio, the inflation rate, and the domestic savings rate. I include the domestic savings rate to control for the impact of a large pool of local capital on the need to appeal to foreign investors. When short-term debt or total government debt is included in the models, the coefficient estimates are not statistically significant.

Table 6.7 suggests that a depreciating exchange rate is significantly associated with a higher level of foreign currency denomination; negative movements in the nominal exchange rate are associated with a higher level of foreign currency denomination. The coefficient on inflation also is statistically significant; a higher inflation rate, however, implies a *lower* level of foreign debt issuance. And the coefficient on government budget balance is neither statistically significant nor in the expected direction. Finally, the coefficient on the domestic savings level is not statistically significant and does not have the expected sign. These results are robust to the inclusion of lagged values as independent variables, or to the omission of the savings variable. Again, then, foreign currency denomination in developed nations does not appear to be simply an effect of economic fundamentals.

Foreign currency denomination benefits governments by providing wider and cheaper access to international capital markets. Foreign currency denomination's cost to governments takes the form of assumption of exchange rate risk. Governments must generate foreign currency to repay their debt obligations; at the extreme, depreciation of the local currency

---

[80] I estimated several other specifications of these models, using both the EMI and the Missale measure of foreign currency denomination and employing other macroeconomic indicators, including long-term interest rates. These specifications did not produce results different from those reported.

can lead to default.[81] Such problems were present in public debt markets in Mexico in 1994 and in private debt markets in Asia in 1997 and 1998. Therefore, government efforts to improve bond market access may serve to exacerbate foreign exchange market concerns. For advanced industrial democracies, both the costs and the benefits of foreign currency denomination are less pronounced. The benefit of foreign currency denomination occurs in the form of lower interest rates. And the increased borrowing costs that accompany exchange rate depreciation will likely not be great enough to drive governments into default.[82] This suggests that, although foreign currency denomination likely is a necessity – and therefore an additional sort of constraint – for some emerging market economies, it remains a strategic choice for governments of advanced democracies.

This brief review of investor-insulating strategies implies a continuum of access to international capital markets. Governments with low levels of investment risk issue bonds denominated in their own currencies. Governments with slightly higher risk profiles can issue indexed bonds, thereby assuming inflation risk. Governments with even higher investment risk issue bonds denominated in an international currency, assuming inflation as well as foreign exchange risk. Finally, governments marked by very high investment risk must borrow from banks or from international financial institutions.

Strategies of Government Insulation

The third set of government strategies insulates governments, to varying degrees, from financial market activity. Capital controls, a more comprehensive means of insulation, shield governments from the vagaries of global capital markets but also reduce the pool of capital available to public and private borrowers. Lengthening the maturity structure of government debt insulates governments by requiring less frequent refinancing of government obligations. And increasing reliance on resident investment may serve to make governments accountable to a more forgiving class of investors.

---

[81] Grabel 1999, Missale 1999, Moses 2001. Of course, the reverse also is true: when a nation's currency appreciates repayment of foreign currency–denominated debt is less expensive.

[82] The credit rating of the Australian government, however, was downgraded in mid-1998 by major ratings agencies, which cited the nature of government debt – a large portion of which was short-term and denominated in foreign currencies – as the reason for the downgrade. *Financial Times*, June 19, 1998, p. 7.

Controls on Capital Flows

Governments place a variety of limitations on flows of capital in and out of their borders. These limitations vary both in the instruments they cover (foreign direct versus equity investment, for instance) and in degree (such as complete closure versus a tax on flows).[83] During the Bretton Woods era, and even until the early 1990s, many developed democracies retained capital account restrictions. Capital controls, particularly prevalent among Scandinavian social democracies and more likely under left-leaning governments, were accepted internationally as a legitimate tool of economic management. Controls shielded economies from capital flight, possibly facilitating the maintenance of large welfare states.[84] Recent work by Lemmen and Effinger, in fact, finds that capital controls in Europe were more stringent in nations with high inflation and large government budget deficits.[85]

The general trend during the last two decades, in both developed and developing nations, has been toward the liberalization of capital flows. Although closure to international flows insulates nations from global financial pressures, it also precludes access to a wide pool of funds, thereby greatly reducing the economic efficiency of savings and investment.[86] For this reason, the international financial community generally has encouraged capital account liberalization.[87] In the wake of recent financial crises, however, several prominent economists and policymakers have discussed publicly the merits of capital market restrictions, particularly temporary, ex ante restrictions on shorter-term flows.[88] Moreover, in the late 1990s, the IMF failed to garner the support necessary to amend its Articles of Agreement to *require* capital account liberalization.

Advocates of controls on short-term capital flows often cite Chile as an example. From 1991 to 1998, Chile imposed a tax on all nonequity capital entering the nation; the rate of the tax depended on how long investment remained in the country, so that shorter-term flows were taxed most heavily.[89]

[83] Keynes 1936 proposes a transfer tax on equity transactions. Tobin 1978 suggests a turnover tax on foreign exchange trading. On the Tobin tax, also see Helleiner 2001, Porter 2001.

[84] Simmons 1999. Giavazzi and Pagano 1988 assess the argument that, in addition, capital controls facilitated the success of the European Monetary System.

[85] Lemmen and Eijffinger 1996.

[86] Bisignano 1994, Calvo et al. 1996, Thompson 1997.

[87] IMF 1997a.

[88] For example, see Eichengreen 1999, *Financial Times*, April 7, 1998, p. 20, September 4, 1998, p. 23. Joseph Stiglitz, quoted in Reuters, June 29, 1998.

[89] Grabel 1996a, Lee 1997.

The rationale behind these controls was that, if exit were costly for portfolio investors, only investors with longer time horizons would locate in Chile. Hence, capital market volatility would fall, and the government would be able to set interest rates somewhat independently of the global financial environment. Along these lines, Edwards finds that, after the Mexican peso crisis, Argentina experienced a spillover of interest rate volatility, but Chile did not.[90] Critics of the Chilean controls, however, note that Chile was more able to impose controls because of its strong macroeconomic fundamentals; that Chile's interest rates were higher than they would have been otherwise; that Chile's high domestic savings rate enhanced its ability to impose controls; and that investors simply learned to evade controls.[91]

Despite these criticisms of the Chilean model – as well as criticisms of Malaysia's imposition of ex post controls in 1998 – many observers continue to view capital controls as a means of reducing the vulnerability of domestic financial systems during transitions to more market-oriented economic systems. Under some conditions, capital controls also lower rates of interest in the domestic economy, as local rates are unaffected by global conditions. A recent study by Edison and Reinhart of capital controls in East Asia finds that controls were effective in achieving greater interest rate stability and a higher level of policy autonomy in Malaysia, but not in Thailand.[92] More generally, such controls can provide governments with the insulation necessary to strengthen their domestic financial systems or to pursue autonomous macroeconomic policies.[93] And Rodrik argues that, once the effects of other key variables are controlled for, the presence or absence of capital controls has no perceptible effect on growth or inflation.[94]

The Effects of Capital Controls   If capital controls afford governments greater policy autonomy, we can imagine that, with controls in place, governments will pursue a different set of policies. Governments may use their autonomy to pursue a more restrictive set of economic policies, as Chile

---

[90] Edwards 1998. Interestingly, Edwards finds that, in the wake of the Asian financial crisis, Chile's interest rates actually were *more* volatile. More generally, Dooley 1996 reports that capital controls are of little use in preventing speculative attacks against countries with "inconsistent policy regimes."

[91] *Economist*, April 11, 1998, p. 54; IMF Survey, October 28, 1996; *New York Times*, February 6, 1998, p. C1.

[92] Edison and Reinhart 2001.

[93] Eichengreen 1999, Grabel 1999, Grilli and Milesi-Ferretti 1995.

[94] Rodrik employs data on 100 nations for the 1975–1989 period.

did, or they may employ their autonomy to pursue more expansionary policies.[95] The expected effect of capital controls on interest rates also is not immediately obvious: controls may lower rates, by allowing governments to set artificially low interest rates; or they might raise rates, by forcing domestic borrowers to access a small pool of local capital.

In order to assess the effects of controls on capital flows, I employ two relatively simple measures of capital market openness. The first, Kim's dichotomous measurement,[96] which uses IMF surveys of balance of payments restrictions, codes any sort of restriction on cross-border capital flows as 0 and codes full capital market openness as 1. Most developing nations have some sort of capital controls during the 1981–1996 period: 47 of 59 nations are coded as 0 in 1981, 53 of 59 nations are coded as 0 in 1988 (the peak of capital account restrictions), and 47 of 59 nations are coded as 0 in 1996. For analysis involving the advanced democracies, I also employ Quinn's measure of capital market openness (see Chapter 3). This measurement ranges from 1 to 4, where 4 represents the highest degree of legal capital market openness. Over the course of the 1980s and early 1990s, this measure increased from a moderate level to a nearly full level of capital market openness. Although both measures evaluate overall legal, rather than actual, openness, previous empirical analyses suggest that legal measures do capture general trends in capital market openness.[97]

In evaluating the utility of capital controls in developing nations, I analyze data for the 1981–1996 period for a set of 59 developing countries, listed in Appendix 6.1.[98] Table 6.8 displays the average levels of deficits, inflation, and government debt for two groups of nations, those with and those without capital controls. Nations with capital controls tend to have less market-friendly macroeconomic fundamentals: on average, nations with capital controls have higher government budget deficits, higher rates of inflation, and higher debt/GDP levels.[99] This result suggests that capital controls do allow for the pursuit of divergent – in terms of the prevailing market ideology – policies.

---

[95] Lemmen and Eijffinger 1996, Grilli and Milesi-Ferretti 1995. Also see Dooley 1996 for a survey of the literature on the effects of capital controls

[96] Kim 1997.

[97] Garrett 1998b, Quinn 1997.

[98] The availability of data varies across indicators, so that some analyses draw on a larger group of these nations and years, and others draw from fewer nations.

[99] The macroeconomic data in this section are from the World Bank, *World Development Indicators* CD-ROM, 1998 and the World Bank, *Global Development Finance*, 1998.

Table 6.8. *Capital Controls and Macroeconomic Indicators in Emerging Markets*

Capital Controls	Mean Government Balance/GDP	N	Mean Annual Inflation Rate	N	Mean Government Debt/GDP	N
Controls	−3.29	468	115.5	534	56.54	270
No Controls	−2.26	112	27.4	131	45.93	56

Note: Each observation represents a country-year.

Table 6.9. *Capital Controls and Macroeconomic Indicators in Developed Democracies, 1981–1986*

Capital Controls	Mean Budget Balance/GDP	N	Mean Annual Inflation Rate	N	Mean Government Debt/GDP	N
Controls (0)	−3.72	134	7.66	150	59.57	130
No Controls(1)	−3.54	156	3.54	161	69.71	143

Note: Capital Controls variable is Kim's 1997 measure. Each observation is a country-year.

In nominal terms, though, governments pay a price for this autonomy: the average nominal interest rate spread (over the London InterBank rate) is 47.6% ($n = 445$) for nations with controls and 26.7% ($n = 112$) for nations without controls. Likewise, the average nominal deposit interest rate is 138.2% in nations with controls, but 22.0% in nations without controls. A good portion of this difference likely is due to differences in inflation; real interest rates are, on average, *lower* in nations with capital controls (2.9% vs. 10.7%).

Among developed democracies, nations with capital controls also have larger government budget deficits and higher inflation. In Table 6.9, based on data for the 1981–1996 period, the difference in average deficits is quite small, but the difference in rates of inflation is substantial.[100] In terms of interest rates, nominal rates are higher in nation-years with any sort of capital controls (11.76% vs. 8.72% for long-term rates, and 12.15% vs. 8.43% for short-term rates), but, as earlier, real rates are lower when capital controls are present. The average annual volatility of short-term and

---

[100] This finding is consistent with Grilli and Milesi-Ferretti's 1995 study of capital controls in advanced industrial democracies; they find that capital controls are more likely where government is larger, inflation is higher, and current account imbalances are larger.

Table 6.10. *Regression Results for Capital Controls in Developed Democracies, 1981–1996*

	Coefficient Estimate	Standard Error	$P > t$
Government Balance	−0.063***	0.024	0.010
Inflation	0.593***	0.027	0.000
Current Account	−0.0747**	0.035	0.032
Capital Controls	−1.020***	0.221	0.000
Constant	7.530***	0.240	0.000

Note: $N = 261$; $R^2 = 0.81$, $p > F = 0.0000$; transformed Durbin–Watson = 1.98.

long-term interest rates, however, is not significantly different (at the 95% confidence level) between the two groups of countries.

The average level of government debt, though, is *lower* in nations with capital controls – the reverse of the situation in developing countries. Additionally, as overall capital market openness increases, so does the average level of government debt. This difference between groups of nations in the debt–controls relationship may reflect variance in default risk. In developed nations, open capital markets expand the total pool of capital available and facilitate the growth of public debt.[101] Because default risk is low, governments can sustain high levels of borrowing. In developing countries, by contrast, the existence of default risk likely serves to limit the amount of government debt accumulated. And, if developing nation governments borrow from multilateral agencies or bilateral creditors, which often are not covered by capital controls, governments can amass large debts without financial market openness.[102]

Finally, for developed nations, a Cochrane–Orcutt regression analysis of annual data (1981–1996) suggests that capital controls – using Quinn's measure – are associated with lower interest rates on government bonds. In Table 6.10, long-term interest rates on government bonds are the dependent variable. As in Chapter 3, higher inflation, a smaller government budget balance, and a smaller current account balance are significantly associated with higher interest rates. Independently of macroeconomic fundamentals, capital controls are associated with higher interest rates. These results suggest, contrary to other evidence, that capital controls may be costly for governments. The association, however, may be spurious: certain types of economies – for example, states with small capital markets – may

---

[101] Corsetti and Roubini 1996, Bisignano 1994, p. 29.
[102] *IMF Survey*, October 20, 1997, p. 327.

be more likely both to impose capital controls and to pay high borrowing costs.

The Determinants of Capital Controls   Studies of capital controls in the developed world suggest that controls reflect deliberate choices regarding economic management: governments view controls as a means of preserving policy autonomy.[103] The pressures emanating from global capital markets at time t + 1 are a direct result of government policy choices at time t,[104] and governments undoubtedly are aware of their agency in this process. Additionally, the preceding data imply that the imposition of capital controls in the developing world likely reflects a desire to pursue some sort of autonomous economic policy. As Chapter 5 points out, a government facing external financial pressures may conform to (e.g., by lowering inflation) or resist those pressures (e.g., by insulating its capital markets). For instance, increases in capital controls in Latin America – in Bolivia, Mexico and Peru, among others – in the mid-1980s served to insulate national economies in the wake of the debt crisis. Similarly, Malaysia's 1998 controls aimed to stem capital flight.

Despite the potential advantages of capital controls, developed nations have been characterized by steady increases in capital market openness. Likewise, in developing nations, movements toward controls are rare: in Kim's data set, there are 10 changes from openness to closure, all in Latin America, and 7 in the 1980s. That said, among nations with equally good or equally bad economic fundamentals, choices regarding capital controls vary. For instance, Malaysia was the only nation to respond to the Asian financial crisis by imposing limitations on capital flows.

Although capital controls are unlikely to be used broadly as an insulating device, especially in the developed world, any decision to use them is likely to reflect domestic distributional concerns. For instance, where local firms demand access to global capital markets and are politically powerful, governments are less likely to attempt insulation via capital controls.[105] Drawing on Spain's experience, Lukauskas maintains that democratization may provide political leaders with incentive to open their capital markets, as they face greater pressures to provide economic goods.[106] Using a broader

---

[103] E.g., Lemmen and Eijffinger 1996.
[104] Sinclair 2001.
[105] Eichengreen and Mussa 1999, Haggard and Maxfield 1996.
[106] Lukauskas 1997.

sample of OECD nations and analyzing the 1950–1988 period, Quinn and Inclan find that capital openness is more likely under left governments with abundant skilled labor. Capital controls, meanwhile, are more likely with left governments and scarce skilled labor, as well as with right governments and disadvantaged business sectors. These partisan effects, however, appear to fade over time.[107] In a more recent and geographically broader analysis, Garrett finds that the extent to which a country is democratic has no impact on capital account openness; where trade unionization is higher, however, capital account closure is more likely.[108] In the contemporary era, then, we can expect governments to seek balance between the contending aims of greater economic efficiency and greater domestic policy autonomy in ways that reflect local interests, institutions, and ideologies.

Debt Maturity Structures

A more common means of government insulation is the management of the maturity structure of public debt. *Maturity structure* refers to the overall composition, in terms of time to maturity or repayment, of debt securities.[109] Governments with shorter maturity structures are more susceptible to financial market pressures, as they expose themselves more frequently to market discipline.[110] For such governments, short-term market movements have direct implications for the costs of government borrowing and, therefore, for budget outlays.[111] This effect is particularly salient in high-debt nations.

A high proportion of short-term debt also renders financial crises more likely. A government that must refinance a large amount of debt on certain days is vulnerable to sudden swings in market sentiment.[112] As recent experiences in emerging markets demonstrate, financial crises are more likely, all factors equal, with short debt maturities or unevenly distributed debt stocks.[113] Along these lines, short maturity structures appear to have facilitated the Mexican financial crisis. The average time to maturity of Mexican

---

[107] Quinn and Inclan 1997.
[108] Garrett 2000a.
[109] Agell et al. 1992, Tobin 1963.
[110] E.g., Calvo and Mendoza 1996a, 1996b. On other uses of maturity structures, for example, to deal with shocks to public finances, see Calvo and Guidotti 1990, Missale 1999.
[111] Barro 1997b, p. 18.
[112] Alesina et al. 1990, Foresi et al. 1996.
[113] Canzonero 1995, Frankel and Rose 1996, Giavazzi and Pagano 1990, Grabel 1999.

government debt fell from 293 days in January 1994 to just 206 days in December 1994.[114] Additionally, a developed nation with shorter-dated debt, such as Sweden in the mid-1990s,[115] finds itself more constrained than a similar nation with a longer debt maturity structure.

On the other hand, governments with longer-term structures can be much less concerned with the implications of shorter-term market move-ments.[116] For instance, the Canadian government recently noted that, by reducing the amount of short-term debt in its outstanding portfolio of debt – from 47% in 1993–1994 to 33% in 1997–1998 – it insulated itself from changes in world interest rates.[117] Interviews with officials of other governments likewise confirm the insulating effects of longer maturity structures.[118]

Although using long-term financing instruments does promise greater government autonomy from financial markets, it often entails costs.[119] Under most circumstances, the yield curve is upward sloping, so that shorter-term borrowing rates are lower than longer-term rates.[120] Issu-ing longer-term debt in such a situation entails higher interest rate costs and may be impossible for some emerging market economies.[121] Especially where outstanding debt is high, governments may find long-term debt to be very expensive, as market actors charge large risk premia.[122]

Therefore, governments seem to face a trade-off between the costs of long-term debt instruments and the benefits of greater policy autonomy. The higher borrowing costs that may be associated with greater insulation have implications for government spending in other areas.[123] Along these lines, Missale suggests that governments have incentives to behave as private borrowers, pursuing a strategy of "funding at least cost and risk."[124] The

---

[114] Cole and Kehoe 1996, Calvo and Mendoza 1996a, *IMF Survey* December 11, 1995, p. 397.

[115] See Chapter 5.

[116] Dornbusch and Draghi 1990, Cole and Kehoe 1996.

[117] Canadian Treasury 1997.

[118] Interviews, Bank of Belgium, April 1997; French Ministry of Economy, May 1997; and German Bundesbank, May 1997. Also see Government of Italy, Treasury Department, *Economic Bulletin* No. 26, February 1998, p. 40.

[119] Agell et al. 1992, Cole and Kehoe 1996.

[120] Agell et al. 1992, Campbell 1995, Cebula 1995.

[121] IMF 2000b.

[122] Cañzonero 1995, Missale and Blanchard 1994, Missale 1999.

[123] Tobin 1963.

[124] Missale 1999, Mylonas et al. 2000, OECD 1993. Missale notes, however, that defining *risk* satisfactorily is difficult for governments and debt management officials.

Canadian Department of Finance, for instance, embraces the objective of "striking a balance between cost, risk and market considerations."[125] Even the U.S. government, which has paid relatively low interest rates in recent years, is sensitive to the costs of longer-term financing. In the late 1970s, the U.S. government undertook deliberate efforts to lengthen debt maturity. In early 1993, however, the Clinton administration noted that significant reductions in financing costs could be realized via the shortening of debt maturities; the Treasury began shifting $50 billion per year in new debt issues from longer (30- and 7-year notes) to shorter (2- and 3-year notes and 90-day Treasury bills) maturities.[126]

Figure 6.5 depicts the trade-off between financing costs and insulation via longer maturity structures.[127] The vertical dimension represents financing costs, in the form of interest rates on government bonds, and the horizontal dimension indicates the term structure, in terms of the average maturity of outstanding government bonds. Quadrant IV represents an ideal situation, in terms of insulation and costs. Investors view countries in Quadrant IV as good credit risks, so they can borrow with long maturities at relatively low interest rates. For these nations, little or no trade-off exists. A possible example is the United States in the mid- to late 1990s: because U.S. government securities are highly desirable investments, the U.S. is able both to borrow at low rates and to have a relatively long average maturity structure. Likewise, the British government succeeded in maintaining a very long average term to maturity during the 1990s and did so at a relatively low cost.[128] Moreover, in Asia, during the mid-1990s, Malaysia, Thailand, and Korea issued bonds with maturities of 11, 7, and 6 years, at very low spreads above developed nation bonds.[129]

The situation represented by Quadrant I, on the other hand, is least desirable. As poor credit risks, nations in Quadrant I must borrow at short maturities but still pay relatively high financing costs.[130] These nations are

[125] Government of Canada, Department of Finance 1997, p. 5. Also see the Treasury, Government of Australia 1998, p. 17, and Interviews 16 and 48 for similar statements. Missale 1999 reports a survey of national debt management agents, sponsored by the Swedish National Debt Office, in which all respondents mention the objective of containing interest costs.

[126] Campbell 1995.

[127] Missale et al. 1997.

[128] Missale notes, however, that the United Kingdom also maintained a long maturity structure in the 1970s and 1990s, when inflation was relatively high.

[129] Goldstein and Turner 1996.

[130] Blanchard and Missale 1994, Dornbusch and Draghi 1990, Miller 1997.

Financing Costs (Interest Rates)

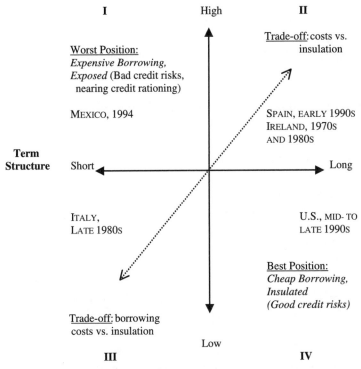

Figure 6.5 Term structure trade-offs.

very exposed to changes in international market sentiment and also may be pressed to pursue adaptive strategies, such as the issuance of indexed or foreign currency–denominated securities. The Mexican government's situation in mid-1994 represents such a case: market actors were willing to buy *tesobonos* only at high interest rates and short maturities, rendering the government very susceptible to a sudden change in market sentiment.[131] Mexican debt management in the mid-1990s provided neither insulation nor low borrowing costs. For nations in Quadrant I, the maturity structure

---

[131] A similar case from the interwar period is France, which faced a market confidence crisis in the mid-1920s, as debt climbed dramatically and the exchange rate plummeted. In order to continue to sell public debt, the French government had to offer very short-term securities (with maturities of one to three months) and to raise interest rates repeatedly. Canziani et al. 1994.

of government debt likely is determined by a nation's economic situation, in that high investment risk creates pressures to shorten maturities. Along these lines, Missale finds that, in high-debt developed nations (with debt levels greater than 100% of GDP), there is an inverse relationship between debt levels and debt maturity.[132]

Quadrants II and III represent "trade-off" situations: governments in the second quadrant pay relatively higher borrowing costs in exchange for longer maturities. Insulation is possible, but at a price. For instance, in the mid- and late 1980s, Italy pursued a Quadrant II strategy: the government attempted to decrease the risks of frequent refinancing by borrowing at longer maturities, even when this meant higher interest rates.[133] Governments in the third quadrant are in the opposite situation: they pay relatively low borrowing costs in exchange for short maturities.[134] The term structure of debt for nations in Quadrants II and III reflects deliberate choice; term structure is not determined fully by macroeconomic fundamentals or financial market demands. Governments may pay lower borrowing costs and be more exposed to the international bond market, or pay higher borrowing costs and be less exposed.[135]

Debt Maturity and Macroeconomic Conditions Figure 6.5 assumes that, especially for developed democracies, macroeconomic fundamentals do not fully determine the maturity structure; most governments find themselves in Quadrant II or III. Previous work on this subject suggests that governments do exercise *some* autonomy over the maturity structure of debt, and that different governments make different types of trade-offs. Missale and Blanchard, as well as a more recent study by Missale, do not find a systematic relationship between debt levels and debt maturity in most OECD nations during the 1960–1996 period. Some governments elect to borrow more cheaply and at shorter maturities; others elect to pay the premium

---

[132] Missale 1999; also see Blanchard and Missale 1994, Miller 1997.

[133] Alesina et al. 1990, Conti and Hamaui 1994, Gowland 1990.

[134] Missale et al. 1997 suggest that governments that are overseeing fiscal stabilizations choose to reduce the term structure of their debt when they otherwise cannot credibly commit themselves to the stabilization program. Although borrowing at short maturities creates refinancing risk, it is cheaper, and, more importantly, it can serve to convince market actors of the government's resolve. A government that borrows in short instruments has little incentive to inflate away debt. In this model, the government chooses short maturities until it convinces markets of its commitment; then it is able to choose long maturity structures.

[135] Dornbusch and Draghi 1990. IMF 2000b recommends the latter course of action for many emerging market governments.

Table 6.11. *Maturity Structures and Government Debt, 1996*

Country	Average Time to Maturity of Government Debt (EMI data)	Government Debt/GDP Ratio	Annual Rate of Inflation
UK	10.1	62.2	2.4
Netherlands	6.4	76.6	2.1
Austria	6.1	69.5	1.9
France	5.3	63.0	2.0
Ireland	5.3	76.2	1.7
Denmark	5.3	70.8	2.1
Germany	4.7	64.9	1.5
Belgium	4.5	126.9	2.1
Finland	4.4	58.0	0.6
Italy	4.3	123.7	3.8
Portugal	3.2	68.1	3.1
Spain	3.1	74.8	3.6
Sweden	2.7	79.4	0.8
AVERAGE FOR SAMPLE	5.0	78.0	2.1

Source: OECD Statistical Compendium; European Monetary Institute *1998 Convergence Report.*

for longer maturity structures.[136] For example, in Ireland in the 1970s and 1980s, as the level of public debt grew, so did the time to maturity of government debt.[137] Similarly, beginning in 1989, the Spanish Treasury worked to lengthen the maturity of its debt (despite the additional costs of doing so) in order to reduce the risks associated with frequent refinancing.[138]

Table 6.11 provides a recent snapshot of debt maturity, inflation, and government debt in Western European nations. Again, this table indicates that the relationship between average term to maturity and government policy outcomes varies cross-nationally. Some nations have relatively high debt but intermediate maturity structures (Belgium); others have relatively low debt and shorter-term maturity structures (Portugal). Additionally, the average term to maturity often moves in the opposite direction from fiscal policy outcomes. In Italy, average maturity increased from 2.8 years in 1991 to 4.3 years in 1996, despite high and (through 1994) increasing levels of government debt. Likewise, Spain's average debt maturity grew

[136] Italy's debt management, cited previously, fits this pattern.
[137] Calvo and Guidotti 1990, p. 222.
[138] Cañzonero 1995.

Table 6.12. *Maturity Structures and Macroeconomic Indicators in Emerging Markets*

	Coefficient Estimate	Standard Error	$P > t$
Inflation	0.0020***	0.0007	0.006
Debt	−0.0840**	0.0329	0.012
Current Account	−0.4329***	0.1137	0.000
Constant	20.41***	2.6147	0.000

Note: $N = 105$; $R^2 = 0.29$; $p > F = 0.000$; transformed Durbin–Watson $= 1.37$ (Prais–Winsten AR(1) regression).

from 1.4 years in 1991 to 3.7 years in 1996, while Spain's debt/GDP ratio increased from 50.4 to 74.1. In both cases, EMU-generated credibility may have offset other economic fundamentals. In Ireland, the pattern was the opposite: the average maturity of debt shrank from 6.7 years in 1991 to 5.3 years in 1996, but Ireland's debt level fell, from 97% of GDP to 76% of GDP. In developed economies, then, it appears that governments are able to make strategic choices regarding debt management. Nations with poor economic fundamentals, however, are more limited in their range of choices: a developed nation with mediocre economic fundamentals may have a choice between an average maturity of 2 years and one of 4 years, but not between an average maturity of 2 years and one of 10 years. Moreover, in developing nations, governments likely have less autonomy in the selection of maturity structures. In emerging market economies, therefore, shorter-term debt is used extensively and likely reflects, to some degree, economic fundamentals.[139]

Two sets of empirical analyses assess further these expectations. An analysis of data for the 1989–1996 period, using the same 59 nations, suggests that economic fundamentals are significantly associated with the maturity structure of government debt. In Table 6.12, the dependent variable is the percentage of government debt that is short-term, with less than one year to maturity.[140] The independent variables are inflation, government debt, and the current account balance.

The results display a significant and positive association between inflation and short-term debt; where inflation is higher, governments borrow

---

[139] Erb et al. 1999.

[140] This is the best measure available for developing economies: although the World Bank also provides a measure of the average time to maturity of *new* government borrowing, it does not provide data regarding the average time to maturity of *outstanding* commitments.

more at the short end of the maturity scale. The magnitude of this co-efficient, however, is quite small.[141] Additionally, larger current account deficits are associated significantly with higher levels of short-term debt, and the effect of this variable is much more pronounced. Governments facing large current account deficits experience pressure to achieve balance via the capital account, and possibly to depreciate the currency. Both of these effects likely lead investors to offer only shorter-term loans. Finally, whereas the association between government debt and the percentage of short-term debt is statistically significant, the sign is not in the expected direction. The negative sign implies that, as the level of government debt climbs, the percentage of short-term debt falls. This result may imply some sort of nonlinearity in the relationship between overall debt and short-term debt: nations with very high overall debt borrow short-term, whereas nations with moderate to high levels of debt have greater choice about the maturity composition of debt. Alternatively, this result may hint at problems in our measures of debt: total debt includes borrowing from multilateral agencies and banks as well as from disintermediated capital markets. If the highest-debt nations borrow more heavily from multilateral agencies and banks, which tend to make longer-term loans, they have a lower ratio of short-term debt.

Although the results in Table 6.12 do not provide definitive evidence, they do support the general expectation that developing nations with high inflation and poor current account positions tend to issue shorter-term instruments. Furthermore, in this sample, the average real interest rate (the nominal rate less inflation) for nations with high levels (20% or higher) of short-term debt is 7.7%, but the average real interest rate for nations with low levels (less than 20%) of short term debt is 2.74%.

For the advanced industrial democracies, I employ data for the 1990–1996 period, from Missale, who uses national sources to calculate the conventional and effective maturities of government debt for most of the advanced capitalist democracies.[142] The dependent variable in the analysis reported in Table 6.13 is Missale's measure of the conventional average term to maturity of government debt. This measure ranges from 1.26 years to 12.43 years, with a mean of 5.17 years and a standard deviation of 2.34 years.

---

[141] Similarly, Missale finds that inflation is associated with shorter maturities only in Finland, Ireland, Italy, and Spain. Missale 1999, p. 188.

[142] Missale 1999. The ECB (formely EMI, until January 1999) also provides average term to maturity data for EU members for the 1990s.

Table 6.13. *Maturity Structures and Macroeconomic Indicators in Developed Democracies*

Variable	Coefficient	Standard Error	$P > t$
LongShort	0.040	0.133	0.763
Inflation	−0.218***	0.058	0.000
Exchange Rate	−0.066	0.043	0.132
Government Debt	−0.043***	0.007	0.000
Constant	9.45***	0.679	0.000

Note: $N = 106$; $R^2 = 0.33$; $p > F = 0.000$; transformed Durbin–Waston $= 1.98$ (Cochrane–Orcutt regression).

Results using this measure are quite similar to those obtained using the EMI's measure, or other of Missale's maturity measures.

The macroeconomic fundamentals included as independent variables are the exchange rate, the inflation rate, and the government debt/GDP ratio. In order to assess the impact of debt financing costs on securities of different maturities, I also include a measure of the differential between short- and long-term government bond rates (LONGSHORT). If governments choose maturity structures on the basis of borrowing costs – rather than on the basis of a desire for insulation – we should observe a negative and significant relationship between LONGSHORT and the average time to maturity of government debt.

These results suggest that macroeconomic fundamentals sometimes are associated significantly with the maturity structure of government debt, but that fundamentals by no means determine the maturity structure of government debt.[143] Higher inflation is associated significantly and negatively with the average term to maturity. A 1% increase in the rate of inflation implies a 0.22-year decline in the average term to maturity, so that a nation with a 7% annual rate of inflation has a maturity structure one year shorter than that of a nation with a 2% annual rate of inflation. Similarly, the coefficient on government debt is statistically significant and negative; a 10% increase in the debt/GDP ratio is associated with a reduction of 0.43 year in the average term to maturity of government debt. Ceteris paribus, a nation with a debt/GDP ratio of 100% has an average term to maturity that is two years less than that of a nation with a debt/GDP ratio of 53%.[144] This effect is not overwhelming: accumulated debt may make the difference between

[143] Missale 1999 notes a similar pattern.
[144] Models using the budget balance rather than government debt produce similar results.

238

a maturity of 6 years and one of 4 years but does not move a government from a maturity of 10 years to a maturity of 2 years. Additionally, the effect of changes in the nominal exchange rate is both small and statistically insignificant.

Last, the coefficient on LONGSHORT is positive, but does not approach statistical significance; this suggests that the cost of borrowing at short versus long maturities may not be so relevant to government maturity structure decisions. This model implies that the maturity structure of government debt is not fully driven by macroeconomic fundamentals. In developed democracies, governments play an important and autonomous role in the selection of debt management policies.[145] Likewise, Giovannini observes that "macroeconomic models do not provide unambiguous recipes for government debt management, but a rich menu of cases to choose from."[146] In other words, on most occasions, governments of developed democracies *do* find themselves in Quadrants II and III in Figure 6.5 – with a strategic choice between borrowing costs and insulation. Ultimately, governments often must decide whether to impose risk and costs on investors or on taxpayers.[147]

Resident Investment

Another potential means for governments to insulate themselves from certain types of market pressures is by encouraging residents to purchase government bonds. When investors can hedge against exchange rate risk via forward markets, they should be indifferent between domestic and foreign assets with the same risk–return profiles. Despite hedging, though, there is evidence that resident investors and nonresidents act differently. For example, governments with high levels of indebtedness, such as Belgium and Italy, are quick to point out that most of their debt is owed to residents, rendering them less susceptible to financial market pressures. Moreover, several studies have noted a home country bias in investment: investors

---

[145] Mylonas et al. 2000 note, however, that there is a trend in OECD nations toward the appointment of politically independent debt managers, which have the sole objective of "meeting the government's borrowing requirements" and are supposed to "prevent the interaction of debt issuance with the conduct of monetary and fiscal policy." But also see OECD 1993, which points out that there are a variety of ways to structure the relationship between debt managers and political actors.

[146] Giovannini 1997, p. 45.

[147] Missale 1999.

do not diversify internationally to the extent that economic theory predicts.[148] And, in their study of the 1994 European bond market, Borio and McCauley find that higher levels of bond market volatility are strongly correlated with higher proportions of nonresident investors.[149] Therefore, when policy outcomes are poor, the loyalty of resident investors may provide governments with a cushion.[150]

Three potential causal mechanisms underlie the resident–nonresident distinction. The first is regulation: if the government imposes penalties on nonresident investors, or if the government offers inducements to resident investors, residents and nonresidents act differently. During the 1950s and 1960s, many OECD governments imposed restrictions on banks, including the compulsory holdings of government securities or credit allocation rules. Additionally, the capital controls in many European nations into the 1980s and early 1990s prevented domestic residents from investing abroad.[151] These rules both served prudential purposes *and* allowed governments to finance deficits at lower rates of interest.[152] Although the EU has attempted to eliminate these regulations, some developed nation governments continue to tax resident and nonresident bondholders differently or to tax income from domestic bonds and income from foreign bonds at different rates. And in Latin America as well as in Western Europe, public pension systems include – even after market-oriented reforms – requirements that some percentage of pension assets be invested in government debt.[153] Lebanon offers an extreme version of resident investors' regulatory incentives: in the late 1990s, U.S. dollars accounted for 65% of Lebanese bank deposits. In early 1998, the central bank banned local banks from investing in emerging markets, leaving a nearly captive supply of resident dollars.

---

[148] Bisignano 1994, French and Poterba 1991, Obstfeld 1993, Obstfeld 1998, von Mises 1912/1953 p. 379. Ahearne et al. 2001 provide evidence that home-country bias in U.S. investors' equity holdings is a result of low information quality in many foreign countries.

[149] Borio and McCauley 1996. On turnover of foreign investment in Spain, see Quiros 1993. Barth and Zhang 1999 find evidence that, in Indonesia, Korea, Taiwan, and Thailand in the late 1990s, foreign investors led market movements. On the other hand, Choe et al. 1998 find no evidence that trades by nonresident investors had a destabilizing effect on Korea's stock market during the 1996–1997 period.

[150] On the choice of loyalty rather than exit, see Hirschman 1970.

[151] Calvo et al. 1996, Gordon and Bovenberg 1996, p. 1059.

[152] Edey and Hviding 1995, Bisignano 1994, Tobin 1963.

[153] Blommestein and Funke 1998 provide a summary of these regulations. Also see Mylonas et al. 2000, OECD 1993. French and Poterba 1991 suggest that behavioral, rather than institutional (including regulatory) factors explain lack of diversification in investors' equity holdings.

Not surprisingly, Lebanon's September 1998 dollar-denominated bond issue was oversubscribed, even though Lebanon's government deficit/GDP ratio was 14%.[154]

The second mechanism is information: resident investors may know more about the implications of various events for key government policy outcomes, they may be able to obtain information more cheaply, and they may be more certain about the information they possess.[155] Along similar lines, Gordon and Bovenberg argue that asymmetric information between investors in different countries underlies the lack of international portfolio diversification.[156] Moreover, because nonresident investors tend to have only a small percentage of their holdings in any given market, their incentives to gather additional information about a particular country are low.[157] Of course, better-informed domestic investors may also be more likely to exit home markets early, as in Mexico in 1994 and Malaysia in 1998.[158]

The third explanation for the resident–nonresident distinction are differences in the types of investors in each category. When government officials argue that resident investors behave in a less volatile fashion, they often refer to individual investors – to "Belgian dentists and Italian grandmothers" – rather than to institutional investors.[159] The market for Italian government securities, in fact, traditionally was characterized by a high proportion of household investors; institutional investors played a relatively marginal role, holding only 11% of bonds in the early 1990s. During the same period, institutional investors held approximately 45% of outstanding bonds in the United Kingdom and France.[160] These investors may act differently not because of nationality, but because of type: individual investors and institutional investors may have very different asset allocation processes.[161] For example, household investors may be less willing to incur (or to hedge

---

[154] *Economist*, September 19, 1998, p. 88.
[155] Aronovich 1999, Frankel and Schmulker 1997, Kaufmann et al. 1999, Shukla and van Inwegen 1995, Interviews 6 and 8. Interview, French Economics Ministry, May 1997.
[156] Gordon and Bovenberg 1996. Also see Eichengreen and Mussa 1999.
[157] Cañzonero 1995, Gavin et al. 1996.
[158] Gil-Diaz and Carstens 1996, Friedman 2000, p. 127. In addition, Barth and Zhang 1999 argue that, during the late 1990s, foreign investors were market leaders, rather than followers, in Asian markets.
[159] Interview, BIS Monetary Affairs Department, May 1997.
[160] Conti and Hamaui 1994, De Felice and Miranda 1994.
[161] Bisignano 1994 and Wilcox 1999 discuss differences in behavior across types of investors.

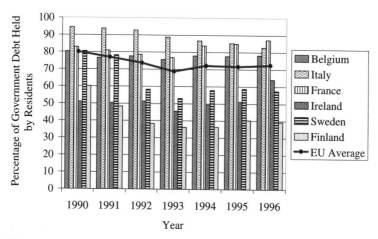

Figure 6.6 Resident investment in European nations.

against) exchange rate risk and, therefore, less willing to buy foreign securities rather than domestic securities.

The potential differences in resident–nonresident behavior likely stem from some combination of these mechanisms – from regulation, information, and investor identity. The mechanisms have similar implications for financial market–government relations: nations with a greater level of resident investment should be more insulated from international financial market pressures. Of course, the resident investment strategy has costs: borrowing only from resident investors may increase (depending on the level of regulation in domestic capital markets) interest rates, as a smaller pool of capital is available.

Therefore, governments in advanced industrial democracies make trade-offs: some encourage high levels of resident investment and may pay slightly higher interest rates, whereas others encourage nonresident investment, possibly paying lower interest rates. Figure 6.6 provides data regarding resident investment in government securities in a sample of European nations.[162] Italy and France display resident holding levels consistently higher than 80% of outstanding debt; Finland, Sweden, and Ireland rely much less on resident investment. Data for Japan and Canada reinforce the picture of cross-national variance: during the 1985–1996 period, over 90% of Japanese debt was held by resident investors. Canadian residential debt

---

[162] These data are drawn from the European Monetary Institute 1998.

Table 6.14. *Resident Investment and Macroeconomic Indicators in Advanced Economies*

Variable	Coefficient	Standard Error	$P > t$
Government Balance (t − 1)	−1.12***	0.37	0.004
Inflation (t − 1)	2.32***	0.49	0.000
Exchange Rate Change	0.48*	0.25	0.060
Constant	59.83***	2.95	0.000

Note: $N = 110$; $R^2 = 0.20$; $p > F = 0.000$; Cochrane–Orcutt regression; transformed Durbin–Watson statistic = 2.00.

holdings, on the other hand, are just a few percentage points higher than the EU average.[163]

Resident Investment and Macroeconomic Conditions Resident investment and macroeconomic fundamentals may be related via two different mechanisms. Governments with poor macroeconomic fundamentals may attempt to appeal to resident investors; when fundamentals improve, they may appeal to foreign investors as well. In Italy, for instance, the proportion of resident investment remained relatively high throughout the 1990s but declined later in the decade as Italy's economic fundamentals improved. This mechanism would produce a statistical association between economic fundamentals in the previous period and current resident investment. In the second pathway, governments already characterized by high levels of resident investment may have the autonomy to choose divergent (that is, non-market-friendly) policies. This mechanism leads to a statistical relationship between resident investment in prior periods and current economic fundamentals.

The analysis reported in Table 6.14 suggests that the first mechanism is more accurate: as fundamentals deteriorate, resident investment increases. The dependent variable in this regression analysis is the percentage of government debt held by residents in EU nations during the 1990–1996 period. The strongest coefficient is on the inflation rate variable: a 1% increase in the rate of inflation in the previous year is associated significantly with a 2.3% increase in resident investment in the current year. The government budget balance coefficient also is significant and negative, implying that when the government deficit is high at time t − 1, the percentage of

[163] Data for 1983–1996 for G-7 nations are drawn from IMF 1998b, p. 190. Because these data are not directly comparable with EMI data, they are not employed in later analyses.

Table 6.15. *The Influence of Resident Investment on Macroeconomic Outcomes*

Dependent Variable	Coefficient on Resident Investment	Confidence Level	N	Implied Effect, One Standard Deviation Change in Resident Investment
Budget Balance	0.1848	99%	97	0.8659
Government Debt	−0.2910	99%	97	−1.3636
Inflation	−0.0136	35%	96	−0.0636

resident investment at time t is higher.[164] Finally, increases in the exchange rate are associated with increases in resident investment: where domestic currency is appreciating, resident investment is higher. When a nation's currency increases in value, so do its government bonds, making nonresident purchases more expensive.

In order to consider resident investment as an independent variable – to test whether higher resident investment facilitates divergent policies – I estimate three bivariate regression equations, reported in Table 6.15. In each model, the annual amount of change in a macroeconomic variable is the dependent variable, and the independent variable is the lagged annual change in resident investment.[165] These simple models suggest that resident investment does not serve as an impetus for the selection of less market-friendly policies. Increases in resident investment are not associated with less market-friendly policies. Resident investment may protect governments once they pursue certain economic policies, but it does not appear to motivate the choice of these policies.

Finally, I consider the association between resident investment and interest rate volatility. If resident investors *do* act differently – and more forgivingly – than nonresident investors, the level of resident investment should be negatively associated with interest rate volatility. Table 6.16 confirms these expectations. The dependent variable is the annual standard deviation of long-term interest rates.[166] Not surprisingly, higher inflation and larger government budget deficits are significantly and positively related to

[164] If we include government debt rather than government budget deficit as the indicator of fiscal policy, the results are very similar. When a measure of the current account balance is included, its coefficient estimate is not statistically significant.

[165] The annual change in resident investment ranges from −19.9% to 17% with a mean of −1.1% and a standard deviation of 4.69.

[166] This variable ranges from 0.0829 to 3.241, with a mean of 0.569 and a standard deviation of 0.403.

Table 6.16. *Interest Rate Volatility and Resident Investment in Advanced Economies*

Variable	Coefficient	Standard Error	$P > t$
Resident Investment (t − 1)	−0.0099***	0.0027	0.000
Government Budget Balance (t − 1)	−0.0474***	0.0118	0.000
Inflation (t − 1)	0.0721***	0.0146	0.000
Constant	0.8704***	0.1908	0.000

Note: $N = 102$; $R^2 = 0.25$; $p > F = 0.0000$.

volatility.[167] Resident investment is significantly and negatively associated with volatility: nations with higher levels of resident investment in the previous period experience less interest rate volatility in the current period. The implied effects of a one standard deviation change in resident investment are similar to those implied by a one standard deviation change in the other indicators. These results suggest that, although resident investment is not associated with less market-friendly economic policies, it does insulate governments from financial sector volatility.

The Costs and Benefits of Resident Investment   Resident investment facilitates borrowing by governments with suboptimal macroeconomic fundamentals, and resident investment appears to reduce interest rate volatility. But, because residents may represent a smaller available pool of capital, interest rates may be higher. The bivariate correlation between government bond rates and resident investment is quite moderate (0.38), suggesting some – but not a very strong – trade-off between resident investment and the costs of borrowing. And the bivariate correlation between national savings rates and resident investment is very small for the 1990s (−0.15). Although larger nations may find it *easier* to attract resident investment, the level of resident investment reflects more than simply the potential pool of domestic savings.[168] Finally, we may conceive of resident investors as one group of domestic political constituents: a government that relies heavily on resident investment is insulated from the international financial markets, but not insulated from the demands of local investors. Therefore, by encouraging high levels of resident investment, a government actually may

---

[167] When the exchange rate variable is included in this analysis, its coefficient is not statistically significant.

[168] Data on the domestic savings rate are taken from World Bank, *World Development Indicators* CD-ROM, 1998.

create stronger domestic preferences against inflation.[169] This puts an interesting twist on the cost–benefit analysis: a government that uses resident investment to insulate itself from external capital market pressures may find itself facing similar pressures from within.

Conclusion: The Interaction of Government Strategies

In addition to highlighting the variety of ways in which governments can interface with global capital markets, this chapter suggests that government strategies should be thought of not in isolation, but as complements or alternatives to one another. Governments may use different institutions that are functional substitutes for one another, or they may employ different policies that are complements. Especially in the developed world, choices over how to link into international capital markets reflect a variety of influences. The character of economic policymaking institutions, the use of investor-insulating tools, and the use of government-insulating measures reflect interplay among domestic political considerations, economic fundamentals, and international financial market pressures. In general, governments of developed democracies have more autonomy in selecting policies than governments of emerging market economies. The percentage of variance in the use of these policies explained by macroeconomic fundamentals is relatively small, leaving plenty of space for political considerations of costs and benefits. Although the data on emerging market policies are less complete than the data for developed democracies, preliminary evidence supports this conclusion.

The three sets of policies examined in this chapter are by no means mutually exclusive. A government, for instance, may pursue an overall program of insulation via *some* lengthening of debt maturities and *some* encouragement of resident investment. Or a government may alter its fiscal and monetary institutions to improve its policy credibility and, therefore, its ability to borrow at longer maturities and in the domestic currency. In fact, simple bivariate correlations suggest that some types of government strategies frequently are used together in advanced industrial democracies. Table 6.17 reports the correlations for the 21 potential pairs of strategies; bold type indicates correlations greater than 0.50. In some cases, strategies appear to reinforce one another. Independent central banks and

---

[169] And ultimately against default; see Alesina and Perotti 1995.

Alternative Domestic Responses

Table 6.17. *Government Policies, Bivariate Correlations*

	Central Bank	Fiscal Institution	Foreign Currency	Indexed Debt	Debt Maturity	Resident Investment
Fiscal Institutions	**0.51**					
Foreign Currency	−0.04	**−0.51**				
Indexed Debt	0.06	0.31	−0.09			
Debt Maturity	0.27	**0.74**	−0.41	**0.66**		
Resident Investment	−0.14	0.28	**−0.89**	0.05	0.28	
Capital Controls	0.33	0.33	−0.16	0.25	0.32	−0.10

independent fiscal institutions go together; an independent central bank may be frustrated by politically dependent fiscal institutions, as expansionary fiscal policy works at cross-purposes with tight monetary policy. At the EU level, the ECB's concerns about fiscal profligacy – and the Stability and Growth Pact – evidence this concern. In similar, but weaker relationship between fiscal institutions and foreign currency debt exists; independent fiscal institutions are associated with less foreign currency denomination. And the correlation between indexed debt and the maturity of debt is 0.66, suggesting that indexation may allow for a longer maturity structure.[170]

Other pairs of strategies may be seen as alternatives: nations that borrow largely from residents have little need to issue foreign currency–denominated securities, as is evidenced by a strong negative correlation between the two measures. For example, in 1996, 83% of Italy's government debt was held domestically and, at the same time, only 7% was denominated in currencies other than lire. Likewise, residents held 78% of Belgium's debt in 1996, and only 7% of Belgian debt was denominated in foreign currencies. Moreover, other types of strategies, such as commitments to an externally based monetary rule, may serve as a substitute for an independent central bank.[171]

[170] See Calvo and Guidotti 1990.
[171] Giavazzi and Pagano 1988 make this argument with respect to EMS.

Therefore, government strategies should be thought of not in isolation, but as complements of or alternatives to one another. Governments may use different institutions that are functional substitutes for one another, or they may employ different policies that are complements. And, as I suggest in the concluding chapter, the utility of various strategies and combinations of strategies changes as the nature of international capital markets changes.

7

History Repeating Itself?

FINANCIAL MARKETS AND NATIONAL GOVERNMENT POLICIES BEFORE THE FIRST WORLD WAR

Globalization is not a new phenomenon. Governments always have been constrained. Globalization really is a catch-word.... Domestic constraints still matter, and international constraints are not much different than they were during the 19th century.[1]

In its international methods, as in these internal methods, nineteenth century society was constricted by economics. The realm of fixed foreign exchanges was coincident with civilization.... Though, as a rule, such considerations [the need for balanced budgets] were not consciously present in the minds of statesmen, this was the case only because the requirements of the gold standard ranked as axiomatic. The uniform world pattern of monetary and representative institutions was the result of the rigid economy of the period.[2]

Polanyi's 1944 account of the collapse of the gold standard regime, and the international economic openness required and facilitated by that regime, implicates the primacy of market forces. Although economic integration was not, in and of itself, detrimental to the functioning of democratic societies, economic integration without an accompanying system of social protection was doomed to failure. Leaders gave priority to the maintenance of external balance over all other goals, but their publics ultimately rejected the notion that currency values were the penultimate policy achievement. If the gold standard's rules – coupled with the evolving domestic political ambitions of governments – sowed the seeds of its demise, can the same be said for contemporary financial globalization? To what extent are Polanyi's criticisms of the late nineteenth and early twentieth centuries relevant today?

[1] Interview, adviser to German chancellor and former IMF official, May 1997.
[2] Polanyi 1944, pp. 252–253.

This chapter addresses these questions by comparing government–financial market relations in the pre–World War I period with government–financial market relations in the contemporary era, as described in preceding chapters. Extant discussions of globalization sometimes point out the parallels between the economic openness of today and the economic openness of the 1870–1914 period.[3] Often, these discussions imply that, because government autonomy was not compromised fully by earlier financial internationalization, that autonomy in the present period also will remain largely unaffected. Although this conclusion provides a much-needed antidote to the popular notion that financial openness renders national states powerless, it is not based on a careful comparison of the characteristics and implications of different periods of financial globalization.

I take an initial step toward filling this lacuna. I assess the similarities and differences between the two eras of financial globalization, with an eye to identifying the ways in which the pre–World War I experience is instructive for scholars and policymakers. After a brief summary of the levels of economic integration and the nature of government borrowing prior to World War I, I identify similarities and differences between the pre–World War I and the contemporary period. My comparison focuses on three dimensions: the structure of the financial industry and, therefore, of sovereign borrowing practices; the governance of capital flows, both nationally and internationally; and the policy commitments and ambitions of national governments. After this discussion, I examine cases of sovereign lending during the 1880–1914 period, identifying the conditions under which borrowers face lower or higher levels of financial market pressures. This examination includes a discussion of four nations' borrowing, as well as evidence from a larger set of archival data, drawn from approximately 70 lending episodes.

From the theoretical comparisons and the empirical evidence, a mixed picture emerges. Governments survived an earlier era of "capital market constraints," during which individual investors looked to financial intermediaries as information sources, and intermediaries took measures to compensate for default risk. Sovereign borrowers with strong economic prospects and unblemished credit histories or sovereign borrowers with political importance paid the lowest rates of interest and were least subject to bankers' involvement in their domestic affairs. Additionally, commitments to an international currency regime further served to limit

[3] E.g., Garrett 1998c, Hirst and Thompson 1996, Held et al. 1999.

governments' courses of action but also reduced investors' perceived currency risk. Today, the situation is similar, although the movements of capital and information are swifter. It also is the case, however, that the needs of governments – in terms of the range of programs for which they sought funds – were more modest before World War I. Governments prior to the First World War usually were not concerned with redistributive aims. Moreover, contemporary governments may find their policies affected not only by portfolio investors, as in the past, but also by direct investors, who are increasingly active in the international movement of funds and production. Therefore, financial activity during the gold standard era suggests that, particularly with the advent of EMU and the increased popularity of currency boards, governments may well find themselves facing a historically unprecedented range of financial market influences.

Economic Internationalization before the First World War

High levels of economic interdependence, facilitated by a combination of hegemonic leadership, currency stability, and technological advances,[4] characterized the late nineteenth and early twentieth centuries. Indeed, the era of the classical gold standard (1870–1914) is regarded by many as a "high water-mark in the free movement of capital, labor and commodities among nations."[5] Many European economies displayed levels of trade openness not again seen until the 1980s. Table 7.1 provides comparative levels of trade openness, measured as the ratio of merchandise trade to GDP, for the pre–World War I and contemporary periods. Labor markets also were significantly integrated, as cross-border migration effected a competitive narrowing of cross-national wage differentials.[6]

Financial markets likewise were internationally linked. Governments have long relied on international borrowing to meet their fiscal needs, with the modern financial order dating to sixteenth-century Antwerp.[7] By the

---

[4] Hirst and Thompson 1996, O'Rourke and Williamson 1999, Zevin 1992. For instance, the installation of the transatlantic telegraph cable (in 1866) reduced the settlement time for intercontinental transactions from approximately one and one-half weeks to several hours, leading one economist to label this advance as "perhaps more significant than anything that has been achieved since." Obstfeld 1998.

[5] Obstfeld and Taylor 1998 p. 353. Also see Hirst and Thomson 1996 and Held et al. 1999.

[6] Feenstra 1998, Williamson 1995.

[7] Germain 1997, Thompson 1997, Zevin 1992. Germain notes, however, that cross-border capital flows existed long prior to the sixteenth century (pp. 35–36).

Table 7.1. *Trade Openness, 1890–1990*

Country	1890	1913	1960	1970	1980	1990
Australia	15.7	21.0	13.0	11.5	13.6	13.4
Canada	12.8	17.0	14.5	18.0	24.1	22.0
Denmark	24.0	30.7	26.9	23.3	26.8	24.3
France	14.2	15.5	9.9	11.9	16.7	17.1
Germany	15.9	19.9	14.6	16.5	21.6	24.0
Italy	9.7	14.4	10.0	12.8	19.3	15.9
Japan	5.1	12.5	8.8	8.3	11.8	8.4
Norway	21.8	25.5	24.9	27.6	30.8	28.8
Sweden	23.6	21.2	18.8	19.7	25.0	23.5
United Kingdom	27.3	29.8	15.3	16.5	20.3	20.6
United States	5.6	6.1	3.4	4.1	8.8	8.0

Source: Feenstra 1998, p. 33.

early 18th century, low information costs and the absence of serious currency exchange barriers facilitated speculative cross-national flows. Transactions in foreign capital markets covered not only the developed economies of Europe, but also the developing economies of Asia and Latin America. In the early 1820s, for example, bond issues by Latin American governments accounted for the largest share of foreign government securities sold on the London stock exchange. Much of this capital financed railways and public utilities, as well as the conversion of existing debts.[8] By the 1830s, a secondary market for government debt existed in London.[9] Although the nineteenth century was characterized by some contractions in international capital flows – for example, after the defaults in Latin America in the late 1820s and again during the 1873–1896 depression[10] – the international financial system was highly integrated by the late nineteenth century.

The gold standard exchange rate regime assumed – and required – the mobility of capital.[11] The gold standard was established formally in 1878;

[8] Cottrell 1975, Manzocchi 1999, O'Rourke and Williamson 1999, Salter 1951. Marichal 1989 estimates that 39% of loans to Latin America in the 1850–1875 period funded public works, while 44% funded debt refinancing.

[9] Cottrell 1975, p. 18.

[10] For discussions of the cyclical nature of capital flows during the nineteenth century, see Lindert and Morton 1990, Lipson 1985, Marichal 1989.

[11] Nations with weaker economies, however, tended to be less able to maintain their commitments to the international monetary system. See Eichengreen 1996, Fishlow 1985, and Held et al. 1999.

initially, participation was limited to the wealthy economics of Europe, North America, and Australia. By the early twentieth century, the reach of the gold standard had expanded to include other European nations, Latin American nations, Japan, and some colonial areas. Cross-border movements of gold and currency facilitated balance of payments adjustment, promoted development of closely integrated financial markets, and channeled investment from the developed to the developing world. In 1914, there was approximately $8.2 billion of British direct investment abroad. In the same year, the United States owned $2.7 billion, Germany $2.6 billion, and France $1.8 billion of foreign direct investments.[12]

Throughout the pre–World War I period, Britain – specifically, the London market – was the major source of foreign capital flows, accounting for 62% of foreign investment stocks in 1870 and 44% of foreign investment stocks in 1914.[13] France and Germany also accounted for significant outflows.[14] For some debtor nations, including Canada, Australia, and Argentina, borrowing on international capital markets funded up to half of domestic capital investment.[15]

Although scholars differ in their precise assessments of the magnitude of contemporary (relative to historical) financial internationalization, they agree that the pre–World War I era was one of great financial openness.[16] In some respects, levels of financial openness in 1913 have only recently been surpassed; in other respects, 1913 levels remain the height of financial internationalization. For instance, Obstfeld points out that average current account positions, which indicate the amount of borrowing (deficits) or lending (surpluses) from abroad, reached a higher level in 1914 than at any time since.[17] Table 7.2 contains Obstfeld and Taylor's data on this subject,

---

[12] Hirst and Thompson 1996, Manzocchi 1999.

[13] Feis 1930 notes that, by the turn of the twentieth century, approximately one-half of current British savings was invested abroad. For a discussion of the relationship among British capital exports, the British economy, and British trade, see Cottrell 1975, chapter 5. As Britain declined in importance as a source of foreign investment, the United States increased. Nevertheless, in 1914, only 8% of foreign investment stocks originated in the United States. Held et al. 1999, p. 193.

[14] Taken together, Britain, France, and Germany accounted for about three-quarters of capital outflows prior to 1914. Bloomfield 1968, Verdier 1998.

[15] See Bloomfield 1968, O'Rourke and Williamson 1999, Tanzi and Schuknecht 2000.

[16] For example, see Bloomfield 1968, Feis 1930, Held et al. 1999, Obstfeld and Taylor 1998, O'Rourke and Williamson 1999, Zevin 1992.

[17] Obstfeld 1998. One could argue, however, that this measure of openness would decline over time if financial market participants became more averse to current account deficits. Governments would find it more expensive, in interest rate terms, to run current account

Table 7.2. *Extent of Capital Flows, Measured by Current Account/GDP*

Period	Argentina	France	Italy	Sweden	UK	All[a]
1870–1889	18.7	2.4	1.2	3.2	4.6	3.7
1890–1913	6.2	1.3	1.8	2.3	4.6	3.3
1919–1926	4.9	2.8	4.2	2.0	2.7	3.1
1927–1931	3.7	1.4	1.5	1.8	1.9	2.1
1932–1939	1.6	1.0	0.7	1.5	1.1	1.2
1947–1959	3.1	1.5	1.4	1.1	1.2	1.9
1960–1973	1.0	0.6	2.1	0.7	0.8	1.3
1974–1989	1.9	0.8	1.3	1.5	1.5	2.2
1989–1996	2.0	0.7	1.6	2.0	2.6	2.3

Note: Totals are based on a 12-country sample (Argentina, Australia, Canada, Denmark, France, Germany, Italy, Japan, Norway, Sweden, United Kingdom, and United States).
Source: Obstfeld and Taylor 1998, p. 359.

indicating the mean absolute value of the current account/GDP for select periods.

Prior to World War I, government borrowing was completed largely through sovereign debt issues. Governments issued bonds in one or more of the key financial centers, which included London, Paris, New York, Amsterdam, or even Berlin.[18] Although France and Germany had been sovereign borrowers themselves in the early and midnineteenth century, by 1870, they were self-sufficient, providing capital to other nations.[19] Just as today, the volume and type of capital flows from financial centers depended on interest rate movements, domestic and foreign business opportunities, the financial status of sovereign borrowers, global market conditions, and war or expectations of war.[20] Investors sought safety at home, but high returns abroad.

Therefore, in the 1880s, as the yield on British government securities (consols) fell and defaults in the developing world became a more distant memory, capital outflows from Britain resumed.[21] A similar pattern occurred in Germany; as interest rates declined in the 1880s, lower quality sovereign debt found a market in Berlin.[22] In the early 1890s, as a result

deficits and would make greater efforts to align national savings with national investment. See Held et al. 1999.
[18] Germain 1997, Held et al. 1999, Lipson 1985, Platt 1986.
[19] Fishlow 1985, p. 399.
[20] Feis 1930, p. 11.
[21] Cottrell 1975, Kindleberger 1993.
[22] Feis 1930.

Table 7.3. *Destinations of European Foreign Investment, 1913–1914*

Destination	Britain (% of Total Outflows)	France	Germany
Russia	2.9	25.1	7.7
Turkey	0.6	7.3	7.7
Other Eastern Europe (including Austria-Hungary)	0.7	10.4	20.0
Western European periphery	1.3	11.6	7.2
Western European core	0.4	3.3	5.5
Europe (not specified)	0.5	3.3	5.1
Total Europe, including Asian Russia and Turkey	6.4	61.1	53.2
Asia and Africa, excluding Asian Russia and Turkey	25.9	21.1	12.8
Latin America	20.1	13.3	16.2
North America and Australasia	44.8	4.4	15.7
Other (not specified)	2.8	0.0	2.1
TOTAL	100	100	100

Source: O'Rourke and Williamson 1999, p. 229, using data from Feis 1930, pp. 23, 51, 74.

of the Baring Crisis, flows from London again subsided. But by the early 1900s, spurred by not only a search for higher returns, but also a desire to escape increased taxes in Britain, investors again expanded their foreign activities, turning toward non-European markets.[23] Likewise, German investors retreated after the costly defaults of the early 1890s but resumed foreign lending around the turn of the century.

Table 7.3 provides information regarding the geographic distribution of European outward investment on the eve of World War I. Imperial areas, including Canada, Australia, and India, attracted nearly one-half of British investment, while Latin America and the United States attracted over 20%.[24] The majority of investment from the Paris market, on the other hand, remained in Europe; although French investment in Latin America increased after 1900, Russia remained the most popular destination in 1914.[25]

[23] Bloomfield 1968. Taking a longer view, Cottrell points out that, between 1820 and 1914, British investors supplied more long-term capital to Latin America than to any other geographical region. The major recipients over this period were Argentina, Brazil, Chile, Mexico, and Uruguay; substantial flows also went to Colombia, Peru, and Cuba.

[24] Also see Feis 1930, p. 23, for data on the geographic distribution of British investment in 1913.

[25] Feis 1930, pp. 33–38. Also see Kindleberger 1993, p. 221.

Capital outflows from Germany were less important, with less than one-tenth of current German savings invested abroad during the 1900–1914 period.[26] Of long-term German capital that was invested abroad in 1914, 53% was invested in Europe, with the greatest amounts to Austria-Hungary, Russia, and Turkey. Finally, the United States became a net exporter of capital in the late nineteenth century[27] but lagged behind European markets in importance until after the First World War.

In 1913, governments with the highest levels of external indebtedness included Russia, Australia, Japan, Brazil, Argentina, Turkey, South Africa, Mexico, Canada, and Egypt.[28] In order to complete a bond issue, governments retained the services of one or more merchant (investment) banks.[29] These banks, including Baring Brothers, N. M. Rothschild, J. P. Morgan, J. S. Morgan, Hope and Company, and Hambro and Sons, issued bonds and provided other services to governments, such as paying interest to bondholders and managing the redemption of bonds. For borrowing governments, issuing debt via a well-known merchant bank increased the perceived quality of the issue,[30] reducing borrowing costs. For merchant banks, debt issues were a steady source of income.[31] Government bonds were denominated in relatively small increments, were redeemable at maturity (usually between 10 and 50 years), and paid interest annually to lenders. Prior to the public sale of any bond, the merchant bank published a prospectus, which detailed the issue price and interest rate of the bonds, provided information about the borrower, and – in some cases – discussed the purposes for which the loan would be used.

In the middle and late nineteenth century, merchant banks issued sovereign debt in one of two ways: first, the issuing house could purchase the bonds outright, giving the government its loan immediately, and sell them to investors at a higher price. The difference between the purchase price and public sale price was the bank's profit, but any issues not sold to the public became a liability for the issuing house. Second, the issuing

---

[26] Feis 1930, pp. 61–62.

[27] Eichengreen and Fishlow 1998.

[28] Lindert and Morton 1990.

[29] Cottrell 1975 notes that merchant banks were the single most important group in the London market; they were responsible for at least 37% of all overseas issues between 1870 and 1914 (pp. 30–32).

[30] Ziegler 1988, p. 10.

[31] For example, Orbell 1985 estimates that, during the 1880s, it was not unusual for a merchant bank to achieve a gross profit of £50,000 on an issue, although ordinarily it would have been between £15,000 and £30,000.

house could offer the bonds for sale to the public on a commission basis. Borrowing governments received the amount of bonds sold, less the merchant bank's commission. In this case, borrowing governments bore the risk of unsold issues, which were simply cancelled. Once issued, bonds usually were quoted and sold on secondary markets, such as the London Stock Exchange.

Issuance on a commission basis was a low-risk strategy for merchant banks and, therefore, was common in the 1870s and 1880s. But even with commission issuance, a succession of undersubscribed issues was damaging to a merchant bank's reputation among private investors.[32] To address this functional problem, in the late nineteenth century, merchant banks developed a third instrument, the practice of underwriting.[33] The merchant bank issuing the loan arranged for a syndicate (a collection of other merchant banks) to purchase large amounts of a bond issue, for a commission, before offering the bond publicly. These underwriters, in turn, often divided their loan participation among subunderwriters. Each participating underwriter received a commission and took up any bonds, on a prorata basis, not subscribed for by investors.[34] In some ways, underwriting was a means of portfolio diversification. The syndicate arrangement guaranteed that an issue would be fully subscribed, either by financial entities or by the public. The latter, obviously, was better for borrowing governments, as it helped to maintain their access to capital.[35]

Then versus Now: Similarities and Differences

In broad terms, the 1870–1914 period was characterized by relatively high financial openness and by many governments' reliance on disintermediated capital markets. Individual investors vetted sovereign debt issues in the late nineteenth century, just as fund managers do in the contemporary era.[36] How, then, do government–financial market relations during this period compare to those in the contemporary era? In this section, I examine three

---

[32] Orbell 1985; see later discussion.

[33] Platt 1986, Ziegler 1988.

[34] This section draws on Ziegler's 1988 description of the merchant banking industry. In a few cases, merchant banks bought issues, or large amounts of issues, themselves, rather than using an underwriting syndicate. According to de Cecco 1974, it was this practice that rendered Baring Brothers vulnerable to the Argentine crisis in 1890.

[35] Eichengreen and Fishlow 1999, pp. 23–24.

[36] Eichengreen and Fishlow 1999, p. 24.

dimensions of financial market–government relations in the pre–World War I period: the structure of the financial industry and of sovereign borrowing practices, the national and international governance of capital flows, and the policy commitments and ambitions of national governments.

The Financial Industry and Sovereign Borrowing Practices

Individuals, Intermediaries, and Information   One key difference between the pre–World War I investment industry and today's financial sector is the management of portfolios by individuals rather than by professional investors and fund managers. A key similarity, on the other hand, is investors' reliance on financial intermediaries as sources of information.

Today's investment portfolios are managed, to a large extent, by professional investors. As I discuss in Chapter 2, the delegation of investment authority to fund managers is an efficient solution to individuals' functional problems of diversification and information. Individual investors can collect – especially given recent improvements in technology and data standards – a wide range of information about hundreds of sovereign issues and corporate securities, but doing so is expensive, in terms of opportunity costs. Similarly, portfolio diversification by individuals is possible, but only with high transaction costs. Therefore, individual investors, whether they have $1,000 or $1,000,000 to invest, tend to delegate control over investment to a fund manager, who has thousands of similar clients. Fund managers' collection and evaluation of information provide an efficient solution.

Prior to the First World War, individuals retained the management of most portfolios;[37] investment trusts, the forerunner to the modern mutual fund, were not developed widely until the 1920s.[38] Mostly individuals ultimately purchased government bonds, so that a large number of investors held each bond issue. One implication of this difference for governments is the present-day opportunity for sudden shifts in large quantities of investment. Despite similar levels of market concentration in pre–World War I merchant banking and contemporary fund management, the degree and speed of aggregate market responses should vary, not only because of technology, but also because of the diffusion of control of investments. Where a tight-knit, relative performance–oriented group of fund managers controls the preponderance of investment, we should see pronounced responses to

[37] Manzocchi 1999, Suter 1992.
[38] Cassis 1990, Eichengreen and Fishlow 1999.

changes in policy outcomes, political events, and economic developments. But where a large and diffuse set of individuals controls the bulk of investment, responses are slower *and* more diverse. For governments, this implies that the punishing (and rewarding) effects of the "herd" are more severe today than they were a century ago.

Recent research by Paolo Mauro and his colleagues confirms this expectation. In a comparison of sovereign debt issues in emerging markets in the 1870–1913 period with similar issues from the 1992–2000 time frame,[39] they find greater volatility in contemporary than in 1870–1913 emerging markets. Although financial crises, associated with sharp rises in sovereign risk premiums, were not unheard of before World War I, they were far more common in the 1990s. Global crises, in which nearly all emerging markets experienced sharp jumps in sovereign spreads, are a particular phenomenon of the contemporary era. The authors also discover a greater amount of common cross-national variation across spreads in the contemporary era: when one emerging market economy experiences a jump in interest rates, so do others. Finally, Mauro and associates' work suggests that, whereas country-specific events were the usual correlates of changes in spreads in the 1870–1913 period, global events were the more common cause in the 1990s.

This pattern is due, in part, to a greater cross-national synchronization of economic cycles, but it also reflects different patterns of investor behavior. Whereas individuals prior to World War I did not have the resources (given transactions costs) or even the desire (given time horizons) to move holdings in response to small changes in market conditions, fund managers have both the means and the motive to do so. Especially when dealing with emerging markets, today's fund managers pay less attention to country-specific events. Therefore, "push factors" often drive market movements. For governments of developing nations, this suggests reduced autonomy: as I discuss in Chapter 4, even the "right policies" may not be sufficient to insulate governments from increases in borrowing costs or reductions in market access.

Despite the difference between the periods in the identity of portfolio managers, a similarity remains – the reliance on financial intermediaries as providers of information. The incentives to collect and employ information

[39] Mauro et al. 2000. The 1870–1913 sample consists of either 8 or 14 nations, depending on the specification, and the 1992–2000 sample includes 10 nations, all of which issued Brady Bonds.

and the need to collect information relevant to default risk drive contemporary differences in the treatment of developed and emerging market nations. Investors in the nineteenth century also worried about default risk (discussed later), particularly in developing nations, and this intensified their needs for information. Whereas intergovernmental organizations, credit ratings agencies, and fund management firms serve as information providers today, merchant banks were the key information providers in the past.

Individual investors were attracted to foreign securities because they often offered higher yields than domestic securities, even after controlling for investment risk.[40] These investors had a wide range of assets from which to choose, such as American railroads, Peruvian guano, and South African gold mines.[41] The financial press, including the *Economist* and the *Financial News*, provided regular coverage of such investments.[42] Investors, however, often worried about the quality, as well as the quantity, of this information. Private investors turned to merchant bankers not as a means of pooling risk and diversifying investments, but as an intermediary between borrowing governments and them.[43] In many cases, investors were relatively ignorant about foreign regions; their only indication of the quality of an asset was the reputation of the issuing house.[44] In the pre–World War I period as today, then, the role of financial intermediaries revolved around reducing transaction costs, making international investment a profitable undertaking for individuals.[45]

---

[40] Ferguson 1999, Salter 1951. As in the contemporary era, investors' interest in foreign securities was characterized by periods of mania and periods of panic, as well as periods of normal market operation. See Eichengreen 1991.

[41] Obstfeld 1998.

[42] Alternatively, Mauro et al. 2000 argue that investors' lack of information did not characterize the late nineteenth century; investors had access to all the information necessary, and some devoted substantial time to analyzing it. Also see Flandreau 1998.

[43] Marichal 1989, Salter 1951. Ziegler 1988 notes that "the British investor was ignorant of almost everything to do with Latin America, confusing Argentina with Chile and Mexico and wholly unable to follow the intricacies of Argentine internal politics. They depended on the judgment of Baring as to whether or not their money would be safe. On the whole their confidence was justified" (pp. 233–234).

[44] Carosso 1987. Germain 1997 notes that pre–World War I securities issued in London were a mixture of good and bad, and that reputation was the only means by which investors could distinguish among securities. On information problems and biased media coverage in the 1820s, see Dawson 1990.

[45] Germain 1997 discusses the role of information flows in facilitating the rise of different financial centers. Also see Cottrell 1975 on the importance of "international networks of

Merchant banks often had close relations with national governments and access to data regarding national political and economic conditions. They also had well-developed communications networks among financial centers, relying first on private couriers and later on telegraphic transmissions.[46] In return for commissions and possible profits on government securities,[47] merchant banks provided investors with information regarding the quality of assets. Sovereign lending was profitable for merchant banks as long as they were able to sell issues to the investing public (as well as to underwriting institutions). As a result, they faced incentives to protect their reputation – in other words, to provide high-quality information and to price issues to reflect accurately this information.[48] Therefore, in order to make sovereign issues that appropriately – in size, maturity, and price – reflected default risk, merchant bankers demanded information about the political and economic conditions in borrowing nations and, where issues were perceived to be of lower quality, demanded assurances against the risk of default.

An early example of merchant banks' concern with reputation and information is Barings' response to Argentina's default, in 1828, on its 1824 sovereign loan. During the 15 years after the default, Baring was "preoccupied" with settling the default in a way that would satisfy, at least partially, private investors who had invested on their recommendation. Baring held part of this loan and had bought back more to protect the price; its main concern, though, was with the amount that remained in private hands:

No merchant banker who wished to survive as a leading house could afford to ignore the woes of the bondholders who had bought stock from them. If a loan backed by Barings ended in such abject failure, who would trust their judgment in the future?[49]

correspondents" in gathering credit information about sovereign borrowers and in facilitating transactions in the London capital market.

[46] Carosso 1987, Ferguson 1999.

[47] Turner 1991. Eichengreen 1990 considers the extent to which, in the 1920s, these commissions reflected considerations of investment risk. He suggests that, although commissions do not fully capture sovereign risk, they may reflect the degree of familiarity with the particular economic situations of individual nations.

[48] Ziegler 1988, p. 10. During the 1931–1932 U.S. Senate Foreign Bond Investigation, the banking community made a similar argument about their disincentives to deceive individual investors. They noted that established firms had no incentive to promote questionable investments because "such securities would damage the underwriter's credibility with investors, making it more difficult for the underwriter to sell securities in the future" (quoted in Eichengreen 1990, pp. 122–123).

[49] Ziegler 1988, p. 107. Also see Marichal 1989.

And after the 1890 financial crisis in Argentina, Baring behaved in a similar fashion.[50]

This is not to say that merchant banks never made incorrect lending decisions, or that private investors always blindly followed investment banks' recommendations. In the 1850s and 1860s, Barings had a mixture of success and failure when trying to market debt issues to the public.[51] The investing public was "less than enthusiastic" about Argentine debt in 1866 and 1873; the 1866 Argentine loan was not fully bought by the public until 1869.[52] For this reason, in the early phase of its sovereign issuing business, Baring tended to avoid issues by "distant governments," on the grounds that it was difficult to create a market for these.

Additionally, in some cases, investment banks acquiesced to the temptation to mislead or provide false information to investors in order to make short-term gains. Some of the securities that ended up in the hands of the public – rather than in the hands of underwriting syndicate members – were "often those whose prospects the promoting or financing groups held in doubt."[53] In 1933, Winkler observed, "Individual investors were prevailed upon to succumb to the impressive statements contained in the prospectuses descriptive of foreign loans."[54] Along these lines, he provides a good deal of anecdotal evidence regarding the misinformation – or lack of information – contained in some prospectuses. The prospectuses were a marketing tool, designed to sell bonds, and did not always provide sufficient information regarding a nation's finances, nor the means by which borrowing governments were able to achieve balanced budgets. Moreover, Feis suggests that individual investors' propensity to purchase poor-quality issues was more pronounced in France, where investors were more venturesome (and banks were more prone to lead them astray), but less pronounced in Germany, where investors "retained more independence of judgment," journalists were better informed and more honest, and banks were therefore less likely to encourage lower-quality investments.[55]

The reliance of individuals on merchant banks as an information source, and the resulting centrality of reputation to merchant banks, imbued merchant banks with strong incentives to evaluate sovereign issues

---

[50] Ziegler 1988, chapter 15.
[51] Orbell 1985.
[52] Ziegler 1988.
[53] Feis 1930. Also see Marichal 1989.
[54] Winkler 1933, p. xv.
[55] Feis 1930.

appropriately. Merchant banks that repeatedly offered government securities at inappropriate rates of interest or prices would fail, over time, to retain
the confidence of investors. If this happened, they would lose out on profits and commissions stemming from public offerings. Particularly for large
houses with long legacies of lending, merchant banks did not try intentionally to mislead investors; if an issue began to fare poorly on the secondary
market, the issuing house might buy back additional amounts as a way
of supporting the price. Therefore, just as current mutual fund managers
worry about the reputation they will earn if the assets under their management perform poorly, issuing houses worried about the repercussions
of selling poorly performing securities.[56] Merchant banks would take great
care to evaluate the risks, particularly default, associated with sovereign
issues.

For governments in the pre–World War I period, this meant that merchant banks demanded evidence of the willingness and ability to pay, as
well as information about current government revenues and expenditures.
These demands were more pronounced for lower-credit-quality borrowers, which often were asked to pledge some sort of security for the loan or
to make frequent deposits – to cover interest payments – with the issuing
bank. In this way, then, the constraints on borrowing governments are quite
similar in the two periods.

Competition for High-Quality Loans Today governments compete with
one another, as well as with private entities, in order to attract investment.
In order to attract funds, a sovereign borrower must offer rates of return
that not only compensate in absolute terms for inflation and default risk, but
also are consistent in relative terms with rates offered by other borrowing
nations. As I detailed in Chapters 3 and 4, governments characterized by
low levels of default risk and solid economic prospects have the easiest and
cheapest access to funds, and governments with higher default risk and
more uncertain prospects have the most difficult access. Put differently,
investors clamor to invest in high-quality assets, driving down government
borrowing costs, whereas governments must clamor to find buyers for low-
quality assets, driving up government borrowing costs. This general pattern
is most pronounced during periods of global crisis, when investors seek the
safety inherent in assets such as U.S. Treasury Bonds.

---

[56] For instance, Carosso 1987 notes that reputational concerns led the Morgans to decline
many accounts; they wanted to keep foreign issues of a high quality.

A similar pattern characterized the pre–World War I period, in that merchant banks often jockeyed among themselves to put out issues for high-quality, high-expectation borrowers. As a result, a mixture of competition (to be the lead issuer) and cooperation (to prevent governments' from playing banks off against one another and to share in issues of sovereign debt) characterized pre–World War I merchant banking. On the competitive side, because banks earn commissions from sovereign issues and bond sales and because long-term lending to governments often lead to other, more profitable activities (such as issuing short-term credits),[57] each merchant bank had an incentive to become the financial agent for borrowing governments.

On the cooperative side, banks often were bound together through underwriting, syndicates, and personal contact. Additionally, although a single merchant bank or group of banks was responsible for placing a sovereign issue, this placement often depended on consultation with other financial institutions. A sovereign lending decision reflected the lead bank's concerns, as well as the concerns of other participating financial institutions. Although merchant banks ultimately were interested in marketing sovereign issues to the public, they also were interested in attracting participation by other well-informed financial institutions. Moreover, despite their competition with one another, banks were sensitive to governments' efforts to play them off against one another. For example, around the turn of the twentieth century, Baring and J. S. and J. P. Morgan competed to lend to the Argentina government; this competition peaked in 1908, as Argentina opened negotiations with J. P. Morgan for a new loan of $10 million pounds. The Argentine government, hoping to win better terms, attempted to secure separate bids from each house. In the end, however, the banks cooperated to issue the loan jointly. Officers of Barings expressed concern about the way in which the Argentine government had treated them.[58] In other cases, merchant banks went even further to consider the views of their colleagues. Especially among the "old school" investment banks, like Barings, Rothschild, Schroeders, and Hambros, it was quite commonplace to respect "spheres of influence."[59] By the mid-19th century, for instance, it was clear that the Rothschilds were agents for Brazil, and Barings were

---

[57] Burke 1989, pp. 32–33, Carosso 1987, p. 201.
[58] Burke 1989, Carosso 1987, Ziegler 1988.
[59] Feis 1930, p. 10.

agents for Argentina. In many ways, then, the merchant banking industry was close-knit and cooperative.[60]

But where banks attempted to enter new markets, or to establish positions as sovereign lenders, competition could be fierce; the overall degree of competition increased throughout the pre–World War I period. Pursuing "other banks' clients" was more common among up-and-coming banks, such as J. P. Morgan, J. S. Morgan, Peabody, and Speyer.[61] For example, in 1904, Baring considered issuing sovereign debt for Cuba. When its agents arrived in Havana, they were frustrated to discover that the Cuban government was negotiating simultaneously with representatives of other investment banks. Ultimately, Speyer and Company offered better terms and placed the loan. Baring, along with some of its underwriting partners, expressed dismay that the Cuban government had succeeded in securing better terms via competitive pressures.[62]

What did the nature of merchant banking imply for governments, especially in relation to contemporary sovereign borrowing? Just as the degree of influence on today's governments depends on their overall attractiveness to investors, such was the case prior to 1914. Governments that issued low-risk assets or that had strong economic prospects gained better terms and were not required to provide security for their loans or to alter their domestic policies and institutions. These governments could solicit bids for sovereign issues from a variety of institutions, improving their market treatment.[63] Higher-risk borrowers with poor track records, on the other hand, were likely to receive less favorable terms. Merchant banks were reluctant to compete for this sort of business. Higher-risk new borrowers might fare slightly better,[64] as merchant banks were sometimes eager to establish an exclusive relationship. As in the contemporary era, though, the borrowers with the most room for maneuver were those with the lowest risk: those who could prove that they did not need financing had the easiest time getting it.[65]

---

[60] Wilkins 1991.

[61] Burke 1989, Carosso 1987.

[62] Baring Archive, ref. 200090.

[63] This parallels lending to developing nations in the 1970s: as international banks sought to increase their market shares, interest rate spreads narrowed dramatically. Cohen 1986, Devlin 1989.

[64] On the difference in market treatment between unproven borrowers and better-known borrowers, see Tomz 2001a.

[65] Mauro et al. 2000.

The Range, Velocity, and Scope of Financial Activities Within the rubric of the financial industry, another basis for comparison between historical and contemporary globalization concerns the broader nature of financial markets. First, today's governments interact with a variety of financial instruments. Although bank-based lending has declined in importance over the last decade, portfolio capital has grown in salience. Portfolio instruments include traditional bonds and equities, as well as new, derivative instruments. Additionally, foreign direct investment is increasingly important to national economies, especially in the developing world, where inflows of direct investment have recently grown to exceed inflows of portfolio investment. Net long-term capital flows to developing nations in 1997 were 56% foreign direct investment (FDI) and 44% "international capital markets," including debt and equity. When emerging markets were hit by financial crises in 1998 and 1999, the role of FDI became even more pronounced, accounting for between 64% and 80% of net long-term flows.[66]

How does this compare with the pre–World War I period? Generally, gross capital flows at the end of the 1990s were much greater than gross flows prior to the First World War.[67] In terms of instruments, bonds and equities were the rule of the day.[68] As scholars have pointed out in recent years, however, foreign direct investment was not absent in the late nineteenth century, and it began to increase sharply during the early twentieth century. In 1890, British direct investment in Latin America exceeded holdings of bonds there; this investment, however, was concentrated in Argentina, Mexico, and Brazil.[69] By 1913, 46% of British investment in Latin America was direct investment in private industry, 38% was in government loans, and the remaining 16% was portfolio investment in private industry.[70] The differences between instruments, however, suggest that, *even if* contemporary governments face similar bond market constraints, they may face greater overall capital market constraints, as they strive to satisfy direct investors as well as foreign exchange markets.

---

[66] World Bank, Global Development Finance 2000, table 2.1, p. 36.

[67] E.g., Brittan 1998, Friedman 2000. It is possible to argue, however, that measurements of gross flows greatly exaggerate the amount of activity in financial markets. These statistics often include a large number of orders that are not transacted or that are made on margin. Additionally, Manzocchi 1999 notes that, for developing nations, the pre–World War I era was characterized by the highest ever stock of gross foreign investment.

[68] Lipsey 1999. The long-standing scholarly consensus is that portfolio flows dominated the pre–World War I era, accounting for perhaps 90% of total international flows.

[69] Lipson 1985. Also see Stone 1977.

[70] Stone 1977, p. 698.

Moreover, contemporary financial markets are broader in geographic scope. Although developing nations, including Argentina, Brazil, India, Mexico, and Russia, were very active in international borrowing before World War I, many developing nations and colonial territories were not involved in the global capital market.[71] On the other hand, at present, involvement in global capital markets has become the rule, rather than the exception, as developing nations clamor to garner the label of "emerging market." Therefore, the number and nature of governments that are potentially affected by international capital markets – in both negative and positive fashions – have expanded dramatically.

Finally, we may consider the long-run significance of recent changes in communications technologies. These changes have facilitated dramatic increases in the velocity of financial flows; this velocity, coupled with the increasing complexity of financial instruments, contributes to regulatory challenges for national governments.[72] Increased velocity also can lead to stronger market influences on government policy choices. Undoubtedly, velocity can generate more immediate financial market pressures, but are these pressures also more pronounced? That is, does the compression in time of financial market influence also imply an increase in strength?

These differences in the nature of financial activities give us reason to expect that contemporary governments are *no less subject to influence* by financial openness than were governments before the First World War. Given the centrality of information and reputation to financial intermediaries, or the competition to lend to high-quality borrowers, we can expect to see some similarities in government–financial market relations. At the same time, given the greater role of professional investors, as well as the broader range of financial instruments and the compression in time of financial activity, we can expect governments – especially in developing nations – to experience the positive and negative effects of globalization in a more intense fashion.

National and International Governance of Capital Flows

A second dimension of comparison between these two eras of globalization is the governance of capital flows: to what extent do political authorities, at the national or international level, oversee or intervene in private capital

---

[71] Friedman 2000, Marichal 1989, chapter 5.
[72] For instance, see Dryzek 1996, Held et al. 1999, Turner 1991.

markets? Intervention and oversight may have several different effects on capital markets, including the emergence of moral hazard among lenders and individuals, the faster resolution of sovereign financial crises, and the alteration of the degree of market access of some borrowers. In this section, I suggest that pre–World War I great-power governments were more able and willing than their contemporary counterparts to intervene in sovereign debt markets, particularly where politically important borrowers were concerned. The willingness to intervene, however, varied across governments and declined throughout the early twentieth century. This intervention has a contemporary analog, at the international level, where the IMF sometimes serves to create moral hazard for private investors and sometimes allows political considerations to alter its own lending practices. Ultimately, this implies that – in both periods – politically important or otherwise "too big to fail" nations receive easier treatment in financial markets than their objective economic and political conditions warrant.

National Protections for Investors   The potential effects of great-power governments on merchant bankers' activities rest on two mechanisms – governments' willingness to offer protection from other governments' defaults and governments' propensity to pressure banks to lend for geopolitical reasons. These pathways are not necessarily independent of one another; both can serve to generate a certain level of moral hazard. In the pre–World War I era, great-power governments responded to sovereign default in a variety of ways, which ranged from indifference to or support for debt administration councils to diplomatic pressure and, more rarely, armed intervention.[73] Governments occasionally were willing to intervene directly in response to sovereign default, but this willingness declined over time.[74]

The British government's stated policy regarding assistance to investors in cases of default left it some latitude but fell squarely on the side of nonintervention.[75] The Palmerston Circular of 1849 established the principle that dishonest governments "could not count on too much forebearance," but, at the same time, noted that "imprudent investors could not count on

---

[73] Germain 1997, Suter 1992. On military intervention in Mexico by the United States, Britain, and France in the 1860s, see Marichal 1989.

[74] Suter 1992.

[75] Lipson 1985, Platt 1968.

aid."[76] In the face of moratoria and defaults in the 1870s (in Latin America, Spain, Turkey, and Egypt), the British government refrained from intervention, on the grounds that government action on debtors' behalf would "give false security and increase the government's obligation to take measures against defaulting debtors."[77] Likewise, the British government left the settlement of Argentina's 1891 default – the most serious default prior to the First World War – to the Argentine government and the private bondholders. The British government was similarly restrained when dealing with default in Europe in the 1890s; its actions toward Greece and Portugal went no further than "friendly remonstrance."[78] Refraining from intervention allowed the British government to avoid thorny involvements in the domestic politics of developing nations.[79] As an alternative, the British government encouraged the development and use of the Corporation of Foreign Bondholders, a private consortium of investors that dealt collectively with sovereign defaults.

In France, the government's most common response to potential default was diplomatic pressure.[80] Likewise, most German government activity in support of investors took the form of friendly, moderate diplomatic intervention. The United States government was even more restrained: it had a stated policy, dating back at least to 1885, of not intervening to collect debts.[81] Particularly in the early twentieth century, however, the U.S. government sometimes *did* become involved in the fiscal affairs of various Central American and Caribbean nations, as a stated means of preventing future default.[82] For instance, in 1905, Speyer and Company issued a new loan to the government of Costa Rica, allowing the government to return to

---

[76] Feis 1930, p. 103.

[77] Feis 1930, p. 106. The British government, however, did place official pressure on Turkey and Egypt, after their suspensions of payments in 1875–1876. Also see Lipson 1985, Platt 1968.

[78] Feis 1930. In the case of Greece, the British government did provide a guarantee for the 1898 loan, promising to make interest payments if the Greek government could not. This was an exceptional case, driven by a strong political interest: "The mechanism of a British government guarantee was adopted to make it possible, for political reasons, to raise a loan on relatively easy terms in the European money markets on behalf of a country with no credit standing of its own" (Platt 1968, p. 12).

[79] Lipson 1985. Lipson notes, however, that the British government was much more willing to intervene to protect foreign direct investments.

[80] Feis 1930.

[81] Finnemore 2002.

[82] Lipson 1985.

private capital markets after its defaults of 1874 and 1891. The new loan was secured with a first charge on customs revenues, as well as with proceeds from the liquor monopoly. Beyond this security, American investors had the U.S. government's backing: the loan agreement stated that bondholders could apply to the U.S. government for aid in enforcing the agreement and for protection against its violation.[83]

Likewise, the Honduran 1911 loan negotiations with the Morgans were contingent on a 1911 convention between the United States and Honduran governments. In the convention, the Honduras government, which had outstanding defaults on debts issued in the 1860s and 1870s, promised that it would use the loan (secured via a customs guarantee) to put its fiscal house in order. The U.S. government was given the right to appoint the head of Honduran Customs as well as the right of prior consultation on any change in Honduran customs duties.[84]

On rare occasions, and against weaker borrowers, great-power governments assumed a more active role regarding default. The most startling of these instances occurred in Venezuela in 1902. In response to the Venezuelan government's proposed default,[85] the German, Italian, and British governments presented ultimatums, and then their naval forces. This was a somewhat exceptional event, in which national governments used military means to protect their investors.[86] Similar episodes occurred later in the period – the United States Marines invaded and took over customs revenue collection in the Dominican Republic in 1905,[87] and a British battleship appeared in Guatemala in 1913, in response to debt repayment problems – but became increasingly rare.

The decline in overt government involvement in debt collection may reflect changes in governments' understandings regarding legitimate uses of force and the relationship between sovereignty and government debt.[88]

---

[83] U.S. Congress 1905–1906.

[84] Paredes 1912. Ultimately, the treaty, which had been negotiated secretly, was attacked by the Honduran National Congress as an infringement on the country's sovereignty and independence.

[85] Platt 1968 suggests, however, that the British government had other, more salient grievances (such as interference with shipping) against the Venezuelan government, pp. 339–344.

[86] Finnemore 2002.

[87] Lindert and Morton 1990. Also see Lipson 1985 for a more general discussion of U.S. practices in the Caribbean.

[88] Finnemore 2002 argues that the change in practices surrounding intervention and default reflected not a change in the utility of military intervention, nor a change in state interests, but a change in states' beliefs and in international norms.

The defining moment for this change was the 1907 Hague Peace Treaty, which outlawed military force as a means to collect sovereign debts and encouraged the use of international arbitration. After 1907, European governments continued sometimes to express concerns about debt and to employ diplomatic tools, but they generally avoided the use of force. This change in state practice also should have reduced investors' propensity for moral hazard, causing a more careful consideration of default risk.

Today, although the settlement of outstanding debts is of concern to governments (for instance, as it was in the Russian case), individual governments usually do not use – or even threaten – military force to collect debts; nor do they demand involvement in fiscal policymaking. In general, then, great powers were more involved than their contemporary counterparts in protecting bond investors, but this involvement was neither extensive nor regular. Rather, it depended on geopolitical concerns, as well as on the perceived egregiousness of the default. What this implies for investors, then, is only a moderate contribution of national governments to moral hazard. Therefore, private investors had incentives to consider governments' willingness and ability to pay.

Pressures from and Control by Governments   Pressures from home governments also can influence investors' behavior. If the home government encourages merchant banks to lend to a particular government, and if this encouragement generates expectations of bailout, investors are less inclined to consider default risk. In such cases, the logic of moral hazard operates to change risk–return calculations. If, on the other hand, home governments neither encourage certain types of investments nor offer guarantees regarding them, investors should not experience moral hazard problems. Rather, they must concern themselves with assessing and appropriately pricing investment risk.

Some observers suggest that prior to the First World War there was an intimate connection between finance and diplomacy.[89] Merchant bankers generally were averse to international conflict, especially on a broad scale, because conflict was bad for business.[90] In some cases, political power took

---

[89] See Polanyi 1944, Viner 1929. On the connection between more recent U.S. foreign policy and international bank lending during the 1970s and early 1980s, see Cohen 1986.

[90] Although financial houses stood to gain, at least in the short term, from financing localized wars, more widespread conflict depressed financial markets and weakened national

precedence over profit, as governments closed national markets to certain sovereign borrowers.[91] And the desire to maintain international stability, coupled with the desire to maintain friendly relations with home governments, sometimes led to close consultations of financial actors and national governments. Some banks, such as J. P. Morgan in the United States, refused to take part in foreign loans that were not sanctioned by home governments.[92]

There was substantial cross-national variation in government involvement in sovereign lending in the pre–World War I period. The British government was least involved in merchant banks' activities. The German, and particularly the French, governments were more intimately involved in issues of international finance.[93] In Feis's account, the main goal of the French government was to make capital outflows serve the state's political aims. This goal was served by preventing lending to unfriendly governments, by making the listing of foreign securities on the Paris market contingent on political promises, and by utilizing connections with financial actors and media to facilitate borrowing by political allies.[94] For instance, from the late 1880s, loans issued and listed in Paris required not only the approval of the French government, but also the approval of the Russian government. This immediately closed the French capital market to Austria; for several more years, the market remained open to Hungary. In 1909, however, Russia's concerns about the rise of Austria-Hungary led to a

---

currencies. Of N. M. Rothschild and Sons, Polanyi 1944 writes: "They were anything but pacifists; they had made their fortune in the financing of wars; they were impervious to moral consideration; they had no objection to any number of minor, short or localized wars. But their business would be impaired if a general war between the Great Powers should interfere with the monetary foundations of the system. By the logic of the facts it fell to them to maintain the requisites of general peace... every war, almost, was organized by financiers, but peace also was organized by them" (p. 11). Similarly, Ziegler 1988 notes, "Though their views on foreign policy might differ from time to time, on one thing all the partners of Barings were united: that if war broke out between two major European powers, then, irrespective of who won or lost, 'as far as banking and commercial circles are concerned, the result would be disastrous'" (p. 279). Also see Ferguson 1999, Viner 1929.

[91] Feis 1930, Germain 1997, Polanyi 1944, Viner 1929.

[92] Carosso 1987 also notes that, in exchange for their sensitivity to political considerations, home governments provided banks with valuable information on the political and economic characteristics of borrowing governments.

[93] Cohen 1986, Cottrell 1991, Fishlow 1985, p. 386, Germain 1997, Lipson 1985, Platt 1968, Viner 1948.

[94] Feis 1930. Also see Cohen 1986, Eichengreen and Fishlow 1998.

direct refusal of an official listing for a Hungarian loan.[95] Additionally, with appeals to "patriotism," the French government pressed merchant banks to extend economically risky loans to Russia, Romania, and Morocco.[96] Moreover, the French government drew an explicit connection between trade and finance, pressing, or even requiring, sovereign borrowers to buy French products.[97] As a result, pre–World War I French foreign lending often was influenced not only by objective assessments of risk and return, but also by "antipathies and sympathies, traditional, emotional and political."[98] For borrowing governments favored politically by France, this pattern of home government–bank relations served to loosen constraints.

In Germany, the government was less active in directing lending for explicitly political purposes.[99] Although the government hoped that international lending would facilitate the achievement of political ends,[100] it generally trusted the large German banks to be conscious of these ends. Explicit German government direction of sovereign lending became more common as the First World War approached; German banks developed the practice of consulting the German Foreign Office with regard to any loans in which it might have a political interest. On only three occasions – with Serbia in 1893 and 1906 and with Russia in 1906 – did the German government intervene to prevent loans. More common were interventions to encourage banks to make new loans, including those to Italy in the 1880s, Turkey and Hungary in 1910, Romania in 1913, and Bulgaria in 1914.[101]

---

[95] In the same year, for prudential as well as political reasons, the French government refused to grant listing to a Bulgarian loan. In 1913, anticipating that any loan would be used for military purposes, the French government refused to approve listing for a Romanian loan. The loans eventually were issued in London, Brussels, Berlin, and Amsterdam. See Feis 1930 and Viner 1929.

[96] De Cecco 1974, Germain 1997.

[97] Feis 1930.

[98] Feis 1930, p. 50. Reflecting in 1913 on his tenure as French finance minister, Calliaux stated, "I have conducted the public finances for six years; I have admitted to quotation only those foreign loans which assured France political and economic advantages" (quoted in Feis 1930, p. 123).

[99] On occasion, particularly as war approached, the German government stated that capital should fund German projects rather than foreign ones. In 1913–1914, the Prussian finance minister intervened to bar a bond issue by the Mexican government, arguing that Germany could not afford any foreign capital outflows. Feis 1930, p. 170.

[100] Feis 1930.

[101] This passage draws on Feis 1930, pp. 163–181.

The British government took a much less activist stance with respect to directing private capital flows.[102] Interaction between financial institutions and the British government was "irregular, a matter of informal choice, indirect and unrevealed."[103] Members of the British investing public prided themselves on their independent decision making. During the nineteenth century, capitalists in Britain maintained, in a fashion consistent with dominant laissez-faire ideology, that it was their right to invest as they wanted; the government went along with this notion.[104] Because British foreign policy was largely aloof from political struggles of the Continent, the government could take this passive stance more easily.

Moreover, British capital flowed in greatest volume to nations with which the British government had friendly political relations; if only for self-interested economic reasons, British investors tended to avoid countries with which the government had poor political relations. For instance, when a British syndicate offered shares of a sovereign loan – to repay debt, disband troops, and improve industry – to China in 1912, it did so over the British government's protests. The public did not subscribe to 60% of the loan, leaving that portion with the underwriters. In 1913, another loan to China, issued by the same consortium but without British banks, was oversubscribed. Although the 1913 loan was "ill conceived," implicit government endorsement made the difference: "There was a sense that the continental European governments would not permit default."[105]

When, on occasion, the British government had strong opinions regarding capital flows (for instance, to Turkey, Egypt, Greece, and India), its influence traveled through informal channels. There was no formal requirement that merchant banks consult the government before issuing foreign loans. Informally, the Bank of England's board meetings drew together representatives of the largest merchant banks, and the bank was in regular contact with the Treasury, as well as the Foreign Office and the Board of Trade. Prominent investment bankers, such as Nathaniel Rothschild and Lord Revelstoke (John Baring), were also prominent political figures, further blurring the line between government and the financial sector.[106]

---

[102] Viner 1929.

[103] Feis 1930, pp. 85, 88.

[104] Platt 1968.

[105] Feis 1930, pp. 449–452.

[106] Feis notes that "the feelings and decisions of the investors showed substantial identity with those of the government in power." Feis 1930, p. 88. Also see Platt 1968, p. 74.

Within the rubric of these general patterns, Feis's and Viner's accounts of prewar capital markets focus on cases of loans in which home governments' political considerations played some role, and in which changes in political allegiances were associated with changes in lending behavior. These include Italy, Portugal, the Balkans, the Ottoman Empire, China, and Japan. Italy's main source of sovereign borrowing shifted from France to Germany, and again back to Germany, during the 1880–1914 period. In such cases, the existence of overt political interests generated moral hazard; investors believed that a given nation was "too important to fail." This sentiment may have allowed Serbia to borrow excessively, for instance.[107]

In most pre–World War I lending episodes, bankers were unaffected by this type of moral hazard. Where borrowers were politically important, however, as in the case of Russia, merchant bankers did accede to pressures from home governments. As a result, they were less vigilant about default risk and often ignored economic realities.[108] Therefore, politically important – and friendly – borrowers could escape financial market pressures, and politically unimportant borrowers could not; politically important but unfriendly borrowers – as well as financially desperate borrowers[109] – were in the least desirable position.

The relationship between finance and diplomacy in the prewar period is considerably tighter than that in the contemporary period, reflecting not a contemporary separation between politics and economics, but governments' *inability* to direct private sector behavior. Contemporary governments cannot easily convince bankers "to participate in risky and unattractive transactions" or to be the "passive, and in some cases unwilling, instruments of the diplomats."[110] Similarly, if a U.S. or a European investment fund wants to purchase a certain asset, and the U.S. or EU governments forbid those purchases, the investment funds can move their

---

[107] Beginning with independence, in 1878, Serbia borrowed large amounts on international markets. Serbia was inexperienced financially, but European states – especially France – were eager to gain influence in the Balkans. This eagerness spilled over to the banking sector. See Feis 1930.

[108] Along these lines, Fishlow 1985 suggests that political considerations drove borrowing in Europe (including Russia), whereas market-oriented considerations drove lending to peripheral nations (North America, Latin America, Oceania).

[109] Persia in the 1910s provides such an example; from 1912 to 1914, it was bankrupt and forced to negotiate advances. The British government, aiming to increase its influence in the region, took the lead in proposing and negotiating advances. By 1914, Persia was dominated by the nations that provided financing (Feis 1930).

[110] Viner 1929, p. 84.

operations offshore. As Germain suggests, private investors now have greater control (than public officials) over access to credit.[111] This is not to say that today's investors do not consider geopolitical conditions when assessing default risk; as Chapter 4 suggests, these sorts of considerations can be particularly important for lower-quality borrowers. It is to say, however, that borrowing governments' probability of receiving "easier treatment" from private lenders because of a political allegiance with a great power is substantially lower. On this dimension of government involvement, then, contemporary borrowing governments should face greater private market constraints.

International Governance   A final way in which private capital flows may be governed is international; intergovernmental institutions may fulfill some of the same functions as national governments, helping to ensure against default and to establish certain types of policies in borrowing nations. International institutions also may create rules that reduce the likelihood of financial collapse or provide higher-quality information to private sector actors.

Before World War I, there was little international governance of capital markets. The gold standard regime, to which many European nations subscribed, and to which several peripheral nations pegged their currencies, set broad parameters for government behavior, requiring them to privilege external adjustment and to allow for the unfettered movements of capital.[112] British political power surely helped to enforce this system,[113] but there existed no formal international institution to monitor or encourage compliance with its rules. Likewise, there was no international lender of last resort to provide liquidity in times of crisis; rather, France and Germany sometimes fulfilled this function.[114] Furthermore, investment banks had to collect information themselves or rely on third parties to do so.[115]

---

[111] Germain 1997.

[112] Eichengreen 1992.

[113] Kindleberger 1973.

[114] Broz 1997.

[115] For a discussion of the development and practices of Credit Lyonnais's research department, which is analogous somewhat to contemporary emerging markets risk research by investment professionals, see Flandreau 1998, who argues that the Credit Lyonnais department fulfilled some of the same functions currently fulfilled by the IMF.

Today, a variety of global and regional financial institutions exist, most notably the International Monetary Fund, but also the G-7 and the BIS. These institutions are not always effective in their efforts to prevent crises or to enforce international rules;[116] for instance, the international system lacks an adequate mechanism for the resolution of sovereign defaults.[117] International financial institutions, however, do provide global capital markets with a greater degree of formal structure than pre–World War I markets had. The IMF is, as nineteenth-century merchant banks were, a transmitter and monitor of information from potential sovereign borrowers to investors. Moreover, these institutions undertake some of the same functions performed historically by national governments. For instance, through its conditionality based lending, the IMF influences the fiscal policy choices of national governments. This may be seen as akin to, although not exactly an analog of, governments' occasional direct fiscal involvement (recall the United States and Honduras in 1911, in which the United States hoped to gain political influence via its role in fiscal policy) before the First World War. Because actors in private capital markets often use the conclusion of and compliance with IMF stand-by agreements as a seal of approval, this IMF activity serves as a centralization (and standardization) of government-imposed limits on governments. In fact, given that conditionality is a standard component of IMF lending, and that the scope of conditionality has expanded over time,[118] the government-based constraints on contemporary poor-credit borrowers are just as great as, if not greater than, those on pre–World War I poor-credit borrowers.

Additionally, through the potential for rescue and bailouts that it creates, the IMF can serve as a source of moral hazard for investors, much as great-power governments occasionally did before the First World War. Along these lines, autopsies of financial crises in Mexico and Russia suggest that private investors believed that the IMF (and, by extension, the U.S. government) would not allow these nations to default. The IMF's treatment of the Russian government throughout the 1990s – allowing it continued access to credit despite its failure to meet specific conditions – gives credence to this argument.[119] Similarly, Thacker's study of IMF lending from 1985 to 1994 suggests that nations that are moving toward U.S. policy positions

---

[116] See Eichengreen 1999, for instance, for a summary of recent critiques of the IMF.
[117] Eichengreen 1999, Suter 1992.
[118] See Gould 2001, as well as the discussion in Chapter 4.
[119] E.g., Stone 2002.

are more likely to receive loans; these effects are more pronounced in the post–Cold War era.[120] In both periods, investors are most subject to moral hazard when they lend to politically important borrowers.[121] Ultimately, then, although the means of governance of international capital flows are different in the current and the historical eras, the implications for government policy are similar: borrowing governments can escape from some of the influence of capital markets when they are politically important but otherwise find themselves scrutinized in terms of their ability and willingness to repay obligations.

Policy Commitments and Ambitions of National Governments

The third and final dimension for comparison of the pre–World War I and contemporary eras includes two types of government policies – their exchange rate commitments and their welfare state aims. The former represents another type of constraint on government decisions, one that can serve to alter borrowing costs, but also to limit policy flexibility. The latter provides insight regarding the extent to which there is something to constrain: governments that aspire to do very little are less affected by the same financial market pressures than those that aim to do quite a lot.

Exchange Rate Regimes   During the 1870–1914 period, many nations adhered – to one degree or another – to the gold standard exchange rate system. The central rule in this system was the maintenance of the

---

[120] After controlling for a variety of macroeconomic factors, such as debt levels and balance of payments position, Thacker finds that, where a government's position is moving in the direction of the U.S. position, as measured by key UN General Assembly votes, that government is more likely to conclude an agreement with the IMF. For the post–Cold War data, both a nation's absolute policy position and its direction of movement are associated positively with the conclusion of IMF agreements. Thacker 1999.

[121] Similarly, Eichengreen 1990 and Salter 1951 discuss the successful placement of several League of Nations loans to Central Europe in the 1920s. Although the sovereign lending climate was generally unfavorable in the early to mid-1920s, these loans were successful: not only did they offer high risk premia, but they also offered monitoring of government finances. League loans required governments to engage in discussion with the league's Financial Committee, which focused on reducing fiscal deficits, reforming central banks, and controlling future expenditures. Here, as in the contemporary period, external monitoring – and perhaps implicit guarantees by sponsoring governments – reduced concerns about default risk.

convertibility of the national currency into gold at the established rate of exchange (par).[122] Core European nations adhered quite stringently[123] to the standard, whereas greater instability in gold standard commitments prevailed in Southern Europe as well as in Latin America.[124]

The classical gold standard regime served as both a constraint and an opportunity for governments, similarly to present-day currency boards (see Chapter 6), or to the Economic and Monetary Union. Because it required automatic adjustment in response to balance of payments imbalances, as well as the free flow of capital and goods, the gold standard privileged external commitments (the maintenance of par values) over nations' internal conditions. Governments' monetary policy autonomy was surrendered in service to the gold standard regime.[125] At the same time, commitment to the gold standard allowed governments to access international capital markets at lower rates of interest; gold convertibility appeared to signal sound government finances, as well as future debt servicing capacity.[126] Because financial market participants viewed credible commitments[127] to the gold standard as insulating them from exchange rate and inflation risk, sovereign borrowers in peripheral gold standard nations appear to have paid lower rates of interest, all other factors equal, than sovereign borrowers in non–gold standard nations.[128] This suggests that, even though financial market participants did not always impose strong constraints on governments in the form of conditions on loans, their preference for the gold standard placed indirect constraints on national governments. Along these lines, O'Rourke and Williamson posit that the difficulties in obtaining foreign capital that were faced by nations in the Mediterranean periphery were due, in part,

---

[122] Bordo and Schwartz 1994.

[123] Albeit not perfectly, and not in precisely the same fashion. See Eichengreen 1996.

[124] During the gold standard era, Argentina, Brazil, Chile, Italy, and Portugal all suspended convertibility in some periods.

[125] Eichengreen 1992, Obstfeld and Taylor 1998, von Mises 1912/1953, p. 416. Bordo and Schwartz 1994 note, however, that the gold standard allowed for opt-outs in cases of well-understood, exogenously generated shocks.

[126] Bordo and Schwartz 1994.

[127] Turner 1991. Eichengreen 1996 notes that during the pre–World War I era, and particularly for core nations, market participants viewed commitments to the gold standard as credible. Therefore, capital flows served to stabilize the system. This stands in contrast to the interwar years – or the 1990s – when credibility of fixed rate systems was on the wane, and speculative capital flows often served to attack these systems.

[128] Bordo and Rockoff 1996, Bordo and Schwartz 1994, Ferguson 1999, Obstfeld 1998, O'Rourke and Williamson 1999, Salter 1951.

to a lack of commitment to the gold standard, and the resulting levels of investment risk.[129]

Adherence to a fixed exchange rate regime undoubtedly constrains monetary policy in a way that adherence to a floating regime does not. In the *most* fixed systems – such as currency boards, dollarization, and EMU – the money supply is fixed exogenously, so that fiscal policies also face limits. On this basis, Polanyi suggests that policymakers rarely even *consider* deviating from the economic orthodoxy implied by the fixed rate system.[130] Some contemporary scholars, however, take a more moderate view of the constraints imposed by the international gold standard. For instance, Held and associates argue that governments – particularly those in the developing world – often chose to buffer their economies from the impact of the international economy, imposing trade protection, regulating markets, and failing to comply fully with the gold standard's rules. They also suggest that investors' investment in developing nations mediated the impact of the gold standard: "The willingness of investors in surplus countries to lend to deficit countries meant that as long as current account deficits were covered by long-term financial flows from surplus countries, there would be limited pressure to adjust."[131]

In other words, borrowing governments that appeared to be "good prospects," in terms of their continued ability to attract capital, were able to deviate a bit from gold standard commitments without adverse effects. This allowed some room for policy maneuver. How do the pressures emanating from the gold standard exchange rate regime compare to pressures emanating from contemporary currency regimes? The contemporary era is characterized by a mixture of exchange rate regimes, with a recent trend toward bifurcation. Many nations have adopted fully flexible rates, regaining a degree of monetary policy autonomy but also having to reassure investors regarding currency risk. Other nations have moved toward strongly fixed systems, such as currency boards (Argentina, Hong Kong, and a few others), dollarization (adopted recently in El Salvador, and under discussion in other Latin American nations), and monetary union (12 EU members).

---

[129] O'Rourke and Williamson 1999. They note, however, that a lack of commitment to the Gold Standard does not fully explain variation in capital flows: despite a shaky adherence to the Gold Standard in the late 19th century, Argentina remained able to attract large investment flows, with a risk premium of approximately 3% over British rates.

[130] Polanyi 1944.

[131] Held et al. 1999, p. 197.

The former category of nations faces fewer exchange rate–based constraints than pre–World War I gold standard nations did. At the same time, where these nations' currencies are subject to volatility, and particularly where governments are of lower credit quality, they either pay an interest rate premium for currency risk or employ other strategies (including foreign currency denomination and indexation, as discussed in Chapter 6) that serve not only to ameliorate risks for investors but also to limit governments' freedom of action. The latter group of nations face exchange rate–based constraints similar to those on pre–World War I governments: their commitments effect a reduction in borrowing costs but also a limitation in freedom of maneuver. And when their commitments to fully fixed systems lose credibility, their access to financial market also suffers, as Argentina's experience in late 2000 and 2001 demonstrates.

Welfare State Policies   If exchange rate–based limits on contemporary governments are no greater than, or perhaps not quite equal to, those facing pre–World War I governments, what about their policy ambitions? Do today's governments aspire to do more in the contemporary period, and do they therefore have greater need of funds and approval from international capital markets?

Before World War I many governments, especially in peripheral areas, relied heavily on global capital markets, accumulating debt/GDP ratios similar to those seen in many contemporary developing nations. Therefore, governments had incentives to please financial markets, in order to maintain their access to funds. There *is* a significant difference, however, in the uses of financing and the ambitions of governments in the two periods. Prior to the First World War, governments' policy aims were not nearly as far-reaching; in many nations (especially newer ones), several components of the modern welfare state did not exist. Governments aimed to provide infrastructure and national defense but often did not attempt to supply income redistribution or social insurance. Tanzi and Schuknecht note that, among 18 advanced nations, the average level of government expenditure/GDP was 13% in 1913; this figure represents growth from the 1870s but is much lower than the 1960 average of 28% and the 1996 average of 46%.[132] It was not until after World War I and the Great Depression – and as a result of broader suffrage, popular mobilizations, and changes in electoral institutions – that national

---

[132] Tanzi and Schuknecht 2000.

governments embraced the role of social protection.[133] In fact, the classical gold standard system rested on the political domination by the wealthy of less prosperous groups. As long as governments could force large segments of domestic society to accept the costs of domestic economic adjustment, they were able to maintain their commitment to gold.[134] It was only during the interwar period, when governments faced increased demands from expanded domestic constituencies, that they faced the choice between their exchange rate commitments and their commitments to domestic interest groups.[135]

Today's governments, then, have a greater variety of domestically based demands placed on them, in terms of providing not only infrastructure and national defense, but also education, health care, and social security. The greater ambition of governments means that financial market pressures can have a greater impact, even if they are of the same strength as during the pre–World War I era. There is, in a sense, more room for financial markets to affect governments – more policy dimensions for which market reactions matter – than there was a century ago. Ultimately, then, pre–World War I governments may have been more limited by their exchange rate commitments, but they were also less affected by these constraints because of their modest policy ambitions.

Similarities and Differences: Summing Up

Thus far, I have offered three broad areas for comparison of the pre–World War I and contemporary eras. Developing expectations regarding

---

[133] On the development of modern welfare states, see Esping-Andersen 1990, Keohane and Nye 1977, Polanyi 1944, Przeworski 1985, Ruggie 1982, and Tanzi and Schuknecht 2000. On domestic political changes between the prewar and interwar periods, and the resulting impact on economic policymaking, see Eichengreen and Simmons 1995, Simmons 1994.

[134] E.g., Keohane and Nye 1977, O'Rourke and Williamson 1999, Simmons 1994.

[135] Obstfeld and Taylor 1998, p. 380. For a discussion of the conditions under which governments subsume domestic politics to international exchange rate commitments, see Simmons 1994. Simmons finds that, during the interwar period, the countries most likely to adhere to their international monetary commitments were those that were small, highly trade-dependent, led by stable governments, and characterized by a quiescent labor force. On the other hand, unstable governments tended to overconsume, running large current account deficits, and allowed their currencies to depreciate much more than stable governments.

similarities and differences between the periods allow us to assess the extent to which contemporary financial globalization, and its implications for governments, is "something new." Table 7.4 summarizes these comparisons, as well as their implications for government policy.

The structure of the financial industry suggests that governments prior to World War I faced a less fickle, slower-moving, and less variegated global capital market. But despite these differences in speed and volatility, those governments were subject, as are their contemporary analogs, to investors' concerns regarding default risk. Merchant banks, seeking to maximize profits and to preserve their reputation, often sought formal assurances regarding governments' willingness and ability to repay their obligations. These concerns sometimes led to quite overt investor influence on government policies, especially in areas such as revenue collection. And, as today, competition was weaker – and investors' influence greater – where borrowers had lower credit quality and more modest economic potential. The governance of capital markets before World War I reinforced investors' incentives to evaluate carefully government policies, as national governments were more often than not unwilling to bail them out in cases of default. The development of the Corporation of Foreign Bondholders, the primary mechanism for collective behavior by lenders, helped to increase investors' leverage on previously delinquent governments.

In cases of politically important borrowers, however, national governments *did* pressure banks and investors to extend funds, thereby reducing their concerns about credit quality. As today, nations with geopolitical status found themselves less influenced by private capital markets. Finally, policy ambitions and commitments created a mixed environment for pre–World War I governments: on one hand, they faced similar, if not stronger, exchange rate regime pressures; on the other hand, their scope of public policies was less extensive. Ultimately, then, today's financial globalization is of a different variety from that of the pre–World War I era; in some respects, these differences imply greater market pressures for today's governments. In other respects, the market pressures are much the same. In the next section, I evaluate cases of pre–World War I sovereign borrowing, as a means of highlighting these similarities and differences, as well as of exploring the conditions under which political importance and economic prospects ameliorated financial market pressures on some borrowers.

Table 7.4. *The Pre–World War I and Contemporary Eras: Similarities and Differences*

Dimension	Pre–World War I	Contemporary	Implications
Financial Industry			
Primary actors: individuals vs. firms	Individuals	Investment firms	Greater volatility in market movements, and domination of global factors, in contemporary period
Role of financial intermediaries	Merchant banks that provide information to individual investors and focus on preserving their reputations as information providers	Individuals who defer to fund managers; managers who collect and respond to information; manager focus on preserving reputation	Intermediaries concerned about reputation, leading to consideration of default risk and influence in government policymaking
Competition for high-quality loans	Merchant banks that compete for high-quality borrowers and new borrowers with strong prospects	High-quality borrowers who pay low rates of interest; little default risk considered	Cheaper and greater access for high-quality borrowers
Range, velocity, and scope of instruments	Focus on portfolio investment, with some role for FDI; relatively slow speed of activity and limited geographic scope	Greater innovations, including derivatives, as well as greater role for FDI; greater velocity and wider geographic involvement	Potential for more numerous financial market-based influences on governments; potential for quicker market reactions to government policies
Governance			
National protection for investors	Limited; self-organization, including corporation for foreign bondholders	Likewise limited	Serves to limit moral hazard; in both periods, investors need to consider willingness and ability to pay

Pressures from and control by national governments	Some government pressures, with cross-national variations	National governments less able to direct financial activity	Sovereign borrowers of importance to great-power governments that have easier access
International governance	Rules of gold standard affect governments at the center as well as some at the periphery, but no international institutional governance of capital markets	International Monetary Fund, G-7, and others as framework for governing capital flows	Important borrowers that may get better treatment can generate moral hazard; can also centralize constraints on governments, e.g., stand-by arrangements
Policy Commitments and Ambitions Exchange rate regime	Gold standard that privileges external commitments over internal conditions but also reduces investors' risk	Floating exchange rates in most nations, but currency boards, EMU, and foreign currency denomination used to reduce investors' risk	Nations adhering to gold standard, currency boards, or EMU that face an additional constraint, as a result of past policy choices
Welfare state policies	More modest government policy ambitions; focus on infrastructure rather than on social policy	Government focus on both infrastructure and social policy; retention of existing social policies key domestic politics issue	More policies to "be constrained" in the contemporary period

Borrowing Governments and International Capital Markets: Assessing Market Influences

In the previous section, I reviewed three central dimensions of pre–World War I financial globalization and their implications for the constraints placed on governments. In that era, I expect negotiations between merchant bankers and sovereign borrowers to reflect concerns about the ability and willingness to repay debt; these concerns will be more pronounced for less developed and lower-credit quality borrowers, and where there is less competition among merchant banks; and these concerns will be less pronounced where governments intervene for political reasons or commit to bailing out investors.

How well do these expectations fit the empirical record? Anecdotally, we can observe an intense concern with default risk in many cases of lending during the 1880–1914 period. Particularly after periods of defaults, as in the 1880s, investors were not willing to lend freely.[136] Rather, they were responsive to borrowing governments to the extent that nations had "fresh vitality or important resources awaiting the steam shovel, the locomotive, the plow or the mining shaft."[137] Investors' desire to fund productive investments with a greater likelihood of prompt repayment is reflected in the distribution of British capital in 1913. Approximately 25% of this capital funded loans to national and state governments, 41% was invested in government-issued railway securities, and the remaining 24% funded "other productive investments."[138] Moreover, in an analysis covering fourteen European nations from 1880 to 1913, Flandreau and associates[139] find a positive association between debt/GDP levels and interest rate risk premia. Although this relationship is nonlinear – suggesting that market discipline only occurred as debt reached high levels – it does indicate some degree of concern with total indebtedness and with default.

Another reflection of investors' concerns with default risk was their insistence on the creation of public debt administrations, the purpose of which

---

[136] Tomz 2001a.

[137] Feis 1930, p. 26. For instance, Feis notes that French investment in Russia was sustained by "a sense of vast, hardly exploited agricultural and mineral riches of Russia, the giant character of the economic life that might arise therein, once it was properly managed" (p. 52). In the contemporary period, Kingstone 1999 argues that nations with large markets are less constrained by financial market pressures. Investors, eager to be in important economies, "will come no matter what the economic policy regime is" (p. 10).

[138] Data are calculated from Feis 1930, p. 27.

[139] Flandreau et al. 1998.

was to provide security for investors in the event of default. For example, in Turkey, the Ottoman Public debt administration was created in the early 1880s to assure debt payments in the face of continuous large budget deficits.[140] The debt administration controlled the government salt and tobacco monopolies; stamp, spirits, and fishing taxes; the tax on raw silk production; any excess customs from rate increases; and the annual tribute due from Bulgaria. Creditors' consent was required for any changes in tax laws that would reduce revenues; as the government contracted new debts, additional revenues were put under the debt administration's control.[141]

Likewise, Balkan nations – also characterized by high levels of default risk – maintained access to capital markets by promising control over revenues to their creditors. In order to guarantee repayment of an 1895 consolidation loan, the Serbian government put revenues into a special fund run by the Monopolies Administration.[142] And in 1898, the Greek government transferred control of revenues set aside for debt repayment to the International Financial Commission. The agreement that established the commission also included measures designed to keep public finances healthy; the existence of the commission enabled Greece to borrow more cheaply than it could have otherwise.[143] And, in 1909, when considering a loan to Honduras – which had previously defaulted on a loan – J. P. Morgan insisted that the loan be secured by customs revenues *and* that the U.S. government collect these revenues.[144] Although more recent scholarship questions the *extent to which* investors accounted for default risk in the prewar period,[145] there is compelling evidence that investors often considered default risk salient.

---

[140] Lindert and Morton 1990 note that Turkey's problems of fiscal mismanagement date back at least to the Crimean War loan of 1854. Also see Suter 1992, who observes that most of Turkey's foreign borrowing in the pre–World War I period funded budget deficits rather than productive investments.

[141] Feis 1930.

[142] Feis 1930, p. 268.

[143] Feis 1930.

[144] Carosso 1987, p. 590. Ultimately, the loan was not issued, because the U.S. government and the Honduran government did not ratify the formal treaty to guarantee the loan.

[145] Lindert and Morton 1990 examine the degree to which, in the 1850–1973 period, foreign governments paid appropriate risk premia when borrowing on international capital markets. They find that, whereas investors charged risk premia to foreign borrowers, these ex ante premia did not capture sufficiently ex post risk. Moreover, investors seemed to pay little attention to borrowers' past repayment records, even though borrowers with earlier defaults were more likely than other borrowers to default in later periods.

In order to evaluate more systematically the expectations developed in the previous section, I examine archival materials from five merchant banks: N. M. Rothschild, Baring Brothers (now ING Barings), J. P. Morgan, Morgan Grenfell (now Deutsche Morgan Grenfell), and Hambro and Sons (now Hambros Bank). Because London was the major market during the period, the analysis is weighted toward issues made in London. The total market value of government bonds traded in London in 1875 was £3 billion (approximately 2.73% of British GDP), and £4 billion (2.2% of British GDP) in 1905.[146] Activity in the London market can be taken as broadly representative of (although possibly less politicized than) activity in other markets. In fact, many sovereign debt issues negotiated in London occurred simultaneously in other markets.[147]

Each of the five banks was a major actor in merchant banking and government finance prior to the First World War.[148] The Rothschild family gained ascendancy in European state finance by the 1820s; despite the bank's relative decline after 1880, N. M. Rothschild was the largest private bank in London, and one of the largest banks in the world, on the eve of World War I. They were responsible for over one-fourth of public issues of foreign securities in London between 1865 and 1914, and their business was weighted heavily toward government issues.[149] Baring Brothers also was active in government finance in the nineteenth century; between 1890 and 1914, Baring handled – either alone or in conjunction with other merchant banks – multiple government debt issues for the United States, Argentina, Russia, and Britain, as well as issues for Belgium, Canada, China, Egypt, Japan, and Turkey.[150] Morgan Grenfell, often in cooperation with J. P. Morgan, also made numerous loans to governments, particularly in the Western Hemisphere. Hambro and Sons focused their efforts on Northern Europe, reflecting the family's Scandinavian roots, but also led loans in Southern Europe.

The archival materials from Baring Brothers are the most complete; the collection contains extensive records of correspondence, organized according to proposed and actual bond issues. The archival materials for the

---

[146] Calculated from data in Mauro et al. 2000, p. 7. Platt 1986 also provides data on the levels of British foreign investment on the eve of World War I.

[147] E.g., Stone 1977.

[148] See Marichal 1989, appendix D, for a guide to banking houses involved in Latin American finance during this period.

[149] Ferguson 1999.

[150] Orbell 1985.

other banks are more sparse and less systematic. Nathaniel Rothschild ordered that all correspondence be destroyed after his death; what survive are copies of outgoing correspondence from London for the 1906–1910 period. Although the Hambro collection contains a range of correspondence and is, in most cases, sorted by lending episode, only a portion of the overall lending materials survives; the same is true for J. P. Morgan's investment banking collection. The Morgan Grenfell archives likewise are spotty; some materials were retained, others were destroyed, and past archivists have found little rationale for the retention of materials.

I employ these materials in two ways: first, using a set of 70 sovereign lending episodes for which complete or partially complete files exist, I create a database of lending episodes. This database covers 22 sovereign borrowers, during the 1880–1914 period, and provides aggregate evidence regarding sovereign lending. Second, drawing primarily on Barings's materials, I provide brief examinations of lending experiences of four countries – Argentina, Japan, Russia, and Cuba. Argentina, Japan, and Russia all accessed the London capital market on several occasions prior to the First World War; Cuba negotiated for a loan in 1903–1904, but Barings ultimately declined this issue. Both types of evidence suggest that lenders were quite cognizant of default risk, particularly for poorer borrowers, but that competition from other banks and political pressures from home governments sometimes served to mute these concerns.

Aggregate Archival Evidence

The database of lending episodes includes 70 cases; in 11 cases, loans ultimately were not issued, because negotiations broke down at some stage in the process. All of the case materials contain – to different degrees – discussions of the proposed issue, correspondence between merchant banks and governments, correspondence among participating banks, and information regarding the final terms of the loans. Using these materials, I coded several dimensions of the loans, including their terms (amount, duration, interest rate, and interest rate spread, currency denomination, and issue price), their discussion of willingness and ability to pay (including the mention of government finances, the pledging of security, and other promises made by borrowing governments), the salience of interbank competition for loans, and the existence of pressures from home country governments.

Table 7.5 contains summary statistics for the database, in terms of the interest rates, interest rate spreads (defined as the difference from the London

289

Table 7.5. *Summary Statistics, Database of Sovereign Lending Episodes*

	Mean	N	Minimum	Maximum
Interest Rate	4.76	61	2.75	6.0
Interest Rate Spread	1.23	61	−2.0	4.0
Loan Amount, £millions	12.76	60	0.31	80.0
Loan Issue Price (par = 100)	91.64	38	77	101
Loan Duration, years	25.69	32	1	75
Loan Yield[a]	5.36	35	2.79	7.5

[a] Yield is calculated by dividing the interest rate by the issue price. Because of data availability, this measure is available for only 35 cases.

bank rate), amount, and duration. Of these loans, 47 are denominated in British sterling, 11 are denominated in gold, and 8 are denominated in U.S. dollars or other currencies. The purposes of loans varied; the most popular were the refinancing of existing debt (29 cases) and construction of railways and other infrastructure (20 cases). Other purposes included short-term advances (5), currency reform (5), military operations (5), and social policy (2).[151]

The overall picture that emerges is one in which bankers often attempt to guarantee repayment of the principal and interest. In over half (37) of the cases, government debt and deficits are discussed during the negotiation process. More than half of the loan prospectuses[152] on file contain information regarding past and current government revenues, as evidence of governments' ability to service their debt. In approximately half (33 of 67) of the lending episodes, the borrowing government pledged some sort of security for the loan; the most popular form of security was customs duties (20 cases), followed by other taxes and revenues (10 cases), then general revenues (5 cases), and revenues from state monopolies (5 cases).[153] In one-third of the "security" cases, the borrowing governments also promised to make monthly or semiannual deposits of funds, to cover interest payments, to either the lead bank or its designated representative. In six of the "nonsecurity" cases, governments pledged to make annual payments into a sinking fund, used eventually to repay the principal.[154] In three other

[151] Of the case files 44 included a discussion of the loan's purpose. Some loans had 2 purposes; hence the purposes total 69.

[152] Loan prospectuses exist for 23 lending episodes.

[153] Again, some loans included two forms of security.

[154] Sinking funds also were used with four of the loans with pledges of security.

"nonsecurity" cases, governments promised to refrain from future borrowing for a specified period.[155]

To what extent are the loan terms, the pledging of security, and the concerns with ability and willingness to pay related to borrowers' credit quality, home government pressures to lend, competition among investment banks, and the exchange rate regime? To begin, there is a substantial negative association between interest rate differentials and the pledging of security for a loan. For loans with pledges of security, the average interest rate differential is 1.75% ($n = 32$); for loans without such promises, the average differential is 0.64% ($n = 27$).[156] Where credit quality was low (as indicated by high differentials), lenders were more likely to attempt to ensure repayment by tying loans to particular government revenues.

Additionally, in the 10 cases in which home governments pressured banks to extend loans, average interest rate differentials are lower (0.95%, versus 1.28% for the remaining cases), the average duration of loans is longer (32 years, versus 24.8 years), and the average loan amount is larger (£24.7 million, versus £10.6 million). Although none of these differences is significant at a 95% level of confidence – in large part because of the small number of "government pressure" cases – they do imply that, where home governments have political reasons to encourage borrowing, borrowers face looser terms.

In the six cases containing mention of a high level of competition among investment banks, the average interest rate spread is 0.83%, compared with the overall sample mean of 1.23%. For 16 cases containing mention of only a moderate level of competition, the spread is 1.39%. Whereas low or moderate competition does not advantage borrowers, high competition does, in terms of borrowing costs. On the other hand, where investment banks display an overt concern with their reputation vis-à-vis individual investors, borrowers pay higher interest rate spreads (1.53%, in 10 cases, versus 1.17%, in 51 cases). Concern with reputation, then, appears to be associated with a greater desire to compensate for investment risks.[157]

Moreover, the currency denomination of loans is associated with their terms, suggesting that denomination in gold transferred risk from investors to borrowing governments, much as foreign currency denomination does

---

[155] These promises were made in eight cases total.
[156] This difference is significant at a 95% confidence level. For lending episodes with yield data, the average yield for loans without security is 4.35% (11 cases); for loans without security, the average yield is 5.86% (22 cases).
[157] These differences are not significant at a 95% confidence level.

today. The mean interest rate differential for gold denominated loans ($n = 41$) is 1.17%, compared with 1.34% for loans denominated in pounds, dollars, and other currencies ($n = 20$). Gold-denominated loans also were larger, averaging £13.56 million (compared with £10.74 million). Furthermore, the pledging of security for the loan was more common for nongold loans (62% of cases) than for gold loans (44% of cases). Loan durations, however, were substantially shorter for gold-denominated loans (19 years versus 41 years), suggesting perhaps that lenders worried that sovereign borrowers' commitments to the gold standard, or at least their commitment to repayment of loans in gold, were subject to change in the long run.

Cases: Cuba, Argentina, Japan, and Russia

The general picture that emerges from the collection of archival cases is consistent with the expectations developed earlier in this chapter: lenders generally were concerned with default risk, so that borrowers with high credit quality received better treatment from lenders. The pressures exerted by lenders, however, were less severe with high levels of competition among investment banks, or with pressure to lend from home governments. Here, I present brief summaries of bankers' interactions with four countries. These cases were selected because they include a new borrower for which a moderate to high level of competition exists (Cuba); a borrower with a history of default, but with strong economic prospects and high competition (Argentina); a borrower with high political importance (Russia); and a borrower with a combination of moderate to strong economic prospects and moderate political importance (Japan).

Cuba Cuba exemplifies a low-income developing nation, attempting to access international capital markets for the first time.[158] Representatives of Barings were very concerned about default risk, going as far as to seek assurances from the U.S. government of assistance in case of default. Ultimately, however, the Cuban government's room for maneuver was enhanced by competition from a rival investment bank.

In October 1903, the Cuban government initiated discussions with Barings regarding a loan to Cuba, the purpose of which was quite general. The bankers viewed Cuba's economic prospects as quite modest, and, from

---

[158] These materials are drawn from the Baring Archive, file 200090. Cuba played a very minor role in the London capital market, accounting for only 0.22% of total government bonds (excluding British consols) traded in London in 1905. Mauro et al. 2000, table 1.

the beginning, default risk played a major role. In their private memos, the bankers noted that investors would not be interested in a Cuban bond unless they were convinced that, in case of default, the U.S. government would lend support to the collection of security for the loan. Although they did not demand an official U.S. government guarantee, Barings wanted some sort of U.S. government support, such as a U.S. commissioner to look after the bondholders' interests. Barings's potential underwriting colleagues echoed this sentiment; for instance, in February 1904, Paribas noted that Cuba was more likely to default than Mexico, making U.S. government involvement essential. In the end, however, the U.S. government did not provide any assurances regarding repayment of the proposed loan.

Barings also informed the Cuban government that a loan would require a specific guarantee of customs revenues; in their view, the existing laws authorizing foreign borrowing promised customs revenues as security only in a general way. Barings demanded that Cuba provide, as security, the amount due for each interest payment, plus a 10% cushion. During the negotiation process, Barings sent detailed information regarding the legal structure and language of specific customs guarantees in Mexico and Argentina – a clear effort at diffusion of "best practices."[159] Moreover, Barings reminded the Cuban government that the bond and interest were to be repayable in gold, as this served to eliminate currency risk: "In the event of any change taking place in the nature of the legal currency in Cuba, it is important that it should be made clear that this will not affect the service of the Loan."[160] All in all, the loan negotiations in late 1903 and early 1904 reflected a strong concern with default risk – fully expected for a low-income borrower with little credit history, especially when the U.S. government had refused to promise any sort of protection.

Ultimately, however, a combination of external political factors and competition from another merchant bank led to the breakdown of negotiations between Barings and Cuba. Barings was concerned about the political situation in the Far East in 1904 and therefore reluctant to tie up $35 million in a loan to Cuba. In February, when diplomatic relations between Russia and Japan broke off, Barings and their colleagues withdrew from the negotiations; Barings maintained that it was unfortunate to lose the business, but it was not prudent to lend in the current global climate. At the same time, Speyer and Company, a German bank, offered to make the issue; Speyer had

[159] Meyer et al. 1997.
[160] November 6, 1903, letter from Baring to Vanderlip.

made counteroffers throughout the course of the negotiations, prompting John Baring (Lord Revelstoke) to observe that their attitude "savours only of blackmail." Speyer was willing to offer a loan regardless of the situation in the Far East, and the competition between merchant banks served to reduce the constraints on the Cuban government. Perhaps because they were new to financial markets – and therefore seen as having potential for a longer-term lending relationship – they were able to access credit markets with some success. Their loan totaled $35 million, with $20 million taken immediately and the rest optioned for a later date; the loan lasted 40 years, was priced at 91, and was secured by 1.5% of Cuban customs duties. It also was relatively cheap, in terms of interest rate differentials, issued at 5% – only 1% above the London bank rate. The 1904 loan from Speyer was subscribed twice over, indicating strong public interest in this loan, even without formal U.S. guarantees.

Argentina   Argentina exemplifies a middle-income developing nation that in the two decades prior to World War I, was only moderately constrained by international financial markets.[161] A large portion of capital flow to Latin America was directed at Argentina;[162] these funds were used primarily for public works, rather than for debt financing, especially in the 1880s.[163] Although Argentina's 1890 default – which set off the Baring Crisis and threatened European capital markets[164] – gave rise to concerns about the country's future ability to pay, these concerns were balanced by a strong sense of its economic potential and by the resulting competition among investment banks.[165] By the turn of the century, Argentina had satisfied its external creditors via an austerity program and a restoration of gold convertibility, and Barings had renewed its major role in Argentine finance. In the early twentieth century, Argentina had a rapidly growing population, a very large foreign trade sector, an ambitious program to develop its infrastructure, and good standing with foreign investors.[166]

Two episodes illustrate bank–government relations in Argentina: in 1898 and 1899, Argentina sought loans to refinance some of its debt at lower rates

---

[161] These materials are drawn from the Baring Archive, files 200058, 200059, 200060, and 200061.

[162] In 1905, Argentina accounted for 2.18% of all government bonds (excluding British consols) traded on the London market. Mauro et al. 2000, table 1.

[163] Marichal 1989.

[164] Orbell 1985.

[165] Marichal 1989, p. 145; Bordo and Schwartz 1994, p. 34.

[166] Platt 1986.

of interest. Argentina was not in desperate need of refinancing, and several merchant banks provided competing offers. At the same time, Barings was concerned that the proceeds of the loan would fuel political tensions between Argentina and Chile. Barings pressured the Argentine government to resolve its conflict with Chile and to commit itself to make no new issues in Europe without first giving preference to Barings. Ultimately, though, the Argentine government was in a strong position – refinancing was desirable, but not imminently necessary. The government declined the terms offered by Barings; later, in March 1900, the government received a short-term advance (without the political strings attached) for the same purpose from Barings.

The next year, Barings approached the Argentine government with a proposal to undertake debt refinancing. Barings's representative in Buenos Aires pointed out that Argentina's outstanding debt was lower than that of similar nations; nevertheless, Barings pressed for a customs guarantee for this loan. They noted that a similar guarantee – offering 60% of customs revenues as security for the loan – was well received by investors in Mexican securities. Along similar lines, in July 1901, J. P. Morgan – a possible underwriting participant – wrote to Barings that they would prefer to see a budget surplus in Argentina. After these pressures, the Argentine government introduced into parliament a law setting aside customs revenue as a loan guarantee. Ultimately, however, the 1901 loan negotiations collapsed in the face of domestic political resistance: there was staunch opposition to the customs guarantee legislation. Local observers reported that this was related to issues much larger than sovereign debt. Again, Argentina failed to complete a borrowing contract but – given that these operations were about refinancing, rather than about procuring new or desperately needed funds – remained able to take a relatively firm stance with investors. Whereas Argentina's 1902 refinancing loan from Barings included security, its loans later in the decade (from both Barings and J. P. Morgan) did not. The confluence of economic prospects, competition, and less than immediate need for capital provided Argentina with room for maneuver.

Russia Lending to Russia is the most politically motivated of the cases examined and perhaps the most politically motivated of all pre–World War I lending.[167] Despite looming political instabilities and questions of financial mismanagement in Russia, investment banks were quite willing to provide

---

[167] Kindleberger 1993.

loans in 1906 and again in 1909.[168] Discussions of default risk were almost nonexistent, as was competition among banks, but pressures from home governments were substantial. Therefore, Russia represents an instance of a government whose political importance – coupled with a vague sense of economic prospects in the distant future – served to mediate the influences of international financial markets.

Foreign investment in Russia increased steadily during the prewar period, funding an almost-uninterrupted budget deficit from 1893 to 1912. In 1895, foreigners held 30% of Russia's debt; this amount reached 48% in 1914. Of the debt outstanding in 1914, 80% was held in France and 14% in the United Kingdom. Russia's relations with each of the major European capital exporters were colored by political considerations. In France, Russian borrowing was tightly linked with the Russo-French political alliance.[169] There, each set of sovereign debt negotiations was accompanied by official discussions of the uses of borrowed capital and of foreign policies. During the Russo-Japanese War, Russia relied almost exclusively on the French market. By the end of that war, however, Russian credit in Paris was nearly exhausted, and Russia sought new capital on the London market.

Political considerations long had precluded financial flows from London to Russia; British investors, for example, had lent only to Japan during the Russo-Japanese War. Although Barings had a long-standing relationship with the Russian government, this relationship fell off considerably in the 1870s and 1880s.[170] The house of N. M. Rothschild was hostile to Russia because of the government's treatment of Jews, although it had lent to them in the 1880s and 1890s.[171] These negotiations, which began immediately after the conclusion of the Russo-Japanese War, were very secretive.[172] In September, Barings consulted the British government, in order to ensure that they did not object to Barings's involvement. Government officials responded that, the deeper the financial connections between Russia and the United Kingdom, the more peaceful their political relations would be. In October, Lord Revelstoke traveled to Saint Petersburg to conduct these

---

[168] In 1905, Russia accounted for 11.68% of all government bonds (excluding British consols) traded on the London market. Mauro et al. 2000, table 1.

[169] Feis 1930, pp. 218, 223; Kindleberger 1993, Viner 1929.

[170] Orbell 1985.

[171] See Davis 1983, Ferguson 1999, pp. 379–380.

[172] These materials are drawn from the Baring Archive, files 200164, 200165, 200166, 200167, and 200168.

negotiations directly. Early in the negotiations, Revelstoke asked for a general outline of the state of Russian finances; the government promptly provided a statement of imports and exports, as well as a statement of total gold holdings.

After this point, however, Russian government finances were rarely mentioned. Rather, the political importance of the loan to both the Russian and the British governments – along with discussions over which banks should be included in the syndicate – drove the negotiations. In October 1905, Revelstoke observed that the negotiations were very time-consuming, "out of all proportion to the profit to be earned." But, given his sense that a British financial presence in Russia was "vitally important," Revelstoke continued his work on the Russian issue. The negotiations for the loan were suspended temporarily in December 1905, when Russia entered a state of domestic political upheaval; at this time, the British government representatives reported that Russia needed money more than ever and could be counted on not to repudiate its obligations. Meanwhile, Russia's financial troubles deepened, and criticism in Paris and London of the Russian government's absolutist tendencies and economic policies intensified.[173]

Negotiations reopened in March 1906, and the British authorities continued to express geopolitical concerns. For instance, in April 1906, the British representative in Saint Petersburg noted that the Russian government would be in a very bad position if it did not get the loan, and this would damage British political and economic interests. The government's revenues were decreasing, leaving the government in even more dire straits. "Without a loan, the government cannot meet the expenditures already incurred, the government will be on the verge of bankruptcy, and this could facilitate a revolution."[174]

Later that month, the loan to Russia was issued; the 5% loan (at 1.5% over the London bank rate, and priced at 89) totaled £80 million and was raised in European capital markets; Barings handled the London tranche of £13,101,000. This loan allowed the government to suppress revolution and to remain on the gold standard; it also marked the large-scale opening of the London financial market to the Russian government. The largest share of the loan was taken by France; other portions were financed in

---

[173] A major concern at the time was the Russian Duma, which was not to open until May 1906. Liberal opinion in London and Paris suggested that Russia should not be permitted to contract a loan without Duma approval; others were curious about the constitutional status of debt issued without the Duma's consent. Viner 1929.

[174] From Spring-Rice letter, April 1906, Baring Archive.

Austria, the Netherlands, and Russia.[175] It is interesting to note that there was little competition for this loan, perhaps reflecting the size of the issue and the dominance of political considerations. Ultimately, bankers were willing to overlook economic considerations because of political concerns. Although the loan was authorized by the Russian legislature, the bankers paid little attention to the purposes of the loan or to Russia's potential ability and willingness to repay its debt. Some contemporaneous observers, noting the initial success of the issue, but the fall of bond prices by mid-1906, suggested that bankers should have paid more attention to Russia's fiscal position.[176] Similarly, Lindert and Morton note that although Russia did repay its loans during the pre–World War I period, the proceeds of loans were used in questionable ways, such as for railroads with military (rather than commercial) purposes and for bribery of the French financial press.[177]

In 1908 and 1909, Russia negotiated another international loan; as in the 1906 negotiations, Russia's political state was more important than its fiscal state to the ability to borrow. This loan was contracted to repay treasury bonds that would fall due in May 1909 and to provide fresh financing for railroads and the army. As in 1906, the negotiations reflected little, if any, consideration of the legitimacy of the purposes of the loan – although the bankers did request that the general purposes be included in the loan prospectus – and contained no discussion of default risk. The British government again leaned on bankers to provide credit. Moreover, the Russian government appeared quite able to use its political connections with France – and its easy access to French capital markets – to demand better terms for its loans. In August 1908, for example, the Russian finance minister informed Barings that a 5% loan was impossible, as that was a "wartime rate," and he needed to demonstrate to the Duma the advances made in Russian credit. Ultimately, his request was granted; the interest rate on the 1909 loan was 4%, only 1% above the London bank rate. Again, Russia's political importance – and competition from French lenders – overrode considerations of default risk and economic status.

---

[175] Anan'ich and Bovykin 1991 note that the Russian government initially wanted the loan to have an international flavor. The French government, however, insisted on Russia's unreserved support in the French conflict with Germany over Morocco. As a result, German banks withdrew altogether.

[176] The Rothschilds were among these observers. See the 1906 letters file, as well as Ferguson 1999.

[177] Lindert and Morton 1990.

Japan   Of these four cases, Japan[178] demonstrates the greatest economic potential, as well as a moderate level of political importance and moderate interbank competition. Although investment banks made some mentions of default risk and sometimes requested loan guarantees, they generally were willing to make large loans at competitive rates of interest.[179] This combination rendered Japan one of the less constrained sovereign borrowers in the pre–World War I period.

Japan took out its early loans – in 1870, 1873, 1897, and 1899 – in the London capital market. Japan established a gold standard in 1897 and adhered to the standard until 1917.[180] In 1901, with its finances in poor shape, Japan began negotiating for loans in all major capital markets.[181] At the time, given Russia's concerns about Japan and France's alliance with Russia, Japan had difficulty accessing the French market. Japan found the British market more accommodating, particularly after a 1902 Anglo-Japanese political alliance was cemented. For the next several years, and throughout the Russo-Japanese War, Japanese loans found a receptive market in London. Although the British government refused to provide official loan guarantees for Japan, it did take an unofficial "benevolent interest" in the flotation of these loans.[182]

Barings was involved in several issues to the Japanese government in the early 1900s. In 1902, correspondence between N. M. Rothschild and Barings indicated that the British government "regard[ed] it as a matter of political importance that Japan should be able to raise the money it needs in the UK rather than elsewhere."[183] Talks for a loan to Japan, with Barings as a participant, and for the purpose of railway construction (totaling £5.1 million), were concluded very quickly, in less than one week, and with little reference to Japan's financial position.[184] Japan had assured bankers that the loan would not increase the government's total debt stock, and its gold standard commitment served to allay investors' concerns.

In 1904, Baring was involved in the development of two loans to Japan. Although they officially withdrew from Japanese financing when hostilities

---

178 These materials are drawn from the Baring Archive, files 200186, 200187, 200188, 200189.
179 In 1905, Japan accounted for 1.93% of all government bonds (excluding British consols) traded on the London market. Mauro et al. 2000, table 1.
180 Bordo and Schwartz 1994.
181 Feis 1930, Viner 1929.
182 Viner 1929.
183 Baring Archive, file 200186.
184 Orbell 1985.

between Russia and Japan commenced, the bank was quite involved in behind-the-scenes negotiations. The first loan, for £10 million at 6% interest, was issued in May, against the backdrop of political tensions between Japan and Russia. The majority of this loan was to insure gold convertibility, and therefore most of the proceeds remained in London for use in exchange market intervention. Unlike the 1902 loan, and probably as a result of the prevailing international political climate, this loan included security guarantees in the form of customs revenues and was at a 3% premium over the London rate.[185] Interestingly, however, the customs guarantees were less specific than those attached to loans of less-developed borrowers, such as Mexico. Moreover, the negotiations reflected some concerns about competition from other banks.

The second 1904 loan was issued in November; again, the bankers expressed concerns about security for the loan. In September, they suggested that, given political tensions between Japan and Russia, some sort of security for the loan – preferably customs revenue – was necessary for a successful issue. And again, the participants in these negotiations expressed concerns about competition from a rival investment bank. In the end, a loan of £12M, offered in both London and New York, was issued. The loan was secured by a second charge on the customs receipts of the Japanese empire; the loan prospectus provided information about customs revenues in the previous five years. This guarantee reflected some concern with default risk, but again the concern was less pronounced than that expressed about lower-income borrowers. The Japanese government appeared satisfied with the outcomes of these loans; in January 1905, the finance minister reported to Barings that the emperor was "very satisfied with how the syndicate has treated them, and plans to come to them for future borrowing needs."[186]

In 1905, Japan accessed the London capital market three times – in March, July and November – borrowing a total of £100 million at 4.5% interest.[187] Again, these loans were negotiated relatively quickly, with modest attention to default risk and little mention of the purposes of these loans. The March loan was secured with revenues from the tobacco monopoly; the Japanese government seemed quite willing to trade a loan guarantee for a large loan at a small interest rate premium, and there was little negotiation

---

[185] The premium on the 1902 loan was 2%.
[186] Baring Archive, file 200188.
[187] This was a premium of 0.5% to 2% over the London bank rate, depending on the month.

Table 7.6. *Argentina, Cuba, Japan, and Russia*

Case	Economic Prospects	Political Importance	Interbank Competition	Overall Constraints
Argentina	Moderate: sense of potential, despite earlier problems	Low to moderate	Low to moderate: tension between Baring and Morgan	Moderate: Baring demand for specific guarantee, government refusal to grant; no loan issued
Cuba	Low to moderate	Low: U.S. government unwilling to guarantee loan	Moderate: Speyer very interested in capturing Cuban government account	Moderate to high: Baring demand for specific loan guarantee; Speyer willing to make loan
Japan	High	Moderate: some British government pressure	Moderate, particularly in 1904	Low to moderate: guarantee loans using customs revenue, but able to borrow large amounts
Russia	Low; moderate in the distant future	High: very important to British government	Moderate: little interest from Rothschild, but competition from French banks, especially in 1908	Low: little discussion of loans' purposes or government's ability to repay

301

on this matter. The July loan also was characterized by limited negotiation; it was secured by another charge on tobacco revenues. In both March and July, the lending syndicate faced competition from Speyer, which offered the government better financing terms. Finally, in November, an issue of £50 million, for the purpose of converting outstanding debt – with any surplus to be used as the government deemed necessary – was made. This issue, put forward by a large international syndicate, was enormously oversubscribed by the public, although there was no security offered. Japan, then, provides an intermediate case: a borrower with some political importance (although less than Russia), for which there was some competition from other investment banks, and whose economic prospects were favorable. As we expect, Japan was moderately constrained by international capital markets, in that it was often required to provide guarantees for its loans, but it also was able to borrow large amounts frequently.

Table 7.6 summarizes these four cases according to their economic prospects, political importance, level of interbank competition, and overall financial market constraints. These cases provide support for our expectations that investment banks often considered governments' willingness and ability to pay – and, therefore, constrained government policy choices – in the pre–World War I era but that these constraints were affected by political as well as economic factors.

Conclusion

This chapter compares two eras of financial globalization: the contemporary era and the pre–World War I era. By analyzing the similarities and differences between the periods, I suggest the extent to which recent influences of financial markets on government policy have historical parallels. I employ three axes of comparison: the structure of the financial industry and, therefore, of sovereign borrowing practices; the governance of capital flows, both nationally and internationally; and the policy commitments and ambitions of national governments. Although there are many similarities between the periods, there also are some differences; for instance, the currency regime created greater constraints for *most* pre–World War I governments, whereas less ambitious social policies mean that pre–World War I governments were *less* affected by financial market pressures. All in all, I expect that today's governments are at least as influenced by capital markets as those in the 1880–1914 era; history may be repeating itself today, but it is doing so more loudly.

In the latter section of the chapter, I draw on archival materials from investment banks to assess the extent to which different factors influenced government–bank relations. For instance, I consider the extent to which geopolitical importance and interbank competition relieved borrowing governments from financial market pressures, as well as the extent to which national commitments to the gold standard served to allay investors' concerns (but also, of course, to impose another set of limitations on government policy). The larger database and the case studies suggest that – as is true today – sovereign borrowers with strong economic prospects and unblemished credit histories and sovereign borrowers with political importance receive the most lenient treatment from global capital markets.

8

Financial Market–Government Relations in the Twenty-First Century

> The government of an internationally integrated economy is far from powerless. It is merely somewhat constrained.[1]

The final years of the twentieth century witnessed a dramatic rise in grassroots protests against the IMF, the WTO, the G-7, and the Organization of American States (OAS), among others. The common threat binding together these disparate protest actions was accountability: to what extent could intergovernmental organizations be held responsible by member governments and by individual citizens? Had the democratic process in these institutions become so indirect as to be meaningless? Did the focus on efficiency and effectiveness in international political and economic relations result in a failure to attend to issues of equity and representation? In many ways, this book addresses the same theme of accountability: to what extent, and via what mechanisms, do contemporary governments retain policymaking autonomy vis-à-vis international financial markets? Has the locus of government policymaking shifted from cabinets and legislatures to central banks[2] and bond markets? Or do governments and domestic groups remain the ultimate arbiters of national policy choices? As many scholars of international institutions would point out, and as I demonstrate, governments' freedom of action *is*, in some ways, reduced by international involvement *but* remains intact, or is even expanded, in others.

Key Findings

This book contributes to a wide literature on economic globalization by focusing on the behavior of market participants and its implications for

---

[1] Martin Wolf, *Financial Times*, May 13, 1997, p. 18.
[2] E.g., Berman and McNamara 1999.

government policymaking. It offers answers to two questions: how do financial market participants evaluate government policy? How important are these evaluations to government policy choices? The theoretical framework underlying the "strong but narrow" and "strong and broad" conceptions of government–financial market relations is a micrologic of financial market decision making, based on the types of investment risk that are salient to market participants, as well as on market participants' demands for information.

Our central argument is that the consideration of government policies by financial market actors varies markedly across groups of countries. In the advanced capitalist democracies, market participants consider key macroeconomic indicators, but not supply-side or microlevel policies. Governments are pressured strongly to satisfy financial market preferences in terms of overall inflation and government budget deficit levels but retain domestic policymaking latitude in other areas. The means by which governments achieve macropolicy outcomes, and the nature of government policies in other areas, do not concern financial market participants. So, whereas many governments have converged cross-nationally in the pursuit of lower inflation and lower government budget deficits, they have not converged in a variety of other areas, including overall government consumption, the structure of tax systems, and the role of labor market institutions within the economy. Particularly in developed nations, governments retain a significant amount of policy autonomy and political accountability. If, for domestic reasons, they prefer to retain traditional social democratic policies, for instance, they are quite able to do so.[3]

Chapter 2 introduced a set of theoretically grounded expectations regarding financial market influences on government policy. I defined financial market influence on government policy in two dimensions: strength and scope. As international capital mobility increases, so should strength of financial market influence. Scope depends on the signaling dynamic between governments and investors and market participants' resulting incentives to gather information. Drawing from recent literature in finance and economics, I suggested that the relative costs and benefits of employing information determine the range of government policy indicators that are salient to investors, and that this range varies across types of countries.

---

[3] Iversen 1999 argues, however, that many traditional social democratic policies are ill suited for current economic conditions, so that, even if governments can pursue them, they may not want to.

Where default risk is essentially nonexistent, market participants can exclude many types of indicators from consideration; on the other hand, where default risk is highly salient, investors have material incentives to consider a wide range of information. Therefore, I hypothesized that, in the contemporary era, financial markets exert a "strong but narrow" influence on government policy choices in developed nations. Financial market participants are able to exact harsh punishment of governments that pursue suboptimal policies, but this punishment is meted out on the basis of a small set of indicators. By contrast, emerging market governments face a strong and broad market constraint: market participants consider many dimensions of government policy when making asset allocation decisions.

To evaluate these expectations, Chapters 3 and 4 presented a variety of types of empirical evidence. In the first section of Chapter 3, I utilized interviews with financial market participants in London and Frankfurt. These interviews strongly support the portrayal of financial market influence in OECD nations as "strong but narrow." Because investors are confident that governments are willing and able to repay their obligations, they are mainly concerned that governments "get the big numbers right." The strength of financial market influence, which stems from capital mobility, is reinforced by the fact that market participants tend to rely on a similar set of decision-making indicators. And the narrow nature of the financial market constraint is reinforced by the relatively short time horizons that prevail within the market.

In order to reinforce the interview data, the remainder of Chapter 3 presented a quantitative assessment of financial market reactions to government policies in advanced democracies. Using pooled cross-sectional time series analysis for the 1981–1995 period, I tested the relationship between interest rates on long-term government bonds and various policy outcomes. I find that the strongest determinants of long-term interest rates are inflation and U.S. long-term interest rates. Government fiscal balances, current account balances, and exchange rate levels also are significantly and somewhat strongly associated with government bond rates. I then examined the influence of microside indicators on government bond rates. Here, the quantitative analysis provides mixed evidence: the most aggregate of these indicators, such as the total size of government, are associated significantly with long-term interest rate levels. The strength of these associations, however, is rather small, so that the cost to governments of divergent policies is not great. The least aggregate of these indicators, including the balance between workers' and employers' social security contributions, are not significantly associated with interest rate levels, as the strong but narrow constraint predicts. Moreover, bivariate analyses of the relationship between macro- and microindicators suggest that micropolicy divergence in the face of macrolevel convergence is quite possible.

The question of financial market–government relations in the developing world was the subject of Chapter 4. I expected that, given uncertainty about governments' types and the resulting salience of default risk, emerging market governments would face a broader range of financial market influences than developed democracies. And because of their need to attract external financing, most emerging market economies are very exposed to international capital markets. To assess the expectation of "strong and broad" financial market pressures, particularly the role of default risk, I provided empirical evidence from a variety of sources – simple quantitative analyses, a second round of interviews with as well as surveys of financial market participants, and the methodology and outputs of sovereign credit rating agencies. This evidence suggested that, although there is some cross-national and over-time variation in the extent to which emerging market nations are constrained by financial market pressures, governments of emerging market economies generally have less policymaking autonomy than governments of advanced industrial democracies.

In Chapters 5 and 6, I considered the implications of financial market pressures for domestic political processes and outcomes. How do domestic political institutions and ideas serve to mediate and refract the pressures exerted by international capital markets? Moreover, by what means do governments seek to ameliorate the influence of international financial markets on domestic policymaking? I addressed the issue of domestic politics in two ways. First, in Chapter 5, I generated expectations regarding the sources of variation in government responses to financial market constraints. I hypothesized that, where governments were more sensitive to economic outcomes (as elections approached, or when they were more clearly responsible for policymaking), where governments were more vulnerable to capital market pressures (as in emerging market economies), and where interest rate changes were larger, governments would be more likely to accede to financial market pressures. Therefore, a variety of national features, including the type of electoral system, the degree of federalism, the size of the welfare state, trade openness, and debt management policies, are likely to affect national responses to financial market pressures. As a preliminary assessment of these expectations, I considered several cases of government response to financial market activity during the 1994 government bond market turbulence.

Among developed nations, it appears that even governments that experience strong external pressures retain a certain degree of policymaking autonomy, responding – as did Sweden – to pressures in a way that fits with national conditions. The Australian social commentator Richard Neville captures the "constraint/autonomy" combination in his description of life under Labour: "There is perhaps an inch of difference between an Australia governed by the Labour Party and an Australia governed by the Right. But, believe me, it is an inch worth living in."[4] Governments do not have full autonomy – as they likely never have had – but they retain control over many issues that affect the daily lives of their citizens.

Chapter 6 considered domestic politics from another angle, by exploring the various means by which governments can influence the nature of their relationship with international capital markets. These means include policies that alter market participants' expectations regarding macroeconomic outcomes, policies that insulate particular groups of investors from certain kinds of investment risk, and policies that insulate governments from activity in international financial markets. In general, particularly in advanced capitalist democracies, governments have *some significant degree* of choice regarding these policies: they are not forced by financial market pressures to make particular institutional changes. Rather, the policies pursued reflect governments' considerations of the costs and benefits of particular policies, depend on domestic distributional concerns as well as external economic pressures, and, therefore, vary cross-nationally.

As Chapters 2 through 4 suggested that we could learn a great deal about financial market–government relations by considering the issue across geographic regions, Chapter 7 highlighted the value of considering financial market–government relations over time. In that chapter, I assessed the issue for an earlier period of capital market openness, the pre–World War I era. This analysis drew from the primary materials of four investment banks, specifically considering cases of lending to Argentina, Cuba, Japan, and Russia, as well as on a larger set of lending episodes. I reviewed the many similarities between contemporary investment banking and pre–World War I merchant banking. For instance, individual investors have long looked to financial intermediaries – investment banks, institutional investors – as sources of information. And these intermediaries were as

---

[4] Cited in Radice 1996, p. 139.

concerned, if not more concerned, with default risk prior to World War I. Concerns about default risk, however, were mitigated by the geopolitical importance of certain borrowers and, earlier in the period, by governments' willingness to intervene on behalf of investors. Here we see additional parallels – investors' treatment of Russia, a borrower that was "too important to fail," and the more general problem of moral hazard that is introduced by implicit bailout guarantees. At the same time, however, we must be conscious of the differences in governments across historical eras: prior to the First World War governments usually were not concerned with redistributive aims. Moreover, many governments adhered to the gold standard regime, which served to reduce investors' perceived currency risk but also constricted monetary policy autonomy.

Implications for Policy

A central finding of this book is that governments often retain significant policymaking autonomy vis-à-vis international capital markets. Particularly in advanced capitalist democracies, participants in the government bond market care about overall policy performance, but not about the varying ways in which governments can achieve this performance. For example, smaller deficit/GDP ratios can be achieved via reductions in government expenditures or via increases in government revenues. And an expenditure reduction or a revenue increase can be achieved in a variety of ways as well. Therefore, we should expect – as we do – to observe continued cross-national divergence in a variety of government policy areas. In emerging market economies, governments' room for maneuver is less but remains intact nonetheless: developing nation governments that experience market pressures to reform their social security systems, for instance, often do so in different ways.

In terms of policymaking autonomy, then, there is a significant degree of freedom left for many governments. Although there are pressures for lower rates of inflation and smaller budget deficits, governments can achieve these in a variety of ways. This is particularly true where domestic constituents are willing to pay – either in terms of taxation or in terms of higher interest rates – for certain publicly provided goods. Especially in such cases, domestic policymaking processes remain key determinants of national policies, so that democratic accountability continues to affect the actions of elected leaders.

This book also serves to remind policymakers and scholars that the pressures governments experience are the result of past policy choices. Although governments often are inclined to claim that they have "no choice" when responding to external economic pressures, we should not forget that their current positions are the result of past political choices. For instance, government decisions regarding the type of exchange rate regime later affect the type of government policies that are most obtainable. Where capital is internationally mobile, a nation with a fixed exchange rate or even a currency board loses monetary policy autonomy. On the other hand, flexible rates can serve to restore monetary policy autonomy, but with a cost to fiscal policy freedom. Likewise, broad choices about capital market openness, which are driven by political considerations as well as by technological pressures,[5] create future opportunities and constraints for governments. On a slightly smaller scale, previous decisions about the amount and nature of borrowing affect current behavior: where a government has a high level of debt and/or must roll over its debt frequently, it is more susceptible to financial market pressures. As Chapter 6 reminds us, there are many choices a government is able to make when structuring its relationship with international capital markets. Some of these choices – such as controls on certain types of capital flows or borrowing from residents – serve to dampen the economic benefits of capital market openness, but also serve to insulate governments from the pressures of such openness. At present, when considering options such as currency boards and currency unions, governments should do so with an awareness of the trade-offs involved. Currency boards can serve to reduce investors' exchange rate risk considerations and to improve governments' anti-inflation credibility, but they also limit the extent to which governments can address macroeconomic downturns or aid ailing financial institutions.

The theoretical and empirical findings presented in Chapter 4 highlight the fact that, in emerging market economies, the nature of financial market pressures can vary markedly over time. This variance, in turn, can alter the extent to which government activity is limited by financial market openness: where a mania situation prevails in global capital markets, governments can do no wrong in the eyes of return-hungry investors. Governments are able to pursue any number of policies, including those that are politically beneficial in the short run but economically detrimental in the long run. But where a panic situation prevails, governments often can do nothing

[5] Garrett 2000b.

to please risk-averse investors. In such situations, investors often fail to distinguish "lemons" from "cream puffs," avoiding all emerging market economies.[6] For scholars, this behavior provides another type of over-time variation to explain: under what conditions do market participants become more risk-averse or risk-acceptant? Are these shifts systematic in nature or purely stochastic?

For policymakers, a similar question exists: if the optimal capital market environment is a normal one, in which interest rate premia are consistent with key economic fundamentals, how can governments and international institutions best ensure that such a climate prevails? In other words, what sorts of factors push financial market participants from fundamentals-based to herding-based behavior, and how can these factors be controlled or even eliminated? In the wake of the financial crises of the 1990s, this issue has been at the fore of the "international financial architecture" debate. Some scholars identify moral hazard as a key problem: investors are more likely to behave in a manic fashion if they believe they will be bailed out in the event of a crisis. Others cite information as a central defect: where investors swing from mania to panic, the cause often is the release of new information that is very much at odds with older information. Still others locate many problems in the structure of contemporary bond markets, both in terms of the way in which sovereign bond contracts are designed,[7] and in terms of the structure of the investment management industry. For instance, because fund managers must generate funds to meet redemptions in the case of a downturn, they often are left to sell off the best-performing assets, leading "good" countries into crises of their own. Most likely, each of these problems – and several others – contributed to recent manias and the subsequent panics.

For international institutions, the question is whether or not the political will to address these problems exists. In terms of the practices and structure of the IMF, little is likely to change. Between those alleging that the IMF does "too little" and those complaining that it does "too much," policymakers seem poised to conclude that the present degree and structure of IMF activity are "just right." In terms of the investment management industry, efforts at stricter national regulation are likely to lead firms to exit to less strict jurisdictions. And international efforts on this front would encounter similar problems, as individual states would face large incentives to

---

[6] Akerlof 1970.
[7] Eichengreen 1999.

defect – witness Luxembourg as well as a range of Caribbean nations. In information, the IMF has made some progress in its efforts toward the creation and adoption of an international data standard.[8] The SDDS has 50 subscribers at present, including all developed nations except New Zealand, and efforts to ensure full compliance by subscribers are now under way. Although there remains a difference between access to and use of information, these efforts eventually may help to reduce the occurrence of manias and panics.

Issues for the Future

Changes in Financial Market–Government Relations

How might the key determinants of the strength and scope of financial market influence change in the near future? As the analysis in Chapter 7 makes clear, the relationship between the government bond market and national governments varies over time. For instance, as the degree of international capital mobility changes, so should the strength of financial market influence. And as the number of potential investment locations and the type of investment risks change, so should the scope of financial market pressures. Two recent changes in developed nations may serve to alter the future character of financial market–government relations.

The Euro   First, the advent of a single currency in Europe should lead to, among other effects, a more unified financial market.[9] Because investors will no longer face currency risk among EMU member nations, monetary integration should increase the development of European markets, for sovereign and corporate debt, as well as for equities.[10] On the corporate debt side, this suggests that Europe could catch up with English-speaking nations, which tend to have deeper and more liquid corporate fixed income sectors.[11] In the first two quarters of 1999, for instance, corporate bond

---

[8] Mosley 2000b.

[9] Gros and Lannoo 2000 discuss the effects of EMU on derivatives markets. On the consequences of EMU for wage bargaining in Europe, see Soskice and Iversen 1999.

[10] OECD 1999, Sassen 1999, *Economist*, October 24, 1998, p. 85; *Economist*, September 18, 1999, p. 83; *Economist*, May 5, 2001, survey p. 20. After EMU, European investment funds also are not affected, within the euro-zone, by local currency exposure regulations.

[11] BIS 1998, Mylonas et al. 2000.

issues in EMU nations tripled from their 1998 levels.[12] In equity markets, EMU appears to be leading to higher market capitalization, as well as to a movement away from intermediated, bank-based financing.[13] Fund managers have begun to allocate by sector within Europe, rather than by country.[14] Although a proposed merger of the London and Frankfurt stock exchanges collapsed late in 1999, equity market integration can be expected to intensify.

On the sovereign side, the euro-denominated debt market now is almost equal in size to the U.S. Treasury Bond market.[15] The advent of the euro (and euro-denominated debt instruments) may have two effects central to government–financial market relations:[16] it can heighten the salience of default risk *and* it can dilute the impact of resident investment. Prior to the advent of EMU in January 1999, investors in Europe worried little about default risk; rather, inflation (and therefore currency) risk was the main determinant of spreads between sovereign borrowers. The key economic fundamentals were those discussed in Chapters 2 and 3 – exchange rates, inflation rates, government budget deficits, and current account balances, as well as expectations regarding EMU. With the launching of the single currency, cross-national differences in inflation and currency risks disappeared. Italian government bonds and German government bonds now both are denominated in euros and are affected by a common monetary policy.

Spreads on government bonds have declined among the euro-area nations, reflecting the disappearance of currency risk as well as cross-national fiscal consolidation. These spreads, however, have not disappeared fully. As do Canadian provinces, EU member states continue to pay different borrowing rates, although the spreads among them rarely exceed 50 basis points.[17] The continued existence of different interest rates reflects the renewed (albeit still minor) salience of default risk, as well as low liquidity in some markets.[18] All debt now issued by EU member governments is essentially foreign currency–denominated: in the event that a government does not have the resources to repay its debt, it cannot solve its problem by

[12] *Economist*, September 18, 1999, p. 83.
[13] Gros and Lannoo 2000, Lannoo 1998.
[14] *Economist*, February 21, 1998, p. 72; OECD 1999.
[15] *Economist*, November 21, 1998, p. 71; Gros and Lannoo 2000.
[16] Also see BIS 1998, p. 96; *Economist*, September 19, 1998, p. 94; Prati and Schinasi 1998.
[17] Lannoo 1998.
[18] Alesina et al. 1992, BIS 1998, Lemmen and Goodhart 1999.

printing domestic currency.[19] Rather, the ECB controls the money supply. Therefore, provided that Article 104b of the Maastricht Treaty, which states that the member governments will not be bailed out, remains credible, default risk is again salient for the EU-12. Investment analysts anticipated this in 1997 and 1998:

> There is no default risk when the government runs its own printing presses, so the risks associated with bonds will change with EMU. The foreign exchange and inflation risks will disappear, but the default risk will emerge. And countries facing market discipline could have greater instabilities.[20]

> After EMU, there will be less to say about bond markets in Europe. It will all be about spreads, and about political risk. This means looking at default risk, something that doesn't get much attention right now ... but it will come back post-EMU, as market actors worry about the potential effects of asymmetric shocks, and about disparities in growth in Europe.[21]

The renewed salience of default risk is evidenced in sovereign credit ratings. In late 1997, the 11 future EMU members shared a long-term local currency rating of AAA – the highest possible sovereign debt rating.[22] Despite the variation in their levels of debt and, to a lesser extent, deficits, all of their benchmark government bonds were assumed to be virtually risk-free. Governments' ratings for foreign currency issues were more variable, ranging from AA– in Portugal to AAA in Austria, France, Germany, and the Netherlands. This variability reflected the higher risk sometimes associated with foreign currency–denominated debt. When EMU membership was announced in May 1998, the major ratings agencies collapsed members' local currency and foreign currency ratings into a single measure. As a result, most ratings fell: in late 1998 (as well as presently), six of the EU-11 received an AAA rating: Austria, Denmark, France, Germany, Luxembourg, and the Netherlands. The remaining five received ratings of AA+ (Belgium, Ireland), AA (Finland, Italy, Spain), or AA– (Portugal).[23] Ratings agencies judged these five nations to have slightly lower credit quality, or higher default risk. In its October 1999 discussion of Belgium's rating, for instance, Standard and Poor's noted that Belgium had achieved

---

[19] Giovannini 1997, Gros and Lannoo 2000.

[20] Interview 38.

[21] Interview 64.

[22] Standard and Poor's Creditweek, November 5, 1997.

[23] Standard and Poor's Creditweek, November 4, 1998; November 3, 1999; November 1, 2000. Finland's rating was upgraded to AA+ in 1999, as was Spain's.

the fiscal consolidation necessary to enter EMU but that its "high public debt burden still constrains its long-term rating."[24]

It is useful to inquire, then, about the extent to which EMU marks a break-point in financial market–government relations for the euro-area nations. Some observers have suggested, for instance, that the market for government debt in the euro-zone may eventually resemble the market for state-level debt in the United States, or, perhaps more accurately, the market for provincial debt in Canada. Most federal entities pay relatively low rates of interest, but they are distinguished according to default risk. Moreover, if default risk becomes a central consideration for market participants, to what extent will financial market influence in Europe increase in scope? Will the existence of a more coherent European bond market also spark investors to make more rigorous comparisons of national macro- and micropolicies?[25] And will investors begin to consider not only overall fiscal outcomes, but specific tax and expenditure policies?[26]

Next, as I note in Chapter 6, a major rationale for home country investment is regulation: where pension funds and life insurance companies are required to hold assets in the same currencies as liabilities, or where these institutional investors must hold a certain amount of local currency-denominated debt, they are essentially required to invest in home country instruments. EU-licensed insurance companies, for instance, are required to hold 80% of assets in the same currency as their liabilities; that usually means domestic currency. At the end of 1998, European insurance companies had invested over half of their assets in home country government and government-guaranteed securities.[27] With EMU, however, the investment regulations become irrelevant: the euro is the local currency, so any euro-denominated asset qualifies.[28] Some regulatory barriers do persist, however: for instance, EU members to date have failed to agree on a common withholding tax framework for bond investors.[29]

But, in general, individual European governments may have lost part of their captive audience for government securities.[30] We can expect

[24] Standard & Poor's, Belgium – Sovereign Rating, October 1999. Also see *Financial Times*, February 25, 1997, p. 6.
[25] Tanzi and Schuknecht 2000.
[26] Lemmen and Goodhart 1999.
[27] Vota 1999.
[28] Giovannini 1997, Lannoo 1998, OECD 1999.
[29] Gros and Lannoo 2000 summarize many of the other cross-national differences in tax regimes.
[30] *New York Times*, November 14, 1998, p. C1.

institutional investors to rebalance their portfolios away from domestic assets, although this rebalancing may occur rather slowly. If resident investors and nonresidents do act differently, as empirical evidence suggests, then this loss may serve to heighten the constraints on national governments. At the very least, governments will have to make greater efforts to make their bonds attractive to European investors: for instance, since 1998, the Irish debt management agency has embarked on an effort to make Irish debt more attractive to non-Irish investors. This effort, mostly aimed at increasing bond market liquidity, was motivated by the concern that, after EMU, with no exchange rate risk, there would be little motivation for Irish investors to buy Irish paper.[31] These efforts may include routine debt management practices, such as creating liquid markets for certain classes of bonds, but they may also include more pronounced measures, such as changing tax rates or altering fiscal policymaking institutions.

Falling Debt in the OECD   Second, the overall trend – not unrelated to EMU – toward falling debt levels in advanced industrial nations will serve to limit the supply of low-risk, low-yield government bonds. These instruments often are staples of international portfolios; as supply decreases and demand remains constant, governments will find interest rates on benchmark instruments dropping, possibly to new lows. For instance, in April 2000, as way to effect debt reduction, the U.S. Treasury began to buy back outstanding Treasury bonds. In doing so, it drove up demand for Treasury bonds and notes and was able to finance its operations more cheaply.[32] Likewise, in May 2000, the costs of borrowing for the British government fell dramatically, as the budget surplus as well as a windfall from the sale of mobile phone licenses led to a contraction in the supply of gilts. Because many pension funds' rules require that they buy long-term sovereign debt, the spread between corporate bonds and UK government bonds then widened dramatically.[33]

The advantages, in terms of borrowing costs, for governments of the movement toward debt consolidation, however, could be mitigated by concerns about liquidity. If governments drastically reduce their issues of certain instruments, the markets for these instruments will become less liquid. Where instruments are less liquid, investors will demand a premium – a

---

[31] *Financial Times*, October 14, 1998, p. 16.
[32] *New York Times*, April 9, 2000, p. C3.
[33] *Economist*, May 13, 2000, p. 78.

liquidity risk rather than an inflation risk or default risk premium, but a premium nonetheless.[34] But, particularly when investors are risk-averse, and if other European nations achieve budget surpluses, demand for developed nation bonds likely will far outstrip supply. When refinancing debt, then, governments should find that interest rate costs decrease. In some ways, then, this virtuous circle could allow another sort of autonomy for governments. When borrowing costs fall, funds previously used for interest payments can be used for other purposes. Therefore, although the emergence of default risk could preserve differences among EMU nations, overall trends in debt should facilitate a general lowering of rates: even if Belgium pays more to borrow than Germany, both will pay less than they did 5 or 10 years ago. Moreover, this implies that, in the twenty-first century, the reward for being one of the set of developed country nations, as opposed to being an emerging market or frontier market nation, will be even greater.

The Diversity of International Investment

The second, broader challenge for the future, both intellectually and practically, is to consider how *different types* of international capital interact to influence government policymaking. This book focuses on a very likely source of financial market influence, the market for sovereign debt; the causal mechanisms it traces provide a theoretical foundation that is consistent with many of the empirical realities in developed and developing nations. As we know, however, globalization is a multifaceted process;[35] on the financial side alone, bond markets, equity markets, foreign exchange markets, and foreign direct investors may influence government policymaking. Different types of investors may well exert different sorts of pressures on national governments. Moreover, investors' preferences are likely to vary across categories of government policies: some policies are highly salient to some types of investors; other types of policy are far beyond investors' concerns.[36]

To begin, equity investors are likely to emphasize different factors than do investors in sovereign debt. The importance of sectoral, rather than national, factors to the performance of many firms generates some of these

[34] Mylonas et al. 2000, OECD 1999.
[35] Also see Burgoon 2001, Sinclair and Thomas 2001, Thomas 2001.
[36] Burgoon 2001 evaluates a similar expectation, using data for 18 OECD nations. Also see Brooks and Mosley 2000.

317

differences. The importance of government policies to equity investors also is likely to vary across groups of nations: in emerging markets, a great deal of investors' analyses focus on top-down allocation: in what countries should they invest? Government policy can be very central to top-down decisions. In more mature equity markets, however, allocation is often bottom-up, so that investors focus primarily on firms and industries. In such cases, government policy is much less important.[37] This suggests that investors' pattern of looking closely at government policy in emerging markets, but not in developed nations, may hold on the equity side as well.

Additionally, whereas portfolio investors may, all factors equal, favor reductions in government education expenditures, foreign direct investors may favor maintenance of or increases in education spending. This leaves a large question unanswered: when both portfolio and direct investors are active in a nation, how are their competing interests resolved? Most investigations of the effect of global capital markets on government policy, including this one, evaluate the effects of one type of investment – foreign direct investment, portfolio investment, or foreign exchange flows – on government policy.[38] These investigations do not consider the aggregate effects of, and interactions among, different types of foreign capital.

In reality, nations are inserted differently in the global economy. High international integration in one economic area, such as portfolio finance, does not necessarily go hand in hand with high integration in another economic area, such as direct investment.[39] In fact, there is a relatively weak correlation between a nation's level of international portfolio investment and its level of foreign direction investment.[40] Moreover, particularly in times of financial crisis, direct investment tends to behave differently than portfolio investment; for instance, in 1998, despite the turbulence in shorter-term global capital markets, global FDI remained at a stable, relatively high level.[41] These differences likely have important consequences for the patterns of government spending and policy change across nations.[42] Therefore, scholars of international political economy now face the

---

[37] Also see Interview 59.

[38] Maxfield 1997, chapter 3, discusses different types of investors, particularly within the category of portfolio investment. Garrett and Mitchell 2001 examine the potentially different impacts of direct investment and portfolio capital flows in OECD nations.

[39] Garrett and Mitchell 2000.

[40] Garrett 2000a, 2000b. For a large sample of nations, this correlation was 0.27 in the 1990s.

[41] BIS 2000, p. 38.

[42] Armijo 1999, p. 23.

challenge of considering the interaction among different classes of foreign investment.[43]

Finally, in a much larger sense, scholars are left to consider the overall impact of economic globalization. We gain a better understanding of the precise causal mechanisms linking markets and governments when we consider each of the constituent parts of globalization separately – when we think about how trade influences government policy outcomes, about how financial markets influence government policy outcomes, and about how the freer flow of ideas and individuals influences government policy outcomes. In the end, however, if we want to understand more fully the contemporary policymaking process, we must put these pieces back together. For example, capital market openness may generate enhanced pressures for reduced government budget deficits, and trade openness may foster (through domestic political mechanisms) demands for increased government compensation.[44] A government facing these contending pressures may opt to increase compensation and increase taxation (reducing the budget deficit but compensating dislocated workers), to increase compensation but cut other areas of government spending, or simply to cut public spending. At the end of the day, then, we must ask not only about the extent to which governments retain policymaking autonomy and accountability in the face of capital market integration, but about the extent to which they retain such capacities in the face of capital market, trade, and production integration.

[43] Brooks and Mosley 2000 offer an initial exploration of this issue.
[44] E.g., Dryzek 1996, Rodrik 1997.

Appendix 2.1

Financial Market Interviews

Interview Number	Firm	Date
1	Salomon Bros.	March 5, 1997
2	Matushita UK	February 25, 1997
3	Cursitor-Eaton	January 28, 1997
4	Henderson Inv. Mgmt.	March 21, 1997
5	AXA Law and Equity Inv. Mgmt	January 27, 1997
6	Yamaichi Investment	March 26, 1997
7	Deutsche Bank	April 4, 1997
8	UBS	January 28, 1997 March 25, 1997
9	British Aerospace Pension Mgmt.	January 31, 1997
10	IBJ International	March 27, 1997
11	Commerzbank Investment	May 27, 1997
12	Deutsche Bank Asset Mgmt.	May 22, 1997
13	J. P. Morgan Investment	May 27, 1997
14	J. P. Morgan Investment	May 27, 1997
15	Prudential Inv. Mgmt.	February 11, 1997
16	BZW (Barclay's)	May 12, 1997
17	Salomon Bros.	May 9, 1997
18	Paribas Inv. Mgmt.	March 10, 1997
19	Nikko Europe	February 13, 1997
20	Kawasaki (UK)	February 25, 1997
21	Dresdner Bank	April 8, 1997
22	Merrill Lynch	April 25, 1997
23	Institutional Fund Mgrs'Assoc.	February 3, 1997
24	Deutsche-Morgan Grenfell	February 20, 1997 March 20, 1997

(continued)

Appendix 2.1 *(continued)*

Interview Number	Firm	Date
25	Honda UK	March 24, 1997
26	Mikita UK	February 21, 1997
27	HSBC-James Capel	March 12, 1997
28	Genesis Inv. Mgmt.	January 20, 1997
29	Commerzbank Asset Mgmt.	April 16, 1997
30	Zurich Investment Mgmt.	April 14, 1997
32	Lombard St. Research	February 19, 1997
33	Cursitor Eaton	January 28, 1997
34	Hambros Bank	March 11, 1997
35	BHF Bank	April 17, 1997
36	Allianz	April 21, 1997
37	Deutsche Bank Rsch.	April 9, 1997
38	Smithers Research	February 19, 1997
39	Dresdner Bank Rsch.	April 18, 1997
40	Generale de Banque	May 7, 1997
41	Deutsche-Morgan Grenfell	February 20, 1997
42	J. P. Morgan Investment	May 27, 1997
43	AIWA Industries	March 3, 1997
44	IBM (UK)	March 5, 1997
45	AMP Inv. Mgmt.	March 20, 1997
46	Robert Fleming Inv. Mgmt.	February 21, 1997
47	Robert Fleming Inv. Mgmt.	February 27, 1997
48	Deutsche Bank Research	May 21, 1997
51	Goldman Sachs Asset Management	October 21, 1998
52	Donaldson, Lufkin and Jenrette	October 16, 1998
53	ANZ Investment Bank	October 12, 1998
54	Nomura	October 6, 1998
55	Prudential	October 16, 1998
56	Moore Capital Management	October 15, 1998
57	HSBC	October 14, 1998
58	Genesis Investment Management	October 9, 1998
59	Credit Suisse First Boston	October 9, 1998
60	Guinness Flight Asset Management	October 8, 1998
61	Deutsche Morgan Grenfell	October 20, 1998
62	CIBC	October 12, 1998
63	Morgan Stanley Asset Mgmt.	October 21, 1998
64	CIBC	October 7, 1998

Appendix 3.1

Data Definitions and Sources

CAPOPEN: Legal capital market openness (the existence or absence of capital controls) from Quinn 1997. This measure uses the IMF's Annual Reports on Capital Exchange Restrictions to assess the severity of a nation's restrictions on the payment and receipts of capital. This measure ranges from 0 to 4 where 4 indicates fully free payment and receipts of capital.

CORPTAX/PROF: Ratio of corporate income taxes to net operating surplus of domestic producers (profits) (From Swank 1998b).

CURRACCT: The current account balance as a percentage of GDP. Negative numbers indicate a current account deficit (OECD Statistical Compendium, various years).

ELECTION: A 0–1 dummy variable, coded 1 for an election during that month and 0 for no election (Swank 1998b).

ERCHANGE: Monthly change in the nominal trade-weighted effective exchange rate (Datastream [electronic publication]).

GCAPITAL/GDP: Government capital spending as a percentage of GDP (World Bank, World Development Indicators, various years, CD-ROM).

GCONSUMPTION/GDP: Total government consumption spending as a percentage of GDP (OECD Statistical Compendium, various years).

GOODS/GDP: Government spending on goods and services as a percentage of GDP (World Bank, World Development Indicators, various years, CD-ROM).

GOVBAL: The general government budget balance as a percentage of GDP, where a negative number indicates a deficit (OECD 1997).

GOVDEBT: The ratio of government debt to GDP, where larger numbers indicate larger debt shares. The OECD definition of debt/GDP ratios, which includes all levels of government, as well as social security liabilities, differs slightly from the European Commission's (Maastricht Treaty) definition (OECD 1997).

GOVERNMENT/GDP: The total size of government, including consumption and capital spending, as a percentage of GDP (OECD Statistical Compendium, various years).

GTAX/GDP: Government tax revenue as a percentage of GDP (OECD Statistical Compendium, various years).

GWAGES/GDP: Government spending on wages as a percentage of GDP (World Bank, various years).

HEALTH/GDP: Current Public Expenditure on health, as a percentage of GDP (Health figures are from the OECD Health Data 1995; these figures and GDP statistics are found in Huber et al. 1997).

IND/CORPTAX: Ratio of taxes on individuals to taxes on corporations (Swank 1998b).

INFLATE: Monthly change in the level of consumer prices (IMF, International Financial Statistics CD-ROM, various years, and Datastream).

LECTC: The percentage of cabinet seats held by left-party ministers. Annual data are converted to monthly data on the basis of election dates. Where an election occurred after the 15th day of the month, the change in cabinet seats is recorded for the following month (Swank 1998b).

LEFTGS: The percentage of legislative seats held by left parties that are part of the governing coalition. Annual data are converted to monthly data, as with LEFTC. A score of 0 indicates that no left parties with parliamentary representation are part of the governing coalition (Swank 1998b).

LTRATE: Market-determined interest rates on long-term, benchmark government bonds (IMF, International Financial Statistics CD-ROM, various years, and Datastream).

OPENNESS: General international economic openness. This measure includes restrictions on payment and receipts of capital (CAPOPEN), restrictions on payment and receipts of goods and invisibles (current account openness), and participation in international agreements on these issues. OPENNESS ranges from 0 to 15, where 15 indicates full openness to external economic flows (Quinn 1997).

PAYTAX/GDP: Payroll taxes on employers as a percentage of GDP (Swank 1998b).

TRANSFERS/GDP: Social security transfers as a percentage of GDP. Includes benefits for sickness, old age, family allowances, social assistance grants, and welfare (OECD, Historical Statistics, various years, table 6; available from Huber et al. 1997).

USLT: Long-term U.S. interest rates, also for benchmark government bonds (IMF, International Financial Statistics CD-ROM, various years).

WOR/EMPCON: Ratio of workers' to employers' social security contributions (Swank 1998b).

Appendix 3.2

Full Results for Macroindicators Model

Variable	Coefficient	Standard Error
USLT	0.2538979***	0.0192141
USLT – Lag 1	0.0684961***	0.0201333
USLT – Lag 2	0.0791859***	0.0188864
INFLATE	0.1022192***	0.0173127
INFLATE – Lag 1	0.0801053***	0.0177536
INFLATE – Lag 2	0.0516412**	0.0171877
GOVBAL	−0.050101*	0.0240537
ERCHANGE	−0.0231955***	0.0049851
ERCHANGE – Lag 1	−0.0106435*	0.0049967
CURRACCT	−1.479957	1.329048
CURRACCT – Lag 1	3.801062	2.615207
CURRACCT – Lag 2	−2.599915*	1.322194
CAPOPEN	0.0633982	0.1776917
LEFTC	0.0019679*	0.0010034
ELECTION	0.0830383*	0.0392404
ELECTION – Lag 1	0.0914585*	0.039239
Constant	4.608673***	0.717962

Note: $^*p < .05$, $^{**}p < .01$, $^{***}p < .001$; two-tailed test.

Appendix 4.1

The Components of the SDDS

Prescribed Indicators	Components of Prescribed Indicators	Encouraged Indicators	Periodicity	Timeliness
Real Sector				
National Accounts	GDP by major expenditure category and/or by sector	Saving, gross national income	Quarterly	[With a lapse of no more than] one quarter
Production Indexes	Industrial, primary, commodity, or sector, as relevant	Forward-looking indicators, e.g., business confidence surveys; monthly or quarterly	Monthly, or as relevant	Six weeks; one month encouraged
Labor Market	Unemployment, employment, wages/earnings		Quarterly	One quarter
Price Indexes	CPI and PPI		Monthly	One month
Fiscal Sector				
General Government/ Public Sector	Revenue, expenditure, balance, and domestic and foreign financing	Interest payments	Annual	Two quarters

(continued)

Appendix 4.1 *(continued)*

Prescribed Indicators	Components of Prescribed Indicators	Encouraged Indicators	Periodicity	Timeliness
Central Government Operations	Budgetary accounts: revenue, expenditure, balance, domestic and foreign financing	Interest payments	Monthly	Monthly
Central Government Debt	Domestic and foreign, as relevant, with breakdown by currency and maturity (revised)	Debt service projections (interest and amortization on medium- and long-term debt)	Quarterly	One quarter
Financial Sector				
Analytical Accounts of the Banking Sector	Money aggregates, domestic credit by public and private sector, external position		Monthly	One month
Analytical Accounts of the Central Bank	Reserve Money, domestic claims on public and private sectors, external position		Monthly; weekly encouraged	Two weeks (one week encouraged)
Interest Rates	Short-term and long-term government security rates, policy variable rate	Range of representative deposit and lending rates	Daily	May be released as part of other data products, which are widely available from private sources
Stock Market	Share Price Index		Daily	See interest rates

The Components of the SDDS

Appendix 4.1 *(continued)*

Prescribed Indicators	Components of Prescribed Indicators	Encouraged Indicators	Periodicity	Timeliness
External Sector				
Balance of Payments	Goods and services, net income flows, net current transfers, select capital account items	Foreign direct investment and portfolio investment	Quarterly	One quarter
International Reserves	Gross official reserves, denominated in U.S. dollars	Reserve-related liabilities, as relevant	Monthly; weekly encouraged	One week
Merchandise Trade	Exports and Imports	Major commodity breakdowns	Monthly	Eight weeks (four to six weeks encouraged)
International Investment Position			Annual (quarterly encouraged)	Two quarters (one quarter encouraged)
Exchange Rates	Spot rates and 3- and 6-month forward rates		Daily	See interest rates
Addendum Item: Population		Key distributions by age and gender	Annual	

Appendix 4.2

Rating Agency Methodologies

I. Euromoney

Method: Euromoney surveys economists and political analysts for their views on the creditworthiness of 179 countries. These survey results are combined with quantitative indicators to produce "a sensitive measure of the riskiness of investing in these economies." Scores range from 0 to 100.

Indicators

1. Economic data (25%): Based on global economic projections for current and future year performance, as forecasted by 20 economists at leading financial institutions.
2. Political risk (25%): Risk analysts, risk insurance brokers, and bank credit officers rate countries, with a perfect score for "no risk of non-payment" and a zero score for "no chance of payment being made."
3. Debt indicators (10%): Calculated by using data from the World Bank World Debt Tables for the previous year. Indicators include the ratio of debt service to exports, the current account balance as a percentage of GDP, and the ratio of external debt to GDP.
4. Debt in default or rescheduled (10%): Based on the amount of debt in default or rescheduled during the last three years.
5. Credit ratings (10%): The average of sovereign ratings from IBCA, Moody's, and Standard and Poor's.
6. Access to bank finance (5%): Calculated from disbursements of private, long-term, unguaranteed loans as a percentage of GDP.
7. Access to short-term finance (5%): Scores calculated by taking coverage available from U.S. Export–Import Bank, NCM UK, ECGD, and membership of OECD consensus groups.

8. Access to international bond and syndicated loan markets (5%): Euromoney's estimation of how easily a country might access the markets now.
9. Access to and discount on forfaiting (5%): Reflects the average maximal tenor available and the forfaiting spread over "riskless" countries such as the United States.

II. Institutional Investor

Method: Bankers at 75 to 100 leading international financial institutions are asked to grade each country on a scale of 0 to 100, with 100 representing those nations with the least chance of default. Banks are not permitted to rate their home countries, and the individual responses are weighted, with more importance given to responses from banks with greater worldwide exposure and more sophisticated country-analysis systems. Scores range from 0 to 100.

III. Standard and Poor's

Method: Ratings are based on two categories of risk, economic and political. Economic risk addresses the government's ability to repay its obligations on time and is a function of qualitative and quantitative factors. Political risk addresses the sovereign's willingness to repay debt and is based on qualitative assessment. Possible ratings are AAA, AA, A, BBB, BB, B, CCC, CC, C, and D. Plusses and minuses may also be assigned. A rating of AAA indicates "extremely strong" capacity to meet financial commitments, whereas D indicates that a government presently is in default.

Indicators

1. Economic Risk
   a. Economic System and Structure: market or nonmarket economy; resource endowments and degree of diversification; size and composition of savings and investment; rate and pattern of economic growth.
   b. Fiscal Policy and Public Debt: public sector financial balances; currency composition and structure of public debt; public debt and interest burdens; contingent liabilities, including banks; debt service track record.

c. Monetary Policy and Inflation: trends in price inflation, rates of money and credit growth, exchange rate policy, degree of central bank autonomy.

d. Balance of Payments Flexibility: impact on external accounts of fiscal and monetary policies; structure and flexibility of the capital account; adequacy and composition of capital flows.

e. External Financial Position: size and currency composition of public and private external debt, maturity structure and debt service burden, level and composition of reserves and other assets.

2. Political Risk

a. Political System: form of government and adaptability of institutions, degree of popular participation, orderliness of leadership succession, degree of consensus on economic policy objectives.

b. Social Environment: living standards, income, and wealth distribution; labor market conditions; cultural and demographic characteristics.

c. International Relations: integration in the global trade and financial system; security risks.

Sources: Hue 1997, Shapiro 1997; Standard and Poor's 1995; Standard and Poor's 1997.

Appendix 4.3

Rating Agency Outcomes, 1997

Country	Institutional Investor Ranking	Institutional Investor Rating	Euromoney Rating	Euromoney Ranking	Euromoney Ranking, II set	S&P Rating	S&P Rank
Switzerland	1	92.5	93.7	10	10	AAA	1
Germany	2	91.5	94.65	8	8	AAA	1
Japan	3	91.3	93.04	13	13	AAA	1
United States	4	91.2	97.09	2	2	AAA	1
Netherlands	5	89.7	95.66	5	5	AAA	1
United Kingdom	6	88.4	95.73	4	4	AAA	1
France	7	88.2	92.4	14	14	AAA	1
Luxembourg	8	87.3	99.3	1	1	AAA	1
Norway	9	84.7	94.74	7	7	AAA	1
Austria	10	84.6	93.35	12	12	AAA	1
Singapore	11	83.9	96.16	3	3	AAA	1
Denmark	12	81.6	95.04	6	6	AAA	1
Canada	13	80.8	94.4	9	9	AAA	1
Belgium	14	80.7	91.1	18	18	AAA	1
Taiwan	15	77.1	90.44	19	19	AA+*	3
Ireland	16	75.7	93.44	11	11	AAA	1
Finland	17	74.9	92.06	15	15	AAA	1
Spain	18	74.7	87.51	21	21	AAA	1
Sweden	19	74.3	89.17	20	20	AAA	1
Italy	20	74.3	85.39	25	24	AAA	1
Australia	21	72.2	91.68	17	17	AAA	1
New Zealand	22	71.7	91.68	16	16	AAA	1
South Korea	23	71.4	87.04	22	22	AA−*	6
Portugal	24	69.6	86.52	23	23	AAA	1

(continued)

Appendix 4.3 *(continued)*

Country	Institutional Investor Ranking	Institutional Investor Rating	Euromoney Rating	Euromoney Ranking	Euromoney Ranking, II set	S&P Rating	S&P Rank
Malaysia	25	67.5	83.32	28	27	AA+	2
Hong Kong	26	64.9	84.61	27	26	A+	7
Malta	27	63.4	70.91	44	41	AA+	2
Czech Rep.	28	62.8	74.54	37	35	A*	9
Chile	29	62	79.94	32	30	AA	4
Thailand	30	61.1	77.09	34	32	AA	4
UAE	31	60.8	80.3	31	29		
Iceland	32	60.1	85.04	26	25	AA+	2
China	33	58	70.5	45	42	BBB*	13
Cyprus	34	56.8	80.38	30	28	AA+	2
Kuwait	35	54.2	75.18	36	34		
Saudi Arabia	36	53.7	73.5	40	37		
Oman	37	52.8	69.92	47	44	BBB−*	15
Qatar	38	52.4	77.39	33	31	BBB*	13
Israel	39	52.2	75.59	35	33	AA−	5
Slovenia	40	52.1	73.97	38	36	AA	4
Indonesia	41	51.6	70.95	43	40	A+	7
Greece	42	51.3	73.26	41	38	BBB−*	15
Mauritius	43	50.9	67.82	49	46		
Bahrain	44	49.7	71.13	42	39		
Botswana	45	49.5	61.76	57	54		
Poland	46	47.9	56.58	62	59	A−	10
Colombia	47	47.7	63.68	52	49	A+	7
Hungary	48	47.6	70.06	46	43	A−	10
India	49	46.3	64.61	50	47	BBB+	11
Tunisia	50	46.3	62.86	55	52		
S. Africa	51	46.0	69.88	48	45	BBB+	11
Slovakia	52	43.9	63.46	53	50	A	8
Mexico	53	42.6	64.14	51	48	BBB+	11
Philippines	54	42.3	63.14	54	51	A−	10
Barbados	55	41.9	52.81	71	68		
Uruguay	56	41.7	62.46	56	53	BBB	12
Turkey	57	40.8	53.39	67	64	B*	21
Argentina	58	39.9	59.17	59	56	BBB−	14
Morocco	59	39.7	53.65	66	63		
Trinidad and Tobago	60	39.7	59.53	58	55		
Brazil	61	38.8	59.11	60	57	BB	18
Egypt	62	36.7	54.73	64	5161	A−	10
Costa Rica	63	34.5	50.23	77	74		

Appendix 4.3 *(continued)*

Country	Institutional Investor Ranking	Institutional Investor Rating	Euromoney Rating	Euromoney Ranking	Euromoney Ranking, II set	S&P Rating	S&P Rank
Jordan	64	33.8	53.2	70	67	BBB−	14
Estonia	65	33.6	53.21	69	66		
Sri Lanka	66	33.2	49.19	79	76		
Venezuela	67	33.1	49.08	80	77	B*	21
Romania	68	32.7	51.65	75	72	BBB−	14
Papua New Guinea	69	32.5	47.68	85	82		
Vietnam	70	32.5	52.41	73	70		
Zimbabwe	71	32.3	42.0	95			
Paraguay	72	32	54.04	65	62	BBB−	14
Peru	73	32	48.19	83	80		
Swaziland	74	31.8	53.36	68	65		
Lebanon	75	31.5	48.98	81	78		
Ghana	76	30.6	47.85	84	81		
Panama	77	30.2	52.36	74	71	BB+*	17
Croatia	78	29.3	57.58	61	58	A−	10
Latvia	79	29.1	55.04	63	60	A−	10
Libya	80	28.7	20.15	163	125		
Kenya	81	27.9	41.22	96	92		
Pakistan	82	27.7	48.94	82	79	B+*	20
Jamaica	83	27.5	44.15	90	86		
Bangladesh	84	27.4	42.65	94	90		
Lithuania	85	27.4	52.52	72	69		
Seychelles	86	27.3	50.51	76	73		
Ecuador	87	26.6	46.57	86	83		
Iran	88	26.1	29.44	135	112		
Nepal	89	25.2	40.11	99	95		
Syria	90	25	39.78	100	96		
Bolivia	91	24.9	45.93	88	84		
Gabon	92	24.1	43.47	92	88		
Guatemala	93	24.1	43.27	93	89		
El Salvador	94	23.9	49.39	78	75	BBB+	11
Russia	95	23.5	43.97	91	87	BB−*	19
Algeria	96	23.2	38.53	102	98		
Bulgaria	97	22.5	35.07	111	102		
Dominican Republic	98	22.5	45.36	89	85	B+*	20
Myanmar	99	21.3	32.92	118	105		

(continued)

Appendix 4.3 *(continued)*

Country	Institutional Investor Ranking	Institutional Investor Rating	Euromoney Rating	Euromoney Ranking	Euromoney Ranking, II set	S&P Rating	S&P Rank
Kazakhstan	100	20.9	40.25	98	94	BB+	16
Malawi	101	19.8	32.44	121	106		
Senegal	102	19.8	40.84	97	93		
Cote d'Ivoire	103	18.9	38.84	101	97		
Honduras	104	18.3	37.46	104	100		
Tanzania	105	18.1	28.49	139	115		
Cameroon	106	18.1	32.02	122	107		
Burkina Faso	107	17.7	38.43	103	99		
Uganda	107	17.7	36.7	105	101		
Ukraine	109	17.6	29.31	136	113		
Uzbekistan	110	17.1	33.03	117	104		
Mali	111	16.7	30.78	125	108		
Togo	112	16.7	29.75	132	109		
Zambia	113	16.1	21.84	157	123		
Ethiopia	114	16	20.88	159	124		
Benin	115	16	34.79	112	102		
Mozambique	116	14.9	22.87	152	120		
Nigeria	117	14.8	26.78	144	117		
Belarus	118	14.5	22.7	154	121		
Albania	119	14.3	29.58	133	110		
Congo	120	14	27.29	142	116		
Guinea	121	13.8	29.55	134	111		
Grenada	122	12.9	19.9	165	126		
Angola	123	12.5	24.64	148	118		
Nicaragua	124	11.9	23.32	150	119		
Haiti	125	11.4	28.99	137	114		
Cuba	126	10.8	10.35	175	132		
Sudan	127	10.4	16.4	170	128		
Yugoslavia	128	9.9	19.83	166	127		
Georgia	129	9.5	14.03	173	131		
Iraq	130	8.3	5.98	177	133		
Zaire	131	8.1	14.74	172	130		
Liberia	132	6.9	15.19	171	129		
Sierra Leone	133	6.6	21.86	156	122		
Afghanistan	134	6.3	4.09	178	134		
North Korea	135	5.8	3.08	179	135		

* All Standard and Poor's ratings are for local currency debt, except where denoted by *. The ratings denoted * are for foreign currency debt.

Appendix 6.1

Nations in Capital Controls Data Set

Argentina	Georgia	Pakistan
Armenia	Guatemala	Panama
Azerbaijan	Honduras	Paraguay
Bangladesh	Hungary	Peru
Belize	India	Philippines
Bolivia	Indonesia	Poland
Botswana	Israel	Romania
Brazil	Jamaica	Russia
Bulgaria	Jordan	Slovak Republic
Chile	Kazakhstan	Tanzania
China	Kenya	Thailand
Costa Rica	Korea	Tunisia
Croatia	Latvia	Turkey
Czech Republic	Lebanon	Ukraine
Dominican Republic	Lithuania	Uruguay
Ecuador	Malaysia	Venezuela
Egypt	Mexico	Vietnam
El Salvador	Moldova	Zambia
Estonia	Mongolia	Zimbabwe
Ethiopia	Nigeria	

References

Achen, Christopher H. 2000. "Why Lagged Dependent Variables Can Suppress the Explanatory Power of Other Independent Variables." Paper presented at the Annual Meeting of the Political Methodology Section of the American Political Science Association, July 20–22, UCLA.

Ackermann, Carl, Richard McEnally and David Ravenscraft. 1999. "The Performance of Hedge Funds: Risk, Return, and Incentives." *Journal of Finance* 54: 833–874.

Adserà, Alícia and Carles Boix. 2002. "Trade, Democracy and the Size of the Public Sector: The Political Underpinnings of Openness." *International Organization* 56.

Agell, Jonas, Mats Persson and Benjamin J. Friedman. 1992. *Does Debt Management Matter?* Oxford: Clarendon Press.

Ahearne, Alan G., William L. Griever and Francis E. Warnock. 2001. "Information Costs and Home Bias: An Analysis of U.S. Holdings of Foreign Equities." Board of Governors of the Federal Reserve System. *International Finance Discussion Papers* 691 (May).

Aitken, Brian. 1996. "Have Institutional Investors Destabilized Emerging Markets?" *IMF Working Paper* 96/34-EA.

Aizenman, Joshua, Michael Gavin and Ricardo Hausmann. 1996. "Optimal Tax and Debt Policy with Endogenously Imperfect Creditworthiness," *NBER Working Paper* 5558 (May).

Akerlof, George. 1970. "The Market for Lemons." *Quarterly Journal of Economics* 54: 488–500.

Alesina, Alberto and Robert J. Barro. 2001. "Dollarization." *American Economic Review* 91, No. 2 (May): 381–385.

Alesina, Alberto and Vittorio Grilli. 1992. "The European Central Bank: Reshaping Monetary Politics in Europe." In *Establishing a Central Bank: Issues in Europe and Lessons from the US*, edited by Matthew B. Canzoneri, Vittorio Grilli, and Paul R. Masson, 43–77. Cambridge: Cambridge University Press.

Alesina, Alberto and Roberto Perotti. 1995. "The Political Economy of Budget Deficits." *IMF Staff Papers* 42 (March), 1–31.

1996a. "Fiscal Discipline and the Budget Process." *American Economic Review* 86: 401–407.

1996b. "Budget Deficits and Budget Institutions." *NBER Working Paper* 5556 (May).

1996c. "Income Distribution, Political Instability and Investment." *European Economic Review* 40: 1203–1228.

Alesina, Alberto and Howard Rosenthal. 1995. *Partisan Politics, Divided Government and the Economy*. Cambridge: Cambridge University Press.

Alesina, Alberto and Nouriel Roubini with Gerald D. Cohen. 1997. *Political Cycles and the Macroeconomy*. Cambridge, MA: MIT Press.

Alesina, Alberto and Lawrence Summers. 1993. "Central Bank Independence and Macroeconomic Performance: Some Comparative Evidence." *Journal of Money, Credit and Banking* 25: 151–162.

Alesina, Alberto and Guido Tabellini. 1988. "Credibility and Politics." *European Economic Review* 32: 542–550.

Alesina, Alberto, Mark De Broech, Alessandro Prati and Guido Tabellini. 1992. "Default Risk on Government Debt in OECD Countries." *Economic Policy* 7: 427–463.

Alesina, Alberto, Rudi Hommes, Ricardo Hausmann and Ernesto Stein. 1996. "Budget Deficits and Fiscal Performance in Latin America." *NBER Working Paper* 5586 (May).

Alesina, Alberto, Alessandro Prati and Guido Tabellini. 1990. "Public Confidence and Debt Management: A Model and Case Study of Italy." In *Public Debt Management: Theory and History*, edited by Rudiger Dornbusch and Mario Draghi, 94–118. Cambridge: Cambridge University Press.

Allen, Christopher S. 1989. "The Underdevelopment of Keynesianism in the Federal Republic of Germany." in *The Political Power of Economic Ideas: Keynesianism across Nations*, edited by Peter A. Hall, 263–289. Princeton, NJ: Princeton University Press.

Allsopp, Christopher and David Vines. 1998. "The Assessment: Macroeconomic Policy after EMU." *Oxford Review of Economic Policy* 14: 1–23.

Alt, James and Robert Lowry. 1994. "Divided Governments, Fiscal Institutions and Budget Deficits: Evidence from the States." *American Political Science Review* 88: 811–828.

Alter, Alison B. and Lucy M. Goodhart. 2001 "Electoral Exuberance? Political Business Cycles and the Stock Market." Paper presented at the Annual Meeting of the Midwest Political Science Association, April 19–21, Chicago.

Anan'ich, B. V. and V. I. Bovykin. 1991. "Foreign Banks and Foreign Investment in Russia." In *International Banking. 1870–1914*, edited by Rondo Cameron and V. I. Bovykin, 253–290. New York: Oxford University Press.

Anderson, Christopher J. 2000. "Economic Voting and Political Context: A Comparative Perspective." *Electoral Studies* 19: 151–170.

References

Anderson, Nicola, Francis Breedon, Mark Deacon, Andrew Derry and Gareth Murphy. 1996. *Estimating and Interpreting the Yield Curve*. New York: John Wiley & Sons.

Andrews, David M. 1994. "Capital Mobility and State Autonomy: Toward a Structural Theory of International Monetary Relations." *International Studies Quarterly* 38: 193–218.

——— 2001. "Financial Deregulation and the Origins of EMU: The French Policy Reversal of 1983." In *Structure and Agency in International Capital Mobility*, edited by Timothy J. Sinclair and Kenneth P. Thomas, 9–26. Basingstoke: Palgrave.

Andrews, David M. and Thomas D. Willett. 1997. "Financial Interdependence and the State: International Monetary Relations at Century's End." *International Organization* 51: 479–511.

Armijo, Leslie Ann, ed. 1999. *Financial Globalization and Democracy in Emerging Markets*. New York: St. Martin's Press.

Armijo, Leslie Elliott. 1996. "Inflation and Insouciance: The Peculiar Brazilian Game." *Latin American Research Review* 31: 7–45.

Aronovich, Selmo. 1999. "Country Risk Premium: Theoretical Determinants and Empirical Evidence for Latin American Countries." *RBE (Rio de Janiero)* 53: 463–498.

Avelino, George, David S. Brown and Wendy A. Hunter. 2001. "Globalization and Social Spending in Latin America, 1980–1997." Paper presented at the Annual Meeting of the American Political Science Association, August 30– September 2, San Francisco.

Axilrod, Stephen H. 1996. "Transformations to Open Market Operations: Developing Economies and Emerging Markets." *International Monetary Fund Economic Issues* 5: iii–17.

Baldez, Lisa and John Carey. 2001. "Budget Procedure and Fiscal Restraint in Post-Transition Chile." In *Presidents, Parliaments and Policy*, edited by Stephan Haggard and Mathew McCubbins. New York: Cambridge University Press.

Balkan, Errol M. 1992. "Political Instability, Country Risk and Probability of Default." *Applied Economics* 24: 999–1008.

Banerjee, Abhijit V. 1992. "A Simple Model of Herd Behavior." *Quarterly Journal of Economics* 107: 797–817.

Bank for International Settlements. 1998. *68th Annual Report*. Basle, Switzerland: Bank for International Settlements.

——— 2000. *70th Annual Report*. Basle, Switzerland: Bank for International Settlements.

Banks, J. and J. Sobel. 1987. "Equilibrium Selection in Signaling Games." *Econometrica* 55: 647–661.

Barro, Robert. 1979. "On the Determination of the Public Debt." *Journal of Political Economy* 87: 940–971.

——— 1997a. *Determinants of Economic Growth*. Cambridge, MA: MIT Press.

——— 1997b. "Optimal Management of Indexed and Nominal Debt." *NBER Working Paper* 6197 (September).

Barro, Robert and David B. Gordon. 1983. "Rules, Discretion and Reputation in a Model of Monetary Policy." *Journal of Monetary Economics* 12: 101–121.

Barro, Robert and Xavier Sala-I-Martin. 1995. *Economic Growth.* New York: MacMillan.

Barth, Michael and Xin Zhang. 1999. "Foreign Equity Flows and the Asian Financial Crisis." In *Financial Markets and Development,* edited by Alison Harwood, Robert E. Litan and Michael Pomerleano, 179–218. Washington, D.C.: Brookings Institution.

Bates, Robert and Da-Hsiang Lien. 1985. "A Note on Taxation, Development and Representative Government." *Politics and Society* 14: 53–70.

Bayoumi, Tamim and Barry Eichengreen. 1995. "Restraining Yourself: The Implications of Fiscal Rules for Economic Stabilization," *IMF Staff Papers* 42 (March): 32–48.

Bayoumi, Tamim, Morris Goldstein and Geoffrey Woglom. 1995. "Do Credit Markets Discipline Sovereign Borrowers?" *Journal of Money, Credit and Banking* 27: 1046–1059.

Beck, Nathaniel and Jonathan K. Katz. 1995. "What To Do (and Not to Do) with Time Series Cross Section Data." *American Political Science Review* 89: 634–647.
    1996. "Nuisance vs. Substance: Specifying and Estimating Time-Series-Cross-Section Models." *Political Analysis* 6: 1–36.

Bekaert, Geert, Claude B. Erb, Campbell R. Harvey, and Tadas E. Viskanta. 1998. "Distributional Characteristics of Emerging Market Returns and Asset Allocation." *Journal of Portfolio Management* (Winter): 102–116.

Berger, Suzanne. 1996. "Introduction." In *National Diversity and Global Capitalism,* edited by Suzanne Berger and Ronald Dore, 1–25. Ithaca, NY: Cornell University Press.

Berger, Suzanne and Ronald Dore, eds. 1996. *National Diversity and Global Capitalism.* Ithaca, NY: Cornell University Press.

Berkowitz, M. K. and Y. Kotowitz. 1993. "Incentives and Efficiency in the Market for Management Services: A Study of Canadian Mutual Funds." *Canadian Journal of Economics* 26: 850–866.

Berman, Sheri and Kathleen R. McNamara. 1999. "Bank on Democracy." *Foreign Affairs* 78: 2–8.

Bernhard, William T. 1998. "A Political Explanation of Variations in Central Bank Independence." *American Political Science Review* 92: 311–328.

Bernhard, William and David Leblang. 1999. "Democratic Institutions and Exchange Rate Commitments." *International Organization* 53: 71–98.

Bianco, William T. 1994. *Trust: Representatives and Constituents.* Ann Arbor: University of Michigan Press.

Bikchandani, Sushil and Sunil Sharma. 2000. "Herd Behavior in Financial Markets: A Review." *IMF Working Paper* WP/00/48 (March).

Bikchandani, Sushil, David Hirshleifer and Ivo Welch. 1992. "A Theory of Fads, Fashion, Custom, and Cultural Change as Informational Cascades." *Journal of Political Economy* 100: 992–1026.

References

Bisignano, Joseph. 1994. "The Internationalisation of Financial Markets: Measurement, Benefits and Unexpected Interdependence." *Banque de France Cahiers Economiques et Monetaires* 43: 9–71.

Block, Fred. 1977. "The Ruling Class Does Not Rule: Notes on the Marxist Theory of the State." *Socialist Revolution* 33: 6–28.

——— 1996. *The Vampire State and Other Myths and Fallacies about the U.S Economy.* New York: Free Press.

Blommestein, Hans J. and Norbert Funke, eds. 1998. *Institutional Investors in the New Financial Landscape.* Paris: OECD.

Bloomfield, Arthur I. 1968. "Patterns of Fluctuation in International Investment before 1914." Princeton Studies in International Finance No. 21 (Princeton University, Department of Economics).

Boix, Carles. 1997a. "Political Parties and the Supply Side of the Economy: The Provision of Physical and Human Capital in Advanced Economies. 1960–1990." *American Journal of Political Science* 41: 814–845.

——— 1997b. "Privatizing the Public Business Sector in the Eighties: Economic Performance, Partisan Responses, and Divided Governments." *British Journal of Political Science* 27: 473–496.

——— 1998. *Political Parties, Growth and Equality: Conservative and Social Democratic Economic Strategies in the World Economy.* Cambridge: Cambridge University Press.

Bordo, Michael D. and Hugh Rockoff. 1996. "The Gold Standard as a 'Good Housekeeping Seal of Approval'." *The Journal of Economic History* 56: 389–428.

Bordo, Michael D. and Anna Schwartz. 1994. "The Specie Standard as a Contingent Rule: Some Evidence for the Core and Peripheral Countries, 1880–1990." *NBER Working Paper* 4860 (September).

Borio, Claudio E. V. and Robert N. McCauley. 1996. "The Economics of Recent Bond Yield Volatility." *BIS Economic Papers,* No. 45.

Branson, William H., Jorge Braga de Macedo and Juergen von Hagen. 1998. "Macroeconomic Policy and Institutions during the Transition to European Union Membership." *NBER Working Paper* 6555 (May).

Brehm, John. 1993. *The Phantom Respondents: Opinion Surveys and Political Representation.* Ann Arbor: University of Michigan Press.

Brittan, Sir Leon. 1998. *Globalization vs. Sovereignty: The European Response.* Cambridge: Cambridge University Press.

Brooks, Sarah M. 2002. "Social Protection and Economic Integration: The Politics of Pension Reform in an Era of Capital Mobility." *Comparative Political Studies* 35: 491–523.

Brooks, Sarah M. and Layna Mosley. 2000. "International Investors and Domestic Policies: Delineating the 'Market Constraint' in Global Perspective." Paper presented at the Annual Meeting of the American Political Science Association, August 31–September 3, Washington, D.C.

Brown, Keith C., W. V. Harlow and Laura T. Starks. 1996. "Of Tournaments and Temptations: An Analysis of Managerial Incentives in the Mutual Fund Industry." *Journal of Finance* 51: 85–110.

Broz, Lawrence. 1997. "The Domestic Politics of International Monetary Order: The Gold Standard." In *Contested Social Orders and International Politics*, edited by David Skidmore, 53–91. Nashville, TN: Vanderbilt University Press.

Buiter, Willem, Giancarlo Corsetti and Nouriel Roubini. 1993. "Excessive Deficits: Sense and Nonsense in the Treaty of Maastricht." *Economic Policy* 16: 57–100.

Burgoon, Brian. 2001. "Globalization and Welfare Compensation: Disentangling the Ties that Bind." *International Organization* 55: 509–551.

Burke, Cathleen. 1989. *Morgan Grenfell 1838–1988: The Biography of a Merchant Bank*. Oxford: Oxford University Press.

Burtless, Gary, Robert Z. Lawrence, Robert E. Litan and Robert J. Shapiro. 1998. *Globaphobia: Confronting Fears about Open Trade*. Washington, D.C.: Brookings Institution.

Calvo, Guillermo A. and Pablo E. Guidotti. 1990. "Indexation and Maturity of Government Bonds: An Exploratory Model." In *Public Debt Management: Theory and History*, edited by Rudiger Dornbusch and Mario Draghi, 52–82. Cambridge: Cambridge University Press.

Calvo, Guillermo A. and Enrique G. Mendoza. 1996a. "Mexico's Balance of Payments Crisis: A Chronicle of Death Foretold." *Journal of International Economics* 41: 235–264.

1996b. "Petty Crime and Cruel Punishment: Lessons from the Mexican Debacle." *American Economic Review* 86: 170–175.

2000a. "Capital-Markets Crises and Economic Collapse in Emerging Markets: An Informational-Frictions Approach." *American Economic Review* 90: 59–64.

2000b. "Rational Herd Behavior and the Globalization of Securities Markets." *Journal of International Economics* 51(1): 79–113.

Calvo, Guillermo A., Morris Goldstein and Eduard Hochreiter. eds. 1996. *Private Capital Flows to Emerging Markets after the Mexican Crisis*. Washington, D.C.: Institute for International Economics.

Camdessus, Michel. 1997. "Toward a Second Generation of Structural Reform in Latin America." Address at the National Banks Convention, May 21, Buenos Aires.

Cameron, David. 1978. "The Expansion of the Public Economy: A Comparative Analysis." *American Political Science Review* 72: 1243–1261.

1996. "Exchange Rate Politics in France, 1981–1983: The Regime-Defining Choices of the Mitterand Presidency." In *The Mitterand Era: Policy Alternatives and Political Mobilization in France*, edited by Anthony Daley, 56–82. New York: New York University Press.

Cameron, Rondo and V. I. Bovykin. eds. 1991. *International Banking, 1870–1914*. New York: Oxford University Press.

Campbell, John Y. 1995. "Some Lessons from the Yield Curve." *NBER Working Paper* 5031 (February).

Campbell, John Y. and Robert J. Shiller. 1996. "A Scorecard for Indexed Government Debt." *NBER Working Paper* 5587 (May).

Canadian Treasury. 1997. *Debt Management Report*. (Ottawa: Government of Canada).

References

Cantor, Richard and Frank Packer. 1996. "Determinants and Impact of Sovereign Credit Rating." *Federal Reserve Bank of New York Economic Policy Review* 2:37–53.

　　1997. "Differences of Opinion and Selection Bias in the Credit Rating Industry." *Journal of Banking and Finance* 21: 1395–1417.

Canziani, P., F. Giavazzi, P. Manasse and G. Tabellini. 1994. "Fiscal Rules for Debt Sustainability: History and Institutions." In *Bond Markets, Treasury and Debt Management: The Italian Case*, edited by V. Conti, R. Hamaui and H. M. Scobie, 85–108. London: Chapman and Hall.

Cañzonero, Gustavo. 1995. "Spain: Unemployment, Debt Management and Interest Rate Differentials." *IMF Working Paper*, European I Department (November).

Capon, Noel, Gavin Fitzsimmons and Roger Prince. 1996. "An Individual Level Analysis of the Mutual Fund Investment Decision." *Journal of Financial Services Research* 10: 59–82.

Carosso, Vincent P. 1987. *The Morgans: Private International Bankers, 1854–1913*. Cambridge: Harvard University Press.

Cassis, Youssef. 1990. "The Emergence of a New Financial Institution: Investment Trusts in Britain, 1870–1939." In *Capitalism in a Mature Economy: Financial Institutions, Capital Exports, and British Industry 1870–1939*, edited by J. J. Van Helten and Y. Cassis, 139–158. Aldershot, England: Edward Elgar.

Castles, Francis G. and Peter Mair. 1984. "Left-Right Political Scales: Some 'Expert' Judgments." *European Journal of Political Research* 12: 73–88.

Cavaglia, Stefano M. F. G., Magnus Dahlquist, Campbell R. Harvey, Peter L. Rathjens and Jarrod W. Wilcox. 1997. "Emerging/Developed Market Portfolio Mixes." *Emerging Markets Quarterly* (Winter): 47–62.

Cebula, R. J. 1995. "An Empirical Analysis of the Likely Impact of Shortening the Maturity Structure of the Federal Government Debt in the United States." *Economic Internazionale* 48: 197–208.

Cerny, Philip. 1993. "The Deregulation and Re-regulation of Financial Markets in a More Open World." In *Finance and World Politics: Markets, Regimes, and States in a Post-Hegemonic Era*, edited by Philip Cerny, 51–82. Brookfield, England: Edward Elgar.

　　1994. "The Dynamics of Financial Globalization: Technology, Market Structure, and Policy Response." *Policy Sciences* 27: 319–342.

　　1995. "Globalization and the Changing Logic of Collective Action." *International Organization* 49: 595–626.

　　1999. "Globalization and Erosion of Democracy." *European Journal of Political Research* 36: 1–26.

Chang, Eric C., Joseph W. Cheng and Ajay Khorana. 2000. "An Examination of Herd Behavior in Equity Markets: An International Perspective." *Journal of Banking and Finance* 24, No. 10 (October): 1651–1679.

Chevalier, Judith and Glenn Ellison. 1997. "Risk Taking by Mutual Funds as a Response to Incentives." *Journal of Political Economy* 105: 1167–1200.

　　1999a. "Career Concerns of Mutual Fund Managers." *Quarterly Journal of Economics* 114, No. 2 (May): 389–432.

1999b. "Are Some Mutual Fund Managers Better than Others? Cross-Sectional Patterns in Behavior and Performance." *Journal of Finance* 54: 875–899.

Choe, Hyuk, Bong-Chan Kho and Rene M. Stulz. 1998. "Do Foreign Investors Destabilize Stock Markets?" Manuscript, Seoul National University.

Christiansen, Hans and Charles Pigott. 1997. "Long-Term Interest Rates in Globalised Markets." *OECD Economics Department Working Papers* No. 175.

Clark, William Roberts. 1998. "Beliefs and Interests: Choosing Monetary Institutions in a World of Global Capital Mobility." Paper presented at the Annual Meeting of the International Studies Association, March 18–21, Minneapolis.

Clark, William Roberts and Mark Hallerberg. 1997. "Strategic Interaction between Monetary and Fiscal Actors under Full Capital Mobility." Paper presented at the Annual Meeting of the American Political Science Association, Washington D.C.

2000. "Mobile Capital, Domestic Institutions and Electorally Induced Monetary and Fiscal Policy." *American Political Science Review* 94: 323–346.

Clayton, Richard and Jonas Pontusson. 1998. "Welfare State Retrenchment Revisited: Entitlement Cuts, Public Sector Restructuring and Inegalitarian Trends in Advanced Capitalist Societies." *World Politics* 51: 67–98.

Cline, William. 1996. "Comment," In *Private Capital Flows to Emerging Markets after the Mexican Crisis*, edited by Guillermo A. Calvo, Morris Goldstein and Eduard Hochreiter. Washington, D.C.: Institute for International Economics.

Cline, William and Kevin J. S. Barnes. 1997. "Spreads and Risk in Emerging Markets Lending." Institute of International Finance, Research Paper No. 97-1 (Washington, D.C.: Institute of International Finance, December).

Coase, Ronald H. 1937. "The Nature of the Firm." *Economica* 4: 386–405.

Cohen, Benjamin. 1986. *In Whose Interest? International Banking and American Foreign Policy*. New Haven, CT: Yale University Press.

1996. "Phoenix Risen: The Resurrection of Global Finance." *World Politics* 48: 268–296.

Cohen, Daniel and Jeffrey Sachs. 1986. "Growth and External Debt under Risk of Debt Repudiation." *European Economic Review* 30: 529–560.

Cole, Harold L. and Timothy J. Kehoe. 1996. "A Self-Fulfilling Model of Mexico's 1994–1995 Debt Crisis." *Journal of International Economics* 41: 309–330.

Commission for the European Communities. 1995. "Green Paper on the Practical Arrangements for the Introduction of the Single Currency." Brussels (May), COM(95) 333 final.

Conti, V. and R. Hamaui. 1994. "Introduction" In *Bond Markets, Treasury and Debt Management: The Italian Case*, edited by V. Conti, R. Hamaui and H. M. Scobie, 1–12. London: Chapman and Hall.

Conti, V., R. Hamaui and H. M. Scobie. eds. 1994. *Bond Markets, Treasury and Debt Management: The Italian Case*. London: Chapman and Hall.

Cooper, Richard 1968. *The Economics of Interdependence: Economic Policy in the Atlantic Community*. New York: McGraw-Hill.

1972. "Economic Interdependence and Foreign Policy in the 1970s." *World Politics* 24: 159–181.

References

Corsetti, Giancarlo and Nouriel Roubini. 1996. "European vs. American Perspectives on Balanced-Budget Rules." *American Economic Review* 86: 408–413.

Cosh, Andrew D., Alan Hughes and Ajit Singh. 1992. "Financial Innovation, Changing Patterns of Ownership and the Structure of Financial Markets." In *Financial Openness and National Autonomy: Opportunities and Constraints*, edited by Tariq Banuri and Juliet B. Schor, 19–42. Oxford: Clarendon Press.

Cottrell, P.L. 1975. *British Overseas Investment in the Nineteenth Century*. London: MacMillan.

——— 1991. "Great Britain." In *International Banking*, edited by Rondo Cameron and V. I. Bovykin, 25–47. New York: Oxford University Press.

Cukierman, Alex. 1992. *Central Bank Strategy, Credibility and Independence: Theory and Evidence*. Cambridge, MA: MIT Press.

Dale, William B. 1983. "Financing and the Adjustment of Payments Imbalances," In *IMF Conditionality*, edited by John Williamson, 3–16. Washington, D.C.: Institute for International Economics.

Davis, E. P. 1988. "Financial Market Activity of Life Insurance Companies and Pension Funds." *BIS Economic Papers*, No. 21.

Davis, Richard. 1983. *The English Rothschilds*. Chapel Hill: University of North Carolina Press.

Dawson, Frank Griffith. 1990. *The First Latin American Debt Crisis: The City of London and the 1822–1825 Loan Bubble*. New Haven: Yale University Press.

De Cecco, Marcello. 1974. *Money and Empire: The International Gold Standard. 1890–1914*. London: Basil Blackwell.

DeBondt, Werner F. M. and Richard Thaler. 1985. "Does the Stock Market Overreact?" *Journal of Finance* 40: 793–805.

——— 1994. "Financial Decision-Making in Markets and Firms: A Behavioral Perspective." *NBER Working Paper 4777* (June).

De Felice, G. and G. Miranda. 1994. "Institutional Investors and Financial Markets: Evidence from an International Comparison." In *Bond Markets, Treasury and Debt Management: The Italian Case*, edited by V. Conti, R. Hamaui and H. M. Scobie, 217–242. London: Chapman and Hall.

Dell, Edmund. 1987. *The Politics of Economic Interdependence*. New York: St. Martin's Press.

Della Sala, Vincent. 1988. "The Italian Budgetary Process: Political and Institutional Constraints." *West European Politics* 11: 110–125.

Del Valle Borraez, Mueen Batlay and Eriko Togo. 1998. "Overview of Fixed Income Securities Markets in Emerging Markets." *World Bank Workshop Paper*.

Detragiache, Enrica. 1996. "Rational Liquidity Crises in the Sovereign Debt Market: In Search of a Theory." *IMF Staff Papers* 43 (September): 545–570.

Deutsche Asset Management Group. 1997. "Frankfurt Fixed Income Group, Global Investment Strategy, Quarter 2." Frankfurt: Deutsche Bank Group, March 26.

Devlin, Robert. 1989. *Debt and Crisis in Latin America: The Supply Side of the Story*. Princeton, NJ: Princeton University Press.

Dombrowski, Peter. 1998. "Haute Finance and High Theory: Recent Scholarship on Global Financial Relations." *Mershon International Studies Review* 42: 1–28.

Dooley, Michael P. 1996. "A Survey of Literature on Controls over International Capital Transactions." *IMF Staff Papers* 43: 639–687.

Dornbusch, Rudiger and Mario Draghi, eds. 1990a. *Public Debt Management: Theory and History*. Cambridge: Cambridge University Press.

1990b. "Introduction." In *Public Debt Management: Theory and History*, edited by Rudiger Dornbusch and Mario Draghi, 1–13. Cambridge: Cambridge University Press.

Doukas, John. 1989. "Contagion Effect on Sovereign Interest Rate Spreads." *Economics Letters* 29: 237–241.

Downs, Anthony. 1957. *An Economic Theory of Democracy*. New York: Harper.

Drake, Paul W. 1989. *The Money Doctor in the Andes: The Kemmerer Missions, 1923–1933*. Durham, NC: Duke University Press.

Drazen, Allan and Paul R. Masson. 1994. "Credibility of Politics versus Credibility of Policymakers." *Quarterly Journal of Economics* 109: 735–754.

Drezner, Daniel W. 2001. "Globalization and Policy Convergence." *International Studies Review* 3: 53–78.

Dryzek, John S. 1996. *Democracy in Capitalist Times*. New York: Oxford University Press.

Duch, Raymond M., Harvey Palmer and Chris Anderson. 2000. "Heterogeneity in Perceptions of National Economic Conditions." *American Journal of Political Science* 44: 635–652.

Dym, Steven. 1991. "Measuring the Risk of Foreign Bonds." *Journal of Portfolio Management* 18: 56–61.

Eaton, Jonathan and Raqual Fernandez. 1995. "Sovereign Debt." *NBER Working Paper* 5131.

Eaton, Jonathan and Mark Gersovitz. 1981. "Debt with Potential Repudiation: Theoretical and Empirical Analysis." *Review of Economic Studies* 48: 289–309.

Eaton, Jonathan, Mark Gersovitz and Joseph E. Stiglitz. 1986. "The Pure Theory of Country Risk." *European Economic Review* 30: 481–513.

Eccleston, Richard. 1998. "The Fiscal-Electoral Nexus in Australia, 1976–1994." *Australian Journal of Political Science* 33: 267–286.

Edey, Malcolm and Ketil Hviding. 1995. "An Assessment of Financial Reform in OECD Countries." *OECD Economics Department Working Paper* No. 154.

Edison, H. and C. Reinhart. 2001. "Capital Controls During Financial Crises: The Case of Malaysia and Thailand." In *Financial Crises in Emerging Markets*, edited by R. Glick. Cambridge: Cambridge University Press.

Edwards, Sebastian. 1984. "LDC Foreign Borrowing: An Empirical Investigation. 1976–1980." *American Economic Review* 74: 726–734.

1986. "The Pricing of Bonds and Bank Loans in International Markets." *European Economic Review* 30: 565–589.

1994. *The Latin American Debt Crisis*. Washington, D.C.: The World Bank.

1998. "Interest Rate Volatility, Capital Controls and Contagion." *NBER Working Paper* 6756 (October).

References

Eichberger, Juergen, Simon Grant and Stephen P. King. 1999. "On Relative Performance Contracts and Fund Managers' Incentives." *European Economic Review* 43: 135–161.

Eichengreen, Barry. 1990. "The U.S. Capital Market and Foreign Lending, 1920–1955." In *Developing Country Debt and Economic Performance*, Vol. 1, edited by Jeffrey D. Sachs, 107–155. Chicago: University of Chicago Press.

———. 1991. "Historical Research on International Lending and Debt." *Journal of Economic Perspectives* 5: 149–169.

———. 1992. *Golden Fetters: The Gold Standard and the Great Depression, 1919–1939.* Oxford: Oxford University Press.

———. 1996. *Globalizing Capital: A History of the International Monetary System.* Princeton, NJ: Princeton University Press.

———. 1999. *Toward a New International Financial Architecture: A Practical Post-Asia Agenda.* Washington, D.C.: Institute for International Economics.

Eichengreen, Barry and Albert Fishlow. 1998. "Contending with Capital Flows: What's Different about the 1990s?" In *Capital Flows and Financial Crises*, edited by Miles Kahler, 23–68. Ithaca, NY: Cornell University Press/Council on Foreign Relations.

Eichengreen, Barry and Ashoka Mody. 1998. "What Explains Changing Spreads on Emerging-Market Debt: Fundamentals or Market Sentiment?" *NBER Working Paper* 6408.

Eichengreen, Barry and Michael Mussa. 1999. "Capital Account Liberalization and the IMF." *Finance and Development* 35, No. 4.

Eichengreen, Barry and Beth A. Simmons. 1995. "International Economics and Domestic Politics: Notes on the 1920s." In *Banking, Currency and Finance in Europe between the Wars*, edited by Charles H. Feinstein, 131–147. Oxford: Clarendon Press.

Eichengreen, Barry and Nathan Sussman, 2000. "The International Monetary System in the (Very) Long Run." *IMF Working Paper* No. 43 (March).

Eichengreen, Barry, Andrew K. Rose and Charles Wyplosz. 1995. "Exchange Market Mayhem: The Antecedents and Aftermath of Speculative Attacks." *Economic Policy* 20: 249–312.

Epstein, Gerald A. and Herbert Gintis. 1992. "International Capital Markets and the Limits of National Economic Policy." In *Financial Openness and National Autonomy: Opportunities and Constraints*, edited by Tariq Banuri and Juliet B. Schor, 167–197. Oxford: Clarendon Press.

Erb, Claude B., Campbell R. Harvey and Tadas E. Viskanta. 1996. "Political Risk, Financial Risk and Economic Risk." *Financial Analysts Journal* 52 (November/December): 28–46.

———. 1997. "The Making of an Emerging Market." *Emerging Markets Quarterly* 1: 14–19.

———. 1998. "Risk in Emerging Markets." *The Financial Survey* (July/August): 42–46.

———. 1999. "A New Perspective on Emerging Market Bonds." *Journal of Portfolio Management*: 83–92.

Esping-Andersen, Gøsta. 1990. *The Three Worlds of Welfare Capitalism*. Princeton, NJ: Princeton University Press.

1996. *Welfare States in Transition: National Adaptations in Global Economies*. London: Sage, UN Research Institute for Social Development.

European Monetary Institute. 1998. *Convergence Report 1998*. Frankfurt: European Monetary Institute.

Evans, Martin D. D. 1998. "Real Rates, Expected Inflation and Inflation Risk Premia." *Journal of Finance* 53, No. 1 (February).

Evans, Peter. 1997. "The Eclipse of the State? Reflections on Stateness in an Era of Globalization." *World Politics* 50: 62–87.

Fabozzi, Frank and Franco Modigliani. 1992. *Capital Markets: Institutions and Instruments*. Upper Saddle River, NJ: Prentice-Hall.

Fama, Eugene. 1970. "Efficient Capital Markets: A Review of Theory and Empirical Work." *Journal of Finance* 25: 383–417.

Fearon, James D. 1994. "Domestic Political Audiences and the Escalation of International Disputes." *American Political Science Review* 88: 577–592.

Federal Reserve Bank of Kansas City. 1997. "Maintaining Financial Stability in a Global Economy." A Symposium Sponsored by the Federal Reserve Bank of Kansas City, Jackson Hole, Wyoming, August 28–30, 1997. Kansas City, MO: Federal Reserve Bank.

Feenstra, Robert C., 1998. "Integration of Trade and Production in the Global Economy." *Journal of Economic Perspectives* 12: 31–50.

Feis, Herbert. 1930. *Europe: The World's Banker: 1870–1914*. New Haven, CT: Yale University Press/Council on Foreign Relations.

Feldstein, Martin. 1994. "Tax Policy and International Capital Flows." *NBER Working Paper* 4851 (September).

Feldstein, Martin and Charles Horioka. 1980. "Domestic Savings and International Capital Flows." *Economic Journal* 90: 314–329.

Ferejohn, John. 1991. "Rationality and Interpretation: Parliamentary Elections in Early Stuart England." In *The Economic Approach to Politics*, edited by Kristen Monroe, 279–305. New York: Harper Collins.

Ferguson, Niall. 1999. *The House of Rothschild: The World's Banker, 1849–1999*. New York: Viking.

Finnemore, Martha. 2002. *The Purpose of Force*. Ithaca, NY: Cornell University Press.

Fishlow, Albert. 1985. "Lessons from the Past: Capital Markets During the 19th Century and Interwar Period." *International Organization* 39: 383–439.

Flandreau, Marc. 1998. "Caveat Emptor: Coping with Sovereign Risk without the Multilaterals." *CEPR Discussion Paper* No. 2004 (October).

Flandreau, Marc, Jacques Le Cacheux, and Frederic Zumer. 1998. "Stability without a Pact? Lessons from the European Gold Standard, 1880–1914." *Economic Policy* 21 (April), pp. 115–162.

Fleming, J. M. 1962. "Domestic Financial Policies under Fixed and Floating Exchange Rates." *IMF Staff Papers* 9: 369–380.

References

Forder, James. 1998a. "Central Bank Independence: Conceptual Clarifications and Interim Assessment." *Oxford Economic Papers* 50: 307–335.

1998b. "The Case for an Independent European Central Bank: A Reassessment of Evidence and Sources." *European Journal of Political Economy* 14: 53–71.

Foresi, Silverio, Alessandro Penati and George Pennacchi. 1996. "Reducing the Cost of Government Debt: The Italian Experience and the Role of Indexed Bonds." *Swedish Economic Policy Review* 3, No. 1: 203–232.

Frankel, Jeffrey. 1986. "International Capital Mobility and Crowding Out in the US Economy: Imperfect Integration of Financial Markets or of Goods Markets?" *NBER Working Paper* 804.

Frankel, Jeffrey and Chudozie Okongwu. 1995. "Liberalized Portfolio Capital Inflows in Emerging Markets: Sterilization, Expectations, and the Incompleteness of Interest Rate Convergence." *NBER Working Paper* 5156 (June).

Frankel, Jeffrey A. and Andrew K. Rose. 1996. "Currency Crashes in Emerging Markets: An Empirical Treatment." *Journal of International Economics* 41: 351–366.

Frankel, Jeffrey A. and Sergio L. Schmulker. 1997. "Country Funds and Asymmetric Information." Unpublished paper.

Franzese, Robert J. 1999. "Central Banks, Governments and Inflation." *American Journal of Political Science* 43: 681–706.

1999. "Partially Independent Central Banks, Politically Responsive Governments, and Inflation." *American Jornal of Political Science* 43: 681–706.

2002. *Macroeconomic Policies of Developed Democracies.* Cambridge: Cambridge University Press.

Freeman, John. 1997. "Democracy and International Finance: An Experimental Study." Zentrum fuer Internationale und Interdisziplinaere Studien, Austria, Occasional Paper 3.

Freeman, John, Jude C. Hays, and Helmut Stix, 2000. "Democracy and Markets: The Case of Exchange Rates." *American Journal of Political Science* 44: 449–468.

French, Kenneth R. and James M. Poterba. 1991. "Investor Diversification and International Equity Markets." *American Economic Review* 81: 222–226.

Friauf, Karl Heinrich. 1975. "Parliamentary Control of the Budget in the Federal Republic of Germany." In *The Power of the Purse: A Symposium on the Role of European Parliaments in Budgetary Decisions,* edited by David Coombes, 66–84. New York: Praeger.

Frieden, Jeffrey. 1991a. *Debt, Development and Democracy: Modern Political Economy and Latin America, 1965–1985.* Princeton, NJ: Princeton University Press.

1991b. "Invested Interests: The Politics of National Economic Policies in an Age of Global Markets." *International Organization* 45: 425–451.

Frieden, Jeffrey and Lisa M. Martin. 2001. "International Political Economy: The State of the Sub-Discipline." In *Political Science: The State of the Discipline,* edited by Ira Katznelson and Helen Milner. Washington, D.C.: American Political Science Association.

Friedman, Benjamin M. 1984. "Comment on 'Stock Prices and Social Dynamics'." *Brookings Papers on Economic Activity* 2: 504–508.

Friedman, Irving S. 1983. *The World Debt Dilemma: Managing Country Risk.* Washington, D.C.: Council for International Banking Studies.

Friedman, Thomas L., 2000. *The Lexus and the Olive Tree: Understanding Globalization*, rev. ed. New York: Anchor Books.

Froot, Kenneth A., David S. Scharfstein and Jeremy C. Stein. 1992. "Herd on the Street: Informational Inefficiencies in a Market with Short-Term Speculation." *Journal of Finance* 47: 1461–1484.

Funke, Norbert. 1996. "Vulnerability of Fixed Exchange Rate Regimes: The Role of Economic Fundamentals." *OECD Economic Studies* 26: 158–176.

Garrett, Geoffrey. 1996. "Capital Mobility, Trade, and the Domestic Politics of Economic Policy." In *Internationalization and Domestic Politics*, edited by Helen Milner and Robert Keohane, 79–107. Cambridge: Cambridge University Press.

1998a. *Partisan Politics in the Global Economy.* New York: Cambridge University.

1998b. "Governing in the Global Economy: Economic Policy and Market Integration around the World." Paper presented at the 1998 Annual Meetings of the American Political Science Association, September, Boston.

1998c. "Global Markets and National Politics: Collision Course or Virtuous Circle?" *International Organization* 52: 787–824.

2000a. "Globalization and Government Spending around the World." Unpublished paper.

2000b. "The Causes of Globalization." *Comparative Political Studies* 33: 941–991.

Garrett, Geoffrey and Peter Lange. 1991. "Political Responses to Interdependence: What's 'Left' for the Left?" *International Organization* 45: 539–564.

Garrett, Geoffrey and Peter Lange. 1996. "Internationalization, Institutions, and Political Change." In *Internationalization and Domestic Politics*, edited by Helen Milner and Robert Keohane, 48–75. Cambridge: Cambridge University Press.

Garrett, Geoffrey and Deborah Mitchell. 2001. "Globalization and the Welfare State." *European Journal of Political Research* 39(2): 145–177.

Garrett, Geoffrey and David Nickerson. 2001. "Globalization, Democratization and Government Spending in Middle Income Countries." Unpublished paper, Yale University.

Gavin, Michael, Ricardo Hausmann and Leonardo Leiderman. 1996. "The Macroeconomics of Capital Flows to Latin America." In *Volatile Capital Flows: Taming Their Impact on Latin America*, edited by Ricardo Hausmann and Liliana Rojas-Suarez, 21–40. Washington, D.C.: Interamerican Development Bank.

Genesis Investment Management Limited. 1997. *Russia: The Re-Integration of the Financial System and the Real Economy.* London: Genesis Investment Management.

George, Robert Lloyd. 1994. *The Handbook of Emerging Markets: A Country-by-Country Guide to the World's Fastest Growing Economies.* Chicago: Probus.

Germain, Randall. 1997. *The International Organization of Credit: State and Global Finance in the World Economy.* Cambridge: Cambridge University Press.

References

Giavazzi, Francesco and Marco Pagano. 1988. "The Advantage of Tying One's Hands: EMS Discipline and Central Bank Credibility." *European Economic Review* 32: 1055–1082.

Giavazzi, Francesco and Marco Pagano. 1990. "Confidence Crisis and Public Debt Management." In *Public Debt Management: Theory and History*, edited by Rudiger Dornbusch and Mario Draghi, 125–152. Cambridge: Cambridge University Press.

Gibbons, Robert. 1992. *Game Theory for Applied Economists*. Princeton, NJ: Princeton University Press.

Gil-Diaz, Francisco and Agustin Carstens. 1996. "One Year of Solitude: Some Pilgrim Tales about Mexico's 1994–1995 Crisis." *American Economic Review* 86: 164–169.

Gilibert, Pier Luigi. 1994. "Living Dangerously: the Lira and the Pound in a Floating World." In *30 Years of European Monetary Integration from the Werner Plan to EMU*, edited by Alfred Steinherr, 105–142. London: Longman.

Giorgianni, Lorenzo. 1997. "Foreign Exchange Risk Premia: Does Fiscal Policy Matter? Evidence from Italian Data." *IMF Working Paper* 97–39.

Giovannini, Alberto. 1997. "Government Debt Management." *Oxford Review of Economic Policy* 13: 43–52.

Goldfajn, Ilan. 1998. "Public Debt Indexation and Denomination: The Case of Brazil." *IMF Working Paper* 98–18.

Goldstein, Morris 1998. *The Asian Financial Crisis: Causes, Cures, and Systemic Implications*. Washington, D.C.: Institute for International Economics.

Goldstein, Morris and Philip Turner. 1996. "Banking Crises in Emerging Economies: Origins and Policy Options." *BIS Economic Papers* No. 46 (October).

Goldstein, Morris and Geoffrey Woglom. 1992. "Market-Based Financial Discipline in Monetary Unions: Evidence from the US Municipal Bond Market." In *Establishing a Central Bank: Issues in Europe and Lessons from the US*, edited by Matthew B. Canzoneri, Vittorio Grilli and Paul R. Masson, 228–254. Cambridge: Cambridge University Press.

Goodman, John B. and Louis W. Pauly. 1993. "The Obsolescence of Capital Controls? Economic Management in an Age of Global Markets." *World Politics* 46: 50–82.

Gordon, Roger H. and A. Lans Bovenberg. 1996. "Why Is Capital So Immobile Internationally? Possible Explanations and Implications for Capital Income Taxation." *American Economic Review* 86: 1057–1075.

Gould, Erica R. 2001. "Financiers as Fund Principals: An Alternative Explanation of Changes in the Activities of the International Monetary Fund." Dissertation, Stanford University.

Government of Sweden. 2001. *Revised Budget Statement*. Stockholm: Ministry of Finance (November). Also available at http://finans.vegeringen.se/

Gowland, D. H. ed. 1990. *International Bond Markets*. London: Routledge.

Grabel, Ilene. 1993. "Crossing Borders: A Case for Cooperation in International Financial Markets," in *Creating a New Economy: Forces of Change and Plans of*

Action, edited by G. Epstein, J. Graham and J. Nembhard, 64–83. Philadelphia: Temple University Press.

1996a. "Marketing the Third World: Contradictions of Portfolio Investment in the Global Economy." *World Development* 24: 1761–1776.

1996b. "Stock Markets, Rentier Interest, and the Current Mexican Crisis." *Journal of Economic Issues* 30: 443–449.

1999. "Rejecting Exceptionalism: Reinterpreting the Asian Financial Crisis." In *Global Instability and World Economic Governance*, edited by J. Michile and J. Grieve Smith, 37–67. London and New York: Routledge Press.

Graham, John. 1999. "Herding among Investment Newsletters: Theory and Evidence." *Journal of Finance* 54: 237–268.

Grilli, Vittorio and Gian Maria Milesi-Ferretti. 1995. "Economic Effects and Structural Determinants of Capital Controls." *International Monetary Fund Staff Papers* 42: 517–551.

Grilli, Vittorio, Donato Masciandaro and Guido Tabellini. 1991. "Political and Monetary Institutions and Public Financial Policies in the Industrial Countries." *Economic Policy* 6: 342–392.

Grinblatt, Mark, Sheridan Titman and Russ Wermers. 1995. "Momentum Investment Strategies, Portfolio Performance, and Herding: A Study of Mutual Fund Behavior." *American Economic Review* 85: 1088–1105.

Grisanti, Alejandro, Ernesto Stein and Ernesto Talvi. 1998. *Institutional Arrangements and Fiscal Performance: The Latin American Experience*. Washington, D.C.: Inter-American Development Bank.

Gros, Daniel and Karel Lannoo. 2000. *The Euro Capital Market*. New York: John Wiley and Sons.

Grossman, Sanford J. and Joseph E. Stiglitz. 1980. "On the Impossibility of Informationally Efficient Markets." *American Economic Review* 70: 393–408.

Group of Thirty. 1982. *Risks in International Bank Lending: First Report of the International Banking Study Group of the Group of Thirty*. New York: Group of Thirty.

Gruber, Martin J. 1996. "Another Puzzle: The Growth in Actively Managed Mutual Funds." *Journal of Finance* 51: 783–810.

Haggard, Stephan. 1985. "The Politics of Adjustment: Lessons from the IMF's Extended Fund Facility." *International Organization* 39: 505–534.

Haggard, Stephan and Robert R. Kaufman. 1995. *The Political Economy of Democratic Transitions*. Princeton, NJ: Princeton University Press.

Haggard, Stephan and Sylvia Maxfield. 1996. "The Political Economy of Financial Internationalization in the Developing World." *International Organization* 50: 35–68.

Haggard, Stephan, Chung H. Lee and Sylvia Maxfield. 1993. *The Politics of Finance in Developing Countries*. Ithaca, NY: Cornell University Press.

Hahm, Sung Deuk, Mark S. Kamlet and David C. Mowry. 1996. "The Political Economy of Deficit Spending in Nine Industrialized Parliamentary Democracies: The Role of Fiscal Institutions." *Comparative Political Studies* 29: 52–77.

References

Hale, David. 1996. "Bond Booms and Busts," *The International Economy*. November/December: 52–57.

Haley, Mary Ann. 1999. "Emerging Market Makers: The Power of Institutional Investors." In *Financial Globalization and Democracy in Emerging Markets*, edited by Leslie Ann Armijo, 74–89. New York: St. Martin's Press.

Hall, Peter. 1986. *Governing the Economy: The Politics of State Intervention in Britain and France*. New York: Oxford University Press.

1999. "The Political Economy of Europe in an Era of Interdependence." In *Continuity and Change in Contemporary Capitalism*, edited by Herbert Kitschelt, Peter Lange, Gary Marks and John Stephens, 135–163. Cambridge: Cambridge University Press.

Hall, Peter and Robert Franzese. 1998. "Mixed Signals: Central Bank Independence, Coordinated Wage Bargaining, and EMU." *International Organization* 52: 505–535.

Hall, Peter and David Soskice, eds. 2001. *Varieties of Capitalism: The Institutional Foundations of Comparative Advantage*. Oxford: Oxford University Press.

Hallerberg, Mark and Scott Basinger. 1998. "Internationalization and Changes in Tax Policy in OECD Countries: The Importance of Domestic Veto Players." *Comparative Political Studies* 31: 321–353.

Hallerberg, Mark and Juergen von Hagen. 1998. "Electoral Institutions, Cabinet Negotiations, and Budget Deficits in the European Union." *NBER Working Paper* 6341.

Hallerberg, Mark and Juergen von Hagen. 1999. "Electoral Institutions, Cabinet Negotiations, and Budget Deficits in the European Union." In *Fiscal Institutions and Fiscal Performance*, edited by James Poterba and Juergen von Hagen, 81–102. Chicago: University of Chicago Press and NBER.

Harless, David W. and Stephen P. Peterson. 1998. "Investor Behavior and the Persistence of Poorly-Performing Mutual Funds." *Journal of Economic Behavior and Organization* 37: 257–276.

Hausmann, Ricardo and Liliana Rojas-Suarez. eds. 1996. *Volatile Capital Flows: Taming Their Impact on Latin America*. Washington, D.C.: Interamerican Development Bank.

Hays, Jude, Helmut Stix and John R. Freeman. 2000. "The Electoral Information Hypothesis Revisited." Paper presented at "Globalization and Democracy" Conference, May 26–27, University of Minnesota.

Held, David and Anthony McGrew, David Goldblatt and Jonathan Perraton. 1999. *Global Transformations: Politics, Economics and Culture*. Stanford, CA: Stanford University Press.

Helleiner, Eric. 1994. "Editorial: The World of Money: The Political Economy of International Capital Mobility." *Policy Sciences* 27: 295–298.

2001. "Financial Globalization and Social Response? A Polanyian View." In *Structure and Agency in International Capital Mobility*, edited by Timothy J. Sinclair and Kenneth P. Thomas, 168–186. Basingstoke, England: Palgrave.

Hibbs, Douglas. 1977. "Political Parties and Macroeconomic Policy." *American Political Science Review* 71: 1467–1487.

355

1982. "Economic Outcomes and Political Support for British Governments among Occupational Classes: A Dynamic Analysis. "*American Political Science Review* 76: 259–279.

Hirscheifler, David, Avanidhar Subrahmanyam and Sheridan Titman. 1994. "Security Analysis and Trading Patterns When Some Investors Receive Information before Others." *Journal of Finance* 49: 1665–1698.

Hirschman, Albert. 1970. *Exit, Voice, and Loyalty*. Cambridge, MA: MIT Press.

Hirst, Paul and Grahame Thompson. 1996. *Globalization in Question*. London: Polity Press.

HM Treasury (UK). 1999. *Debt Management Report, 1998–1999*. London: HM Treasury.

Holmstrom, Bengt. 1982. "Moral Hazard in Teams." *Bell Journal of Economics* 13: 324–340.

Hommes, Rudolf. 1996. "Evolution and Rationality of Budget Institutions in Colombia." Interamerican Development Bank Research Paper.

Huber, Evelyne and John D. Stephens. 1998. "Internationalization and the Social Democratic Model." *Comparative Political Studies* 31: 353–397.

2001. *Development and Crisis of the Welfare State: Parties and Policies in Global Markets*. Chicago: University of Chicago Press.

Huber, Evelyne, Charles Ragin, and John D. Stephens. 1997. "Comparative Welfare States Data Set, Northwestern University and University of North Carolina." Available at http://lissy.ceps.lu/compwsp.htm.

Institute for International Finance. 1999. *Annual Report*. Washington, D.C.: Institute for International Finance.

International Finance Corporation. 1999. *The IFC Indexes: Methodology, Definitions and Practices*. Washington, D.C.: World Bank/Emerging Markets Data Base, July.

International Monetary Fund. 1995. "Social Dimensions of the IMF's Policy Dialogue." Pamphlet Series No. 47.

1996. *World Economic Outlook* (May).

1997a. *International Capital Markets: Developments, Prospects, and Key Policy Issues*. Washington, D.C.: International Monetary Fund.

1997b. *World Economic Outlook* (May).

1998a. *Annual Report*. Washington, D.C.: International Monetary Fund.

1998b. *International Capital Markets: Developments, Prospects, and Key Policy Issues* (September) Washington, D.C.: International Monetary Fund.

1998c. "Dissemination Standards Bulletin Board." Available at http://dsbb.imf.org.

1998d, "IMF Approves SDR 13 Billion Stand-By Credit for Brazil." *IMF Press Release No. 98/59* (December 2).

1999a. *International Capital Markets: Developments, Prospects, and Key Policy Issues*. September. Washington, D.C.: International Monetary Fund.

1999b. *World Economic Outlook* (October).

2000a. *World Economic Outlook* (May).

2000b. *International Capital Markets*. Washington: International Monetary Fund.

References

2001. "Guidelines for Public Debt Management." Prepared by the Staffs of the International Monetary Fund and the World Bank.

Investment Company Institute. 1999. "U.S. Household Ownership of Mutual Funds in 1999." New York: Investment Company Institute.

Ippolito, Richard A. 1989. "Efficiency with Costly Information: A Study of Mutual Fund Performance, 1965–1984." *Quarterly Journal of Economic* 104:1–23.

1992. "Consumer Reactions to Measures of Poor Quality: Evidence from the Mutual Fund Industry." *Journal of Law and Economics* 35: 45–70.

Iversen, Torben. 1999. *Contested Economic Institutions: The Politics of Macroeconomics and Wage Bargaining in Advanced Democracies*. Cambridge: Cambridge University Press.

2000. "Decentralization, Monetarism and the Social Democratic Welfare State." In *Unions, Employers and Central Banks: Macroeconomic Coordination and Institutional Change in Social Market Economies*, edited by Torben Iversen, Jonas Pontusson and David Soskice. Cambridge: Cambridge University Press.

Iversen, Torben and Thomas Cusack, 2000. "The Causes of Welfare State Expansion: Deindustrialization or Globalization?" *World Politics* 52: 313–349.

Iversen, Torben and Anne Wren. 1998. "Equality, Employment and Budgetary Restraint: The Trilemma of the Service Economy." *World Politics* 50: 507–546.

Iversen, Torben, Jonas Pontusson and David Soskice, eds. 2000. *Unions, Employers and Central Banks: Macroeconomic Coordination and Institutional Change in Social Market Economies*. Cambridge: Cambridge University Press.

Jaffee, Dwight M. and Thomas Russell. 1976. "Imperfect Information, Uncertainty and Credit Rationing." *Quarterly Journal of Economics* 90: 651–666.

Japanese External Trade Organization (JETRO). 1996. *The Twelfth Survey of European Operations of Japanese Companies in the Manufacturing Sector*. London: Europe Division.

Kahler, Miles. ed. 1999. *Capital Flows and Financial Crises*. Ithaca, NY: Cornell University Press.

Kahneman, Daniel and Amos Tversky. 1979. "Prospect Theory." *Econometrica* 47:263–91.

Kahneman, Daniel, Paul Slovic and Amos Tversky, eds. 1982. *Judgment under Uncertainty: Heuristics and Biases*. Cambridge: Cambridge University Press.

Kaminsky, Graciela L. and Carmen M. Reinhart. 2000. "On Crises, Contagion and Confusion." *Journal of International Economics* 51, No. 1 (June): 145–168.

Kapur, Devesh. 2000. "Risk and Reward: Agency, Contracts and the Expansion of IMF Conditionality." Unpublished paper, Harvard University, Department of Government.

Kastner, Scott and Chad Rector. 2001. "Choosing Capital Mobility: Domestic Veto-Players, Partisanship, and the International System." Unpublished Manuscript, University of California San Diego.

Katzenstein, Peter. 1985. *Small States in World Markets*. Ithaca, NY: Cornell University Press.

Kaufmann, Daniel, Gil Mehrez and Sergio Schmukler. 1999. "Predicting Currency Fluctuations and Crises: Do Resident Firms Have an Informational Advantage?" *World Bank Policy Research Working Paper 2259*.

Kaufmann, Robert R. 1985. "Democratic and Authoritarian Responses to the Debt Issue: Argentina, Brazil, and Mexico." *International Organization* 39: 473–503.

Keefer, Philip and Stephen Knack. 1997. "Why Don't Poor Countries Catch Up? A Cross-National Test of an Institutional Explanation." *Economic Inquiry* 590–602.

Keefer, Philip and David Stasavage. 1998. "When Does Delegation Improve Credibility? Central Bank Independence and the Separation of Powers." *World Bank Policy Research Working Paper* No. 2356 (May).

Keeler, John T. S. 1993. "Opening the Window for Reform: Mandates, Crises, and Extraordinary Policy-Making." *Comparative Political Studies* 25: 433–486.

Kennedy, Charles R. 1987. *Political Risk Management*. New York: Quorum Books.

Keohane, Robert O. and Helen V. Milner. 1996. *Internationalization and Domestic Politics*. Cambridge: Cambridge University Press.

Keohane, Robert O. and Joseph S. Nye. 1977. *Power and Interdependence: World Politics in Transition*. Boston: Little, Brown.

Keynes, John Maynard. 1936. *The General Theory of Employment, Interest, and Money*. London: McMillan.

Khorana, Ajay. 1996. "Top Management Turnover: An Empirical Investigation of Fund Managers." *Journal of Financial Economics* 40: 403–427.

Kim, Woochan. 1997. "Does Capital Account Liberalization Discipline Budget Deficits?" Unpublished paper, Harvard University.

Kim, Woo-Chan and Shang-Jin Wei. 1999. "Foreign Portfolio Investors before and during a Crisis." *NBER Working Paper* 6968 (February).

Kindleberger, Charles P. 1973. *The World in Depression 1929–1939*. Berkeley: University of California Press.

1993. *A Financial History of Western Europe*, 2nd ed. Oxford: Oxford University Press.

King, Gary, Michael Tomz and Jason Wittenberg. 2000. "Making the Most of Statistical Analyses: Improving Interpretation and Presentation." *American Journal of Political Science* 44: 341–355.

Kingstone, Peter R. 1999. "Brazil: Short Foreign Money, Long Domestic Political Cycles." In *Financial Globalization and Democracy in Emerging Markets*, edited by Leslie Armijo, 151–176. New York: St. Martin's Press.

Kitschelt, Herbert. 1999. "European Social Democracy between Political Economy and Electoral Competition." In *Continuity and Change in Contemporary Capitalism*, edited by Herbert Kitschelt, Peter Lange, Gary Marks and John Stephens, 317–345. Cambridge: Cambridge University Press.

Kitschelt, Herbert, Peter Lange, Gary Marks and John Stephens, eds. 1999. *Continuity and Change in Contemporary Capitalism*. Cambridge: Cambridge University Press.

Knack, Stephen and Philip Keefer. 1995. "Institutions and Economic Performance: Cross-Country Tests using Alternative Institutional Measures." *Economics and Politics* 7: 207–227.

References

Knight, Malcolm. 1998. "Developing Countries and the Globalization of Financial Markets." *IMF Working Paper* No. 105 (July).

Knoester, Anthonie and Wim Mak. 1994. "Real Interest Rates in Eight OECD Countries." *Rivista Internazionale di Scienze Economiche e Commerciali* 41: 325–344.

Kontopoulos, Yianos T. 1996. "Electoral Competition and Debt Build-Up: An Empirical Investigation of the OECD Experience." Unpublished paper, Columbia University, Department of Economics.

Kontopolous, Yianos and Roberto Perotti. 1999. "Government Fragmentation and Fiscal Policy Outcomes." In *Fiscal Institutions and Fiscal Performance*, edited by James Poterba and Juergen von Hagen, 81–102. Chicago: University of Chicago Press and NBER.

Kopits, George, ed. 1992. *Tax Harmonization in the European Community: Policy Issues and Analysis*. Washington, D.C.: International Monetary Fund, July.

Kramer, Claire, Laura Stephenson and Peter Lange. 2000. "Markets, States and Risk: The Effects of Social Context on Economic Insecurity and Political Preferences." Paper presented at the Annual Meeting of the American Political Science Association, August 31–September 2, Washington, D.C.

Kramer, Jorg. 1998. "Determinants of the Expected Real Long-Term Interest Rates in G-7 Countries." *Applied Economics* 30: 279–286.

Krasner, Stephen D. 1999. *Sovereignty: Organized Hypocrisy*. Princeton, NJ: Princeton University Press.

Krueger, Anne O. 2000. "Conflicting Demands on the International Monetary Fund." *American Economic Review* 90: 38–42.

Kupiec, Paul H. 1993. "Do Stock Prices Exhibit Excess Volatility, Frequently Deviate from Fundamental Values, and Generally Behave Inefficiently?" *Financial Markets, Institutions and Instruments* 2: 1–61.

Kurzer, Paulette. 1993. *Business and Banking: Political Change and Economic Integration in Western Europe*. Ithaca, NY: Cornell University Press.

Kydland, Finn E. and Edward C. Prescott. 1977. "Rules Rather than Discretion: The Inconsistency of Optimal Plans." *Journal of Political Economy* 85: 473–492.

Lakonishok, Josef, Andrei Shleifer and Robert W. Vishny. 1992a. "The Impact of Institutional Trading on Stock Prices." *Journal of Financial Economics* 32: 23–43.

———. 1992b. "The Structure and Performance of the Money Management Industry," *Brookings Papers on Economic Activity* Microeconomics Annual: 339–391.

Lannoo, Karel. 1998. "Institutional Investors, Capital Markets and EMU." In *Institutional Investors in the New Financial Landscape*, edited by Hans J. Blommestein and Norbert Funke, 315–332. Paris: OECD.

Larrain, Guillermo, Helmut Reisen and Julia von Maltzan. 1997. "Emerging Market Risk and Sovereign Credit Ratings." *OECD Development Centre Technical Papers* No. 124 (April).

Lawson, Nigel. 1993. *The View from No. 11*. New York: Doubleday.

Leblang, David. 1999. "Domestic Political Institutions and Exchange Rate Commitments in the Developing World." *International Studies Quarterly* 43: 599–620.

Leblang, David and William Bernhard. 2000. "The Politics of Speculative Attacks in Industrial Democracies." *International Organization* 54: 291–324.

Lee, Jang-Yung. 1997. "Sterilizing Capital Inflows." *International Monetary Fund Economic Issues* 7.

Leland, Hayne E., Martin Feldstein, Robert R. Glauber, David W. Mullins, Jr. and Steven M. H. Wallman. 1997. "Symposium on Public Policy Issues in Finance." *Journal of Finance* 52: 1181–1198.

Lemmen, Jan J. G. and Sylvester C. W. Eijffinger. 1996. "The Fundamental Determinants of Financial Integration in the European Union." *Weltwirtschaftliches Archiv* 32: 432–456.

Lemmen, Jan J. G. and Charles A. E. Goodhart. 1999. "Credit Risks and European Government Bond Markets: A Panel Data Econometric Analysis." *Eastern Economic Journal* 25: 77–106.

Lettau, Martin. 1997. "Explaining the Facts with Adaptive Agents: The Case of Mutual Fund Flows." *Journal of Economic Dynamics and Control* 21: 1117–1147.

Lewis-Beck, Michael. 1998. *Economics and Elections: The Major Western Democracies.* Ann Arbor: University of Michigan Press.

Lewis-Beck, Michael S. and Martin Paldam. 2000. "Economic Voting: An Introduction." *Electoral Studies* 19: 113–121.

Lichtensztejn, Samuel. 1983. "IMF-Developing Countries: Conditionality and Strategy." In *IMF Conditionality*, edited by John Williamson, 209–222. Washington, D.C.: Institute for International Economics.

Liebfritz, Willi, Deborah Roseveare and Paul van den Noord. 1994. "Fiscal Policy, Government Debt, and Economic Performance." OECD Economics Department, Working Paper No. 144.

Liederman, Leonardo and Alfredo E. Thorne. 1996. "The 1994 Mexican Crisis and Its Aftermath: What Are the Main Lessons?" In *Private Capital Flows to Emerging Markets after the Mexican Crisis*, edited by Guillermo A. Calvo, Morris Goldstein and Eduard Hochreiter. Washington, D.C.: Institute for International Economics.

Lijphart, Arend. 1984. *Democracies: Patterns of Majoritarian and Consensus Government in Twenty-One Countries.* New Haven, CT: Yale University Press.

Lindblom, Charles. 1977. *Politics and Markets: The World's Political-Economic Systems.* New York: Basic Books.

Lindert, Peter H. and Peter J. Morton. 1990. "How Sovereign Debt Has Worked." In *Developing Country Debt and Economic Performance*, Vol. 1, edited by Jeffery Sachs, 39–105. Chicago: University of Chicago Press.

Lipsey, Robert. 1999. "The Role of Foreign Direct Investment in International Capital Flows." In *International Capital Flows*, edited by Martin Feldstein, 307–331. Chicago: University of Chicago Press.

Lipson, Charles. 1985. *Standing Guard: Protecting Foreign Capital in the Nineteenth and Twentieth Centuries.* Berkeley: University of California Press.

Lohmann, Susanne. 1992. "Optimal Commitment in Monetary Policy: Credibility versus Flexibility." *American Economic Review* 82: 273–286.

References

Lukauskas, Arvid. 1997. *Regulating Finance: The Political Economy of Spanish Financial Policy from Franco to Democracy*. Ann Arbor: University of Michigan Press.

Lukauskas, Arvid and Susan Minushkin. 2000. "Explaining Styles of Financial Market Opening in Chile, Mexico, South Korea, and Turkey." *International Studies Quarterly* 44: 695–723.

Lunde, Asger, Allan Timmerman and David Blake. 1998. "The Hazards of Mutual Fund Underperformance: A Cox Regression Analysis." University of California, San Diego, Department of Economics, Discussion Paper 98–11 (April).

Lupia, Arthur and Mathew D. McCubbins. 1998. *The Democratic Dilemma: Can Citizens Learn What They Need to Know?* Cambridge: Cambridge University Press.

Maddala, G. S. 1998. "Recent Developments in Dynamic Econometric Modeling: A Personal Viewpoint." *Political Analysis* 7: 59–88.

Mahon, James E. Jr. 1996. *Mobile Capital and Latin American Development*. University Park: Pennsylvania State University Press.

Malliaris, A. G. and Jerome L. Stein. 1999. "Methodological Issues in Asset Pricing: Random Walk or Chaotic Dynamics." *Journal of Banking and Finance* 23: 1605–1635.

Mangano, Gabriel. 1998. "Measuring Central Bank Independence: A Table of Subjectivity and of Its Consequences." *Oxford Economic Papers* 50: 468–492.

Manzocchi, Stefan. 1999. "Capital Flows to Developing Economies throughout the Twentieth Century." In *Financial Globalization and Democracy in Emerging Markets*, edited by Leslie Elliott Armijo, 51–73. New York: St. Martin's Press.

Marichal, Carlos. 1989. *A Century of Debt Crises in Latin America: From Independence to Great Depression, 1820–1930*. Princeton, NJ: Princeton University Press.

Martin, Andrew. 2000. "The Politics of Macroeconomic Policy and Wage Negotiations in Sweden." In *Unions, Employers and Central Banks: Macroeconomic Coordination and Institutional Change in Social Market Economies*, edited by Torben Iversen, Jonas Pontusson and David Soskice. Cambridge: Cambridge University Press.

Maug, Ernst and Narayan Naik. 1996. "Herding and Delegated Portfolio Management: The Impact of Relative Performance Evaluation on Asset Allocation." Unpublished Manuscript, London Business School.

Mauro, Paolo, Nathan Sussman and Yishay Yafeh. 2000. "Emerging Market Spreads: Then vs. Now." *IMF Working Paper* WP/00/190.

Maxfield, Sylvia. 1997. *Gatekeepers of Growth*. Princeton, NJ: Princeton University Press.

1998. "Understanding the Political Implications of Capital Flows to Developing Countries." *World Development* 26, no. 7.

Maxfield, Sylvia and Joshua Hoffman. 1996. "International Portfolio Flows to Developing/Transitional Economies: Impact on Government Policy Choice." Paper presented at the 1996 meeting of the International Studies Association, April 16–20, San Diego.

Mayhew, David R. 1974. *Congress: The Electoral Connection*. New Haven, CT: Yale University Press.

McAleese, Dermot. 1990. "Ireland's Economic Recovery." *Irish Banking Review* (Summer): 18–32.

McKenzie, Richard B. and Dwight R. Lee. 1991. *Quicksilver Capital*. New York: Free Press.

McNamara, Kathleen R. 1998. *The Currency of Ideas: Monetary Politics in the European Union*. Ithaca, NY: Cornell University Press.

Meyer, John W., John Boli, George M. Thomas and Francisco O. Ramirez. 1997. "World Society and the Nation-State." *American Journal of Sociology* 103: 144–181.

Milesi-Ferretti, G. M. and A. Razin. 1996. "Sustainability of Persistent Current Account Deficits." *NBER Working Paper* 5467 (February).

Miller, Victoria. 1997. "Political Instability and Debt Maturity." *Economic Inquiry* 35: 12–27.

Min, Hong G. 1998. "Determinants of Emerging Market Bond Spread: Do Economic Fundamentals Matter?" *World Bank Country Economics Department Paper* No. 1899.

Mishkin, Frederic. 1992. *The Economics of Money, Banking and Financial Markets*. 3rd ed. New York: Harper Collins.

Missale, Alessandro. 1999. *Public Debt Management*. Oxford: Oxford University Press.

Missale, Alessandro and Oliver Jean Blanchard. 1994. "The Debt Burden and Debt Maturity." *American Economic Review* 84: 309–319.

Missale, Alessandro, Francesco Giavazzi and Pierpaolo Benigno. 1997. "Managing the Public Debt in Fiscal Stabilizations: The Evidence." *NBER Working Paper* 6311 (December).

Morrow, James D. 1994. *Game Theory for Political Scientists*. Princeton, NJ: Princeton University Press.

———. 1999. "The Strategic Setting of Choices: Signaling, Commitment, and Negotiation in International Politics." In *Strategic Choice and International Relations*, edited by David A. Lake and Robert Powell, 77–114. Princeton, NJ: Princeton University Press.

Morse, Edward. 1969. "The Politics of Interdependence." *International Organization* 23: 311–326.

Moses, Jonathan. 1994. "Abdication from National Policy Autonomy: What's Left to Leave?" *Politics and Society* 22: 125–148.

———. 2001. "Bonded Polity: The Distributional Consequences of Relying More Heavily on Bond-Financed Social Policies." In *Structure and Agency in International Capital Mobility*, edited by Timothy J. Sinclair and Kenneth P. Thomas, 73–92. Basingstoke, England: Palgrave.

Mosley, Layna. 1998. "Focal Points and International Financial Markets: The Maastricht Convergence Criteria." Paper presented at the Annual Meeting of the International Studies Association, March 17–21, Minneapolis.

References

1999. "The Determinants of National Fiscal Institutions: An Agenda for Research." Paper presented at the Annual Meeting of the American Political Science Association, September 2–5, Atlanta.

2000a. "Room to Move: International Financial Markets and National Welfare States." *International Organization* 54: 737–773.

2000b. "The Politics of Information: Emerging Market Finance and the IMF's Data Standards." Paper presented at the Annual Meeting of the American Political Science Association, August 31–September 3, Washington, D.C.

Mueller, Dennis. 1998. "Constitutional Constraints on Governments in a Global Economy." *Constitutional Political Economy* 9: 171–186.

Mueller, Wolfgang C. and Kaare Strom, eds. 1999. *Policy, Office or Votes? How Political Parties in Western Europe Make Hard Decisions.* Cambridge: Cambridge University Press.

Mundell, Robert A. 1963. "Capital Mobility and Stabilization Policy under Fixed and Flexible Exchange Rates." *Canadian Journal of Economics and Political Science* 29: 475–485.

Mussa, Michael. 1979. "Macroeconomic Interdependence and the Exchange Rate Regime." In *International Economic Policy: Theory and Evidence,* edited by Rudiger Dornbush and Jacob Frenkel, 160–204. Baltimore: Johns Hopkins University Press.

Mylonas, Paul, Sebastian Schich, Thorsteinn Thorgeirsson and Gert Wehinger. 2000. "New Issues in Public Debt Management." *OECD Economics Department Working Paper* No. 239 (April).

New Zealand Government. 1994. "New Zealand Budget 1994: Fiscal Policy and Objectives." Available at www.treasury.govt.nz/pubs/bmb/budgets/1994/fiscalpo.htm.

North, Douglass C. and Barry R. Weingast. 1989. "The Evolution of Institutions Governing Public Choice in Seventeenth-Century England." *Journal of Economic History* 49: 808–832.

Notermans, Ton. 1993. "The Abdication of National Policy Autonomy: Why the Macroeconomic Policy Regime Has Become So Unfavorable to Labor." *Politics and Society* 21: 133–167.

2000. *Money, Markets and the State: Social Democratic Economic Policies since 1918.* Cambridge: Cambridge University Press.

Nunnenkamp, Peter and Hartmut Picht. 1989. "Willful Default by Developing Countries in the 1980s: A Cross-Country Analysis of Major Determinants." *Weltwirtschaftliches Archiv* 125: 681–702.

Oatley, Thomas. 1999a. "Central Bank Independence and Inflation: Corporatism, Partisanship, and Alternative Indices of Central Bank Independence." *Public Choice* 98: 399–413.

1999b. "How Constraining is Capital Mobility? The Partisan Hypothesis in an Open Economy." *American Journal of Political Science* 43: 1003–1027.

Oatley, Thomas and Robert Nabors. 1998. "Redistributive Cooperation: Market Failure, Wealth Transfers, and the Basle Accord." *International Organization* 52: 35–54.

Obstfeld, Maurice. 1993. "International Capital Mobility in the 1990s" *NBER Working Paper* 4534.

—— 1998. "The Global Capital Market: Benefactor or Menace?" *The Journal of Economic Perspectives* 12: 9–30.

Obstfeld, Maurice and Alan M. Taylor. 1998. "The Great Depression as Watershed: International Capital Mobility over the Long Run." In *The Defining Moment: The Great Depression and the American Economy in the Twentieth Century*, edited by Michael D. Bordo, Claudia Goldin and Eugene N. White, 353–402. Chicago: University of Chicago Press.

OECD. 1993. *Government Securities and Debt Management in the 1990s.* Paris: OECD.

—— 1999. "Impact of the Euro on Financial Markets." *Financial Market Trends* 72: 21–37.

Ohmae, Kenichi. 1995. *The End of the Nation State.* New York: McKinsey.

Olsen, Gregg M. 1999. "Half Empty or Half Full? The Swedish Welfare State in Transition." *Canadian Review of Sociology* 36: 241–268.

Olzer, Sule and Guido Tabellini. 1991. "External Debt and Political Instability." *NBER Working Papers* 3772 (July).

Orbell, John. 1985. *Baring Brothers and Co, Limited: A History to 1939.* London: Baring Bros.

O'Rourke, Kevin H. and Jeffrey G. Williamson. 1999. *Globalization and History: The Evolution of a Nineteenth-Century Atlantic Economy.* Cambridge: MIT Press.

Orr, Adrian, Malcolm Edey and Michael Kennedy. 1995. "The Determinants of Real Long Term Interest Rates: 17 Country Pooled Time Series Evidence." *OECD Economics Department Working Paper* No. 155 (June).

Otten, Roger and Dennis Bams. 2000. "European Mutual Fund Performance: A Survey." Unpublished paper, Maastricht University, April.

Pacek, Alexander and Benjamin Radcliff. 1995. "Economic Voting and the Welfare State: A Cross-National Analysis." *Journal of Politics* 57: 44–61.

—— 1996. "The Political Economy of Competitive Elections in the Developing World." *American Journal of Political Science* 39: 745–759.

Papaioannou, Michael G. and George Tsetsekos, eds. 1997. *Emerging Market Portfolios: Diversification and Hedging Strategies.* Chicago: Irwin.

Paredes, Juan E. 1912. *The Morgan-Honduras Loan.* New Orleans: L. Graham.

Patel, Sandeep and Asani Satar. 1998. "Stock Market Crises in Developed and Emerging Markets." *Federal Reserve Bank of New York Research Paper* 9809.

Pauly, Louis. 1996. *Who Elected the Bankers? Surveillance and Control in the World Economy.* Ithaca, NY: Cornell University Press.

—— 1999. "Good Governance and Bad Policy: The Perils of International Organizational Overextension." *Review of International Political Economy* 6: 401–424.

Perotti, Roberto and Yianos Kontopolous. 1998. "Fragmented Fiscal Policy." Unpublished paper, Columbia University and CEPR.

Perry, Robert L. and John D. Robertson. 1998. "Political Markets, Bond Markets, and the Effect of Uncertainty: A Cross-National Analysis." *International Studies Quarterly* 42: 131–160.

References

Persson, Torsten and Guido Tabellini, eds. 1994. *Monetary and Fiscal Policy*. Cambridge, MA: MIT Press.

Pierson, Paul. 1994. *Dismantling the Welfare State? Reagan, Thatcher and the Politics of Retrenchment*. Cambridge: Cambridge University Press, 1994.

1996. "The New Politics of the Welfare State." *World Politics* 48: 143–179.

ed. 2001. *The New Politics of the Welfare State*. Oxford: Oxford University Press.

Platt, D. C. M. 1968. *Finance, Trade and Politics in British Foreign Policy, 1815–1914*. Oxford: Clarendon Press.

1986. *Britain's Investment Overseas on the Eve of the First World War*. New York: St. Martin's Press.

Polak, Jacques J. 1991. "The Changing Nature of IMF Conditionality." *Princeton University Essays in International Finance* No. 184 (September).

Polanyi, Karl. 1944 (1957). *The Great Transformation: The Political and Economic Origins of Our Time*. Boston: Beacon Press.

Porter, Tony. 1999. "The Transnational Agenda for Financial Regulation in Developing Countries." In *Financial Globalization and Democracy in Emerging Markets*, edited by Leslie Ann Armijo, 91–115. New York: St. Martin's Press.

2001. "Negotiating the Structure of Capital Mobility." In *Structure and Agency in International Capital Mobility*, edited by Timothy J. Sinclair and Kenneth P. Thomas, 153–167. Basingstoke, England: Palgrave.

Posen, Adam. 1998. "Central Bank Independence and Disinflationary Credibility: A Missing Link?" *Oxford Economic Papers* 50: 335–359.

Posner, Mitchell. 1998. *Profiting from Emerging Stock Markets*. New York: New York Institute of Finance.

Poterba, James. 1996a. "Budget Institutions and Fiscal Policy in the U.S. States." *American Economic Review* 86: 395–400.

1996b. "Do Budget Rules Work?" *NBER Working Paper* 5550 (April).

Poterba, James and Kim S. Rueben. 1997. "State Fiscal Institutions and the U.S. Municipal Bond Market." *NBER Working Paper* 6237 (October).

Poterba, James and Juergen von Hagen, eds. 1999. *Fiscal Institutions and Fiscal Performance*. Chicago: University of Chicago Press and NBER.

Powell, G. Bingham Jr. and Guy D. Whitten. 1993. "A Cross-National Analysis of Economic Voting: Taking Account of the Political Context." *American Journal of Political Science* 37: 391–414.

Prati, Alessandro and Garry J. Schinasi. 1998. "Ensuring Stability in the Euro Area." *Finance and Development* 35, No. 4 (December).

Prendergrast, Candace and Lars Stole. 1996. "Impetuous Youngsters and Jaded Old Timers: Acquiring a Reputation for Learning." *Journal of Political Economy* 104: 1105–1134.

Pringle, Robert. 1992. "Financial Markets vs. Governments." In *Financial Openness and National Autonomy: Opportunities and Constraints*, edited by Tariq Banuri and Juliet Schor, 89–109. Oxford: Clarendon Press.

Przeworski, Adam. 1985. *Capitalism and Social Democracy*. Cambridge: Cambridge University Press.

Przeworski, Adam and Michael Wallerstein. 1988. "Structural Dependence of the State on Capital." *American Political Science Review* 82: 11–29.

Przeworski, Adam, Michael E. Alvarez, Jose Antonio Cheibub and Fernando Limongi. 2000. *Democracy and Development: Political Institutions and Well-Being in the World, 1950–1990.* Cambridge: Cambridge University Press.

Quinn, Dennis. 1997. "The Correlates of Change in International Financial Regulation." *American Political Science Review* 91: 531–551.

Quinn, Dennis and Carla Inclan. 1997. "The Origin of Financial Openness: A Study of Current and Capital Account Internationalization." *American Journal of Political Science* 41: 771–813.

Quiros, Gabriel. 1993. "Investment and Operating Procedures of Non-Resident Agents in the Government Bond Market." *Banco de Espana Economic Bulletin* (October): 47–58.

Radcliff, Benjamin. 1992. "The Welfare State, Turnout, and the Economy: A Comparative Analysis." *American Political Science Review* 86: 444–456.

Radice, Giles, ed. 1996. *What Needs to Change: New Visions for Britain.* London: HarperCollins.

Reich, Robert B. 1997. *Locked in the Cabinet.* New York: Knopf.

Reisen, Helmut and Julia von Maltzan. 1999. "Boom and Bust in Sovereign Ratings." *International Finance* 2: 273–293.

Richards, Anthony J. 1996. "Volatility and Predictability in National Stock Markets: How Do Emerging and Mature Markets Differ?" *IMF Staff Papers* 43, No. 3 (September): 461–501.

Robson, William B. P. 1994. "Digging Holes and Hitting Walls: Canada's Fiscal Prospects in the Mid-1990s." Commentary, C. D. Howe Institute, No. 56.

Rodrik, Dani. 1997. *Has Globalization Gone Too Far?* Washington, D.C.: Institute for International Economics.

  1998. "Who Needs Capital Account Convertibility?" In "Should the IMF Pursue Capital Account Convertibility?" *Princeton University Essays in International Finance* No. 207 (May).

  1999. *The New Global Economy and Developing Countries: Making Openness Work.* Washington, D.C.: Overseas Development Council.

  2001. "How Far Will International Economic Integration Go?" *Journal of Economic Perspectives* 14: 177–186.

Rogoff, Kenneth. 1985. "The Optimal Degree of Commitment to an Intermediate Monetary Target." *Quarterly Journal of Economics* 100: 1169–1189.

Rogowski, Ronald. 1998. "'Globalization' and Convergence: Getting the Theory and the Evidence Right." Unpublished paper, University of California Los Angeles.

Ross, George. 1996. "The Limits of Political Economy: Mitterand and the Crisis of the French Left." In *The Mitterand Era: Policy Alternatives and Political Mobilization in France*, edited by Anthony Daley, 33–55. New York: New York University Press.

Roubini, Nouriel and Jeffrey Sachs. 1989. "Government Spending and Budget Deficits in the Industrial Countries." *Economic Policy* 4: 100–127.

References

Royed, Terry J., Kevin M. Leyden, and Stephen A. Borrelli. 2000. "Is 'Clarity of Responsibility' Important for Economic Voting? Revisiting Powell and Whitten's Hypothesis." *British Journal of Political Science* 30: 669–698.

Rubinstein, Ariel. 1998. *Modeling Bounded Rationality*. Cambridge, MA: MIT Press.

Rudra, Nita and Stephan Haggard. 2001. "Globalization, Domestic Politics and Welfare Spending in the Developing World." Unpublished Paper, University of Pittsburgh.

Ruggie, John Gerard. 1982. "International Regimes, Transactions, and Change: Embedded Liberalism in the Postwar Economic Order." *International Organization* 36: 379–415.

Sachs, Jeffrey, Aaron Tornell and Andres Velasco. 1996. "The Mexican Peso Crisis: Sudden Death or Death Foretold?" *Journal of International Economics* 41: 265–283.

Salter, Sir Arthur. 1951. "Foreign Investment." *Princeton University Essays in International Finance* No. 12 (February).

Sassen, Saskia. 1996. *Losing Control? Sovereignty in an Age of Globalization*. New York: Columbia University Press.

1999. "Global Financial Centers." *Foreign Affairs* 78: 75–87.

2000. "States and the New Geography of Power: Denationalized State Agendas and Privatized Norm-Making." Unpublished paper, University of Chicago.

Scharfstein, David and Jeremy Stein. 1990. "Herd Behavior and Investment." *American Economic Review* 80: 465–479.

Scheve, Kenneth F. and Matthew J. Slaugher. 2001. *Globalization and the Perceptions of American Workers*. Washington, D.C.: Institute for International Economics.

Schultz, Kenneth A. 1995. "The Politics of the Political Business Cycle." *British Journal of Political Science* 25: 79–99.

Schwartz, Herman. 1994. "Small States in Big Trouble: State Reorganization in Australia, Denmark, New Zealand and Sweden in the 1980s." *World Politics* 46: 527–555.

Scruggs, Lyle and Peter Lange. 2002. "Where Have All the Members Gone? Globalization and National Labor Market Institutions." *Journal of Politics* 64: 126–153.

Sherman, Steven J. and Eric Corty. 1984. "Cognitive Heuristics." In *Handbook of Social Cognition*, Vol. 1, edited by Robert S. Wyer and Thomas K. Srull, 209–286. London: Lawrence Erlbaum Associates.

Shiller, Robert J. 1984. "Stock Prices and Social Dynamics." *Brookings Papers on Economic Activity* 2: 457–498.

1989. *Market Volatility*. Cambridge, MA: MIT Press.

1995. "Conversation, Information, and Herd Behavior." *American Economic Review* 85: 181–185.

2000. *Irrational Exuberance*. Princeton, NJ: Princeton University Press.

Shukla, Ravi K. and Gregory B. van Inwegen. 1995. "Do Locals Perform Better than Foreigners? An Analysis of UK and US Mutual Fund Managers." *Journal of Economics and Business* 47: 241–254.

Simmons, Beth. 1994. *Who Adjusts? Domestic Sources of Foreign Economic Policy during the Interwar Years*. Princeton, NJ: Princeton University Press.

——— 1996. "Rulers of the Game: Central Bank Independence During the Interwar Years." *International Organization* 50: 407–444.

——— 1999. "The Internationalization of Capital." In *Continuity and Change in Contemporary Capitalism*, edited by Herbert Kitschelt, Peter Lange, Gary Marks and John Stephens, 36–69. Cambridge: Cambridge University Press.

Simon, Herbert A. 1955. "A Behavioral Model of Rational Choice." *Quarterly Journal of Economics* 69: 99–118.

——— 1982. *Models of Bounded Rationality*. Cambridge, MA: MIT Press.

——— 1995. "Rationality in Political Behavior." *Political Psychology* 16: 45–61.

Sinclair, Timothy. 1994. "Between State and Market: Hegemony and Institutions of Collective Action under Conditions of International Capital Mobility." *Policy Sciences* 27: 447–466.

——— 2000. "Deficit Discourse: The Social Construction of Fiscal Rectitude," In *Globalization and Its Critics*, edited by Randall D. Germain. New York: Palgrave.

——— 2001. "International Capital Mobility: An Endogenous Approach," In *Structure and Agency in International Capital Mobility*, edited by Timothy J. Sinclair and Kenneth P. Thomas, 93–100. Basingstoke, England: Palgrave.

Sinclair, Timothy and Kenneth P. Thomas, eds. 2001. *Structure and Agency in International Capital Mobility*. Basingstoke, England: Palgrave.

Sirri, Erik R. and Peter Tufano. 1998. "Costly Search and Mutual Fund Flows." *Journal of Finance* 53: 1589–1622.

Smith, Adam. 1776 (1979). *An Inquiry into the Nature and Causes of The Wealth of Nations*, Vol I–II. Oxford: Clarendon Press.

Smith, Mark A. 1999. "Public Opinion, Elections, and Representation within a Market Economy." *American Journal of Political Science* 42: 842–863.

Smith, Vernon L. and James M. Walker. 1993. "Monetary Rewards and Decision Cost in Experimental Economics." *Economic Inquiry* 31: 245–261.

Sobel, Andrew. 1994. "Breaching the Levee, Waiting for the Flood: Testing Beliefs about the Internationalization of Securities Markets." *International Interactions* 19: 311–338.

——— 1999. *State Institutions, Private Incentives, Global Capital*. Ann Arbor: University of Michigan Press.

Sobol, Dorothy Meadow. 1996. "Central and Eastern Europe: Financial Markets and Private Capital Flows." *Federal Reserve Bank of New York Research Paper* 9626 (August).

Soros, George. 1998. *The Crisis of Global Capitalism: Open Society Endangered*. New York: Public Affairs.

Soskice, David. 1999. "Divergent Production Regimes: Coordinated and Uncoordinated Market Economies in the 1980s and 1990s." In *Continuity and Change in Contemporary Capitalism*, edited by Herbert Kitschelt, Peter Lange, Gary Marks, and John Stephens, 101–134. Cambridge: Cambridge University Press.

Soskice, David and Torben Iversen. 1999. "Multiple Wage Bargaining Systems in the Single European Currency Area." *Oxford Review of Economic Policy* 15: 121–138.

References

Starr, Pamela K. 1999. "Capital Flows, Fixed Exchange Rates, and Political Survival: Mexico and Argentina, 1994–1995." In *Markets and Democracy in Latin America: Conflict or Convergence?*, edited by Philip Oxhorn and Pamela K. Starr, 203–241. Boulder, CO: Lynne Rienner.

Stein, Ernesto, Ernesto Talvi and Alejandro Grisanti. 1998. "Institutional Arrangements and Fiscal Performance: The Latin American Experience," *NBER Working Paper* 6358.

Steinherr, Alfred. ed. 1994. *30 Years of European Monetary Integration from the Werner Plan to EMU*. London: Longman.

Steinmo, Sven. 1993. *Taxation and Democracy*. New Haven, CT: Yale University Press.

Steinmo, Sven and Duane Swank. 1999. "The New Political Economy of Taxation." Paper presented at the Annual Meeting of the American Political Science Association, September 1–5, Atlanta.

Stephens, John, Evelyne Huber and Leonard Ray. 1999. "The Welfare State in Hard Times." In *Continuity and Change in Contemporary Capitalism*, edited by Herbert Kitschelt, Peter Lange, Gary Marks and John Stephens, 164–193. Cambridge: Cambridge University Press.

Stiglitz, Joseph E. and Andrew Weiss. 1981. "Credit Rationing in Markets with Imperfect Information." *American Economic Review* 71: 393–410.

Stimson, James A. 1985. "Regression in Space and Time: A Statistical Essay." *American Journal of Political Science* 29: 914–947.

Stokes, Susan C. 1997. "Are Parties What's Wrong with Democracy in Latin America?" Paper presented at the XX International Congress of the Latin American Studies Association, Guadalajara, Mexico, April 17–19.

Stone, Irving. 1977. "British Direct and Portfolio Investment in Latin America before 1914." *Journal of Economic History* 37: 690–722.

Stone, Randall. 2002. *Lending Credibility: The International Monetary Fund and the Post-Communist Transition*. Princeton, NJ: Princeton University Press.

Strange, Susan. 1996. *The Retreat of the State: The Diffusion of Power in the World Economy*. New York: Cambridge University Press.

Summers, Lawrence, 2000. "International Financial Crises: Causes, Prevention and Cures." *American Economic Review* 90: 1–16.

Suter, Christian. 1992. *Debt Cycles in the World Economy: Foreign Loans, Financial Crises and Debt Settlements, 1820–1990*. Boulder, CO: Westview Press.

Suter, Christian and Hanspeter Stamm. 1992. "Coping with Global Debt Crises: Debt Settlements. 1820 to 1986." *Comparative Studies in Society and History* 34: 645–678.

Swank, Duane. 1992. "Politics and the Structural Dependence of the State in Democratic Capitalist Nations." *American Political Science Review* 86: 38–54.

1998a. "Funding the Welfare State: Global Taxation of Business in Advanced Market Economies." *Political Studies* 46: 671–692.

1998b. "The Political Economy of Advanced Capitalist Democracies: Pooled Time-Series Data Base." Typescript, Marquette University.

2001. "Political Institutions and Welfare State Restructuring: The Impact of Institutions on Social Policy Change in Developed Democracies" In *The New*

Politics of the Welfare State, edited by Paul Pierson, 197–237. Oxford: Oxford University Press.

2002. *Diminished Democracy: Globalization, Political Institutions and the Welfare State in Advanced Market Economies*. Cambridge: Cambridge University Press.

Tanzi, Vito. 2000. "Globalization and the Future of Social Protection," *IMF Working Paper* WP/00/12.

Tanzi, Vito and Hamid Davoodi. 1998. "Roads to Nowhere: How Corruption in Public Investment Hurts Growth." *International Monetary Fund Economic Issues* 12.

Tanzi, Vito and Ludger Schuknecht. 1996. "Reforming Government in Industrial Countries." *Finance and Development* 33: 2–5.

2000. *Public Spending in the 20th Century: A Global Perspective*. Cambridge: Cambridge University Press.

Thacker, Strom C. 1999. "The High Politics of IMF Lending." *World Politics* 52: 38–75.

Thomas, Kenneth P. 2001. "Expanding the Debate on Capital Mobility." In *Structure and Agency in International Capital Mobility*, edited by Timothy J. Sinclair and Kenneth P. Thomas, 111–126. Basingstoke, England: Palgrave.

Thomas, Lloyd B., Jr. and Ali Abderrezak. 1988. "Anticipated Future Budget Deficits and the Term Structure of Interest Rates." *Southern Economic Journal* 55: 150–161.

Thompson, Helen. 1997. "The Nation State and International Capital Flows in Historical Perspective." *Government and Opposition* 32 (Winter).

Thorbecke, Willem. 1993. "Why Deficit News Affects Interest Rates." *Journal of Policy Modeling* 15: 1–11.

Tiebout, C. 1956. "A Pure Theory of Local Expenditures." *Journal of Political Economy* 64: 416–424.

Tobin, James. 1963 (1971). "An Essay on the Principles of Debt Management," reprinted in Tobin, *Essay in Economics*, Vol. 1. Chicago: Markham.

1978. "A Proposal for International Monetary Reform," *Eastern Economic Journal* 4: 153–159.

Tomz, Michael. 2001a. "Sovereign Debts and International Cooperation: Reputational Reasons for Lending and Repayment." Ph.D. Thesis, Department of Government, Harvard University.

2001b. "How do Reputations Form? New and Seasoned Borrowers in International Capital Markets." Paper presented at the Annual Meeting of the American Political Science Association, August 30–September 2, San Francisco.

Tsebelis, George. 1995. "Veto Players and Law Production in Parliamentary Democracies." In *Parliaments and Majority Rule in Western Europe*, edited by Herbert Doering, 83–111. New York: St. Martin's Press.

1999. "Veto Players and Law Production in Parliamentary Democracies: An Empirical Analysis." *American Political Science Review* 93: 591–608.

Turner, Philip. 1991. "Capital Flows in the 1980s: A Survey of Major Trends." *BIS Economic Papers* no. 30 (April).

References

1995. "Capital Flows in Latin America: A New Phase." *BIS Economic Papers* No. 44 (May).

Turnovsky, Stephen J. and Marcus H. Miller. 1984. "The Effects of Government Expenditure on the Term Structure of Interest Rates." *Journal of Money, Credit and Banking* 16: 16–34.

Ul Haque, Nadeem, Donald Mathieson and Nelson Mark. 1997. "Rating the Raters of Country Creditworthiness." *Finance and Development* 34: 10–13.

United States, 59th Congress. 1906. "The Costa Rica Debt." U.S. Senate Hearing, 1st Session, 1905–1906. Washington, D.C.: Government Printing Office.

Verdier, Daniel. 1998. "Domestic Responses to Capital Market Internationalization Under the Gold Standard, 1870–1914." *International Organization* 52: 1–34.

Viner, Jacob. 1929. "International Finance and Balance of Power Diplomacy, 1880–1914." *The Southwestern Political Quarterly* 9: 1–29.

1948. "Power versus Plenty as Objectives of Foreign Policy in the Seventeenth and Eighteenth Centuries." *World Politics* 1: 1–29.

von Hagen, Juergen and Barry Eichengreen. 1996. "Federalism, Fiscal Restraints and European Monetary Union." *American Economic Review* 86: 134–138.

von Hagen, Juergen and Ian J. Harden. 1994. "National Budget Processes and Fiscal Performance." *European Economy, Reports and Studies* (January).

1995. "Budget Processes and Commitment to Fiscal Discipline." *European Economic Review* 39: 771–779.

von Mises, Ludwig. 1912 (1953). *The Theory of Money and Credit*. New Haven, CT: Yale University Press.

Vota, Scott J. 1999. "The Changing European Bond Market." *Trusts and Estates* 138 (March).

Wallerstein, Michael and Adam Przeworksi. 1995. "Capital Taxation with Open Borders." *Review of International Political Economy* 2: 425–445.

Walter, Norbert. 1996. "Comment." In *Private Capital Flows to Emerging Markets after the Mexican Crisis*, edited by Guillermo A. Calvo, Morris Goldstein and Eduard Hochreiter. Washington, D.C.: Institute for International Economics.

Weiss, Linda. 1998. *The Myth of the Powerless State*. Ithaca, NY: Cornell University Press.

Welch, Ivo. 2000. "Herding among Security Analysts." *Journal of Finance* 58: 369–396.

Wermers, Russ. 1999. "Mutual Fund Herding and the Impact on Stock Prices." *Journal of Finance* 54: 581–622.

Weyland, Kurt. 1996. "Risk Taking in Latin American Economic Restructuring: Lessons from Prospect Theory." *International Studies Quarterly* 40: 185–208.

Wibbels, Erik. 2000. "Federalism and the Politics of Macroeconomic Policy and Performance." *American Journal of Political Science* 44: 687–702.

Wilcox, Jarrod. 1999. "An Investor's Perspective on the Asian Crisis." In *Financial Markets and Development*, edited by Alison Harwood, Robert E. Litan and Michael Pomerleano, 243–267. Washington, D.C.: Brookings Institution.

Wilkins, Mira. 1991. "Foreign Banks and Foreign Investment in the United States." In *International Banking, 1870–1914*, edited by Rondo Cameron and V. I. Bovykin, 233–252. New York: Oxford University Press.

Willett, Thomas D. 1999. "International Financial Markets as Sources of Crises or Discipline: The Too Much, Too Late Hypothesis." Unpublished paper, Claremont Graduate University.

Williamson, Jeffrey. 1995. "The Evolution of Global Labor Markets since 1830." *Explorations in Economic History* 32: 141–196.

Williamson, John, ed. 1983. *IMF Conditionality*. Washington, D.C.: Institute for International Economics.

———. 1995. *What Role for Currency Boards?* Washington, D.C.: Institute for International Economics.

Winkler, Max. 1933. *Foreign Bonds: An Autopsy. A Study of Defaults and Repudiations of Government Obligations*. Philadelphia: Roland Swain.

Wood, Robert E. 1986. *From Marshall Plan to Debt Crisis: Foreign Aid and Development Choices in the World Economy*. Berkeley: University of California Press.

World Bank. 1998a. "Emerging Markets Database." Available at www.worldbank.org.

———. 1998b. *Global Development Finance*. Washington, D.C.: World Bank.

———. 1999. *Global Development Finance*. Washington, D.C.: World Bank.

———. 2000. *Global Development Finance*. Washington, D.C.: World Bank.

Zeckhauser, Richard, Jayendu Patel and Darryll Hendricks. 1991. "Non-rational Actors and Financial Market Behavior." *Theory and Decision* 31: 257–287.

Zevin, Robert. 1992. "Are World Financial Markets More Open? If So, Why and with What Effects?" In *Financial Openness and National Autonomy*, edited by Tariq Banuri and Juliet Schor, 43–84. Oxford: Clarendon Press.

Ziegler, Philip. 1988. *The Sixth Great Power*. New York: Alfred A. Knopf.

Zweibel, Jeffrey. 1995. "Corporate Conservatism and Relative Compensation." *Journal of Political Economy* 103: 1–25.

Index

Index

economic voting, 165–168
Economist magazine, 18, 154
Ecuador, 152
Edwards, Sebastian, 105, 113, 225
Eichengreen, Barry, 115, 152–153, 162, 224–225, 252, 257–258, 260–261, 272, 277, 279
elections, 62–66, 168–169
  in developed nations, 81–82, 89–90
  in developing nations, 116, 129–130
electoral institutions, 65, 90, 166–168, 204, 213
electronic herd, 1, 2, 25
Ellison, Glenn, 30, 31, 43
embedded liberalism, 6–7, 10
emerging markets, 3, 103–109
  volatility of investment in, 111–112, 154–155, 245, 259, 267
  see also developing countries
endogenous growth theory, *see* new growth theory
equity markets, 17, 52–53, 169, 317–318
  in developing nations, 106–109
Euromoney credit ratings, 143–145
European Central Bank, 205
Exchange Rate Mechanism (ERM), 75, 150, 162, 181, 188
exchange rates, 18, 55, 124, 126, 171, 239, 310
  in developed nations, 78, 85, 86
  see also fixed exchange rates; floating exchange rates
exit, threat of, 7, 29, 105, 240

federalism, 167–168
financial crises, 230–231, 252, 259; *see also* Asian financial crisis; Latin American debt crisis; Mexican peso crisis
financial market influence, 165–166
  scope of, 28, 45–46, 102–103, 112–117
  strength of, 28, 31, 45–46, 105, 110–112

financial market operation, 17, 30
Finnemore, Martha, 269, 270–271
fiscal policy, 3, 11, 76–78, 92
  in developed nations, 55, 57, 76–78, 85, 87
  in developing nations, 125, 147–149
  effectiveness of, 86
fiscal policymaking institutions, 124, 200, 208–214
fixed exchange rates, 11, 13, 126, 167, 205
Flandreau, Marc, 276, 286
floating exchange rates, 11, 13
foreign aid, 109
foreign currency denomination, 114, 172–173, 200–201, 219–223, 291–292
  and default risk, 39, 114
foreign direct investment, 107, 251, 266, 318
France, 197, 233
  1997 election, 64, 65
  Mitterand's policies in, 57, 159–160, 196
  pre-World War I capital markets and, 272–273
Franzese, Robert, 63, 80, 89, 159, 205
Freeman, John, 15, 65, 84, 90, 205
Frieden, Jeffry, 171, 205
Friedman, Benjamin, 42
Friedman, Thomas, 1, 25, 105, 152, 170, 187, 198, 241, 266, 267
fund managers, 59, 263; *see also* institutional investors

Garrett, Geoffrey, 5, 7, 12, 14, 79, 80, 88, 111, 140, 226, 230, 318
Germain, Randall, 8, 150, 251, 254, 260, 268, 272, 276
Germany, 64, 162, 274
globalization, 1, 304, 317
gold standard, 163, 249–253, 276, 278–282, 297
Gould, Erica, 127, 277

Index

Index